D1329661

People and Things

People and Things

Social Mediations in Oceania

Edited by

Monique Jeudy-Ballini and Bernard Juillerat

CAROLINA ACADEMIC PRESS
Durham, North Carolina

Published with the aid of the Secrétariat permanent pour le Pacifique, the Ministère de la Culture, the Ministère des Affaires Etrangères and the Maison des sciences de l'homme, Paris.

Library of Congress Cataloging-in-Publication Data

Jeudy-Ballini, Monique, 1955-
    [Relation à l'objet, relation à l'autre. English]
    People and things : social mediations in Oceania / Monique Jeudy-Ballini and
Bernard Juillerat.
        p. cm.
    Includes bibliographical references and indexes.
    ISBN 0-89089-616-X
        1. Exchange--Oceania. 2. Kava (Beverage) 3. Material culture--Oceania. 4.
Oceania--Social life and customs. I. Juillerat, Bernard.

GN663 .J48 2001
306'.0995--dc21

2001052797

Carolina Academic Press
700 Kent Street
Durham, NC 27701
(919) 489-7486
fax: (919) 493-5668
www.cap-press.com

Printed in the United States of America

Contents

Foreword

This collective work was originally conceived as a medium for providing readers in other countries with a more adequate view of French anthropological studies, and gaining readership for the latter. As French anthropologists working in Oceania, we have become aware that the work of our English-speaking colleagues and our own are somewhat cut off from each other, especially when we study regions in which English is the official language. It is our hope, then, that the papers presented here, translated from the French for the benefit of our non-French-speaking colleagues, will help to foster better mutual understanding of our respective studies.

The authors and co-editors wish to thank the following agencies for their financial support for the translation of the original texts or the publication of this book: the Secrétariat permanent pour le Pacifique, the Ministère de la Culture, the Ministère des Affaires Etrangères, and the Maison des Sciences de l'Homme, Paris.

Moreover we owe special thanks to some of our colleagues and friends, Marie-Claire Bataille-Benguigui, Jacques Bertrand, Lorenzo Brutti, Robert Cresswell, Danielle Daho, Nicolas Govoroff, Paul van der Grijp, Hélène Guiot, Don Niles, Cleo Pace and Don Tuzin for their assistance in the preparation of the iconographic material and some parts of the text.

People and Things

Introduction

The Social Life of Objects

Monique Jeudy-Ballini and Bernard Juillerat

The present book is concerned with the analysis of the social and symbolic function of objects in several Pacific societies, which is primarily one of mediation (through gift-giving, exchange, sharing or conservation) in the relations between individuals or groups, or between humans and spirits. Specialists of animal life, and of primates in particular, have pointed out that organized, intentional gift-giving and exchange are a purely human phenomenon. Chimpanzees and rhesus macaques do have a form of social organization, but their exchanges are exclusively of a behavioral nature, involving sex, domination, submission, aggressiveness, affection and reconciliation (de Waal, 1989). They do not give gifts, nor do they barter, any more than they attempt to transmit messages to each other by means of any objects. There is, at most, evidence of some sort of sharing of food, especially by parents (mostly the mother) with their offspring, or by a male with a female, occasionally between females of a same species. Feeding of the young is the only gift-giving behavior, and it is biologically determined, at that, since it ensures the reproduction of the species.

Sharing (Sahlins, 1974) between adults, as an intentional arrangement, does not exist in animals, or at best it may occur marginally. The fossilized remains of earlier hominoids afford little evidence in this respect, but sharing was certainly an earlier evolutionary trait than any form of gift-giving or exchange, and also preceded the use of objects as identifying or communicational signs. There is in fact a considerable evolutionary distance between the spontaneous sharing of a just-killed prey by a group of meat-hungry animals or of a fruit-laden tree by a troop of monkeys, on the one hand, and the measured allocation of individual shares during a meal within a human family, on the other hand. The accumulation of goods linked with the notion of value—a far cry from the simple satisfaction of dietary needs—is another essentially human feature. Accumulation (often a col-

3

lective undertaking) is then inseparably linked with sharing, redistribution and exchange.

The construction and management of human society requires objects to put what cannot be entirely expressed by body language and speech alone into more tangible form. On the one hand, the object transmitted or symbolically addressed reactivates a signification of a conventional order, but on the other hand it helps people to free themselves, partially, from that given signification and to create what may be called additional meaning. This is characteristic of all gift economies, as opposed to commodity economies (Gregory, 1982). In the former, according to Marilyn Strathern, the object coming from one person generates a mediated relation, whereas in a strictly economic transaction (and even in the mother's act of nurturing her child) the relationship is unmediated. If we retain the expression "unmediated" as applying to direct relations between people (sexual intercourse, fighting, contacts of all sorts and even linguistic exchanges), we would say that what is involved is rather a different form of mediation, since it is clear that the mother's gift of nurturing reifies her own love as well as the child's emotional counter-investment. With this reserve, we may concur with Marilyn Strathern when she writes: "By objectification I understand the manner in which persons and things are construed as having value, that is, are objects of people's subjective regard or of their creation. Reification and personification are the symbolic mechanisms or techniques by which this is done" (M. Strathern, 1988: 176).

Meanings and Efficacy of the Object

Objects derive their meaning and efficacy from the economic, social and psychological motivations of individuals within their society. In itself, an object is only a potential signifier that becomes meaningful through the mediating role it is made to play. This meaning is derived from what people project on the object, be it the idea of fertility, relations of kinship or affinity, emotions — both normalized and non-normalized —, physical and spiritual qualities, narcissistic identification, lethal power, the representation of an actual individual or of a spirit. Often objects form a system among themselves, as when a totem is consistently associated with several others, a mask is meaningful in relation to other masks, a plant is symbolically complementary to another plant, the value of a particular shell is established by the hierarchy of shell moneys, and so on. The social semantics with which we are concerned here revolves around three axes: the relations between persons, the relations between objects, and the relations between persons and objects.

In different contexts, the nature of objects conveying a same meaning, and therefore fulfilling the same socio-symbolic functions may differ, like synonyms in a language. Conversely, the same objects may have several different meanings and functions (like homonyms), while still others may have a "specialized" function, which is to say their signification and their social usage will be univocal. The material discussed in the present work pertains to food and drink (the nutritional function of which is often secondary to their symbolic meaning), crafted objects (mats, sculptures, ritual objects, tools, arms), natural objects sometimes reworked (shell money, self decorations), plants personifying divinities and social groups (totemic species, mythic embodiments), wild or domesticated animals partaking in exchanges between individuals or between humans and spirits, and even heads taken from the enemy to become decorated trophies conveying identity. As signs or symbols, things may also serve as vehicles for status, rank, social class or function, and as such they will arouse an appropriate attitude in members of the group when exhibited to the community. During a ritual, a given object may acquire a special symbolic function that is reactivated by the actors, after which it returns to the status of an ordinary thing. During this brief lapse of time, that which is either transmitted (through initiation, for instance) or modified, but also shared, is the meaning conveyed by the thing. The physical features of the object — the material of which it is made, its form and its color — are closely linked to the meaning to be communicated. They may inform the evocative power ascribed to the object and its metaphoric affiliation with, for example, a gender, a body substance or a natural species. These perceptual attributes partake in the symbolic efficacy that devolves on the object in a ritual or a social transaction, through references to myths in particular, as shown by the Australian *tjurunga*, the Wodani cowries and the Yafar sago (see, respectively, Moisseeff, Breton and Juillerat).[1] In some cultures, the "potency" intrinsic in the object is only evidenced through its effects, such as the ability to constitute "gifts of life" in the case of Samoan mats (Tcherkézoff) or life-giving shell money (de Coppet, 1995), or to bestow strength and power, as *kava* does (Douaire-Marsaudon), or again, to legitimate the origin of the group, like the *kwaimatnie* of the Baruya (Godelier), or the right to land, like some of the Aborigines' sacred objects (Glowczewski). The two aspects — the very nature of the object and its socio-symbolic efficacy, which may be reactivated as desired — are linked in varying degrees, albeit fortuitously. Marika Moisseeff shows how "there is a definite connection between the tangible reality of these objects and the invisibility of the agents — spirits, ancestors and the like — held to be brought into play by the rite." When this mediation is operated through a ritual, the object may sub-

---

1. When no date is indicated, the reference is to a paper by the writer to be found in the present volume.

sequently be hidden or even buried in a sacred place, a men's house, a church or a tomb, or left on the site. Or again, it may be abandoned, left to decompose naturally, or destroyed. In New Ireland, some types of *malanggan* were kept once they had fulfilled their ceremonial function, and their painting was refreshed so that they might serve again in later ceremonies. Others, made of the same material, were destroyed by burning, or again, after a funeral rite, they were abandoned with the corpse in a cave, or sometimes burned with the body, and the ashes of the bones and objects might be cast to sea (Derlon, 1997a and herein). Independently of any ecological constraint, the perishable nature of the vegetal constructions that make up most Melanesian masks corresponds to an aesthetic option inseparably tied to a specific efficacy mustered at a given time. This viewpoint contrasts with the Western, museographic perspective which is an attempt to save objects from decaying, to make them immortal, invulnerable to the ravages of time (see Derlon and Jeudy-Ballini, forthcoming, and Jeudy-Ballini, forthcoming). Paradoxically, it was colonialism that enabled numerous objects to be preserved, but many of those that remained in their place of origin were stolen by merchants and by some missionaries—to be sold, or destroyed. Moreover, there are instances, during the period of pacification (the *pax australiana*), of local populations themselves making auto-da-fés of objects connected with practices such as some traditional ceremonies, warring or head-hunting when they were condemned by the government and the missions, or in the context of millenarian movements. Auto-da-fés instigated by some churches may still be seen, to this day.

When the Aranda bury their *tjurunga* in a sacred place of the Dreaming Time, or when the Baruya wrap their clan relics in a secret place, they are setting aside some element of their own being that will be reactivated when the group needs to summon up its origins. As Marika Moisseeff points out, ritual objects "are concretely present; their existence cannot be reduced to the discourse surrounding them. Paradoxically, acts of camouflage, as when ritual objects are covered or placed behind a screen, often reinforce their presence." This was also true of Polynesian *tiki*, or of the wooden *tambaran* sculptures of the lower valley of the Sepik, hidden, respectively, in the *marae* and in nooks in the men's houses, to be taken out exclusively during rituals. The efficacy of the thing is only "awakened" at the proper time then, and for as long as needed: before that and afterward, the ritual object is placed in a state of suspended animation. The same is true of totemic trees or of plants that are either cut for the ritual, then abandoned, or used for ceremonial purposes without being cut, after which they resume their normal status as plants. Since the totem represents the species as a whole, only an individual specimen is then given symbolic treatment.

The meaning and efficacy of an object may be tied to its form or its material, but it may also be expressed by some imagery, by the motif engraved or painted on it. In other cases, the sculpted object itself is a representation. The medium (be it the human body, the ground, the sheath of a plant, a mask, or the like), which often can only retain the representation fleetingly, is sometimes held to be nurtured by the signs and images placed on it (Glowczewski). Some societies prefer graphic representations, which, in this case, are incomprehensible for non-initiates. Australian *tjurunga*, for instance, bear inscriptions that are "neither figurative nor abstract," "representing the unrepresentable" so to speak, that is to say, the existence of the founding hero and the traces left by him on the landscape. Indeed, "the formal framework of the rite indicates that ordinary signifying relationships are for a time abolished" (Moisseeff). At the same time, however, the motif engraved on them refers to an individual or a group and constitutes "a veritable spiritual and geographical ID card" (Glowczewski).

More generally speaking, this meaning is constructed by the way the spatial and temporal dimensions of the object—physical, social and imaginary spatial features and historical, genealogical and mythical time frames—are dealt with.

Social Mobility of the Object in Space and Time

Susceptible of being kept, given, received, appropriated, incorporated, hidden, traded, inherited, loaned, shared, returned, exhibited, destroyed, reproduced . . . objects, clearly, are subjected to all sorts of treatments in which they are often no more than a pretext. In anthropology the key words referring to relations with an object have generally been exchange and gift, but the issue addressed by the present book is what there is behind transactions. While there is no doubt that exchange is omnipresent, our conceptual framework is nonetheless located outside of the three obligations defined by Mauss and already extensively discussed by so many writers.[2] The reference to space and time, as conceived and organized by a given society, is a way of expanding our approach and showing how the object derives its meaning and value from those ever-changing differentials, those stops and starts, time after time, those lapses of time during which it may be put in abeyance, all of which we hold to be just as socially significant as the very acts by which it is transferred. Sometimes, conversely, it is the precipitation with which exchanges are made that enhances the value of the object, as in Wodani society, where a prized cowry may change hands several times within a same day. Its social visibility is maximal at that point, and what counts, in the long run, is not any particular exchange but the circulation

---

2. Among others, see Lévi-Strauss, 1950; Sahlins, 1974; Guidieri, 1984; Kilani, 1990; Babadzan, 1993; Godelier, 1996; Geffray, 2001.

of shell money, which conveys a symbolic reality to society (Breton). The physical distance covered by an object tends to increase with the development of means of communications, as in Australian Aboriginal society today, where some sacred objects are carried for hundreds of kilometers, to be activated in an initiation rite. But sometimes it is the rites themselves (as composite objects made of knowledge, rights and practices) that travel and diffuse when they are given to other groups (Glowczewski).

Paraphrasing Serge Tcherkézoff's expression referring to Samoan mats, we may say that no object of value is kept with the idea that it will never change hands. For a Samoan mat to be valuable, it must of course meet some aesthetic or material criteria regarding its color, fineness or size, but it must also embody a history. The most famous example is yielded by the Kula exchanges (Malinowski, 1922), in which armbands and necklaces, circulating in opposite directions, are personalized (they are gendered, named and given a rank). With each of their movements within the social space their genealogical history gains in depth, and at the same time the withholders of the most coveted pieces achieve greater prestige. The social value of an object is not easily compatible with anonymity, especially when that value is great, and the acquisition of a rare piece depends partly on the "seduction" at stake between the protagonists. This relational aspect accounts for the importance of magic in exchanges.

Traditional objects are the bearers of a mythical or historical memory: most imported objects, which are lacking in both, can therefore never be true replacements, valid in all contexts. In theory, paper money cannot replace shell valuables in ceremonial exchanges, any more than cloth can replace a tapa, or the gift of a crate of tinned meat can replace the gift of a pig raised at home on garden-grown food and given a personal name which sometimes, as in Sulka society, makes it the homonym of a human (Jeudy-Ballini). But as the old objects change or disappear, there arises the necessity to integrate purchased commodities into the various exchanges or ritual productions (Glowczewski). Whereas cash now currently enters into "traditional" exchanges—be they ceremonial gifts, bridewealth or funeral payments, or offerings to the gods (Godelier, 1994)—, the transition to money, as Edward LiPuma writes (1999: 193), is "never simply the replacement of an indigenous form with a foreign alternative." Some authors have shown how its introduction has produced new visions of the social relationships and induced forms of antagonism between elder big men and younger men and women for the control of local exchange (see Foster, 1995; Akin and Robbins, 1999). Thus the value of the object is enhanced by its travels through a particular social time and space. When transferred to a third party or transmitted to an heir, it turns each recipient into a temporary depository or guardian, although the length of time connected with these travels may greatly vary in amplitude. Depending on the society involved, the object received may be put back into circulation immediately, or be immobilized for an entire lifetime, until the death of its holder. In the logic of exchanges among the Yafar of New Guinea, according to B. Juillerat, "everything points to a fear of deferred reciprocation insofar as it may generate conflict. To put off reciprocating is regarded as a 'bad custom' by the Yafar; always paying off debts, alternatively, is a guarantee of social peace." Among the Sulka of New Britain, on the other hand, the excellence of a relationship is evidenced by the fact that one can never conceive oneself being quits. For this people, avoidance of debt, is characteristic of those relations that are least valued, socially: in this case, simple mutual aid as opposed to the solidarity designated by a polysemic term meaning "to hold, to have a hold on each other" or "to hold hands" (Jeudy-Ballini).

Accumulating for the Sake of Redistributing

An object that is stored once and for all is of little value, and in many Pacific societies temporary hoarding is simply aimed at putting the object back in circulation so as to transform its material quality into social value. Indeed, as opposed to the specifically capitalist logic, it is not accumulation in itself that affords prestige and power so much as redistribution, and even agonistic, calculated "generosity," as has been shown in the Melanesian case by the abundant literature devoted to competitive exchanges between big men, especially in the Highlands of Papua New Guinea[3] and in some island groups such as the Siuai of Bougainville (Oliver, 1967) and the inhabitants of the Banks Islands in Vanuatu (Vienne, 1984). Ostentatious gift-giving backed by the talented rhetoric of the givers is a prelude to an even greater counter-gift, offered after a delay that is both politically necessary and likely to create a temporary, asymmetric tie based on debt and credit. Among the Tolai of New Britain (Epstein, 1979), the finality of hoarding, even if it lasts a lifetime, is to reinsert the valuables in the flow of exchanges at funeral. This distribution enacts the dead person's relations with those who are still alive. The dead dissolve, so to speak, into innumerable monetary ties. It is at this very point when they disappear as physical persons that individuals give the full social measure of their existence. The ability of certain men to develop strategies for galvanizing clientele networks clearly illustrates the apparently paradoxical finding that "by constantly giving one certainly does accumulate, however it is not objects that are accumulated, but relationships" (Tcherkézoff). Further, the well-managed accumulation of relations enables one to gain renown (the Melane-

---

3. Sahlins, 1963; A. Strathern, 1971; Feil, 1984; Lederman, 1986; Lemonnier, 1990; Godelier and Strathern eds. 1991.

sians say, "a name"), exhibited in the form of wives, ability to organize festivities, mastery of ritual, decisional power, etc. But it is also a known fact that ostentatious generosity often serves to sustain rivalries between groups or individuals, and under some circumstances may even be a means of inflicting humiliation. Like the potlatch practiced on the American North-West coast, Melanesian ceremonial exchange may be viewed as a way of waging war peacefully (Salisbury, 1962; Mauss, 1954; Young, 1971; Lemonnier, 1990). In addition, and contrary to the individualistic conceptions prevailing in the Western world, the Pacific way of giving gifts does not necessarily imply the definitive loss of what is given, as shown in a variety of ways by the different forms of (sometimes endlessly) ongoing exchanges, some competitive, others not, that characterize social relations in pre-colonial societies. Sometimes renown is connected with an institutional rank, as in the North Vanuatu grade system, where access to a higher rank must be "paid for," and calls for a festivity (Codrington, 1972; Vienne, 1984).

Exchange and Violence

Nonetheless, some objects are not received, exchanged or inherited, nor, literally speaking, redistributed, and are presumably not intended to be alienated. There are some other objects that one can only obtain by seizing them, by means of violence or murder, which is to say, through an act that blurs the relation (at least tacitly contractual) between giver and receiver, or turns it into a unique moment, impossible to duplicate, outside of any reciprocity. For the Marind Anim of Irian Jaya, discussed by Stéphane Breton, the cut off head of an enemy was in some sense a lost object that the hunter intended to recover: "…its capture was an act of repossession. It is as if it appeared as a detached part of the person who subsequently seized hold of it." When captured, the head—which became a trophy, exhibited as a sign of the power of the group and the prestige of the murderer—was only valued for the name it was believed to bear, and to have muttered before falling, so that the killer might offer it to one of his children. This missing part of the person's identity must be reconquered by wresting it from another so as to recover one's own wholeness and construct oneself as a subject through naming. It is, quite literally, the act of giving that provides its significance to this undertaking.

In pre-colonial times it was mostly during conflicts that forced transfers and appropriation of objects took place on a collective scale. Pigs were killed, women and children were kidnapped, and sculptures of divinities sometimes were carried off when considered as sacred and therefore powerful, to be set up as incarnated gods on the altars of the group that had taken them (Juillerat, 1993). Violence does not however represent a disruptive dimension, or one linked to circumstances external to exchange interaction. If, as pointed out earlier, ceremonial exchanges have sometimes been interpreted as a form of war, it is because violence is often a structural part of them (Godelier, Jeudy-Ballini). As Daniel de Coppet has pointed out (1968: 56), it is also because one of the remarkable properties of the rules of equivalence to which they conform is "to include violence, murder and war in [their] overall system, on a par with the tendering of valuable goods, and on a par, too, with other forms of social translation." As Simon Harrison writes (1989: 584), "[the] problem which Melanesian societies pose is precisely the degree to which they seem to 'socialise' violence and evaluate it as inherently no less fully 'social' behaviour than peaceful cooperation."

On Some Paradoxical Forms of Exchange

Receiving without Having Given/Giving without Receiving/Receiving or Not Receiving

As opposed to what Mauss wrote about the obligations that structure the logic of exchange, Melanesian ethnography shows that (the intention of) giving does not necessarily entail the obligation of receiving or reciprocating. In an earlier development we referred to the mother's selfless gift to her child, that on-going gift of a combination of milk, care and love that, at least in the immediate, does not call for any reciprocity.[4] Among the Yafar of New Guinea, this relation is ritually reactivated when, under some special ritual circumstances, the men address a prayer to a coconut palm, the maternal totem, to which it responds by shedding the petals of its flowers, symbolizing the mother's milk which in turn, in this case, means abundant game. After the rite, the mother, the giver *par excellence*, is ritually closed up again. Her generosity, as virtual as it is random, is kept in reserve for the next occasion. More generally speaking, when it is nature that does the giving, people view this as the effect of their tacit relations with the guardian spirits. The spirit of a dead person embodied by a medium may be contented by an areca nut or a little sago

---

4. There is a deferred, long-term reciprocity, however, since it is by dint of the care received during their youth that the erstwhile children, upon reaching adulthood, will be called upon to provide for their aging, dependent parents, or to make repeated gifts to their maternal uncle. According to some local exegeses, it is that same care that justifies the bridewealth payment made to the nurturing parents (biological or adoptive) who raised the girl being married, or the gift of the wife's labor if a boy is being married (see Jeudy-Ballini, 1992, 1998a).

in exchange for a wild pig already given to the hunter, or for the promise of another one.

At the same time, the margin left to an individual—a real person in this case—for refusing a gift is also documented in New Britain. In Sulka society, the main risk threatening the functioning of ritual exchanges is less that of a shortage of resources than of the refusal of a potential receiver to take on that role, thus blocking the process of circulation. Furthermore, in those endless exchanges that pervade Sulka society, a counter-gift definitely is expected, but is not intended to be compulsory. The absence of reciprocity must not prevent a giver from continuing to give to a partner who does not give anything in return (Jeudy-Ballini). Such abstention partakes in strategies of exchange, then, and must be integrated in our conception of the object and of its social mobility. To be sure, refusals to give, to receive, or to return a gift entail risk-taking, even if they are duly motivated in each case. This does not mean that obligation is necessarily the key word in exchanges. In these societies, which are perhaps not as compelling as Mauss imagined in *The Gift*, there is room for choice and calculation as well. As Alain Testart points out (1993), Mauss actually did not consider the relativity of the term "obligation" as it applies to different cultures and contexts.

Incorporating the Object

Aside from food as nourishment, the incorporation of an object, be it edible or not, is the acme of identification (Freud, 1955d). In Gimi society (New Guinea), the eating of their dead kin by the women is suggestive of an identification with a lost object (Gillison, 1993).[5] As seen above, the Yafar ritually consume coconut palm flowers to restore the nurturing relation with the totemic mother; there is nothing surprising about the fact that this takes the form of a ritualized regression to an oral contact with the breast. Nonetheless, this throwback to the mother-child relationship is staged for the sole purpose of accumulating game meat and distributing it at the next feast. This indicates that the cliché of the existence of a taboo on consuming objects or totemic species should be understood as a ritual obligation to consume these at the proper time and place. In the present example, the Yafar have a prohibition on consuming an object (coconut palm flowers), which they usually do not view as food, but which they eat during the rite described above.

Identification is even more evident when the purpose is not so much to possess an object by ingesting it as to be possessed by it, as in the case of

---

5. We have deliberately excluded the many forms taken by cannibalism and sacrifices in latter-day Pacific societies.

the ritual drinking of *kava* by the traditional chiefs of Tonga. The ritual ingestion of *kava* is meant to produce identity, and to produce it muscularly, so to speak. Françoise Douaire-Marsaudon shows that it is a glorification of the divinity. In a way, the physical strength exhibited by the men during these ceremonies represents the physiological attribute of the sacred. Indeed, the only language the ancestors understand is that of virility, conceived in Tonga as the privilege of the chiefs. The all-mighty ancestors place those whom they invest ritually in a position to become ancestors when their time comes by renewing their soul's capacity to survive after death—something commoners are refused. This identity is experienced as an individual transformation, the passage from one state to another (assessed in terms of more or less "sacred"), and at the same time it is construed as reproduction. The chief's status is grounded in his ability, manifested through possession, to assert his filiation, to give himself ancestors while legitimating in advance the fact that he, in turn, will become an ancestor.

Receiving without Consuming

To receive food does not necessarily imply that one consumes it. The Yafar hunter deemed worthy by the spirits of the dead, who give him a wild pig, refrains from eating it in accordance with the prohibition on the game he hunts. For him, the gratification resides in redistributing the meat to the community, and receiving its gratitude and respect. Hunting, which might be assimilated with possession by force in the Western way of thinking, is in fact conceptualized in many societies—not only in Oceania—as a nonpredatory practice, the success of which is subordinated to the good will of the guardians of the wild animals. The violence exerted on the mother forest then takes place with the consent of the dead, who serve as mediators. Hunters only receive what is granted them. Abstinence, along with social generosity, "redeem," so to speak, the offense towards nature. Bernard Juillerat demonstrates that, conversely, "if he loses the spirits' trust, the unfruitful hunter at the same time loses that of the group."

Another widespread rule in Melanesia prohibits one from consuming the fruits of one's own labor, or from giving them to certain categories of relatives, more especially to the ascendants.

Hiding, All the Better to Show (Showing, All the Better to Hide)

"Consumption of the object tends to be confused with and dissolved into its display," says Stéphane Breton in this volume, speaking of symbolic exchange in Melanesia; its display is at the same time its contemplation.

Photo 1: Arranging shell valuables for ritual display in the Nggwal Bunafunei spirit house in Ilahita, an Arapesh-speaking village in the interior Sepik region of Papua New Guinea. The cassowary-bone dagger shown piercing one of the shell rings is intended to be used to kill a sacrificial human victim, in payment of an initiation debt (Photo D. Tuzin, 1971).

"For them [the Wodani], he notes, the aesthetic realm is entirely coextensive with the realm of shell money." Money, as an object of "aesthetic pleasure," "is irresistibly beautiful only because it is a part of the self." Contemplation in this case is an act of narcissistic appropriation, as is the exhibiting of all kinds of ritual objects. In the latter instance, what is at stake for the initiated men who crafted them is the contemplation, through the gripping emotions of the spectators, of their own power over other humans and perhaps over the gods as well. But such exposure may only represent a very brief moment in the life of the object, especially if it is not intended to survive the ritual, and it is then quite disproportionate to the time required to fashion it. This is true of both the *malanggan* and the Sulka masks, secretly crafted over a period of many months, and whose sudden, dramatically staged revelation maximizes the emotional shock and aesthetically overpowers spectators (Derlon, 1997a; Jeudy-Ballini, 1999b). The efficacy of the object is all the greater for its lightening-like appearance, and therefore the brevity of the pleasure of those who attend the event.

In some instances, the only reason for exhibiting an object is to make conceivable that which escapes ordinary sensory and cognitive perception and which thus subverts the conventional link between signified and signifier calling for a completely different register of comprehension. Moisseeff, writing about *tjurunga*, notes that "by showing something in order to better dissimulate, new meaning is created." "If the rite is to preserve its exceptional character and the [supernatural] forces their putative potency, it is of the greatest importance that their invisibility be safeguarded by this object." The entities (Dreaming beings) responsible for the fertility and the continuation of the group must remain essentially unrepresentable, and that is why the motifs on the *tjurunga* do not *represent* anything. This is reminiscent of what we know about Tahitian *to'o*, those oblong, non-anthropomorphic objects decorated with red feathers and containing a single piece of wood which did "represent" some gods or ancestors, and which were ritually "undressed" and exhibited on some occasions (Babadzan, 1993).

In many parts of New Guinea, to inform people that he has been initiated, a man says he "saw" the ritual objects; and to announce that preparations for initiations are being made, those in charge of the ceremonies say that they are going to "show" those objects (to the boys). Showing — bamboo flutes, masks, bull-roarers or relics — is equivalent to "initiating," and to see them is "to be initiated." Conversely, during the periods between rituals there is a prohibition on the exhibition of the ritual objects, whose sound is held by women and non-initiates to be the spirits' voice. These objects, which legitimate the existence of the divinities and the ancestors, and therefore the power of men, are then guarded within the village ceremonial houses (Bateson, 1958; Tuzin, 1980; Godelier, 1982; Hauser-Schäublin, 1989, Juillerat, 1993), in small, sacred constructions deep in the forest (Barth, 1975), or in remote caves.[6] To unveil what the sound of flutes or the existence of a mask owes to human intervention is tantamount to revealing knowledge that the new initiate, threatened with various sanctions, must keep secret, along with the existence of the objects themselves. At the same time, however, this revelation is also the disclosure of the institutional deception of women, and in some cultures where ritual objects have no religious signification (Fajans, 1997), their *raison d'être* may simply be to perpetuate hierarchical sexual discrimination (Lattas, 1989). Andrew Lattas (1992) shows that the way men regard the fiction they transmit to non-initiates, and consequently, their view of gender relations, may constitute both a way of conceptualizing the dichotomy between image and reality and a way of comprehending history and the relations between black and white people. Having undergone the influence of missionaries for several decades, and consequently having given up men's rituals, some men in certain Lower-

---

6. In the ceremonial houses of the Lower-Sepik, a small room occasionally housed a sculpture of a *tambaran* (a protective divinity) that no man, except its appointed guardian, dared gaze upon directly (Juillerat, 1993).

Sepik and Ramu communities decided to play the sacred flutes in the presence of the women, so as to show them, belatedly, that the spirits they supposedly invited to the men's ceremonial houses for their copious feasts (prepared by the women) were nothing but a subterfuge.

Some societies set apart objects that are neither intended to circulate nor to fulfill any ritual function, and which are only meaningful for those people who are aware of their existence. Sometimes—although rarely—men decide to exhibit a relic to back the legitimacy of a claim touching on their identity and provide material proof of their origins. The object then acts as a genealogy or a myth. Valued objects may also draw their power from the fact that they remain hidden. Some objects are withdrawn from social life and kept invisible, and as such are held to ensure the social mobility of other objects, different or similar in nature—the disjunction occasionally operates within a same category—, which do circulate. Annette Weiner (1992: 10) was the first to note that the "ability 'to keep' empowers [the] ability to attract. In other words, things exchanged are about things kept." In Samoa, according to Serge Tcherkézoff, some buried mats are viewed as the reference for those intended for circulation in exchanges. In Mandak society, in New Ireland, very ancient specimens of strings of beads, excluded from the sphere of exchanges and hidden in the recesses of homes, are clan property and confer a "basis," an "anchorage" to the group's legitimacy, according to Brigitte Derlon (forthcoming, 2002). Similarly, those shell rings that convey the greatest prestige among the Sulka of New Britain are carefully wrapped in a strip of tapa or cloth and practically never leave their hiding place, except when given to a member of a sub-clan as part of an inheritance. The valuable objects that do not partake in rituals are believed to have the power to "attract" other shell money by favoring the reproduction of these currencies and their mobility (Jeudy-Ballini). Serge Tcherkézoff speaks of a "set point," a sacred locus "harboring the social motor of exchange" in Polynesia, while Maurice Godelier refers to "anchor points," "stable, fixed points [...] which stand outside the sphere of exchange and at the same time enable it to exist."[7]

The hidden object elicits fear. The cultural centers recently created in Australia at the initiative of the Aborigines to conserve those sacred objects returned by Western museums are viewed by many of the natives as dan-

---

7. In the Western world, the idea of a standard referring to a prototypic model kept secret to ensure the legitimacy of things in circulation is applied to currencies (the banks' gold standard validates the paper money in circulation) as well as to other measures (such as the standard meter). Juillerat (1991) uses this concept to define mythic knowledge, kept secret and simply transmitted from one generation to the next, and which, according to the Yafar, validates the meaning of the multiple public versions of the myths. This is suggestive of Plato's reference to an intelligible model, the original of its perceivable copies.

gerous places, to be avoided, which only the elders are capable of managing (Glowczewski).

Inalienability: Possessing without Putting into Circulation

By its very existence, an object belonging to a group (be it a family, clan, local group or "tribe") may testify to the origins of that group, its entitlement to bear a given name, or to live on a given piece of land. What is transmitted, then, is the right to the guardianship and symbolic use of the object, which remains physically totally immobilized. Its own origin is inalienable, by definition.

C.A. Gregory (1982) differentiates between alienable and inalienable possessions, in that something that has been "paid for" by a purchaser becomes inalienably his or hers, whereas an object given may, under some circumstances, generate a debt—with the giver retaining a claim to the object. Annette Weiner (1992), followed by Maurice Godelier (1998), adopted the notion of inalienability, but they used it in a different sense to designate objects which can be neither given nor sold, since they embody the identity of the group and therefore have neither usage value nor exchange value. It is their permanent identification with a person, a group, or a function that makes them inalienable. According to Barbara Glowczewski (in this volume), Aboriginal ritual objects and the knowledge and cults associated with them, controlled by appointed guardians, epitomize such inalienable objects, in this sense of the term. Among the Mandak of New Ireland, it is less the objects than the copy rights for a given *malanggan* pattern which are put in circulation, for transmission among kin. However, the initial withholder of these rights recovers them at the death of the person to whom they had been temporarily transferred, for they must return to their clan of origin, so that the younger generations will not be deprived of their legitimate right to control the objects (Derlon). In short, this is an original actualization of the principle of inalienability. In certain societies, objects became inalienable possessions only since the colonial era. John Liep, for instance, writes that while the movement of high-ranking shells became much more restricted in the Massim, "low-ranking shell money increasingly took on the role of an internal cash" (Liep 1999: 143-144).

In those societies in which there is no private possession of real estate, land belongs to the category of inalienable valuables, even if history has played havoc with that rule. The anticolonialist struggles led by the Kanak and the Australian Aborigines, in particular, are based on the argument that their earlier occupation of the land gives them a right to it (Saussol, 1979; Dauphiné 1989; Merle, 1995; Glowczewski, 1998a; Naepels, 1998). Culture too is an inalienable possession, irrespective of the objects that represent it (Glowczewski, Bensa; Welsh, 1997; Strathern, 1999). What happens, then, when the traditional object that has disappeared surfaces again, when its inalienability is recovered after having been confiscated for many years? What happens when the creation of a Cultural Center enables some societies to (re)discover ancient objects that the younger generations had never seen, but which nonetheless inform their present culture and the new relations they entertain with their past? The examples of the Kanak (Bensa) and the Aborigines (Glowczewski), and those of Polynesia and North America as well, indicate "how difficult it is to reduce contemporary Pacific art work to the function of unambiguous props for cultural identity" (Bensa). The meaning attributed to an object in its society of origin does not exhaust all of the meanings it takes on at a given point in history. As Alban Bensa again tells us, the materiality of the object shows how multiple, contingent and unstable its interpretation may be. Some Australian Aboriginal groups, for instance, demand that their ceremonial objects—that part of themselves that has been detached and kept in Western museums—be returned to them, but have not solved the issue, on which they are divided, of what, concretely, to do with these things that belong to their ancestors: of how to take repossession of them, culturally speaking, while protecting them and protecting themselves from them (Glowczewski).

Objects, Personhood and Society

Within a given society, the mediation operated by the object in the accomplishment of the social subject is informed by shared conceptions of equivalence which subvert the Western premise of a strict separation between persons and objects. A.C. Gregory already stressed this opposition between the commodity economy that characterizes the world of money and the gift economy, in which exchanges are defined in symbolic, social and/or cosmological rather than strictly economic terms (Gregory, 1982; de Coppet, 1985; N. Thomas, 1991; de Coppet and Iteanu, 1995).

For the members of a given community, the object must signify the same thing, and while different people regard it differently, their visions form a whole. Exchanges or transfers of valuables, which validate social ties, are predicated on a shared conception of equivalence and perhaps even of replaceability: for the Mandak, a *malanggan* pattern is equivalent to a pig, which in turn is equivalent to the right to work a piece of land for a lifetime (Derlon). While the Anga allow for the exchange of a woman for another woman and/or for some valuables, conversely, "a game-gift cannot be replaced by a shell-gift, and a shell cannot replace a piece of pork" (Lemonnier, 1993 and herein). In agonistic exchanges, as Maurice Godelier points

Photo 2: In the Arapesh-speaking village of Ilahita, in the interior Sepik region of Papua New Guinea, gigantic long yams (*Dioscorea alata*) are decorated and displayed by men of one of the residential wards, as testimony to their spiritual power (Photo D. Tuzin, 1970).

out, the "war of gifts is possible only if the objects given are comparable, even though their value may differ."

The Object as Person

We will not linger here on the innumerable situations in which the object, be it an edible plant or animal, is treated like a person or the abode of a spirit or an ancestor. The long yams of which some New Guinea societies are so proud are (like) persons and are exhibited during ceremonial exchanges. Women mourn when the pigs they nurtured are killed. In Polynesia, the main sea-dwelling species are treated with respect. Tongan fishers, for example, use an "honorific language" and songs when addressing the shark they wish to attract and capture, and generally speaking, the relationship they entertain with it is "a gendered, hierarchical relation [...] in an ecosystem from which women are excluded" (Bataille-Benguigui, 1994). Elsewhere, the situation is reversed: the animal-object incorporates the human subject, as in Mono-Alu (Solomon Islands), where the ashes of incinerated nobles were thrown to the sea and had to be swallowed by certain species of fish, which in turn were personifications of the status of "grandmothers," so that the deceased person might gain access to the world of the ancestors (Monnerie, 1996) — evoking a return to the ancestral womb.

In many cases, the ritual treatment given an object and the fact that equivalence may — or may not — be applied to it in the exchange context refer to conceptions of the person and of his/her component parts. This is true for the *malanggan*, since "the logic of the circulation of their rights expresses local theories of conception." Thus, the painted, sculpted object is held to "symbolize the 'blood' transmitted along paternal lines that comes and goes between dual groups" (Derlon); it is true for Baruya salt, "secretly associated with semen, with male strength" and the *kwaimatnie*, which "contains the power to make humans grow" (Godelier, 1969 and herein); it is true of the Wodani cowries, the circulation and use of which in compensation for human losses within the group (women given in marriage, men killed) guarantee the agnatic continuity of society (Breton); and again of *kava*, "a plant substitute for the ancestral seminal substance, regenerating strength (a sign of *mana*) and life" (Douaire-Marsaudon). It is also the case for the equivalence posited by some Anga groups between women and wealth, suggesting the conceptual "division" of wives into such components as their fertility, productivity and sexual availability. Payment of bridewealth becomes meaningful as a symbolic cutting up of the bride's body (Lemonnier). The Wodani view each cowry as paying for a part of the bride's body, but it is possible to construe the anatomy of the cowry as the body of the dismembered bride, which body is sexless and essentialy composed of paternal organs. When a woman has been entirely paid for, she is said to have been eaten (Breton). Again, money may be seen not as paying for the bride, but rather as a substitute sister, to be exchanged. This attitude is adopted by the Baruya: when a wife-taker does not have a sister to give in exchange for the wife he receives, he gives his brother-in-law some valuables later on (Lemonnier, 1993 and herein). This is the function assigned to the object in marriage and homicide payments, when it is held to be the effigy of a person and as such given a name, an anatomy, a history or powers susceptible of endowing it with a specific identity. The *malanggan*, as well as the funeral effigies (*rambaramb*) of Malekula, may also personify a deceased person. Through these "person-things" (Godelier), these "fictions," or "metaphoric persons" (Breton), society defines, contemplates, recognizes and reproduces itself.

However, we must not confuse anthropomorphization of the object, functioning on the basis of analogy (sufficiently documented to obviate the need for examples), and identification with the object. The thing anthropomorphized remains independent, whereas, conversely, the thing with which the person identifies is not necessarily anthropomorphized. Identification posits the projection of the subject onto the object—or its opposite, an introjection of the object, which amounts more or less to the same thing—but also the projection of the other onto the thing. As early as 1925, in his essay, *The Gift*, Marcel Mauss (1954) had already pointed out that something of the giver departs with the object offered, and for him this accounts for the ensuing obligation to give something in return. Identification, then, is generated by the very gesture of giving in a specific context. With identificatory objects such as totems, relics, emblems, bull-roarers or *tjurunga*, however, gift-giving and the relation it creates with others by making one a creditor or by the expectation of reciprocity are absent. Rather, identification is linked here to the need to make up for the ontological lack constitutional of every subject, both individual and collective (Lacan, 1994). In this case the object is what ties the subject to others: that is, to society.[8]

Marilyn Strathern, again referring to Melanesia, has advanced a conception of the relationship between the individual and the object (primarily in gift-giving) closely tied to a theory of the person. According to her, the latter is not unified, but composed of (or broken down into) his or her social relations. This parallels Freud's earlier description of the constitution of the subject. In exchanges, gender no longer has anything to do with one's sexual anatomy, it amounts to a dimension of the person that always contains male and female elements. For Strathern, the person is endowed with parts that relate to each other, to other people or to objects in a same-sex or cross-sex relation.[9] To this way of thinking, the object, in its mediating function, is not a symbol bearing a conventional meaning, or one that requires decoding. It objectivates the person in his or her relation with the self and/or with others. "Others are created not in contradistinction to persons but out of persons" (1988: 171). For this reason, the object becomes a "relational object" (Moisseeff), and may, when given, be the equivalent of an element or a "detachable" part of the person, partially annexed by the receiver. The name seized by the Marind Anim when

---

8. See, for instance, the ritual attribution to the initiate of the sacred emblem of his lineage among the Murik of Lower Sepik (Lipset, 1997).

9. "Gender refers to the internal relations between parts of persons, as well as to their externalization as relations between persons" (Strathern 1988: 185).

they take their victim's head (Breton) is a particularly striking example of this.

Relation to the Object, Relation to the Other, Object-Relation

If we take the psychoanalytic opposition between subject and object as our starting point, we become aware of entering an ambivalent field in which the "object," in the sense utilized so far, takes on a different signification, and the question of the relation between person and object is posed differently. What psychoanalysis designates as the object-relation[10] is the relation, both real and imaginary, entertained by a subject with another person. Thus, we speak of an object-relation when referring to a child who begins to distinguish the surrounding world from his or her own body, or of the way the mother, then the father, are introjected as unconscious representations, making them imagoes.

It is difficult, obviously, (and theoretically risky) to apply Freudian theory to the way different cultures use objects/things to give meaning to social relations. Nonetheless, there may well be a connection between the way in which a culture identifies a person or a divinity, on the one hand, and the object-relation, on the other hand. This is particularly clear when the object/thing represents a maternal or paternal divinity, but much more complicated when we are dealing with an exchange relationship within the wider framework of kinship. A ritual gift to one's maternal uncle, for instance— a textbook example in cultural anthropology—may constitute a counter-gift for the care and love received from the mother, but again, it may very well be a way of reiterating the bridewealth paid by the father to the man who had given him his sister in marriage. We then realize that the object-relation bearing on the maternal uncle is in turn derived from a cathexis in the mother (and from her reciprocal cathexis in her child) or from the father's (libidinal, psychological and social) investment in the woman he has taken as wife. Object-relations may be transmitted, then, and change from one generation to the next. Often they cover three generations, since a single gift may carry accumulated meanings which both the anthropologist and the people involved find difficult to interpret.[11]

Psychoanalysis may also concern itself with the nature of the object (the thing) itself. The Freudian theory of anal fixation (linked with behavior such as miserliness and generosity, saving and spending) and the use of valuable

---

10. This expression was coined by psychoanalyst Ronald Fairbairns on the basis of the Freudian concepts of cathexis and object-choice.
11. See, for example, Bonnemère (1996) for one Papua New Guinea society.

objects, especially money, to symbolize *faeces* is well known. This symbolism is particularly present in dreams (Freud, 1953a), but it may also be found in all sorts of individual or cultural symbolic productions. Beautiful, shiny objects strongly invested in social relations may lend themselves to interpretations of this type. To return to Melanesia, A.L. Epstein (1979), in the footsteps of Geza Roheim, has suggested this reading for the use and representation of shell money (in the lexical category of *tambu*, "taboo") by the Tolai of New Britain. Referring to the Freudian concept of anal sadism,[12] this anthropologist points out that Tolai shell money is accumulated then used in a calculated manner to acquire prestige and for the political manipulation of social relations. A man who is thought to squander away his shells is looked on with particular scorn. The *tambu* are also ceremonially connected with death and, according to Epstein, contribute to the intrapsychic development of a powerful defense mechanism against loss. His interpretation is in fact supported by one Tolai myth: a child whose parents did not give him the food he requested went off along the seashore and received some shells, called sea excrements, in their natural state, from the neighboring Nakanai. He brought them back to his family,[13] thus introducing the present source of money (quoted in Epstein, 1979: 170). Other examples of the link between money and excrement are provided by the oral tradition of New Ireland (Derlon, in press).

"Cargo cults" too may be given a Freudian reading, especially when the local mythology, reactivated for the occasion, facilitates this interpretation. The Yafar associate the Europeans' wealth mythically with maternal fertility, and the pursuit of commodities is viewed as a regression to the original womb as represented by an imaginary cave which the followers (in the 1981 millenarian cult) attempted to locate. Boundless abundance is thus directly associated with the œdipal fantasies so prevalent in this culture, as shown by other material discussed in the present work. Symbolic offerings to appease the spirits of the forest, which provide game, are a way of ridding hunters of their guilt at having aggressed mother nature, just as a modest offering and some chanting are made to obtain permission to cut down a sago palm belonging to a recently deceased relative (Juillerat). In messianic movements based on a reinterpretation of Christianity, such as the Pomio Kivung of New Britain (Trompf, 1990; Whitehouse, 1995), guilt is

---

12. Here is what Epstein, paraphrasing Freud and Roheim, writes about the young child: "Thus the act of defecation becomes the focus of a struggle for autonomy, ushering in the stage of anal sadism. Faeces, the product of the act, now become an expression of power, which may be used productively or destructively; displaced on the copro-symbols, these may be manipulated creatively or serve as instruments of hostile aggression." (*Ibid.*: 171).

13. This is suggestive of the way small children offer their *faeces* to their mother (seen in Western societies), as a sort of spontaneous "counter-gift" for the love received.

more directly connected with the notion of "sin." For the Sulka activists in this movement, who view sin as saturating virtually all human acts, gifts of food to the dead and the payment of money (literally intended to "pay for" their sins) are believed to achieve redemption (Jeudy-Ballini, 1997).

Libidinal and psychological attachment to the mother throughout adulthood is visible in countless cultures, especially in men (Mead, 1935; Juillerat, 1992, Bonnemère, 1996; Lipset, 1997; Silverman, 2001). Roheim (1970), who is both a psychoanalyst and an anthropologist, views *tjurunga*, inasmuch as they are the equivalent of the subincised penis of the initiate, as a phallic object engraved with motifs representing woman as mother. In this case the object would serve to help the adolescent, to whom a *tjurunga* is given at his initiation, to overcome his nostalgia for his mother and to become a part of the community of men. As Marika Moisseeff shows, anthropological thinking must nevertheless go beyond this level of interpretation, which confines itself to the contrived application to social facts of some aspects of the economy of the individual psyche.

To establish a link between the pursuit of the object and the primordial, intrinsic human lack is already to go further than Roheim. Head-hunting in Marind society provides Stéphane Breton with an opportunity to point to the connection between the beheading of an anonymous enemy and the naming of the child by the father. The name of the victim wrenched from him with his life—the "head name"—only becomes meaningful through this bond of filiation, barring which the name would remain an empty signifier. In this perspective, castration is not central to Marind symbolism: rather, what is involved is the primeval lack, with the "true name" referred to in this society by a term designating the female genitals, which embody *par excellence* an absence rather than a loss. The same is true of Wodani money (cowries, whose sheen speaks of their agitated social history) which, despite its apparent incompatibility with the severed head, is also found to be "a part detached from the subject," continually reconverted into new relations, and which works at establishing the society as a comprehensive whole.

* * *

This introduction has only briefly touched upon the rich semantic material produced by every object wielded socially, be it through exchanges, identification or the projective processes that generate socio-symbolic systems. It has provided a mere glimpse of the extent of the subject, based mainly on contributions to the present book. In the ensuing chapters, the reader will penetrate further into the labyrinth of signifiers and established ways of behaving in Oceania societies, which by now belong to nations freed of colonial domination but not necessarily of exploitation and marginalization. Some categories of objects have disappeared—only to reappear, in

Photo 3: Arrangement of Yafar masks and tools in a window of the Musée de l'Homme, Paris (Photo Musée de l'Homme).

some cases, in the showcases of local museums; the rituals that animated them have faded away or been transformed, other objects have come to create new conceptions of relations and exchange, sometimes to replace the old objects, but outside of the previous relational structures. As for the societies themselves, they are still there and still dynamic, and despite their current integration in the globalized world, they go on weaving the relations among their members and with others through the mediation of material things on which they bestow economic or symbolic values susceptible of satisfying the secret desires of every human being: the desire to reproduce oneself, to establish bonds, to acquire power, to ward off death.

Translated by Helen Arnold

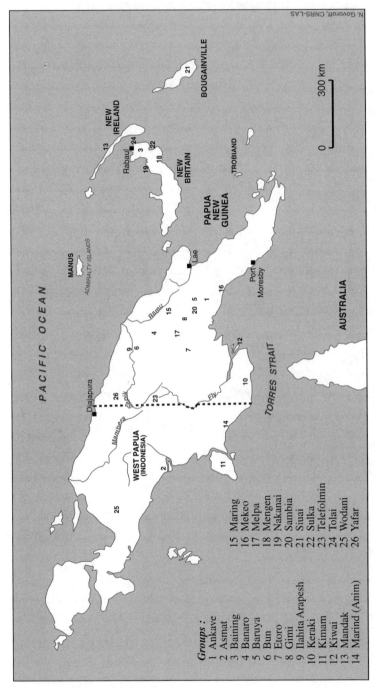

Map 1: New Guinea. Location of the groups mentioned.

Groups :

1 Ankave
2 Asmat
3 Baining
4 Banaro
5 Baruya
6 Bun
7 Etoro
8 Gimi
9 Ilahita Arapesh
10 Keraki
11 Kimam
12 Kiwai
13 Mandak
14 Marind (Anim)
15 Maring
16 Mekeo
17 Melpa
18 Mengen
19 Nakanai
20 Sambia
21 Siuai
22 Sulka
23 Telefolmin
24 Tolai
25 Wodani
26 Yafar

Chapter 1

Subjects and Objects in Samoa
Ceremonial Mats Have a "Soul"*

Serge Tcherkézoff

The Misunderstanding About Some Ceremonial Objects: Are They "Objects"?

When the German administration took control of Western Samoa in 1900, it gave the name of *Alii Sili*, or "supreme chief" of the country, to one of the local leaders. The idea was to weaken the influential groups headed by regional leaders (the "orator chiefs") by establishing some sort of single representative. Not only would this chief represent his country before the Germans, but above all, he was to represent the Kaiser before the Samoans. For indeed, he was asked to proclaim that his position and power were given to him by "His Majesty the Kaiser, the Great King."

That was not the only thing demanded of him. The German administrator knew that in Samoa any enthronement, and more generally any ceremony, was accompanied by a distribution of "fine mats," or *ie toga*. He also knew that these gifts and countergifts between heads of families and influential village leaders were a barometer of the state of relations between families and between villages. To make it clear that a new order had been established, he ordered the "supreme chief" to organize the distribution that was to follow the ceremony enthroning him as "supreme chief" of the country in a very special way. Each of the leaders present were to receive the same

---

* This paper will be published in French as a chapter of my forthcoming book: Tcherkézoff, *La Polynésie et l'Occident. Du malentendu au dialogue anthropologique*, nd 1.

27

number of fine mats. This unheard-of practice revealed very shrewd reasoning on the part of the administrator. Since all of the leaders had received equal treatment, they would all be obliged, in spite of themselves, to acknowledge the supreme power of the Kaiser. They would all become his functionaries, and the power structure would have only two levels: the Kaiser and the local leaders.

However, that idea was grounded in a misunderstanding quite characteristic of modern Western ideology, which posits an absolute split between the subject and the object. Everything would have gone right if the mats had simply been a sort of compensation, a sign of prestige and a means of payment: in other words, medals and money. Had that been the case, it would have been possible to play on the purely quantitative angle. Each leader received the same national decoration, each received the same monetary reward. But mats are not inert. They carry "life," since they represent genealogies. In fact, in some rites mats actually are life-giving objects, as will be seen below.

Another misunderstanding has to do with the idea of inequality. The administrator thought he could disrupt the traditional inequality and present the leaders with the fait accompli of their having been equalized, as the colonial administration desired. Now, putting all of the leaders on equal footing meant making them understand that henceforth the only relevant hierarchical relationship prevailing was between the Kaiser and each Samoan leader. But the Germans had underestimated the ability of the Samoans to systematically reconstruct everything in terms of *hierarchy*. The logic of hierarchy differs from the logic of inequality,[1] however, and is not canceled by a demonstration of equality. When the distribution was over, the prevailing interpretation was not that a new egalitarian order had been established. Simply, the high-ranking leaders were infuriated at not having received the number and kind of mats appropriate to their titular rank (that is, to how far back their genealogy went), and were jealous of the less important leaders, since they wondered what in the world the latter had been doing with the Germans to get "more" than what they were entitled to on the basis of their titular rank.[2]

---

1. We have elaborated on this point elsewhere, using examples from Africa, India and Polynesia (Tcherkézoff 1987, 1994a, 1994b, 1995).

2. This episode, involving Solf and Mataafa, took place in August 1900. It is briefly mentioned in Malama Meleisea's book (1987: 52–53) on the colonial period. The author himself points out the misunderstanding: "foreign observers [...] have tended to see 'fine mats' as economic objects in themselves, as a form of money or capital. The apparent obsession of Samoan chiefs with 'fine mats' has thus often been interpreted as irrational greed. But 'ie toga were not a form of money in the modern sense. Although 'ie toga could be given in 'payment' for services such as house-building or canoe-making, there was no set 'price' for such ser-

The Mandatory Gift, Mauss and Samoa

Pacific island cultures, of which Polynesian, and therefore Samoan cultures are a part, are famous for having based the acquisition of power and prestige on the act of giving. It is by giving—and not by accumulating—that one becomes rich and powerful. This is because someone who has given a great deal may at any point galvanize the network of connections composed of all those people who have been on the receiving end of a gift. That person can obtain help from the others when he has an urgent need to gather a certain number of ceremonial objects to cope with some unexpected event, such as paying a blood-price because some member of his clan has killed a man from another clan, or upholding the clan's renown by making a large contribution to the funeral celebration for the village head, and so on. This is what the "Pacific way" is about: by constantly giving one certainly does accumulate; it is not objects that are accumulated however, but relationships.[3]

Within this context, the Polynesian way of concretizing this logic is through two broad categories of gifts: food and fabrics. The latter may be "fine mats," woven out of strips of cut leaves, or "tapas," made of assembled pieces of beaten bark. Samoa is no exception to this general rule. Today however only the fine mats subsist, at least as objects of gift-giving, practiced by all families. Tapas are now hardly in circulation. In Tonga, on the other hand, both categories may still be found (Douaire-Marsaudon, 1997). In eastern Polynesia (in Tahiti and Hawaii), tapas were the main ritual gift, but the only available observations on them date back to the 19th century (Babadzan, 1993, Valeri, 1985).

In some instances the giver offers—and receives—gifts in both categories. In others, he may give food and receive fabrics, or give fabrics after having received food. Although the names may differ, all Polynesian societies explicitly designate this dualism of objects bestowed.[4] Generally speaking—but this tendency would have to be considerably detailed and qualified—food is produced by men and fabrics are woven by women. However, the sexual identity of the giver and that of the receiver are often independent of this categorization of production. A man may have reasons to give mats, and a woman—in Polynesia, at any rate—may give pigs. As a rule,

---

vices, and the 'ie toga was presented with the same ceremony as on any other occasion to honour the skill of the craftsmen. In Samoan eyes, the number of 'ie toga presented, represented not objects but qualities—respect, prestige, gratitude, deference, recognition, obligation and so on."

3. Godelier, 1982, 1996; Iteanu, 1983; Lemonnier, 1990; Weiner, 1992; Tcherkézoff, nd. 2.

4. Other examples may be found in Douaire-Marsaudon, 1997.

Photo 4: Gift of a fine mat at funerals (Photo Tcherkézoff, 1994).

however, the giver is not an individual, but a family group, and the question of sexual identity may not be at all relevant.[5]

This social character of giving makes it a mandatory act, so to speak. On the one hand, the way the object is brought and presented suggests that it is a gift that the giver was in no way obliged to make. But on the other hand, everyone present is well aware of the truth, which is clear to the outside observer as well. In present-day Samoa, as in the past, if a household does

5. In Samoa, a family that wishes to contribute to the consecration of the village church will offer both types of goods. If, for example, the exchange of gifts takes place between two families whose founding ancestors were respectively a "brother" and a "sister," the gifts may be differentiated.

not make any contribution to ceremonies involving the extended family or village (for births, marriages, funerals, the consecration of a house or a church, the enthronement of a new family or village leader, etc.) this is taken as a sign of its withdrawal from the family or village circle. The threat, which may then be carried out in case of repeated defaulting, is actually an eviction order.

It is a known fact that in Samoa, as in all those Pacific islands that have not yet been converted to the Western system of private property, land "belongs" only to the founding ancestor, and is managed by the representative of that ancestor, the family head (in Samoa: the *matai*). Each household therefore only holds rights to use. To continue to belong to the social group in which one lives, then, one must give gifts. Gift-giving is compulsory, as it were (Tcherkézoff, 1997a).

The apparent enigma of the mandatory gift greatly intrigued Marcel Mauss, the founder of the French school of social and cultural anthropology, and led him to write his famous essay, *The Gift* (Mauss, 1954 [1925]). On the basis of examples collected on different continents by missionaries and administrators during the 19th century, Mauss showed that the practice of giving ceremonial gifts—a truly social act, inescapable for any member of the group—was extremely widespread. What these practices have in common is the "sacred" nature of the object of the mandatory gift (Tcherkézoff, 1997b), which object symbolizes the social group, be it the society as a whole or one of its sub-groups (a "clan" or an "extended family").

The first example chosen by Mauss in the opening chapter of *The Gift* pertains to Samoa. Quoting several texts written by missionaries, Mauss notes that in Samoa gifts may be of two kinds: food and household implements, on the one hand, and "blazoned mats" (mats bearing the history and emblem of the clan or extended family, its "blazon"), on the other hand. Quite remarkably, Mauss immediately had the intuition that only the second kind of gifts—the mats—were relevant to what he was looking for, since those mats were symbols of a group (a family, clan, or other), whereas the objects in the other category seemed to tend to be attached to an individual. He also observed that mats were the only objects that could be transmitted hereditarily as well as given as gifts. This enabled him to link the Samoan example to other instances in which the objects given had the same "comprehensive" character; that is, in which they symbolized the existence and permanence of a social unit (Tcherkézoff, 1997b).

Samoan Mats, Mandatory Gift-giving and Land

The ethnographic writings at Mauss' disposal were extremely slim, and he was guided essentially by his intuition, along with his leanings toward comparative analysis, nourished by extensive reading. Today's anthropologists are much more informed, and we are able to state that known facts about Samoan culture are even more assertive than Mauss could imagine, as to the extent to which "fine mats", *ie toga* (sometimes simply called "mats", *fala*)[6] are the object of a special, extremely sacred type of gift, and for that reason their ritual efficacy is incomparably greater than anything found in any other category, including pigs, implements, and various kinds of food.

Samoan mats clearly symbolize a group (i.e., they symbolize a family name) and never an individual. Conversely, all of the other ceremonial goods, which are not in circulation for as long or do not circulate at all (they are only given once), do not carry the history of a group inscribed on them. They may include pigs, fish, plant food and tools for tattooing, and formerly, canoes and building materials. Nowadays, there are also some very specific tinned foods, as well as paper money.

An old mat is a known and a renowned object. Even if it is kept far from its place of origin, it retains the memory of the family that wove it and gave it away for the first time. It carries with it the genealogy of that family. Nothing of the sort may be said of a pig, a basket of fish or a banknote. Finally, a mat can be used to pay for anything and everything, including the ceremonial gifts required for a marriage, a funeral, etc., but also the gift given to the carpenter who built a house or the craftsman who made a boat. This is true today, as it was yesterday.

But why should one give mats? Why, indeed, are mats the objects used for mandatory gifts, as Mauss had surmised? When the question is put to Samoans, the answer is invariably that one must constantly reassert the bonds of belonging. The absence of an appropriate gift is viewed as com-

---

6. The terminology is extremely complex. *Fala* designates a family of trees (pandanus), the leaves of which may be used to make mats, both coarse and fine. Only the latter are used in the ceremonial context, and are then designated as *ie toga*, or simply as *toga*. "*Ie*" designates the kind of pandanus used for fine mats, and by extension *ie* also designates any sort of fine fabric, be it made locally or imported. The origin of *toga* is debatable. Popular etymology tends to link it to the neighboring kingdom, the Tonga archipelago (see below, the end of the myth of Futa's Mat); my own hypothesis is that the term comes from a proto-Polynesian verb, *to*, or more probably *tao*, which expresses the very idea of "giving," or even more plausibly, "giving in return for while covering an original gift." There are precise reasons for this interpretation, but their explicitation would require a long linguistic discussion (which was commenced at the 1996 conference of the European Society for Oceanists, in the texts contributed by Marshall Sahlins, Penelope Schoeffel, Françoise Douaire-Marsaudon and myself to the session on gift-giving, organized by Paul van der Grijp and Jeff Marck. The papers are available at the secretariat of the Anthropology Department of Copenhagen, 1996 ESFO conference. I have pursued the discussion in several papers (publication pending, Tcherkézoff nd.2). See also Marck, 1999: 339–343.

Photo 5: Tongan islands: young man wearing a Samoan fine mat around his waist for his wedding (Photo M.-C. Bataille-Benguigui, 1983).

ing from a household that is withdrawing, de facto, from membership in the community.

All households are users of the land. They are of course "at home" there ("our land," *lo tatou fanua*), in the sense that they are "heirs," *suli*. But as we know, this right is only a right to use. Being an heir does not give unlimited guarantees. Through the kinship system, an individual inherits a great many names and pieces of land. In actuality, he chooses to give preference to one of the many possible ties when he decides where his main residence will be located, be it in his birthplace or a place he comes to live in later. On every occasion (including a marriage, or payment for some labor done for the benefit of the entire village), each family must necessarily give some mats. To refrain from doing so is like ceasing to claim "I belong here."

Now, everyone always has some cousins who are anxious to establish themselves on the good pieces of the family land. A household that contributes
less than is expected of it loses its prestige and will soon be obliged to yield
up some of its land, to restrict its living space and to abandon some of its
other rights. Its representative loses his authority within the family council,
and so on.

This is of course the other side of the coin in a "customary" land tenure
system, in which land is only "in the family," (*aiga*) (see Tcherkézoff, 1998).
The notion of *aiga* is extremely fluctuating in Samoa, as elsewhere in Polynesia. The group may always expand if the majority decides to adopt an
individual, or even an entire nuclear family. Those involved generally but
not necessarily have some kinship relationship, often distant, with the group.
Furthermore, at any point of time the territorialized group may decide to
exclude one of its members: again, either an individual or an entire household. "Custom" (*aganuu*) does not prescribe any individual right to go
against such decisions.

In short, to not give mats is to lose one's identity as belonging to the
group. The Samoans smile knowingly when they explain their word for
«ceremonial exchange» to an outsider. The expression (*faalavelave*) designates all mandatory gifts, and at the same time designates a "difficulty" or
a "problem." It is "hard" to get the mats together, we "would like to do
something else," they say, but it is "necessary," and explain that through
giving mats they must constantly "show that they have inherited a name
and land" to "be sure we can stay where we are." We are talking about
this logic of circulation at the intra-familial level (*aiga* meaning the extended family), but the same logic prevails between families living in a same
village. In exchanges between families, each family must give enough to
maintain its "place" on the village council. The same is true at the national level, where it formerly applied to warfare and now applies to national
politics.

The Permanence of Mats: Reference to a Set Point and Objects that Circulate

In contrasting mats and food (and implements), Mauss stressed the fact
that Samoan mats represented a stable, unchanging valuable. We do indeed
now know that they are the expression of permanence, through their reference to the origins and history of the clan.

This certainly does not mean that families are not anxious to conserve
these valuables. However, no mat is ever kept with the idea that it should
never circulate. Simply, the more "beautiful" the mat (the older and larger
it is, the fact that it was woven with a very fine stitch or made by the sister

or daughter of a famous old chief), the greater the tendency will be to keep it for an exchange worthy of it. This of course leads to situations (especially nowadays) where some mats will perhaps never circulate again for lack of a sufficiently "worthy" (*mamalu*) occasion. However, only a few families that consistently adopt a "Western" attitude (*faapapalagi*) in life have conceived the idea that a mat should be kept forever.[7]

It is nonetheless just as evident that because they symbolize a group, through the name of an ancestor, the genealogy issuing from that name and the land associated with it, mats always refer to a set point. This constant reference is the ancestral name, the burial site of that ancestor, the place or places linked with the entire history of that name. Furthermore, there are in fact some mats intimately tied to that set point which never circulate, and form a reference for those mats that are subject to exchanges; they are the mats that are buried. These serve as burial shrouds. Those ancestors who successively bore the name of the family chiefs are buried with a mat. The very first mat is the one that shrouded the first ancestor to be buried. Others, later, chosen from among the most beautiful mats in circulation, had the same fate. In the name of that set point, which is both abstract (the name) and concrete (the land, funerary sites, mats in tombs), each generation of women of the family plait mats which are in a sense always replicas of the first mat, and which reassert the bonds of belonging. The notion of the "set point" (the sacred) harboring the social motor of exchange is therefore fundamental, as has already been pointed out by other specialists of Oceania.[8] It is this reference to the origins that must not be dissipated, barring which one loses all sense of the future, and the idea that the group to which one belongs is everlasting.

In Samoa, the family group, or *aiga*, is totally defined by this reference to the origins: it is the name, the land, the funerary site, the "house of the name" (where the chief, invested with the name, receives guests). All this is summed up in what is called the "name-title," or more accurately, the "*matai* name." The Samoans devote much of their social life to discussing titles, and in the old days they spent much of their time warring to gain possession of titles (within a same extended family, but one that might extend over entire provinces). A title is never given, however, nor can it be exchanged. A title can only be borne by a genealogi-

---

7. Significantly, those same families are presently defending the idea of creating a National Museum (for the mats and other treasured objects of their culture). It is worth noting that the same evolution may be seen among the Maori. In present-day Aotearoa-New Zealand the word "taonga," formerly reserved for sacred gifts has now come to designate the general idea of "treasured object of our culture," or "cultural heritage," and to qualify museum collections.

8. See Godelier, 1996.

cal «heir», even if considerable flexibility is introduced by the possibility of adoption and the fact that kinship is reckoned bilaterally. Titles are the most sacred objects in Samoan culture. They are the "sacra" par excellence, the "permanent paraphernalia" for eternity. Without titles and their hierarchy, valid for the entire country, the circulation of mats would be meaningless.

Mats as "Gifts of Life"

The Efficient Object

The object of the gift in the Maussian sense (don obligatoire) is a part of what constitutes the origins—and therefore eternity—and this is why it inherently possesses a sacred power, a "gift of life." On the one hand, as "property" it adequately represents the sub-group that offers it: the mat given belongs to "the family named A." On the other hand, being a sacred object, for the receiver it represents the accumulated life force of the donors. This life force has been demonstrated by the fact that the donor group exists and possesses a genealogy which endows it with an origin and a duration.

The more "beautiful" the mat, the more apt it is to demonstrate that quality embodied in the great length of the genealogy, in the ancestry/value, the value accumulated by the giving group—what Samoans, and Polynesians in general, used to call, or still call, mana. This mana is the power of efficacy, the direct outcome of the amount of time/duration exhibited, of that amount of ancestry/value. One can accomplish miracles with mats of this sort (in the legends, the miracles are magic acts of curing, returning someone to life, victory at war, and so on).

One very tangible miracle, still observable today, is that of a person representing a group that has committed a murder or a serious insult and who saves his life by wrapping himself in a mat. Another, still to be seen in 1950, was the earning of duration and genealogical permanence thanks to a mat or a tapa which made possible the celebration of funerary ceremonies despite the absence of a corpse. These are cases in which an individual died in a far-away place, at sea or in another country. Such a death deprives the descendants of a body to bury. During the 19th century there were also the cases of relatives killed at war and whose soul had escaped. In all of those instances, the soul could be recovered with the help of a mat or a tapa. Some legends also mention bones wrapped in tapa or mats, and which came back to life. Rituals have the same effect (according to accounts from the 1960s): if descendants are bothered too often by the soul of a dead person, they dig up the bones, wash them and wrap them up again in a ceremonial cloth.[9] In the neighboring Tokelau culture, early observers found that an altar for invoking a divinity took the form of an upright stone wrapped in a mat. In Hawaii, tapas wrapped around images of the gods played very much the same role (Valeri, 1985). Numerous examples of this type are found throughout Polynesia.

It is a fact that fine mats and tapas are used in Polynesian ritual as *efficient* objects, meaning that they may create or reveal the presence of the sacred in a given place. Elsewhere this function may be fulfilled by an animal (pigs in Melanesia, holy cows in East Africa and India), copper objects (Indians on the west coast of North America), etc. We will return to this topic in our conclusion. In Polynesia, it is fabrics that are invested with this symbolic function.

The Ifoga *Rite in Case of Murder*

Let us take a close look at the extremely important example of payment of the blood-price or the price of a serious insult. The guilty person, or a member of his family, may appear, alone or more often with some kin, before the offended group to avoid a vendetta by demonstrating his readiness to pay compensation, mostly composed of mats. Following a murder, if one of the murderers is seen by some member of the group that suffered the loss, he runs the risk of being taken and killed. But if the person's intention is to announce the payment of compensation, he arrives wrapped in a mat and seats himself in front of the house of the victimized group. He may wait for hours, sometimes for days, until the offended group agrees to let him enter the house and negotiate. But there is no mention of any instance of a victimized group ever striking a man who came in this way: one does not hit a man through a sacred object. This rite, documented by the earliest reports, dating back to the 19th century, is still practiced today, albeit increasingly infrequently.[10] It applies to all those cases in which a person attempts to obtain forgiveness from another group. The term *ifoga* designates the attitude taken, as a whole, by those who participate in the rite, and means "to abase oneself," *ifo*.[11]

Here is the first part of the most complete narration of an *ifoga* rite, as

9. As opposed to Uvea and Futuna, where printed cotton fabrics may play a role in ceremonies (Douaire-Marsaudon, 1998b), in Samoa people continue to maintain a clear-cut distinction between "fine mats," *ie toga*, made from leaves of one kind of pandanus, to be used in ceremonies, and imported fabrics (called simply *ie*, or *ie solo, ie papalagi*).

10. *Ifoga*, performed with all of the decorum described in the earliest descriptions (see below), have been documented in 1981 (for a murder) and in 1985 (for adultery) (Anders Ryman, personal communication, 1998).

11. *ga* being a substantifying suffix.

narrated by a missionary, Stair, on the basis of some observations made by
him in the 1840s :

> In cases of murder or adultery, the common mode of making com-
> pensation to the injured party or their relatives was by the *Ifonga*, or
> bowing down, accompanied with a *totongi*, or payment of a fine. In
> case the offending party thought it prudent to tender this satisfaction,
> he collected some valuable mats, in number and quality according to
> the nature of the offence, and with his friends prepared to make his
> submission. When it was thought necessary to appear very humble,
> the parties took pieces of firewood, stones, and leaves with them, to
> signify that they put themselves entirely into the power of the aggriev-
> ed party, who might kill, cook and eat them, if they thought proper.[12]
> On nearing their place of destination, which they usually managed
> to reach before or by daybreak, the culprit wrapped some valuable
> mats around his body, and with the rest of his party proceeded to the
> place where they intended to make their submission. If the offended
> party was a chief, they proceeded at once to his residence, where, pros-
> trating themselves before his house, they awaited in silence his deci-
> sion. The position assumed on such occasions was that of bowing on
> their hands and knees, or sitting cross-legged, with the head placed
> between the knees.
>
> Immediately on their arrival becoming known, the chief was informed
> of it, and this was the critical time for the anxious party outside the
> dwelling. The *ifonga*, however, was usually deferred until it had been
> ascertained that the angry feelings first felt had in some measure sub-
> sided; but it occasionally happened that the injured party were unable
> to control their passions on seeing their enemy prostrate before them;
> in which case they rushed out spear and club in hand to inflict sum-
> mary chastisement upon the humbled company. Some of the latter, who
> were on the look-out for such a contingency, narrowly watched the
> movements of the party within the house, and were ready to give prompt
> notice of any meditated onslaught, so that the whole *ifonga* were ready
> to take flight on the first notice of an onslaught, either to the bush, or
> else to their canoes. Severe wounds were often given in such cases, and
> sometimes even lives were sacrificed, where the look-out had been care-
> lessly performed, or the onslaught was unusually fierce.
>
> Generally speaking, the *ifonga* or submitting party were well received,

---

12 Cooking requires an oven. To make a Polynesian oven, one must have wood, stones
and leaves. The burning wood heats the stones to white heat. The food is then placed on the
bed of stones, and the entire set-up is covered with large leaves (thus steaming the food).

and a messenger dispatched to invite them to rise and enter the dwelling to *fai fetalainga*, or hold a consultation. The payment of property was then tenderred, accompanied with an apology on behalf of the transgressor by one of his companions. The chief and his friends replied, and sometimes vented their displeasure upon their visitors in no very measured terms. To this wordy chastisement the *ifonga* replied with all due submission, took their leave and retired, heartily glad to escape with their lives, or indeed with whole heads and limbs.[13]

In this account, Stair clearly states that "the culprit wrapped some valuable mats around his body." But later, as he knelt down and lowered his head as far down as possible, he was practically entirely covered by these mats, which were rolled around his legs, waist and torso. Other accounts that I have heard personally, and other recent observations indicate that the culprit may hide completely under a mat while his companions take the position described above.[14] The culprit is "covered"—*pulou*—by a mat. This term, attested in these cases, is also found in comments in myths.

The Myth of the Mat that Saves by "Enveloping Life"

This *ifoga* rite does in fact correspond to a myth, which in turn shows how a person may save lives by covering himself with a mat. Here is the text of a relatively ancient variant. The mat that is central to this particular myth had been passed down from generation to generation through the women, until it came to play its role, the role of giving life.

In the Manua village of Fitiuta[15] there lived a couple. The husband's name was Mata, the wife was called Fesagai. They had a daughter called Futa, who lived in a place known as Falemao and spent all of her time plaiting a mat. Tagaloa, the creator, went to see her with the

---

13. Stair (1897: 96–98). The account goes on to narrate a fact that occurred during warring, where Stair acted as an intermediary, to convince the chief to offer an *ifonga* and thus obtain reconciliation.

14. I myself have never been present at an *ifoga*. This practice was also observed in 1985 in Western Savaii by a Swedish anthropologist (Anders Ryman, personal communication, 1998).

15. The easternmost village of the whole archipelago, the most important one for the entire Manua group (the three eastern islands) because of its relation with the great title Tui Manua. According to the myths, this is the only village in which the creator of the world, Tagaloa, had accepted to have his own home in the tenth heaven, "the purple home," replicated. Tui Manua may have owed its superiority to its position at the extreme eastern tip of the archipelago. The name Fiti-uta means something like "the other side of Fiji." The Fiji islands are west of Samoa and are located at the westernmost tip of the Samoa-Tonga-Fiji area.

intention of marrying her, but she did not agree, for she felt disgust in his presence. Futa took her mat with her and threw herself into the sea. She swam to the island of Tutuila. She reached the village of Matatula, where she settled and continued to plait her mat.

In that village, she married a man named Feealoalo of Utumea. They had a daughter [...].

The rest of the story may be summarized as follows: Futa gave the mat to her daughter. When the girl grew up, she got married, had a daughter and gave her the mat. The history goes on and on for innumerable generations, with the mother always passing the mat on to her daughter. The last daughter in the series is called Tauolo. Like her predecessors, the girl inherits the famous mat from her mother. This time, the myth says: "From her mother, she inherited Futa's-Mat." Henceforth the mat bears the name of *Fala-o-Futa*, or Futa's-Mat.

Another series of events then begins. One night, Tauolo is fishing in a lagoon by torchlight, with two men (cousins or co-villagers). While they are fishing, a Tongan canoe arrives, commanded by Lautivogia, a Tongan. The latter sees Tauolo and kidnaps all three Samoans, Tauolo and her two companions. As usual, Tauolo was carrying Futa's-Mat under her arm. The Tongan boat returns to Tonga. Now Tui Tonga, the king of the island, was the brother of the kidnapper. The king is immediately subjugated by Tauolo's beauty and wishes to make her his queen. But the abductor, his brother, explains that this is impossible: during the journey, he abused of Tauolo, and she is with child.

The king is so annoyed that he falls ill. His brother orders the two Samoan men prisoners to prepare a good meal for the king. Several attempts are made, but the king refuses to eat. His brother then looks for a way to put an end to the king's sadness. He orders the two Samoans to dig a hole. Then he goes to see Tauolo and tells her: "I am going to die. If the king looks for me, don't tell him anything, and order your two companions not to say anything either." He gets into the hole and kills himself, and the two Samoans cover the tomb.

The king seeks his brother, cannot find him and gets angry with the two Samoans. He announces that he will throw them into the fire. A dignitary suggests that he should begin by making sure his brother is not in Samoa, in case he had left for that country. He sends out a boat. The Tongans arrive on the island of Upolu, whose king is Leutele, and they ask him the question. He tells them: "Send the two Samoans back here, and I will tell you where your king's brother is." The Tongans return home and present their report. The king refuses to give in to this threat, orders that a fire be lit in an enormous oven, and that the two Samoans be cooked in it. Here we return to the text :

The time came when the Samoans were to be taken to the oven.[16]
Tauolo then took her mat and unrolled it so that it would cover[17] all
three of them, herself and her two companions. In that position, they
advanced toward the king. When the king saw the mat, he sent his
wives[18] to try to get a mat of a higher [quality][19] than Tauolo's mat.
The king's wives returned with their mats, but none could be compared with that of the Samoan lady.[20]

The king then proclaimed: "Let the Samoans live." From that day
on, Futa's-Mat was known by its new name of "(Re-)covering life."[21]
Another name given to it was "One but a thousand" because all of
the Tongan mats put together could not compare with that single
Samoan mat.[22]

The three Samoans returned home with the mat. From that day on,
fine mats are called *ie toga*. The travelers reached the village of Fale-
fa and gave the mat to Leutele. Even now, it is the same family which
takes care of[23] that mat.[24]

---

16. *umu*: the bed of white-hot stones placed over burning wood (see note 12).

17. *pulolou*: the plural form of *pulou*, the substantive form of which means "hat" (the
traditional hat affording protection from sunlight is a sort of eyeshade cap made of braided
coconut or pandanus leaves) and the verb form of which means "to cover/to be covered,"
when designating a hat on a head or leaves closing an oven.

18. *autaunonofo*: "the group" *au* of those (men or women) who "live with," *nonofo*.

19. *pe i ai* [if there is] *so latou fala* [one of their mats] *e sili atu* [more than] *i lo le fala
o Tauolo* [Tauolo's mat)]; *e stili atu* "more than," with no other detail.

20. *a e le maua lava* [but they were not at all able to obtain] *se fala e tusa* [a similar
mat] *ma le fala o le tamaitai Samoa* [to the mat of the Samoan lady]; *tamaitai* is an hon-
orary term very similar to the English "lady."

21. *Pulou o le ola* "(Re-)covering of life"; for the first word, see note 18. *ola* = "life, living, to live"; *o* = "of."

22. *ma le isi foi igoa* [and an other new name] *Tasi ae afe* [One but a thousand], *aua o
ie uma o Toga* [because all of the mats of Tonga] *e le tusa* [are not the same] *ma le ie lava e
tasi a Samoa* [to the truly unique mat from Samoa].

23. *teu*: "to look after," "to take care of," "to keep," when speaking of a close relative
or a valuable object.

24. This is my translation based on the Samoan text. The legend is part of the 1955
Herman anthology (text 42), an unpublished, typewritten anthology of which the Marist
Brothers of Pago-Pago (American Samoa) made and distributed several copies under the title
*Tala o le vavau. Samoan Legends. Collected and translated by Brother Herman, published
by the Association of the Marist Brothers' Old Boys, Pago Pago*. The document contains
the texts in Samoan and in English (the translation, by Herman, is generally quite accurate).
Herman, a Marist Brother of German extraction, lived in Samoa as a missionary between
1914 and 1970 (see the Preface to *Tala o le vavau* 1976, a different, much shorter anthology but with the same title, published in New Zealand). His anthology contained legends he
himself had collected, along with others collected by the German anthropologist and admin-

Mauss would certainly have appreciated this myth. In *The Gift*, having observed in his first chapter that Samoan mats belonged to that broad category of objects that are both a (group) property and a "talisman," he reminds the reader of Rivers' comment (1968) on the "talisman" that becomes money and the object of a mandatory gift: "[these are] life-givers, as Rivers put it" (Mauss, 1954 [1925]: 178 n.).

Mats and the Soul

Let us now take a look at another case: the capturing of the soul of a kinfolk who died in a distant place. Elderly people may still be heard to tell how they participated in such ritual action some forty years ago. But thanks to ethnographic writings we can go much further back in time, and this continuity is revealing of the importance of the representations connected with this rite. In the 19th century, the preferred object was the tapa, a ceremonial fabric made of bark, which is practically no longer made in Samoa. Once again, we will be obliged to the missionary, Stair, and his memories of the 1840s. We will then go on to quote Krämer, an anthropologist who worked on genealogies with the collaboration of elderly people in the 1890s.

Stair's account refers to a particular type of occasion, but does not explain

istrator C. Stuebel at the end of the 19th century. The present legend, like the others in this anthology, may therefore have been collected between 1890 and 1950. The fact that it is well known to many Samoans, with some variations in family names, shows that it is an old one (a very similar version was documented by Krämer in the 1890s).

Just a word about the final remark, which says, in short, "this is why the fine mats of Samoa are called 'mats of Tonga' *ie toga*." "*Ie toga*" [pronounced *ie tongua*, like "Tonga," the name of the Tongan kingdom] is definitely the usual Samoan expression designating the mats used in the ceremonial circuit both in the 19th century and at present. However, the Samoan word *toga* must have another etymology (see above, note 6), since the length of the vowel is not the same (*ie tóga*, but Tonga land is *Toga*; see the Samoan and Tongan word *toga*, "wind from the south," which actually exists in all Polynesian languages (cf. *kona* in Hawaii, "leeward wind"). Tonga is south of Samoa. The explanation referring to the kingdom of Tonga is not confined to this particular myth. It is a popular etymology suggested by many Samoans in response to questions about the origin of the expression "*ie toga*," irrespective of whether they are referring to the myth or not. This is true even for young people who are not familiar with the myth. This is not at all surprising. Like the sacred kings, the great, sacred institutions always come from somewhere else. Whereas the Samoan myth claims that the expression designating fine mats comes from the country, "Tonga," in Tonga—where this expression is non-existent—it is said that the first fine mat was brought there by… Samoans. Another example: in both Tonga and Samoa, the art of tattooing is said to have been invented in Fiji, etc. This all simply confirms the fact that Samoa, Tonga and Fiji form a cultural area with a long history of intertwining exchanges, wars and princely marriages. This is the birthplace of Polynesian civilization.

what it is. The death was violent, it took place in an accessible place, and the "body" could be taken, and yet the tapa ritual was necessary. One hypothesis would be as follows. If the place of a violent death is within reach, the deceased is certainly a relative killed at war. If the rite must be performed to recover his soul although the body may be taken, then his enemies must have beheaded him. This practice is corroborated by all of the old sources relative to warring. Furthermore, as we know, in the Samoan conception of the person, the head is the part that is equivalent to the whole, and it is from the head that the soul leaves to travel during sleep, and to disappear, at death. However, Krämer's text suggests a more comprehensive hypothesis. First, any unburied dead person or one who is not buried on his own land becomes a wandering ghost (*aitu, agaga leaga*), irrespective of the circumstances surrounding the death, and he then represents a great danger for his descendants. Secondly, if the death occurs at war, the soul of the deceased escapes but apparently is unable to travel on its own to the island of the dead, where it would become an ancestor. It is the family ceremony that turns the dead person into an ancestor. Contemporary commentary has changed in this respect. There are no longer any wars; however, in case of death at sea, the same individuals say that the soul goes with God, and always did so, in all cases, but that although in their younger days the same belief already prevailed, people thought nonetheless that the tapa rite was necessary. Here is Stair's account, followed by Krämer's text:

> In case a person died a natural death,[25] no anxiety was manifested by survivors respecting his spirit, since it was supposed to have proceeded immediately to the Fafa, whence it either made its way to the "Nu'u-o-nonoa" (the land of the bound) or else to the "Nu'u-a-aitu" (the land of the spirits); but, in case a person died a violent death, much fear was expressed by survivors lest the disembodied spirit should haunt its former abode. To obviate this, a woman proceeded immediately to the spot where the death occurred, if within reach, and, spreading a piece of *siapo* (native cloth) upon the ground, waited until an ant or some other insect crawled upon the cloth, which was then carefully gathered up, and, with the insect, buried with the corpse. The insect was supposed to have received the spirit of the dead, and no further fear was felt respecting its re-appearance; but where the person died in battle, or from some other cause, at a distance, the surviving relatives were often troubled and disturbed by visits from the restless homeless wanderer.[26]

---

25. And, it is inferred, if a funeral is performed.

26. Stair, 1896: 39. Stair then goes on to discuss those cases in which the corpse is not retrievable (because of warring in a distant place or for another reason), and quite curiously, seems to claim that nothing could be done. This is in contradiction with what Krämer says,

This shows how the solidity of the family and the cohesiveness of family ties shape all aspects of the lives of Samoans [...] The family makes sure that the deceased finds rest on his native soil, and that his bones are not scattered in all directions. There is nothing more horrifying than the idea of being buried in a foreign land[27] or [simply] not even being buried. It was believed that even a man who was a victim of homicide, at war, for instance, also became a wandering ghost. If the family of the deceased had the possibility of doing so—and even if some time had elapsed in the meantime—it went to the place where the deceased had lost his life, so as to catch his soul[28], which was wandering around aimlessly. To do so, people spread a piece of white cloth[29] at the place where the death had occurred and waited until any creature whatsoever, such as a cricket, a june beetle or an ant, wandered onto the cloth on its path. They then quickly rolled the cloth up and placed it, with its contents, on the tomb, for they believed that the soul of the deceased had entered the body of the animal. I had an opportunity to witness this procedure recently, following the battle of January 1st, 1899, in Apia. Once the soul has found rest in this way, the family no longer has anything to fear. The soul then goes its way, traveling from East to West, across the islands, diving into the sea each time it reaches the last rock on an island, then climbing onto the next island, until it reaches the fafa,[30] which is the entrance to the subterranean world located near the village of Falealupo[31], in Savaii.[32]

---

and also with the accounts I myself have collected. We may infer that his information was incomplete, and that he came to an overly hasty conclusion.

27. The context of this passage makes it clear that Krämer is speaking of the "familial" native soil *aiga* and not of Samoa as a whole as opposed to the foreign islands.

28. "*um so daselbst noch nachträglich seine umherirrende Seele einzufangen.*"

29. "*Sie breiteten zu dem Zwecke ein weisses Tuch*"; Krämer does not give any other details. The reference to whiteness enables us to exclude ground mats, and in the European vocabulary of the time, it invariably refers to tapas and/or fine mats.

30. Stair (1896: 39) also mentions this trajectory of the souls. Some elderly people have heard their parents tell about this (in my notes from 1982).

31. This village, still in existence (although it suffered enormously from the 1990–91 cyclones), is of course the westernmost point in the entire archipelago.

32. Krämer (1902–3, vol. II: 107); my translation, with the help of Irène Glébov). Krämer is the preeminent source for Samoa in the 1880–1890s. His work is invaluable for the tremendous number of narratives and interviews he took down (unfortunately, for the rite of wrapping the soul, Krämer only gives his personal remarks). In this respect, his two volumes are far superior to anything published by the missionaries (Stair and Turner, whose writings include very few quotations in Samoan), with the exception of the recently unearthed diary of the first missionary (J. Williams, see Moyle, ed., 1984). Although Williams did not stay long, he collected information from a few adventurers who were living there in 1830. An English translation of Krämer (1902) has recently been published (Krämer, 1995). The passage

Mats, the Soul and the Land

The rite of wrapping the soul in a tapa or a mat makes it possible to perform a funeral and to *bury* the dead. To be more accurate, it enables the interment of the symbolic presence of the deceased person. This contents the deceased person who, it is hoped, will not return to haunt his descendants. *But also, if the corpse is not available (in case of death at sea), it makes it possible to erect a tomb on his land.* To this very day, although the rite is not practiced and, fortunately, decapitations during warring no longer exist and people rarely die at sea, it is evident that for families, discussions around the choice of the land on which the dead person will be buried are of the utmost importance.

In these cognatic systems, with the compounding factor of the many adoptions, each individual has numerous kinship ties with a number of different family territories. For example: Vii, a woman, is the daughter of Fiu, her father, and Nifo, her mother. When Fiu was alive, he possessed a title that was very well known throughout the country. But he had chosen to live with the family of his wife Nifo, and therefore in the village of the latter (although the general rule of village exogamy is that the couple lives in the man's village). Nifo and Fiu had several children, some of whom emigrated. One son, Lu, remained in the family home. The parents wanted to build another, more spacious house, with electricity, and established themselves somewhat further away on a piece of land connected with the title of the father of Nifo, the mother (Fiu was a high-ranking civil servant in the administration set up when the country became independent, with a good salary). When Fiu and Nifo died, almost at the same time, their daughter Vii (a married woman with many children and grandchildren), who lived with them, remained in the house. But where should the parents be buried?

The son Lu and the daughter Vii each wanted their parents to be buried as close as possible to their own house. The daughter, Vii, prevailed. She was able to convince her brother for two reasons. One was of a general nature: a brother must respect his sister's decisions. This might not have sufficed, however. The other reason was that Vii lived on a piece of land where the children born to the brothers of Nifo, the deceased mother, could come to settle at any point, since the land was linked with the title of Nifo's father. By erecting the tomb of both of her parents—the tomb of Nifo, which was normal, *but also* the tomb of Fiu—Vii became the special guardian of that land, which had begun to become not only the land

---

quoted is in volume II, p. 115. I myself have a hand-written French translation (by Glébov) of all of volume II and the beginning of volume I (both of which are devoted to ethnographic observations, whereas the rest is a vast collection of genealogies).

of Nifo's father, but also the land of "Nifo and Fiu." Their daughter Vii now has much greater assurance that her own children may also live there if they so desire, alongside of the collateral descendants of Nifo's father, if the latter go there some day.

Mats, the Soul and Symbolism

The Soul and Symbolic Efficacy

There are two salient points here. Politics of relations to land pervade the entire social sphere. Also, the symbolic handling of death is not the simple consequence of some putative belief in a "soul." The idea of some sort of "totemism" (in the 19th century sense of the term) should also be dismissed. Contrary to what Frazer, the specialist of "primitive" logics supposedly functioning in that manner, had to say about this sort of situation, the Samoans definitely do not "confuse" the animal used in the rite of the mat, an animal symbolizing the presence/absence of the deceased person, and that component of the person—*agaga*—that the missionaries translated by the word "soul." If Krämer is to be believed—and here too, the expression smacks of Western materialism—the soul "enters" the animal which serves as a temporary prop. It is not confused with that animal. *As for the efficacy of that symbolic joining, it is provided by the fact that the animal is on/in a ceremonial fabric embodying a genealogical history.*

The Samoans conception of the soul is attested since the writings of the first missionaries. It is the component that leaves the body at death, mounts towards the ridge of the mountain and begins its travels westward, to reach the island of the dead. Although the rite described by Stair, and more surely, the one described by Krämer, date back to a time when the term was already established, it is not mentioned in their writings. I asked the question in my own talks with the elderly people who spoke of the rite (and who did not add anything that Krämer had not already evidenced). The answer came immediately: the insect or the fish "is not the *agaga*." Some people added: "Because the *agaga* is already with God." Yet it was perfectly self-evident for these people that the rite did have to be performed nonetheless.

In his text, Mauss emphasized the "spiritual" character of sacred gifts. The object given contains "some soul" ("*de l'âme*"), a "spirit." There has been endless discussion, since then, on the meaning of that too-famous "spirit of the gift." According to Mauss, sacred objects such as the Samoan "blazoned mats" that are given are containers of a spiritual principle, and as such, a sort of extension of the human being. Those objects have "some soul," they are "things with *mana*," as he wrote. Mauss himself made a clear distinction between the "individual spirit" and the idea of sacredness/*mana*, which links people to the sacred objects that are given. Similarly, to understand the Samoan way of thinking, one may simply replace "soul" by something like "ancestry-value," "genealogical solidity" or "roots." Each time a person gives mats it is as if he was saying: "look, this crisscrossing of fibers shows how numerous and old my genealogy is (expressed by how fine the fibers are)!"[33] The more the mats one gives are "fine," the more one convinces the others, so to speak, of how far back one's genealogy goes, and therefore of one's preeminent rights and of the "sacred power," or *mana*, of one's family. The less one gives to others, the less one shows these, and the less ancestry-value one attributes to oneself.

Here again, the example of the Samoan funeral ceremonies without a body is enlightening. From the "spiritual" angle, there is nothing more to be discovered than in the example of the insect that, once wrapped in the mat, becomes the symbol of a kin who died far away, and who can then be buried. The fish or insect that jumps onto the Samoan mat spread on the waterside when a relative who died at sea is being mourned is not the "soul" of the dead person. That little creature is *a symbol of the soul of the deceased.* Similarly, the "spirit," in the gift of a mat, is not "a soul," but a symbol of the relationship of belonging. The mat does not have a soul. But the intertwined fibers collected from a specific pandanus, washed and dried for days and days and plaited for months by the "sisters" of the family, are *a symbol*, for each of the "heirs," *of belonging* to the genealogy of that family. This, actually, is why the mat or tapa (and in some cases a fabric woven of coconut bark) has the symbolic power to transform an ordinary animal into the vehicle for the soul of an individual. Just as these fabrics, when wrapped around a black stone or a piece of sculpted wood, may cause the divine spirit to be declared present in these objects (in Tokelau, Hawaii and Tahiti).

The Imaginary and the Symbolic

Firstly, we have a distinction between beliefs (and the translation of those beliefs) and symbols, with the latter playing a very real role in social relations. Mats, tapas and coconut fiber fabrics are real, and their "power" in exchanges is very real, despite the fact that this power is the symbol of a belief—belief in the transmission of an ancestral *mana*, as well as the symbol of a long lineage, to which the genealogy testifies. The latter is sufficiently long and rich in details about the generations mentioned to be

---

33. The metaphor of the ancestral divine-entity that is "woven into" the thread of these mats is an attested theme in Polynesian culture. The example of the inhabitants of Rotuma island (attached to Fiji, but peopled by migrants from western Polynesia) is very telling (Hereniko, 1995), but by no means unique.

authoritative as to the beginnings of history, and these beginnings, in turn, are lost in myth, or (in the case of the «greatest» genealogies) in the cosmogony. But there is no reason to accuse these people of believing that their origins are real, since they certainly were real, in one form or another: they did of course have ancestors. That *reality* is definitively invisible (what exactly did that first ancestor do?) but it is perpetuated in an *imaginary* form.

Secondly, we have a distinction, precisely, between the *imaginary* and the *symbolic*, in this case between the imaginary nature of the *references* symbolized by the objects given — and this accounts for the fixity (in the form of beliefs) and the inalienable position of these references — and the symbolic nature of the sacred *objects* — and this accounts for the ability of these objects to participate in the chain of exchanges. Mats refer to unchanging name/titles and permanent origins, and they accumulate value as they circulate, just as genealogies come together at each marriage, producing children who cumulate rights to different name/titles (Godelier 1996).

Generalization

The "spirit of the gift" is the expression of a social relationship of belonging (whole/part). Mats may be the material expression of this in Samoa, and may thus *symbolize* it: such is not the case of pigs. Elsewhere, in eastern Africa for example, this ability to symbolize is devolved on consecrated-and-sacrificed cattle, and not on loincloths, for instance. Here, we are outside of what is socially determined. We are in the sphere of chance attention paid to certain things, of the hazards of symbolic construction. In Polynesia, plaiting — the intertwining of fibers — and wrapping (in a mat or a tapa) have come to symbolize belonging, and even the womb, and the gift of life.[34] In eastern Africa — for the Nyamwezi-Sukuma, for example — it is the fact that an animal has a body with openings and blood that is important. The animal is made to drink sorghum beer. This "establishes" the beer, symbol of the soul of the deceased person (since it is the dead who make plants grow). Afterwards, it is possible to "speak" with the dead person and ask favors of him. He may then be given a final "house": the blood of the animal, which in turn has come to symbolize the soul "drunk" by the animal, may be sent toward the ground, the "country of the dead," when the animal is pierced by the sacrificial knife (Tcherkézoff, 1985). Sig-

---

34. A great many comparisons could be made between the various rituals involving wrapping in mats or tapas, at births, marriages (treatment of the bride) and funerals, and even tattooing, for one thing, and cooking techniques (wrapping in leaves, steaming) for another.

Photo 6: Making a special fine mat. (Photo by Richard A. Goodman.)

nificantly, the same logic *and the same vocabulary* of "entering" and "expelling" is used when these same animals are given in compensation for killing (the blood-price) or for marriage (bridewealth) (Tcherkézoff, 1986, 1993).

In Samoa, mats and not pigs; in eastern Africa, cattle and not loincloths. The need for symbolism allows so many combinations. But be this as it may, it is a fact that some objects definitely are chosen as "*mana* objects.*" For whenever a social group exists, an imaginary core of identifying references is developed, and it is the symbolic manipulation of these that constitutes the very life of the group. The group pursues the only tangible reality residing in all of these representations; that is, its own existence, a wager on eternity. This reality is the feeling of belonging, whence the feeling of existing. It is the tangible side of the imaginary core of identity. The manipulation of symbols of this reality — in this case, fine mats — is aimed at the perpetuation of this reality. This is why these symbolic objects are always promises of life or gifts of life, in one form or another.

Another similar comparison may be made without leaving Oceania. In New Guinea, this essential role is often played by pigs. In Polynesia, and especially in Samoa, pigs are not sacred, and it is ceremonial fabrics — more particularly mats in Samoa, tapas in Tonga and formerly in Hawaii and Tahiti — that play this role. In New Guinea, in what are known as "Big

Men" societies, genealogical memory is often unimportant. What counts above all is success in exhibiting a maximum of wealth so as to become a prestigious leader. Hundreds of pigs are lined up, to be given, for ostentatious generosity is a guarantee of prestige. In Polynesia, the great social affair is the cult of genealogy. What is offered to be seen and heard is not only a given quantity, and not only the tale of earlier exchanges, remembered by all, but also a definite quality, defined by the permanence bestowed by this founding history. When a large, very old mat is given it is accompanied by a whole speech narrating its itinerary within the group and the succession of generations, sometimes dozens of generations, all of which enhances the status of the donor's generation. Sometimes quality may even reverse the reference to quantity. In one exchange that took place in the early 1980s, one family arrived with fifty mats and made fun of another, which had only brought a single mat. Those making fun were unaware that part of the mythical pedigree of the title in the name of which the single mat was given included a reference to a mat "worth a thousand"; precisely that genealogy mentioned in the myth quoted above. They in turn were mocked by the others. In a case like this, the only way to win would be to find a tale in the mythological/legendary corpus that cancels the significance of the other tale. To win, however, one obviously must convince the entire community. Now for ever so long all of the great families — with the help of numerous specialized "orators" — have watched over, cultivated and embroidered on a series of tales, each of which is capable of assimilating many contradictions (in case they are brought up) by going backward "higher and higher" and integrating new genealogical connections in the story. The descendants are necessarily proud to be involved in the new story, and therefore become its supporters in contests involving bouts of oratory and exchanges.

As the saying goes, the more you have the more you get. The only reserve being that in Samoa, wealth is not reckoned according to the number of mats, but on the basis of the number of epic ties and of kinship ties, forming a network whose knots are symbolized by mats ("the mat that was made by family A for the enthronement of chief B who gave it away when his sister's daughter was married…"). Mats that bear stories like that may be worth "a thousand" recently made mats which do not yet have anything to say about the history of Samoan families.

In present-day Samoa, in the early 1980s (at which time the above observations were made), mats were still being made and given away. No modern object, no paper money has been able to replace them, whereas when someone does not have any pigs, he can replace the gift of a pig by the gift of (large) tins of meat (*pisupo*). As long as Samoan women may be seen busily plaiting fine mats, we can be sure that the social reference for all Samoans is still the family group, *aiga*, with its genealogy, and that Samoa continues to be a country-of-families, O *Aiga o Samoa*, and not simply a collection of individuals.[35]

Translated by Helen Arnold

---

35. Recently (since the mid 1990s), it has become increasingly necessary to make a distinction between the "north-western Upolu" region and the rest of the country in any discussion of the relative abandonment or continuation of mat-giving.

Chapter 2

The Kava *Ritual and the Reproduction of Male Identity in Polynesia*[*]

Françoise Douaire-Marsaudon

The *kava* ritual was traditionally one of the major Polynesian rites, in that some crucial issues hinged on it. There were issues of a directly political nature—that is, pertaining to the organization and wielding of power in a particular society—and others pertaining to the construction of the person's identity—that is, to the acquisition of those social attributes that enable individuals to take their place and play their role in society[1]. The present article places emphasis on how one of these identity-linked aspects was dealt with. Its purpose is to show that the *kava* ritual not only partook in the ongoing development of a religious hierarchy, but that it was also the locus of transmission, between those men who assumed leadership, of an idealized form of manliness. If this is truly the case, then the *kava* ritual, which differs considerably from the great initiation ceremonies for men found in so many other Pacific island societies, and especially in Melanesia, may be seen to fulfill the same main function, which is to say the reproduction of (at least one part of) the male identity[2]. Moreover, as will be shown, irrespective of the conception the different Polynesian or Melanesian societies have of the differences between the sexes, there seems to be a specific, essen-

---

[*] First published as «D'un sexe, l'autre : Le rituel du *kava* et la reproduction de l'identité masculine en Polynésie», *L'Homme* 157, 2001: 7–34.

[1]. I have shown how the two aspects, one political and the other identity-related, may be articulated, in two previous articles (1996 and 1998a) on the *kava* ritual.

[2]. See Godelier, 1982; Lemonnier, 1990; Bonnemère, 1996.

tially paradoxical issue at stake in the reproduction of men's identity: that is, the fact that men originate within women.

To make my point, I will discuss the example of *kava* rituals in several Polynesian societies, and more specifically in the kingdom of Tonga. For an understanding of what follows, the reader must be familiarized with the object itself—the *kava*, which is both a plant and a ceremonial drink—within its Pacific island context.

General Remarks on *Kava*

The Consumption of Kava *in the Pacific Islands*

The beverage made from the *kava* plant (*Piper methysticum*) was used for ceremonial consumption in many Pacific societies, and was not confined to any one of the three main South Pacific cultural areas[3]: Micronesia, Melanesia and Polynesia. Polynesia does seem to be the main focus of the kava ritual, however (Newell, 1974: 376). In most Polynesian societies, *kava*-drinking was common on a wide variety of occasions. Here is what Father Bataillon, a French Marist on a mission to Wallis and Futuna in 1838, had to say:

> the cava plant is almost the only thing these people really need. Indeed, they use it to honor their divinities and to propitiate them; they use it to make peace with their enemies, and to maintain the benevolence of kings and chiefs; the guilty owe their pardon and even their lives to it; it serves as talisman, to obtain good health and find lost objects; it presides over all unions and all visits, and over every procedure, be it religious or lay, public or personal, however unimportant; in short, nothing is done without offering cava as a sign of adoration or friendship. (Bataillon, 1841: 10–11)

Because it was a sacred drink, and the drink was the focal point of ritual practices for the worship of "pagan" divinities, *kava* was long condemned by missionaries. In most Polynesian societies, missionaries were obliged to retract their proscription, however.

Kava-drinking has definitely not been abandoned in present times: in some western Polynesian societies the drink is consumed in many more or less formalized contexts. In Tonga, for instance, ceremonial drinking takes

---

3. The other area being Australia, where *kava* was not consumed traditionally. Those Pacific islanders who immigrated to Australia brought it with them (in the 1970s), but the nature of its properties makes the use of *kava* highly controversial and in some cases even prohibited at present (personal communication by Stéphane Lacam).

place during the rites of passage and during political events involving the chiefdom (visits between chiefs, nomination to a position, transmission of a title, etc.), while more informal drinking may be observed every evening, in the village *kava* clubs.

The Plant and the Drink

In Western Polynesia, the word *kava* designates both a shrub and the herb tea made of it[4] . The shrub, *kava*, is generally from 1.2 to 3 meters high. A number of varieties, varying from one group to another, are distinguished, and duly named[5]. The drink prepared by infusion of its roots is grayish or yellowish, but the liquid may take on a green hue if the roots used are fresh or if chewed leaves are added. Its effects depend on the cultivars, the proportions of plant and water and, of course, the amount absorbed. When highly diluted or taken in small quantities it is, according to one eye-witness (a pharmacist in Tahiti), "a tonic, stimulant drink that imparts the strength to endure great fatigue, while procuring a pleasant state of excitement" (Cuzent, 1940: 278). At higher doses, *kava* will be successively "soothing, sudorific, diuretic, narcotic, anaphrodisiac" (*Ibid.*: 282). Its consumption may cause quaking of the limbs, spasmodic contractions of the stomach and esophagus, and even vomiting. Some inveterate drinkers fall into a state of stupor and senselessness, accompanied by hypersensitive hearing. The same pharmacist reports that in Tahiti, old *kava* drinkers have "very poor eyesight, bright red conjunctiva (. . .), dry, scaly skin, with cracks and ulceration" (ibid.: 281). A recent study of the psychotropic effects of *kava* shows it to contain active alpha-pyrones which are soporific, anticonvulsant and locally anesthesic (Brunton, 1989: 5); when consumed in large amounts it may be hallucinogenic.[6] Labeled a narcotic and hypnotic substance, *kava* is viewed as an effective means of warding off anxiety, a fact that is helpful in explaining the convivial atmosphere so often found among *kava* drinkers (Lebot, 1991: 169–183).

---

4. See Churchward, 1959: 257; Missions maristes, 1890: 158.

5. 14 varieties in traditional Hawaiian society (Titcomb, 1948: 109); 14 in Tahiti as well. However, in Hawaii, the Marquesas Islands and the Society Islands, most of these cultivars have now disappeared, along with the traditional knowledge pertaining to them.

6. Ethnopsychoanalyst E. Bott was struck by the ambiguous effects of *kava*, which led her to interpret the ritual as being, among other things, the locus in which contrasting feelings are presented and expressed (Bott, 1987).

Photo 7: Preparation for the *kava* at Mata-Utu, Wallis, 1999 (Photo Hélène Guiot).

The Ritual

In present-day Tonga, *kava* rituals take place in a wide variety of social contexts[7]. A distinction is generally made between village *kava* (*faikava*), chiefs' *kava* ('*ilokava*) and royal *kava* (*taumafakava*) (Helu, 1992).[8] Now, as in the past all *kava* rituals, from the most solemn to the most informal ones, conform to a precise etiquette. In pre-Christian times, the Tongan *kava* rituals were particularly imposing ceremonies:

> Almost all Pacific islanders, living on islands located between the two tropics, are passionately attached to this drink, but nowhere else is it the object of such a strict ceremonial, of such solemn gatherings as have been observed on Tonga-Tabou. (Dumont d'Urville, 1830–35, 4: 252–253)

An exhaustive description of the ritual is unnecessary here, but a brief presentation of one of the formerly most common ceremonials, such as an '*ilokava*, or *kava* of the chiefs, will be useful. The participants are seated

---

7. The description that follows is based on Collocott (1927), Bott and Leach (1972) and Biersack (1991).

8. One *faikava* in particular may be mentioned : the courtship *kava*, a *kava* ritual (*faikava 'eva*) that gives a young man the right to officially court a girl (Rogers, 1975: 395).

in two semicircles, forming a large oval called an *'alofi*. The chief whose *title* is highest in the hierarchy of those present—that is, the man who bears the title of "elder"—is seated at the head of the main semicircle. The rest of the main semicircle is formed by the various chiefs present, alternating with their *matapule*, or chief's attendants. These chiefs are seated in an order based on the genealogical relation between their title and the title of the person who is presiding (the sovereign in royal *kava*).

In the old days, the *kava* roots were cut into pieces and then chewed by adolescent boys and girls chosen, on the basis of a number of criteria, from among the crowd of spectators who attended the ritual without participating in it directly. It is noteworthy that the *kava* drinkers are not the chewers, as is clearly indicated by one 19th century source, according to which the chiefs, present either inside or outside of the *kava* circle, looked down on the chewing of *kava*, which was left to the common people (Labillardière, 1799: 117).[9] According to our pharmacist from French Polynesia, chewing of *kava* roots excites the mucous membranes to the point where it would be impossible for those who chew it to drink the beverage, and if they did, they would immediately vomit.

The criteria for selecting chewers were mainly based on their health (Dumont d'Urville, 1830, vol. 4: 257) and their having reached sexual maturity. The girls had to be pubescent but virgins, and not be menstruating during the preparation of the *kava*. At present, *kava* is no longer chewed in Tonga, but the girls who are allowed to participate in the preparation of the drink still must meet the same requirements. The boys also had to be pubescent, but it is difficult to determine whether they too had to be virgins, although there is good reason to think so.[10]

The young people first rinsed their mouths, then chewed the pieces of *kava* slowly and carefully until they obtained little patties, which were then placed in a wooden bowl, the *tano'a*. Chewing of the *kava* roots has completely disappeared at present, probably on orders from the missionaries. The *kava* roots are crushed between two stones, in a mortar. The celebrants then dissolved the patties by pouring water gently into the *tano'a* until they were reduced to a liquid. Once filtered, using a stringy fiber made of the shaft of bourao (*Hibiscus tiliaceus*) bark, the drink was poured into cups and distributed in the proper order ; that is, according to the hierarchy of the titles present. All of this was—and still is—performed with the utmost solemnity. This is particularly true of the dissolving and filtering processes, for which the celebrant's arms moved in a truly choreographic

---

9. Some findings on this subject are unclear, however (see Williamson, 1975: 77).

10. In Tanna (Vanuatu), the boys who prepare the ritual drink are circumcised but «not initiated to active sex life» (Brunton, 1989: 97).

fashion. The distribution of the cups, for which each participant is called by his title, is another great highlight, since it reasserts, and in some cases modifies, the hierarchy, and each and all may take stock of the situation as they follow the order in which the cups are distributed.

There is generally a distribution of food during the *kava* ritual: a portion of pork meat, sometimes garnished with a piece of a cooked tuber, is placed in front of each of the chiefs, who take the dish but put it aside without eating it. A person who is outside of the *kava* circle goes to fetch it. That person may be the child of a sister, or a grandchild, or again an outsider: that is to say, someone whose position with respect to the chief is one of *fahu*, which, in this context, means "above the taboos". Hocart interpreted the gesture of carrying off the *kai fono* as the sign showing that the chiefs gathered for the *kava* ritual are no longer themselves, but rather represent their ancestors who are divinities (1915: *passim*).

A Ritual Evoking the Ancestral Spirits

In the zone where *kava* is consumed there are indications that its use—as a drink or libation—was formerly linked to funeral rites and to the worship of the spirits of the dead. Indeed, in Polynesia, according to our oldest sources, the ceremonial itself seems to have initially been a rite for the invocation of the ancestors, who were asked to come to "haunt" the chiefs present. The latter spoke in the name of the ancestors, sometimes after copious libations.[11] In Tonga, the chiefs, or *'eiki*, were believed to be of divine origin: to consult their ancestors, then, meant invoking the divinities. In point of fact, the practice of calling high-ranking chiefs by the name of their ancestors during the *kava* ritual was still current in the early 20th century, whereas the representative of the royal family was called by the name of his tutelary divinity (Gifford, 1929: 160).

A Ritual Associated with the Chiefdom and the Title System

In Polynesia, the *kava* ritual was, and still is, closely tied to the chiefdom and the title system. In Tonga, the most exceptional varieties of *kava* were reserved for the chiefs; the same rule is found in Hawaii (Titcomb, 1948: 111). As for the ceremonial drink, it was, and still is, distributed in accordance with the hierarchy of the titles present. The title is an ancestor's name,

---

11. See Martin, 1981: 84–85; Kirch, 1984: 67; Bataillon, 1841.

or to be more accurate, it is a name/ancestor, borne by the recipient and theoretically by all of his ancestors who bore it before him. In Tonga, titles may circulate in extended families of both noble and common birth (for example, the title of village chief is a title for commoners), but in the formal *kava* ceremonies, the chiefs' *kava* (*'ilokava*) or royal *kava* (*taumafakava*), the vast majority of the titles present are *'eiki* or *matapule* titles; that is, titles indicating rank, not for commoners. On some occasions however, some commoners who had proved to be particularly courageous warriors were admitted to those *kava*, including the royal *kava*. These men were called *toa* and their bravery was believed to partake of the *mana*.[12] There were ties binding all of the *'eiki* titles and connecting them to three royal clans in genealogical form, with one title considered the "older brother", or "younger brother" of another. The titles usually conferred authority over land and the people who lived on it. However, the possession of such authority implied that any bearer of a title must be able to protect both the land and the people, by physical force if necessary. This leads us to the third characteristic of the *kava* ritual.

A Male Ritual

Rivers, writing in the early 20th century, had already pointed out the exclusively masculine character of *kava* rituals in Melanesia (1968: 248). In Vanuatu, for instance, in Tanna, not only are women not allowed to attend the ritual, but the men present must avoid any allusion to them (Brunton, 1989: 98). In Polynesia, the degree to which women are tolerated within or on the outskirts of the *kava* ritual varies from one group to another. In the Marquesas Islands, *kava* was "an everyday drink similar to what tea and coffee are for us, and a pleasure every native enjoys in his home" for men, but its use was prohibited for women and children (Cuzent, 1940: 177). In Tahiti, women did not take part in the rituals, but they drank *kava* for prophylactic purposes, to combat venereal disease in particular (Cuzent, 1940: 280). In Tonga and Wallis, women may partake in a *kava* ritual, but they seem to rarely be present. In Wallis, girls were, and still are, allowed to serve as auxiliaries in the preparation and distribution of the ceremonial drink. Furthermore, queen Falakika and queen Amelia (who reigned between 1858 and 1895) drank *kava* during solemn gatherings (Rossille, 1986: 98–99). However, a 20th century source quoted by R. Rossille states that as a rule "women attend *kava* rituals within their homes and in the

---

12. Some of these valiant warriors had their name transformed into a title, a commoner's title, which was then transmitted to their descendants.

family circle, never outside" (ibid.).[13] According to S. Chave, the presence of women was prohibited when the *kava* ritual was a religious ceremony (in honor of the ancestors) (Chave, 1992: 184). In Tonga, during a courtship *kava*, the future bride prepares the *kava* but does not drink it. For her wedding ceremony, the bride presides over the *kava* circle and receives the first cup. Aside from these specific occasions, women only participate in a *kava* circle because of the title they bear and therefore represent: their sex is in no way considered.[14] In Futuna, women generally do not participate in the ritual (Rossille, 1986: 99).

The reason why the *kava* ritual may be viewed as a male affair is not simply because women are not allowed to participate, or only on some occasions and under certain provisos. As S. Chave clearly saw, it is a place where a form of virility—"deliberate movements exhibiting the musculature", "sureness of movement and physical strength", "words pronounced calmly and strongly" is exhibited (Chave, 1992: 142). The representation of gender differences in which physical strength is conceived as a natural attribute of men is certainly a "commonplace" view, not necessarily backed up by nature: what Bourdieu calls a "naturalized social construction" (1998: 9). This representation is nonetheless shared by Tongans, and by Polynesians in general. Physical strength, the strength that wins combats, is viewed as the distinctive attribute of men, and a sign of *mana*. As a gift of the ancestors, and subject to their obscure whims, it may very well suddenly vanish. Lastly, it is the sign and the proof of sexual potency, and makes a man a "rallier", a chief par excellence, one followed by warriors and surrounded by a multitude of women and children.

In Futuna, *kava* was traditionally used for the libations of warriors (Rossille, 1986: 99). In the Society Islands, "*kava* was a reward given to young men who had just fought their first battle," and the use of *kava* "showed that a young man was henceforth a warrior" (Cuzent, 1940: 278). In Tonga, in earlier times, the *kava* ritual was a way of putting an end to hostilities between two clans or two rival groups, but it was also the place for launching the challenges that started wars. Today, in Tonga as well as in Wallis and Futuna, the more informal *kava*—like those that take place every evening in every village of Futuna, for instance—are clearly a part of

---

13. Rossille suggests that it may be the missionaries, rather than any traditional exclusionary practice, who are responsible for the fact that 20th century women do not attend the *kava* ceremony. However, the sources he himself quotes seem to indicate that while some women drank *kava* in the intimacy of their home, the consumption of *kava* during public rituals was reserved for men. Women sovereigns, whose participation rested on their title, would be the only exception.

14. For example, when queen Salote Tupou III, mother of the present king of Tonga, presided over the royal *kava*, in her time, she represented the royal title of Tu'i Kanokupolu.

the socialization process for pubescent boys. This is where men's stories are told, sexually connoted jokes are exchanged, boys are reprimanded if needed: in short, they are taught how to behave, socially, especially with respect to women. Furthermore, the participation of young men in the *kava* circles, in which a specific etiquette is always observed, including in the most informal settings, is viewed as a good way of channeling their manly energies. By the same token, *kava*, as a drink, is viewed as the best antidote to the unbridled consumption of alcohol (mostly in the form of beer), with its attendant problems (brawls and violence of all sorts).

What the Myths Say about *Kava*

In Tonga, the *kava* ritual is connected with two myths of origin: one pertaining to *kava* and the other to the first supreme chief, the Tu'i Tonga. I have published a full, detailed analysis of these elsewhere (1996 and 1998b), and will confine myself to presenting the main conclusions here.

The Sacrifice of the Leprous Girl

The Myth of the Origin of *Kava*

During a fishing expedition, a Tu'i Tonga stops off on a remote island, whose only inhabitants are a couple of poor people and their daughter, Kava'onau, a leper. The couple, realizing that their host is a chief of the highest rank, decides to make an *'umu* (food cooked in a buried oven), but since they do not even possess a pig, they decide to kill their daughter and serve her to the Tu'i Tonga. When the food is placed in front of him, Tu'i Tonga realizes that the parents have sacrificed their daughter for him...He is touched by the gesture, and orders that the remains of the girl be buried. Two plants grow on the girl's remains: on her head, a *kava* bush, on her intestines, a sugar cane plant. In some versions, a rat bites the *kava* bush and is dazed, but retrieves its balance after biting the sugar cane. A very high-ranking chief, Lo'au, gives orders for the two plants to be brought to the Palace, and for the preparation of the *kava* according to certain rules, to make a ceremonial drink.[15]

The myth of the origin of *kava* is the story of a sacrifice. A husband and wife, too poor to provide a real meal (made of tubers and pork meat) for the supreme chief, sacrifice their leprous daughter for him. The myth begins

---

15. Related by Gifford (1924: 71–75) and Bott (1982: 92ff).

Photo 8: Royal *kava* at Mata-Utu, Wallis (Photo P. van der Grijp).

Photo 9: Royal *kava* at Mata-Utu for the fortieth anniversary of the reign of the King of Wallis in 1999 (Photo Hélène Guiot).

by staging an essential opposition structured around an axis based on the status of the protagonists. On the one hand, there are the sacrificers—the parents—, on the other hand, the receiver of the sacrifice—that is, the Tu'i Tonga. The latter actually possesses the highest conceivable rank in the entire group, his person is sacred and everything he touches becomes sacred as well. Conversely, the couple lives on a "remote" island, with no family other than their daughter, and does not even have a pig. In the Tongan system of representations, this is an indication of the worst sort of poverty, as well as the lowest possible status. When the parents kill their daughter and cook her as a substitute for the pig they lack, their gesture is directly motivated by the desire to do their duty (*fatongia*) towards their leader, in this case the supreme chief. The stress placed on the opposing statuses of the protagonists of the story suggests that the man and wife do not simply represent any specific parents, unique in that they acted in this singular way, but rather, they represent all commoners or people with low status. From this viewpoint, the Tu'i Tonga is not only the supreme chief, but all high-ranking chiefs: in other words, all of those titled aristocrats on whose land the tenant farmers live. The parents' sacrifice is presented as an exemplary act, an act indicating, by contrast, what commoners are supposed to do for their chief under "normal" conditions: feed him a real meal, a *ha'unga*, including tubers and pork meat. It is worth noting, in fact, that in present-day Tonga a noble chief who visits the tenant farmers of his *kainga* absolutely must be honored with a *ha'unga*. Not providing such a meal is not only a serious breach of the tradition, it also seriously damages the honor of those farmers.

If we take a look at the sacrifice itself, now, we see that the girl offered to the Tu'i Tonga as food just barely escapes being eaten. The powerful supreme chief does not eat the victim, and her body is destined to be consumed only following its *transformation*. There is a first explanation of this "aborted" act of cannibalism: the Tu'i Tonga does not devour the girl because he does not overstep the limits of his power, and his authority proceeds partly from the fact that he is not a devourer and a tyrant, since he is capable of self-control.[16] One is of course tempted to wonder whether the victim's disease, leprosy, has something to do with the fact that the supreme chief does not eat the girl. Strikingly, her leprosy does not seem to add any *decisive* element to the story, and we may legitimately wonder why this detail is mentioned, since it certainly cannot be gratuitous. Furthermore, the desquamation induced by an excessive consumption of *kava* (see above) may be

---

16. This explanation has been suggested by Valeri (1989: 228) and Biersack (1991: 235). On the social and political implications of the cannibalism of Polynesian chiefs, see also Howard, 1986.

suggestive of the effects of leprosy, although nothing authorizes us to think that the Tongans confused the two. We will put aside the leprosy issue, for the moment, until the comparison of the two myths sheds new light on the question.

In the myth, the "direct" sacrificers are of course the girl's parents. However, inasmuch as the intention behind the killing of the girl was the need to feed the Tu'i Tonga, the latter is indirectly the cause of the tragedy. From this viewpoint, he becomes the sacrificer and the parents, who sacrificed their most precious belonging, are the victims. Everything in the Tu'i Tonga's attitude indicates that henceforth the debt contracted here will bind the Tu'i Tonga to the girl's parents, who may also be viewed as representing all commoners or people with a low status. In exchange for the sacrifice of the leprous girl, the Tu'i Tonga uses his *mana* to cause plants to sprout, just as he caused the *kava* and sugar cane to grow on the remains of the sacrificed girl. The story begins with the contrasted statuses of the protagonists, and shows how their characters are insurmountably opposed. It then goes on to set up a type of relationship which will characterize them from then on.

Here is the second myth connected with *kava*.

The Cannibalistic Murder

The Myth of the Origin of the Tu'i Tonga

One of the Tangaloa gods, 'Eitumatupu'a, falls in love with the daughter of a chief, 'Ilaheva Va'epopu'a. He descends from the heavens by a great iron-tree (*Casuarina equisetifolia*) and makes her pregnant. Upon returning to the heavens, the god 'Eitumatupu'a sends 'Ilaheva a piece of clay and a yam to feed the child. He also gives the child a name, 'Aho'eitu. The child grows up, and asks his mother who his father is. She tells him he is a god who lives in heaven and he decides to go to see him, using the same iron-tree. Once 'Aho'eitu arrives in the sky, he meets his father, who introduces him to his celestial brothers, but the brothers are jealous of his beauty and cut him to pieces, throw his head into a bush and then eat him up. The father then discovers their deed, and orders his sons to fetch 'Aho'eitu's head. He places the head in a *tano'a* (*kava* bowl) and orders them to regurgitate the remains of their brother, his flesh and his blood, into the bowl. Some time later, 'Aho'eitu resuscitates. 'Eitumatupu'a sends his children down to the earth, and entrusts 'Aho'eitu with the supreme leadership, with the title of Tu'i Tonga. His celestial brothers must remain behind him, to help him govern, without any pretension to the royal title.

There are a great many analogies between the myth of the origin of the Tu'i Tonga and the ceremonial drinking of *kava*. The most striking one is no doubt the presence, in the myth as well as in the rite, of the *tano'a*, or *kava* bowl, in which the Tu'i Tonga resuscitates and which is also used for making the ceremonial drink. These analogies have in fact produced a number of interpretations.[17] Some of my own ideas are as follows. The myth of the first Tu'i Tonga revolves around a murder, the killing of the hero, 'Aho'eitu, future supreme chief, committed by his celestial brothers. The murder is followed by an act of cannibalism, the eating of 'Aho'eitu followed by his resurrection. Here too, the story of the cannibalistic murder proceeds by oppositions: in this case, the two contrasting "births" of 'Aho'eitu. One, the first birth, is a "normal" one. 'Aho'eitu, the hero, is first born to a woman. His mother may be the daughter of a chief, she may have been impregnated by a god, but she is nonetheless an inhabitant of this world. The other, second birth, is a prodigiously extraordinary one. The hero is killed and devoured by his divine brothers and is born again, not from his ashes, but from his remains, from the bottom of the *tano'a*, thanks to his father, a god in heaven.[18] The first birth delivers a creature who is definitely different from ordinary human beings, since he is the product of fecundation by a divinity. However, if we retain the Tongan theory of the maternal transmission of bodily substances—according to which it is only the mother's substances that are transmitted to her child—then 'Aho'eitu is not godly *in his body*, even if he was fathered by a god descended from the heavens. There were, indeed, two theories of the transmission of substances in Tonga. One—also found elsewhere in Polynesia—according to which both father and mother jointly transmit their substances to their offspring, while the other—which seems to be specific to Tonga—postulates that only the mother transmits her substances to her children. There are several indications that the exclusively maternal transmission of substances arose with the development of the lineage of supreme chiefs. The distinctive quality of these high-ranking chiefs was indeed transmitted by the women, thus making their nobility unquestionable, since it was grounded in a criterion inscribed in the body. What is involved here is probably this exclusively maternal transmission of substances, then. To return to the myth, we find that the hero's transformation into a unique being, both human and divine, is only completed by the second birth, which gives him access to the highest status. But he acquires this double nature gradually, from the moment he is

17. See Bott and Leach, 1972; Valeri, 1989; James, 1990; Biersack, 1991; Douaire-Marsaudon, 1996 and 1998a.
18. According to Sahlins, the Fijian chief who is «reborn» symbolically in and through the ritual, is also «killed» by drinking *kava* (Sahlins, 1981: 125).

born on earth to his heavenly rebirth, and more specifically, during the initiatory voyage that takes him from the earth to the heavens. It is because he was devoured by his celestial brothers and partook of the intimacy of their bodies that the hero became divine *in his substances*. Cannibalism, in this case, may be considered the equivalent of a second gestation, a most singular gestation that takes place in the heavens, and among men. But also, the fact that the divine sons eat the hero makes them all brothers and by the same token makes those heavenly brothers murderers. For in the traditional Polynesian representations, to be swallowed by a god is the ordinary destiny awaiting most human beings, and an end of this sort cannot by any means be considered a murder. On the other hand, to put to death a person who is one's own kin—that is, someone with whom one shares identical substances—is a definite act of murder. In other words, it is unquestionably the cannibalistic eating of the hero by the celestial sons of the god that transforms both parties into "brothers" and at the same time makes assassins out of 'Aho'eitu's celestial "brothers", and crestfallen assassins at that, when 'Aho'eitu resuscitates.

This cannibalistic murder has several simultaneous effects, then: a) it transforms the hero, 'Aho'eitu, into a man/god; b) it turns the celestial sons of the god and the hero into brothers; c) it transforms the killing retrospectively into a clear case of murder; d) it turns the celestial brothers into murderers and then into repentant culprits. The cannibalistic murder of 'Aho'eitu by his brothers and his resurrection by his father constitute the extraordinary, male, celestial substitute for ordinary, female and earthly procreation. In conclusion to the myth, the murder institutes a debt between the Tu'i Tonga and his celestial brothers, who are obliged to accompany him on earth and remain behind him: in other words, they must help him govern without taking his place. Lastly, by making the supreme chief the son of the god 'Eitumatupu'a, the Ancestor par excellence, it gives all noble titles a divine origin and an impressive genealogical depth (since all titles are genealogically tied to the title of Tu'i Tonga), thus constituting a twofold gage of the legitimacy of power according to the Tongan value system.[19]

---

19. The large number of societies in which the *kava* ritual was tied to the cult of the ancestor spirits suggests that this really was its oldest known function. In Tonga, the myth of the origin of the first Tu'i Tonga is probably a more recent creation, connected with the reinforcement of the lineage of supreme chiefs. The ancient *kava* ritual would then have been reinvested with new, complementary meaning, linked with the transformations in local politics. The *kava* ritual could then be viewed as a rite remythified by history.

Relations Based on Debt

Let us now return to the first myth, and the sacrificing of the leprous girl, which just barely fell short of cannibalism. According to the interpretation advanced here, the outcome of the eating of 'Aho'eitu is that he then partakes of his brothers' substances, and hence, of their divine nature. If we go back to the first myth and apply the same interpretation to the avoided eating of the leprous girl—and there is no reason no to do so, since the same system of representations is at work in the two—we see that the eventuality of the girl's being eaten by the Tu'i Tonga cannot even be envisioned. Through the sharing of his substances, it would make her kin to the Tu'i Tonga, a person who shares at least a portion of his identity, perhaps even his sister. In other words, according to the Tongan kinship system, a person who would rank higher than he himself. The myth excludes any cannibalism, just as the Tongan conception excludes any sharing of substances between the Tu'i Tonga, man/god, and commoners or people with low status.[20] There is even reason to believe that the victim's disease, leprosy, constitutes a distinctive feature that highlights the totally inconceivable character of such sharing. Another tale in the oral tradition actually ascribes the same function to the same disease: a girl's parents avoid having her eaten by making believe she has leprosy.[21]

Each of the two myths relates a primordial action, then: a sacrifice in the case of the young leper, a murder in the case of the first Tu'i Tonga. The outcome of the action in both cases is the transfiguration of the heroes, victims of a sacrifice and a murder. The girl gives birth to two plants, one of which is essential to the ceremonial life of Tongans in general and of its high-ranking chiefs in particular; 'Aho'eitu, who is killed and devoured by his celestial brothers, is changed into a two-sided creature, both man and god. However, the conclusion of the main action—a sacrifice in one case, a murder in the other—also transcends the relations between all of the protagonists. The sacrifice of the leper founds the relations between commoners and high-ranking chiefs. While the former are obliged to provide food for the latter, the latter must, in return, use their *mana* to cause the germination of the fruit of the land. The celestial brothers of 'Aho'eitu, guilty of murdering their brother, must "remain behind him": meaning, clearly, they must help him govern without taking his place. Each of the two actions ends

---

20. In pre-Christian Tongan society—as opposed to many neighboring Polynesian groups—there was a clear-cut boundary between ranking chiefs and commoners (only the former were entitled to an afterlife, for example). Although royal-blooded chiefs, or "chiefs-in-the-body," were viewed as partaking of the two «natures», they were nonetheless thought to be much more divine than human.

21. See Gifford, 1924: 193.

with the institution of paradigmatic relations between the victims and the other protagonists. These relations are grounded in a debt: in other words, in an imperishable commitment composed of duties, conceived as necessary, reciprocal and inextinguishable.

An Ancestral Seminal Substance

Metamorphoses

The two myths, read together, shed light on each other, as we have seen, but it remains for us to discover their exact articulation with the *kava* ritual. The link between the myth of the origin of *kava* and the *kava* ritual seems to be given immediately. Moreover, we have seen that the myth of origin of the supreme chief and the *kava* ritual are connected by various analogies, and especially by the presence of the wooden bowl, or *tano'a*. One wonders, however, whether there is not a more specific relation, perhaps symbolic but not necessarily so, between the central object of the ritual—that is, the ceremonial drink, that muddy water-colored liquid drawn from the roots of the *kava* plant—and the two central objects of the myths, which are the martyred body of the leprous girl, on the one hand, and the cannibalized body of the first supreme chief, on the other hand.

A liminal remark may be made on the basis of the myth, which is unambiguous on one point: the *kava* plant definitely grew out of the body of the girl, but it had to be taken to the palace and prepared according to rules established by the civilizing hero Lo'au before being transformed into a ceremonial drink, and for the specific purpose of doing so. In other words, the ceremonial drink *does not* represent the body of the leprous girl, even if it does come from it. A series of transformations takes place between the body of the leprous girl and the *kava* beverage: there is a definite process, designated by connections to which the myth draws our attention. The *kava* as a plant grows out of the body of the leprous girl, from that plant a liquid—*kava*—is drawn, and from that liquid comes *kava* as a ceremonial drink. While the body of the girl is definitely associated with the *kava* plant, since the latter originates in her, *kava* as a *ceremonial drink* represents something very different from the body of that poor victim.

This reasoning may help us understand the way in which the ceremonial beverage is associated, at the same time, with the cannibalized body of 'Aho'eitu. The *kava* drink ingurgitated by the titled chiefs during the ritual *does not* represent the cannibalized body of the first supreme chief any more than that of the leprous girl. The myth does not suggest that the body of the supreme chief and the *kava* drink are in any way identical. It is the *making* of *kava* in the *tano'a* that serves as a metaphor for the murdering and resurrection of the supreme chief. The *kava* plant, a perfectly secular object, turns into a ceremonial drink, a sacred object, exactly *in the same way as* 'Aho'eitu, a man from the earth, changes into a man/god, thus becoming the most divine, or the most sacred of all of the earth's inhabitants. In both cases, the *kava* bowl, or *tano'a*, is the place where those metamorphoses occur which create the transition from the secular to the sacred, or more accurately, from the less sacred to the more sacred. In both cases it is the intervention of a divine, or deified figure that accounts for this transformation. In the first case it is the Tu'i Tonga, in the second the god 'Eitumatupu'a. The articulation between myths and rites often proceeds by shifts in meaning leading gradually from one signifier to another. This conception leads us to discover another of these signifiers, an essential but one whose message is delivered on another, less "political"level. It is more related to identity than those touching on the institution of relations between the groups forming the political and social pyramid. This requires that we return to the ritual.

On Kava *Roots as Bones and* Kava *Liquid as Semen*

As mentioned above, in Polynesia the *kava* ritual was as a rule, and perhaps originally, linked with the cult of the dead, and was used to invoke the spirits of the ancestors. The ingestion of *kava* was believed to enable the ancestors to enter the body of one of their descendants, to "inhabit" it momentarily—in what the missionaries called a "fit of possession"—and to use that body, and the voice in particular, to communicate with the living. According to the Tongan philosopher and historian Futa Helu, the *kava* roots traditionally represented a sort of plant substitute for the bones of the ancestors.[22] The relationship between the land belonging to a kinship group (*kainga* in Tonga) and the ancestors of that same group, a very strong one in Polynesia, would, in this hypothesis, be vehicled by a material representation, an objectivated sign, that of the *kava* bush that grew on the group's land. In the same vein, it is conceivable that the action of moistening the *kava* roots with saliva first, and then with water, was viewed as a process in which the ancestors' bones were symbolically brought back to life. In the Tongan oral tradition, bones are also linked to a fertilizing substance: for instance, a woman becomes pregnant by stepping over the bones of a hero. As F. Héritier has written, in many cultures the notion of ancestrality is based on the presence of a transmissible substance stored in the bones, a sort of "semen" containing the "principle of the transmission of

---

22. Personal communication.

life" (1989: 109). Inasmuch as the analogy between bones and a fertilizing substance does exist in the Tongan system of representation, we may postulate that in pre-Christian times the liquid produced by chewing and dissolving the *kava* roots—substitutes for the ancestral bones—represented the symbolic equivalent of an ancestral seminal substance. In this perspective, the preparation leading from the roots to the making of the drink may be seen as the imaginary projection of a process in which the bones of the ancestors are believed to produce a seminal substance (re)generating strength and life.[23] When the recipients take this substance into their bodies, it has several concomitant effects. These effects are well known, since they are what *kava* drinkers expect of it when they meet on ritual occasions. First of all, this substance causes the ancestors of their respective lineages to be reborn in them. During a ceremonial *kava*, each participating chief does in fact represent his title/ancestor's name; that is all those men who bore that title before him. Furthermore, on occasions one of those ancestors seizes the descendant and speaks through his mouth. Secondly, and at the same time, this same substance is also believed to make the chiefs physically powerful. This is a sign of *mana*, which makes men strong and able to bear their title gloriously, and to physically defend the land attached to that title. In the rite as well as in the myths, then, *kava* is the agent of a metamorphosis, a transfiguration leading to a more "sacred" state. When the chiefs ingurgitate *kava*, they *are* their ancestors; in other words, they are beings who have become divine, pure emanations of *mana*, as is further signified by the extreme solemnity of the ritual.

However, the myth of the creation of *kava* reminds us that the origin of the latter is the body of a girl from the very lowest strata, and leprous as well. How can this element of the myth be reconciled, in all strict logic, with our hypothesis that *kava* is the symbolic equivalent of an ancestral seminal substance, used by chiefs to revive their deified ancestors within themselves?

It should be remembered that it is not the ceremonial drink that comes out of the leprous girl's body, but the *kava* bush. The myth of Kava'onau is indeed very clear on these two points: 1) it is the *kava* bush, a plant, that grows out of the body of the sacrificed girl; 2) the liquid *kava* is obtained with the help of the instructions given by a high-ranking chief, the civilizing hero called Lo'au. What the myth says is that the ceremonial drink itself definitely does come from the sacrifice of a leprous girl, but only after—and thanks to—acts accomplished by the supreme chief, then by a very high-ranking chief in

---

23. The idea that sperm is a revitalizing substance is widely accepted in many Pacific and Far-East Asian societies, and perhaps elsewhere (Bottéro, 1992). For Polynesia, Bottéro mentions the case of Tahitian transvestites who ingested sperm to fortify themselves (ibid.: 26). In Melanesia, the example of the Baruya is well known : «sperm is life and strength, it is the food that gives strength to life» (Godelier, 1982: 91).

charge of assisting the former in his task. The Tu'i Tonga "fertilizes" so to speak the body of the young leper by causing the first *kava* bush to grow on it; Lo'au then transforms the roots of this bush into a ceremonial drink. Our first remark is that in the myth of the origin of *kava*, symbolic procreation replaces the projected eating of the girl. Secondly, we note that no such manipulation is performed on the sugar cane, which may be consumed directly. Now, in many Polynesian societies, sugar cane has a female connotation.[24] Anthropologist E. Leach has shown that in the Tongan myth of Kava'onau, the sugar cane probably originally grew out of the girl's vagina rather than her "intestines" or her "feet".[25] This sort of association between sugar cane and the female element seems to indicate that the *kava* bush—constantly contrasted with the sugar cane in the myth—is associated with the male element. We may postulate, then, that one of the two plants to come out of the body of the young girl "fertilized" by the *mana* of the Tu'i Tonga, the sugar cane, is a female element, while the other, the *kava*, is male.[26]

But once these structural elements of the myth have been delineated, we discover something else behind these contrasts and associations. If, indeed, we now consider not only the object, *kava*, as a plant or a drink, but the process that leads from one to the other, another significant level of the ritual comes to light, and offers us a clue for interpreting the elements belonging both to the myth and the ritual, as a whole. In the myth of origin and the *kava* ritual there is indeed a parallel between two transformation processes: on the one hand—in the myth—the transformation of *kava* into a sacred drink, and on the other hand—in the ritual—the transformation of a male individual into a "strong" man. The overall meaning suggested by the whole represented by the myth/ritual, then, is that of a double metamorphosis: the body of Kava'onau, symbolically "fertilized" by the *mana* of the Tu'i Tonga, produced two plants, the *kava*, the male element, and sugar cane, the female element, exactly like the body of a woman, symbolically fertilized by the *mana* of high ranking chiefs, may give birth to children of both sexes.[27] But the main idea of the myth/ritual complex is that the agent of this double metamorphosis is the same in both cases. The transformation of the *kava* plant into a ceremonial drink requires the active intervention of high-ranking chiefs *just as they must intervene in the transformation of a male individual into a "strong" man—in*

---

24. See Barrau, 1965: 338.
25. See Bott and Leach, 1972: 264. The «corrected» version was probably the missionaries' doing.
26. The myth also emphasizes the necessary complementarity between the two plants, through the story of the rat who loses, and finally retrieves, its balance.
27. In pre-Christian Tongan society, it was believed that through the *mana* they had received from their deified ancestors, the high ranking chiefs fertilized the land on their domain and initiated the fertilization process in the women in their local group (*kainga*).

other words, into a chief or a valorous warrior. In the same way as the body of a woman may give birth to an individual of either sex, the body of Kava'onau produced two entities, respectively male and female: the *kava* bush and the sugar cane. To become a "strong" man, or if we like, a "true" man, the male individual must submit to a series of operations accomplished exclusively by men and amongst themselves, exactly as the *kava* plant will only become a ceremonial drink through the *mana* of the supreme chief, for one thing, and secondly, through the maneuvers of the civilizing hero. Thus, one and the same mechanism accounts for the creation and function of the ceremonial drink, a substitute for semen, and the production of "true" men. From a "secular" plant that originally grew out of the body of a low-class girl, sacrificed by her poor parents and symbolically fertilized by the supreme chief, *kava* was transformed into a sacred ceremonial drink thanks to the precise rules set down by a civilizing chief. Planted thereafter on the ancestral land of the *kainga* (the local group headed by a chief), the *kava* bush represents the quintessence of the relation between the ancestors and the family domain. The liquid *kava*, a plant substitute for the ancestral seminal substance, is prepared from roots/ancestral bones in accordance with the rules. This produces a metamorphosis making it a sacred drink through which men who are chiefs transmit their maleness from one to another, thus perpetuating it in themselves.

The mythical/ritual complex of which *kava* is the focus is constructed around a series of metamorphoses which may be represented as follows:

sacrificed body	fertilization	*kava* (plant)	preparation→	sacred drink
cannibalized body	regurgitation	*kava* (bowl)	resurrection→	man/god
roots/ bones	chewing	*kava* (bowl)	moistening→	ancestral seminal substance
chiefs	ingestion	*kava* (drink)	possession→	deified ancestors
male individuals	ingestion	*kava* (drink)	enhanced virility→	chiefs/ warriors

The Symbolic Production of Male Identity

The Kava *Ritual and Men's Initiation Ceremonies*

The *kava* ceremony, as practiced in Tonga, may thus be viewed as the locus of the ritual reproduction of chiefs as "true" men. The mythical ritual complex analyzed above is of course specific to Tongan society. One wonders, however, whether one of its conclusions—that one function of the *kava* ritual was to transmit male identity—may not be extended to other Polynesian societies. As already mentioned, throughout Polynesia, as in Tonga, the *kava* ritual is primarily connected with men and with those activities—war, in particular—conceived as typically manly. If we pursue this hypothesis, the Polynesian *kava* ritual may have very much the same functions as male initiations in other Pacific island societies. It is a fact that in New Guinea, some groups still periodically perform men's initiation ceremonies, in which all boys of a given age group undergo ordeals explicitly designed to turn them into adult men (in the old days, warriors).[28] Those anthropologists who have worked on this subject[29] have shown the articulations between these great initiation ceremonies for men and some salient features of their social organization, and more specifically, a marked sexual antagonism and the assertion, both in their practices and in their systems of representation, of the necessary domination of men over women. In these societies, the justification of women's subordination rests on the logic according to which men were obliged to dispossess women of their original (pro)creative power because of the permanent danger they represent for society, especially because they are polluted.[30] In New Guinea, the main objective of men's initiation ceremonies is to remove boys from the women's world, and to construct their male identity *against* women and *with* the help of men, with each of the sexes playing roles in the rituals on registers that vary from one group to another (Bonnemère, 1996: 379–380). For instance, in those groups where ritualized homosexuality is practiced, the function of the latter seems to be a "radical sexual resocialization" putting a definite end to the long period during which the boy lived in symbiosis with his mother (Knauft, 1987: 171).[31] In Baruya society, boys must be "re-delivered" by men, and this process, viewed by the latter as a "great labor", begins at the earliest phase of the initiations and lasts over ten years (Godelier, 1992: 16).

In Western Polynesia, the forms taken by conceptions of sexual dichotomy are quite different. Women's role in everyday practices within the kin-

---

28. See Bonnemère, 1996: 377. In some of these cultures, among the Anga, for instance, men's initiations were actually the main community event, along with war (Bonnemère, 1996: 22).

29. See, especially, Godelier, 1982; Herdt, 1984; Knauft, 1987; and Bonnemère, 1996.

30. See Godelier (1982: 105, 120ff. and 1992: 8, 11, 20). See also Herdt, 1987. However, even in New Guinea, women's subordination is not always consistently referred to women's absolute pollution (see Bonnemère, 1996 : 374).

31. As for girls, there is the idea that they «grow» more easily and more naturally than boys, who must be subjected to the intervention of men in order to achieve their own maturity as men (Godelier, 1992 : 16).

ship group and in rituals is viewed more highly, the opposition between the sexes is not as strongly asserted and the relations between genders are definitely less difficult. In Tongan myths, women's genesic (sexual and reproductive) capacities are stressed, for they are believed necessary for the proper ordering of the world. Women's body, menstruation and child-bearing, very much like the "natural" cycles (and especially the ripening of the fruits of the land) were thought to belong not to some "nature" synonymous with disorder and chaos and therefore requiring domestication, but all the opposite: they were believed to be of a higher order, the order of the ancestors and the divinities (Douaire-Marsaudon, 1998b: 297). The sisters of each *kainga* kinship group, who ranked higher than the brothers, were— and still are to this day—believed to have the power to throw spells on their brothers' lineage, a fearsome power giving them ultimate control over the reproduction of the *kainga* group. Nonetheless, if our hypothesis is correct, and the *kava* ritual is the locus of the transmission, and therefore the reproduction, of male identity by men in positions of chief, it leads us to a discovery. That is, even in societies where the difference between the sexes does not take the form of a pronounced antagonism, and where women's rank is an essential criterion in social and political life, there does exist a social institution through which male identity is transmitted and reproduced generation after generation. Several remarks are necessary at this point.

Firstly, although the *kava* ritual may well be the locus of reproduction of male identity and therefore play the same role as men's initiation ceremonies in Melanesia, it is nonetheless not totally comparable to those rituals, for several reasons. One the one hand, the *kava* ceremony is not the only ritual whose function is to transform boys into adults. In Tonga, and elsewhere in Polynesia, there was a ritual designed to mark sexual identity at the onset of puberty. Between the ages of 12 and 16, a collective rite took place, during which boys were circumcised (in fact, superincised). They were placed in confinement for several days and explicitly kept from any contact with women.[32] On the other hand, the *kava* ritual is performed in a wide variety of contexts, including rites of passage, but also for the acquirement of a title or the visit of a chief, etc, some of which are quite unrelated to men's initiation, whereas in the Melanesian men's initiation rituals, all of the acts, with no exception, are performed for the purpose of transforming boys into adult men. Furthermore, the calm and sort of slow solemnity that prevail during a *kava* circle contrast sharply with the violence and fear that exemplify many initiation ceremonies for men in New Guinea.

---

32. Circumcision takes place in a hospital, nowadays, and the rites that accompanied it are no longer practiced (with the exception of a simple ceremony occasionally performed in private, within the family).

Virility, the Prerogative of Polynesian Chiefs

Lastly, and perhaps most importantly, the imposing initiation ceremonies for men are compulsory for the entire age group, whereas only certain individuals are accepted at the formalized *kava* rituals. It should, indeed, be recalled that the formalized *kava* rituals took place among the chiefs only, even if a few commoners who had proved to be particularly brave warriors might occasionally be invited. Although little is known on the subject, it is highly probable that commoners had their own *kava* circles, at least at the time of their first contact with the outside world. This is suggested by the fact that many Polynesian groups have special cultivars reserved for their chiefs.[33] However, owing to the aristocratic ideology reigning in Polynesia and in Tonga in particular, those *kava* rituals for commoners were no more than very pale imitations of the "true" rituals, those involving the chiefdom. Furthermore, as we have recalled, the Polynesians viewed physical strength as virtually immaterial. It was believed to be given by the *mana*, that emanation of the gods or the ancestors, a power that exceeds individual humans, by definition. This body of representations should explain why, in Tonga, physical strength as well as that "distinction" of which it is both the attribute and the sign—that is to say, virility—is not viewed as belonging to all male individuals in general. Rather, virility and everything pertaining to it—both physical and sexual features—was first and foremost the prerogative of the chiefs. Not only were they supposed to perform the greatest feats at war, but their sexual energy was thought to surpass that of ordinary mortals, as well. The first contacts with Tongan society seem to indicate that only the chiefs were actually polygamous at the time. The prestige of a chief—in other words, his *mana*—was therefore measured both by his exploits as a warrior and by his sexual feats, as measured by how many wives he had and how many children he fathered. This of course does not mean that ordinary men were viewed as devoid of sexual identity. Here, as elsewhere, circumcision was considered a decisive step in the transformation of boys into male adults. But this male identity was felt to be less clear-cut, less well established: in short, less complete than that of the chiefs and, at most, of the *toa*, those commoners who had distinguished themselves by their bravery at war. The rationale for this quasi confiscation of maleness by the chiefs was to be found in the Tongan conception of the socio-cosmic order. Indeed, in traditional society, only the chiefs were entitled to life after death. When they died, their souls were believed to find their way to Pulotu, a paradise inhabited by the divinities from whom their ancestors descended. The divinities and the chiefs shared the same origin

---

33. This supposes that other cultivars were used by everyone.

and the same destiny: they were "kin", so to speak, and therefore had the same access to *mana*. Conversely, the souls of commoners were thought to disappear when they died.[34] There was no afterlife for the commoners, then, and therefore no ancestors, either. It was precisely this refusal of ancestrality that grounded the confiscation of the commoner's virility. Where could they get their physical strength from, since they had no ancestors ? Only a few exceptionally privileged individuals whose warrior exploits had proved that they were not totally abandoned by the gods might hope to modify their fate. So, while it was definitely through the *kava* ritual that one became a real man by absorbing the ceremonial liquid, a substitute for the ancestor's seminal substance, this transmission of virility nonetheless remained strictly confined to and controlled by the chiefs.

Is a Woman Enough to Make a Man?

Lastly, if the *kava* ritual is clearly the locus of the reproduction of male identity, this would suggest that irrespective of the way societies express and experience the difference between the sexes, each of them has a specific way of dealing with the question of the transmission of maleness.[35] This question, which arises out of a universally experienced fact—*female* individuals give birth to children of *both sexes*—may be formulated as follows: "how can men be produced by a woman's body ?" This question may be put and broken down in any number of ways, depending on the society involved. "Are we born of a single person, or of two ?" "Does the same come out of the same, or of the other ?"[36] All are variations on a same theme, that does not pertain so much to sexual identity *per se* as to its transmission.

Human beings produce society, for the purpose of living, as Maurice Godelier puts it, and they are the only social animals to do so (Godelier, 1984: 9). However, this social reproduction itself is grounded in a paradox: if there is no denying that society is composed of individuals of both sexes, and if, consequently, its reproduction requires the combined existence of the

---

34. ...or possibly to have an afterlife, but in the form of an insect doomed to be swallowed by a wading bird, reputedly one of the favorite embodiments of the gods.

35. Unfortunately, I have not been able to discuss the Australian initiation rites for men, which are beyond the scope of this article. However, here is what Testart has to say about the last phase of the Aranda initiation rites, the *engwura*: «the *engwura* is not an individual initiation. Circumcision was a response to the question: was it the men or the women who gave birth to this child, the novitiate? The question posed by the *engwura* is more radical: do women give birth to men, or is it the other way around ?» (Testart, 1992: 166).

36. As Lévi-Strauss put it, in his discussion of the «work» of the Œdipus myth on the same questions (1958: 239).

two sexes, experience shows that only one of the two, the female sex, gives birth to individuals of both sexes. The extraordinary variety of systems of representation that have been developed by different societies to account for the process of reproduction of life is certainly the product of the need to render this paradoxical fact thinkable. It is not inconceivable that the universality of the paradox of female engendering of both sexes may have generated the notion—a phantasy, but one fraught with anxiety—of an entirely effeminate society, not because it excluded men, but because they had been insufficiently masculinized. The same idea is in fact often expressed within our modern Western societies, particularly with respect to the development of the one-parent family, the problems connected with absentee fathers or those who shirk their responsibilities, as well as the issue of the adoption of children by homosexual couples.

In *The making of great men*, Maurice Godelier explains that all of the efforts made by Baruya men to establish their domination, in thought, over the women of the group, are designed to reduce the importance of that unavoidable fact: "it is in the woman's belly that children are conceived and from her belly that they are born, and (...) it is then to her milk that they owe their survival" (Godelier, 1986 [1982]: 229). It has often been claimed that in the Pacific islands, and elsewhere, some ritual practices are a way of providing men with a sort of "cultural" compensation for women's "natural" creativity.[37] In Polynesia, the prevailing symbolism generally acknowledges women's role in procreation, even if much of the control over the life-giving process is confiscated from the mothers, to be handed over to the (men's) sisters. However, the efforts made by Melanesian *and* Polynesian societies to control the symbolic production of male subjects through the essential rituals of group life point to the idea that perhaps the ideological foundations of male domination are to be sought not only in the fact that women give birth to children but *also* in the corollary and equally unavoidable fact that men are born of women.

The *kava* ritual, present in many Polynesian societies and elsewhere, is a complex institution orchestrating a great many aspects of social life. In traditional Tongan society, the mythical/ritual complex developed around what is simultaneously a common plant and a sacred drink—*kava*—constituted the foundations of the social and political hierarchy and structured the relations between the constituent groups. At the same time, through the ritual, those men who occupied the position of chief took control of the symbolic production of male identity. Today, although many of these

---

37. There is also the idea that women's procreative function represents nature's intrusion within the social sphere, and that this intrusion must be culturally controlled (Juillerat, 1986: 516).

representations have disappeared, *kava* circles still play a regulatory role in the socialization of boys.[38] Thus, we discover that the *kava* ritual is one of those social spaces in which the fundamental issues involving both the community and the individual come into play.[39]

Translated by Helen Arnold

---

38. In his book on male initiation in Australia, Testart shows that the initiation rite is tied to *teaching of socialization*, and that this is a fundamental part of the rite, and is «quite like the way teaching is conceived in our own culture, since it is during initiation that boys are taught the basic rules of social life» (Testart, 1993: 16).

39. In other parts of the world, other more or less ritualized social spaces are perhaps (at least partially) invested with the task of forging masculinity. The example of football matches comes to mind (see Bromberger, 1995).

Chapter 3

Surrogates for Humans and for Gods*

Maurice Godelier

I. The Baruya: An Example of a Society with Gift-Exchange, Not Potlatch

The Baruya tribe lives in two high valleys of a mountain chain in the interior part of New Guinea known as the Eastern Highlands. Their reputation as salt-makers made them familiar to many tribes they had never encountered but who bought their salt from tribes that themselves traded with the Baruya. The Baruya's ancestors did not live in the place presently inhabited by their descendants, but in the vicinity of Menyamya, at Bravegareubaramandeuc, today a deserted spot to which the masters of the initiations return every three or four years, at the time of the male initiations, to gather magic plants and collect handfuls of ancestral soil, with its magical properties, in other words full of supernatural powers and the ancestors' force.

At some time, probably around the end of the eighteenth century, the Baruya's ancestors were forced to leave their territory after enemies burned their village and massacred part of its inhabitants. The survivors fled, eventually finding asylum at Marawaka, among the Yoyué, who lived on the slopes of Mount Yelia, at a distance of four or five days' walk. Some generations later, the refugees, abetted by the Ndelie, a clan belonging to the host tribe, drove the rest of the tribe from its territory, and a new group

---

* First published as "Des objets substituts des hommes et des dieux," *Social Anthropology* 3 (2), 1995: 95–114.

Photo 10: First grade initiates who have just had their noses pierced are held by one of their relatives (Photo M. Godelier).

appeared which today bears the name Baruya, from the name of the clan that exercised the most important ritual functions in the male initiations, those which transform boys from children into adolescents and young warriors.

To complete this brief sketch of Baruya history and social organization, I should add that they do not have a power center, a paramount chief, like the Trobrianders, or Big Men who amass wealth and women, and seek to outdo each other in potlatch-like contests of gift and counter-gift giving, like the Melpa (A. Strathern, 1971).[1] They do, however, have men who are "greater" than the others, Great Men whose powers are either inherited (like those of the masters of the male or the shaman initiations) or acquired (like those of the great hunters, the great cassowary hunters, the great horticulturalists and the best salt-makers). Masters of the initiations always come from the same clans, the other Great Men may belong to any clan.

So how do the Baruya deal with *gifts*, *exchanges*, inalienable *objects* (A. Weiner, 1985, 1992) with valuables, with money? They have three categories of objects which, for lack of a better term, I will call sacred objects, valuables and currency.

---

1. See also Godelier and Strathern (eds.), 1991; Lederman, 1986; Lemonnier, 1990, 1993; A. Strathern, 1969.

Baruya Sacred Objects

Chief among the sacred objects of the Baruya are the *kwaimatnie*; these are cult objects kept hidden away by the masters of the initiation ritual and displayed and handled exclusively by them on these occasions. Only the clans descended from the Menyamya refugees possess *kwaimatnie*, with the exception of the Ndelie, the clan that betrayed its tribe and helped the Baruya to seize their hosts' territory. In recognition of the Ndelie's help and also to associate them in the performance of the initiations, the Baruya clan gave them a pair of *kwaimatnie*. In addition to the *kwaimatnie*, cult objects included the dried fingers of the right hand of Bakitchatche, a legendary Baruya hero who led them into battle against the Yoyué and in seizing their lands, and a pair of flint stones, owned by the Andavakia clan, which were used to re-kindle the primordial fire in the big ceremonial house where the initiations are held. Bakitchatche's fingers and the flint stones disappeared when the village in which they were kept was burned down by a young Australian officer during the campaign to pacify the region. All clans also possess bull-roarers. These are slender pieces of polished black palm that are whirled over the head during initiations to produce the loud roaring sound purported to be the voice of the spirits conversing with the men. Bull-roarers are manufactured by men, but their prototype is said to have been an arrow shot by the forest spirits, the *yimaka*, which lodged in a tree trunk next to the head of a Baruya ancestor. The bull-roarers give men death-dealing powers, powers to succeed in hunting and in war.

All the sacred objects described are objects appropriated and used exclusively by men, but that does not mean, as we will see, that they are male objects. The word *kwaimatnie* means "to make grow." A *kwaimatnie* is therefore an object that contains the power to make humans grow. There is no such thing as one *kwaimatnie*. They come in gendered pairs; the stronger or "hotter" of the two is the female *kwaimatnie*. In short, and this is the Baruya's most closely guarded secret, within the sacred object which manifests men's power is contained the women's powers which the men managed to appropriate when their mythic ancestors stole the women's sacred flutes; today women may not touch or look on these flutes. But where did the *kwaimatnie* come from? The Baruya tell us that Sun himself gave them to the ancestors of the clans living at Bravegareubaramandeuc.

Sacred Objects: Gifts from the Sun and the Spirits to the Baruya's Mythic Ancestors

These objects as well as the knowledge that goes with them—the ritual spells, Sun's secret name—are inalienable goods and are withheld from the exchange process. The distribution of the *kwaimatnie* among clans has a religious significance, but also a directly political one, for only the clans that descend from the Menyamya refugees plus the Ndelie take part in the tasks of initiation, though not all in the same positions and not all in the same stages. The entire initiation sequence unfolds between two crucial moments in the male lifecycle: the forcible separation of the boys from the women's world and the passage from the second to the third stage, in other words from the adolescent world to that of young men. It is at this time that a man places on the young warriors' head the beak of a hornbill, which for the Baruya is a symbol of the penis; it is mounted on a sort of tiara terminating in two boar's tusks, which are pressed into the flesh of the forehead; this "crown" is the symbol of the woman vagina. Baruya political relations are structured as hierarchical ranks, and in a hierarchy, truly reciprocal relations do not exist, only non-symmetrical relations of complementarity and interdependence.

What is Concealed Inside a Sacred Object?

A *kwaimatnie* is a long bundle wrapped in a strip of red bark, a *ypmoulie*, the ceremonial headband worn by Baruya men; it is dyed red for the color of the Sun, their father. I once had the privilege of seeing what was inside a *kwaimatnie*. The man who showed it to me arrived with his son, who would inherit it: carefully the father spread the bark, and I saw, lying side by side, a black stone, some bones and a nut. The man did not speak to me, but began silently to weep. After several minutes, with the same care, he re-wrapped the packet and left. Emotion before an object that was not beautiful, but which for him was probably sublime. The black adze-blade-shaped stone was Venus; Venus for the Baruya is a Baruya woman who was given as a present to Python, the master of thunder and rain, who dwells in the sky. The woman changed into Venus, the morning and evening star. One of the bones was from an eagle, the Sun's bird; but the eagle is also the metamorphosis of Djoué, the primordial dog who lived with the first woman before humans appeared on earth. The other bone was a human bone, probably from an ancestor of the man's clan; it was sharpened like the awl-bone used to pierce the noses of the initiates. The nut was a brown disk bearing a design that looked like an eye. The Baruya call it "baby's" eye. This disk is sucked to purify the mouth after talking about sexual matters and is used in magic spells for restoring or giving life. For the Baruya, the *kwaimatnie* are not the "sign" of Venus, they are the real presence of Venus and her powers. In this sense, they are only partly symbols, whereas the hornbill beak is understood and seen as the symbol of the man's penis. The crucial point here is that, for the Baruya, *kwaimatnie* were not made

Photo 11: On the right, the ritual master is brandishing a *kwaimatnie*, a sacred object with which he will strike the initiates' breasts; on the left, a man is holding a stick decorated with cowries and wooden awls used for nose piercing (Photo P. Lemonnier).

by human hands but by beings in the image of man, but who are more powerful—Sun, Moon and so on—and who originally communicated directly with their ancestors. The Baruya therefore consider it their duty to preserve these objects and to use them to reproduce the type of society that Sun and their ancestors left to them.

The sacred is therefore a certain relationship with the origin of things, such that real humans disappear from this origin and in their place appear imaginary duplicates. This is the lesson of the Baruya myths recounting the origin of cultivated plants, tools, weapons, and so on. It is as though human society could not be thought or represented unless it obliterated from the conscious mind the active presence of man at his own origin. One cannot simply state, as Durkheim did, that society is the source of the sacred. It also has to be shown that the sacred conceals something from the collective and individual consciousness, something essential, something contained in social relations which the sacred makes opaque to the conscious mind. In the case of the Baruya, the sources of this opacity are clear. They lie in the existence of two relationships of exclusion which form part of the very foundations of their society, both of which are manifested in the initiation rituals. These rituals largely exclude the participation of women, which is to say one half of society, thereby legitimizing men's general domination of women; but they also exclude from the exercise of power a number of clans descended from the autochthonous groups absorbed by the Baruya.

Sacred objects are a visible synthesis of the real and the imaginary components of social reality. Because of this, they are charged with the strongest symbolic value for the members of the society that produced the code; however sacred objects can never be reduced to the status of pure symbols or to that of simple objects.

Concerning Things Repressed Which Enable People to Live in Society

The Baruya social order is at once a sexual order, a certain type of relationship between the sexes, and a political-religious order, the relationship between the clans of the descendants of the conquerors and those of the descendants of the autochthonous groups. The union and fusion of the sexual and political-religious aspects of the social order are realized in the production of the initiation cycle and in its periodical reproduction. The fact of having revealed the existence of two domains that must be united and fused in order to construct the social order takes us—on a theoretical level—well beyond the individual case of the Baruya, affording us a glimpse of the conditions necessary to all life in society. It is as though human *social* existence were due entirely to two processes of *repression*, which constitute the two sources of the *formation* of the *individual* and of the *collective* unconscious. On the one hand, there is something in human sexuality that is incapable of co-existing with the conscious part of the human psyche and which therefore must be repressed, though it never really disappears; on the other hand, there are components of social relations that have to do with the organizing principles of society, which divide it and make it so that one segment of society can claim singly to represent the whole of society and to govern it in the name of the "common good."[2] Among the Baruya, it is the men who rule, not the women; and among the men, those from certain clans, the Great Men.

I should point out, at the end of this analysis of Baruya sacred objects, that these have a soul, a spirit, *koulie*, and that the same word in Baruya is used to designate "spiritual powers." The concept of *koulie* is therefore the equivalent of the concept of *mana* (Keesing, 1984). Sacred objects, together with the land conquered and passed down by the ancestors, are

---

2. Freud and Marx still offer useful hypotheses and concepts for analyzing the two repression processes necessary for human social existence.

the two things a lineage must guard preciously: these cannot—save in exceptional circumstances—be given or exchanged.

It now remains for us to analyze the two categories of things that the Baruya use in commercial exchanges or in gift-exchanges: salt, which serves as a currency, and a number of valuables, which they procure by trading their salt.

Salt Money and Valuables

We will begin with an analysis of salt, since it is their salt trade which gives the Baruya the means to procure their valuables (Godelier, 1969). The salt is extracted from the ashes of a plant grown in naturally or artificially irrigated zones. Once the salt canes have been cut and dried, they are burned, and the ashes are mixed with water. The salty solution is then slowly evaporated in large salt ovens tended by an expert. This process yields some fifteen bars of crystallized salt weighing between two and three kilograms a piece. The salt in question is not sodium but potassium, which is very salty and a violent poison in high doses. It is not used in everyday consumption but exclusively in ritual contexts. Salt is regarded as a source of strength, which builds up in the liver, where the Baruya believe the individual's entire force is stored. But salt is secretly associated with semen, with male strength. Salt never circulates as a commodity between Baruya; it is a gift-object, redistributed among kin, co-initiates, and so forth. The Baruya regularly make expeditions to exchange their salt with neighboring tribes; they trade it for means of production (stone tools), means of destruction (bows, arrows), means of social reproduction (bird-of-paradise plumes, pearl-shells, large shells) and expendable items (bark-cloth capes, string bags, ropes, etc.). Salt is the only commodity that can be exchanged for all others and, in this sense, serves as a universal equivalent. It is therefore a special kind of commodity because it can be used to measure the exchange value of all other commodities; in other words it functions as a currency. Baruya exchanges are impersonal, they do not feel personally bound to people who buy from them or from whom they buy.

The Baruya use their salt to procure objects that I have called "valuables." These are the large flat mother-of-pearl shells that adorn a woman's breast from the time she begins menstruating and is initiated. It is important to note that the Baruya do not amass these precious objects, whereas they could well do so. They simply buy as many as are needed for everyone to have such ornaments. Yet it is precisely this kind of shell that, in the Highlands groups which practice large-scale potlatch-like ceremonial exchanges, is accumulated for the purpose of giving so many that one hopes the recipient will be unable to give a like quantity in turn. Why this contrast? Why

Photo 12: Exchange of native vegetal salt between a Baruya and a man of another tribe (Photo M. Godelier).

is it that what is practiced in Big-Men and in potlatch societies is not a practice among the Baruya? The presence of certain objects in a society does not explain why the society uses them. The explanation for the difference in these uses lies in the different kinds of social relations. I see two reasons which exclude the accumulation of these valuables for the Baruya, the same things that exclude the accumulation of pigs which, together with shells, feature among the items of wealth exchanged in Highlands potlatches.

The first reason seems to me to lie in the very nature of Baruya kin relations, which are founded on the direct exchange of women between lineages. The Baruya do not have bridewealth, and therefore no wealth in the form of pigs or valuables that might be directly substituted for a woman. The same principle operates in warfare: the death of a Baruya cannot be compensated by anything other than the death of an enemy. The life of a warrior cannot be paid for by a gift of material wealth. It would be an error however to conclude from this that the Baruya do not know about exchanging wealth for a woman. They are familiar with the principle, but reserve the practice for dealing with remote tribes with whom they trade but who do not live on their doorstep and with whom they are not alternately at war or at peace. With their immediate neighbors, on the other hand, the Baruya practice direct exchange of women. We are therefore obliged to conclude that they are familiar with the principle of bridewealth, but that they deliberately do not apply it within the sphere of their political-religious relations. In sum: with the Baruya, we have sacred objects which are not exchanged, and valuables or currency which are exchanged, but not in the form of competitive gift- and countergift-giving, or in other words potlatches. There is one area in which the principle of gift-exchange reigns supreme, and that is the sphere of kinship. Here women are "exchanged" between lineages, and with the women go exchanges of services and goods. The gift of a woman is a "total prestation", which creates a debt that is not cancelled by the return gift of a woman. Analysis of the Baruya case thus enables us to define the significant distance, the structural differences that exist between societies which use gift and countergift as total prestations and those which practice competitive giving between individuals and groups in which the preferential instrument is the gift and countergift of wealth, the agonistic gift-exchange known as potlatch.

Concerning the Sociological Conditions Permitting the Emergence and the Development of Potlatch Societies

Two conditions seem necessary. Apparently something has to happen in two different areas of social life: the area of kinship and the area of political-religious relations. First of all, in the area of kinship, marriage must no longer be governed by the direct exchange of women, and bridewealth must on the whole have replaced "sister exchange."[3] And secondly, a portion of the political-religious power must exist in the form of titles, ranks, names and emblems placed in competition and open to those who successfully establish their superiority over others through prodigal giving, by amassing ever more wealth in order to outdo others in gift-exchange. Give more than your rival, return more: this is the recipe for potlatch, and it relentlessly drives the system to its limits.

---

3. On Melanesian marriage systems, see M. Strathern, 1984, and for an interpretation of the ideology of exchange and gender, M. Strathern, 1988.

In order for this to occur, the curb comprised by the direct exchange of women must have disappeared. For the direct exchange of women keeps the system from running away for two reasons, one quantitative, the other qualitative. The number of exchangeable "sisters" (even "classificatory" ones) is always very small, and unless one imagines that a man monopolizes all his sisters in order to multiply the number of wives he can take, and thereby sentences his brothers to bachelorhood, the sphere of *direct* exchange of women is quantitatively restricted from the start, and has scant room for expansion. This exchange is also qualitatively limited because it is two *concrete* persons that are exchanged. The problem vanishes, however, when, in exchange for a concrete person, one gives wealth, objects or pigs that are raised not to eat but to give. The nature of the elements of the problem has changed: on the one hand, we have a woman; on the other, wealth, objects or pigs that can be multiplied by producing more or by procuring them by other means, and in proportions that are incomparable to the possibilities of multiplying human beings. On the one hand, we have concrete persons, on the other, all sorts of "things" which function as surrogates for these persons. When a woman is exchanged for a woman, it is an exchange of two *identical* "realities" whose social value is presumed *a priori* to be *equivalent*. Their upbringing ensures that all girls will be hard workers, faithful wives and good mothers, that they will all be equivalent. Yet even the best upbringing cannot guarantee that a woman will give birth to viable children or that she will not be sterile. (Among the Baruya it is always the woman who is accused of being sterile, even if it is clearly the husband who is. In such an event, the Baruya say nothing or choose to deny the evidence. A Baruya man simply *cannot* be sterile.)

But when a woman is exchanged for wealth, it is no longer items of an identical nature that are exchanged and take the place of one another, it is items of distinctly different natures, whose equivalence takes on a new, more abstract character. Persons are now equated with things, and things with persons. But the two terms of the equation do not have the same mode of existence. Persons are produced in the framework of kinship relations. Wealth is produced and/or amassed in the framework of the social relations which organize production and exchange. These can be kinship or other kinds of relations, which operate as the social framework of production. It is in this context that material wealth can be accumulated without the limits on its multiplication which apply to the reproduction, the multiplication of persons. Once women can be exchanged for wealth, a veritable political economy of kinship becomes possible. Women procure wealth, wealth procures women. One can amass wealth to get women, one can accumulate women to get wealth.

But the practice of bridewealth, the absence — or the presence of no major social importance — of direct exchange of women do not suffice to draw the society into the exhilarating but perilous round of gifts and countergifts of

Photo 13: Necklaces of cowries or other shells exchanged for native salt by a man whose daughter is about to have her first menstruation. Here two other girls are prepared for the ceremony (Photo M. Godelier).

wealth; it is not enough to subordinate the economy and the moral world of individuals and groups to the constant transfer of wealth from hand to hand, from group to group, from individual to individual. Relations of power, political-social relations must also be unlocked (if they were locked up) or they must be locked up only at certain levels of the political hierarchy, and the rest of the positions must be accessible by competition between groups and between individuals; furthermore, the condition for success in this competition must be the *capacity to amass wealth and to redistribute it*, to give it away. It is by giving away wealth that a man acquires power and fame, just as it is by giving wealth that a man acquires wives. Under these conditions, objects, or at least those that constitute wealth, function not only as *substitutes for per-*

sons, for human beings, but also as substitutes for the sacred objects that are the ultimate source of all human power, their possession attesting a privileged relationship with the gods and the ancestors.

When these two types of structure intersect and mesh—on the one hand, kinship relations in which the alliance between two lineages entails transfer of wealth on the part of the wife-takers and in which direct exchange of women plays only a minor part and is even sometimes explicitly forbidden[4], and on the other hand, political relations in which a number of individuals and local groups can, by vying to outgive each other, use wealth to accede to positions of power and prestige either within their own tribe or in a much broader inter-tribal or regional framework—then all the conditions seem to be present for the emergence of a society in which groups and the individuals who represent them can pursue their interests by making a show of their disinterestedness.

We have thus come full circle. All the elements are now in place to recon-struct the basic structure of societies marked by "an economy and a moral code dominated by gift-giving." This structure combines, in a great vari-ety of ways, kinship relations in which alliances necessitate exchanges of wealth and political relations in which, alongside a number of powerful positions not up for competition, there are a great number of others which are the object of public economic and political competition at the tribal and intertribal levels. In this type of society, the field of competition between groups and between individuals is immense. It cuts across all kinship rela-tions and extends to a large portion of the political-religious relations as well. But the underlying logic is always the same: that of social relations which exist and are reproduced only between persons and between groups, but groups which for the most part act like persons and are regarded as such. There is no trace here (or almost insignificant traces) of imperson-al relations like those found in contemporary Western society, those obtain-ing between citizens equal before the law and the constitutional State.

By political-religious powers, I mean a certain kind of powers which are exercised *over* the entire society and/or are exercised on behalf of the entire society in order that all of the kin groups and all of the local groups which constitute it may be reproduced together, as a whole, united by and over and above their internal divisions, their conflicts of interest, their dis-putes. The field of political-religious relations overspills and encompasses that of kinship because it deals with matters of local-group interests and kin-group interests, which it represents, but on another plane, which is large-ly independent of the area of kinship.

---

4. As among the Mendi in Highlands New Guinea, who forbid direct exchange of women because it prevents affines from vying with each other in competitive gift-exchanges. Cf. Led-erman, 1986. See also my analysis of this example (Godelier, 1991).

The field of power in societies Mauss described as being marked by "an economy and a moral code dominated by gift-giving" are thus divided into ranks and spheres. The highest ranks, the most prestigious titles are (ideally) withheld from the arena of the struggle, of the competition for power. They are associated with possession of the most precious valuables, sacred objects which remain in the clan and are kept out of the frenetic world of gift- and countergift-exchange and that of commercial exchange, where, instead of winning by generous giving, one wins by hard bargaining over the price of the things one wants to buy or sell. But in addition to the highest ranks and most prestigious titles withheld from gift and commercial exchange, there is a whole other store of titles and ranks that confer power and fame, and which are theoretically open to competition between all individuals and groups (with the exception of slaves and persons of low status). To gain access to these titles, a man must sacrifice part of his belongings, of his wealth. He can do this in two ways: by giving them away or by destroying them publicly, but always taking care to show that he can live without this wealth. It is in these socio-political arenas that gift-exchange deploys all of its facets, reaches its height, which necessarily culminates in exchanges in which the goods no longer even change hands but are destroyed in a public display by their owner.

But why does the exchange of gifts and countergifts become, in this type of society, the *privileged* instrument of the *struggle* for power and fame? The first reason is because giving puts others under obligation without the need to resort to violence. The gift, as we have seen, creates *solidarity* between the two partners and at the same time puts one (the recipient) *under obligation* to the other (the donor), installs him in a socially inferior and dependent position, at least until such time as he can in turn give the same thing or its equivalent. But whereas for the Baruya, the goal of heeding the principle of "a woman for a woman" is to enable *all* men to have at least one wife and therefore enable all lineages to reproduce themselves,[5] in societies which practice competitive exchanges of wealth, the avowed goal is to enable only *a few* individuals and groups to accede to the positions, titles and ranks

---

5. In 1981, we witnessed attempts on the part of a number of representatives of Baruya lineages to substitute a system of bridewealth for the traditional system of direct exchange of women, *ginamare*. This gave rise to some sharp debates, collective public discussions in which the bulk of the young bachelors voiced their attachment to the tradition in order to avoid "the rich men" being the only ones able to marry and to "have all the women." Some publicly accused the old men of wanting to "sell" their daughters whereas they had not had to "buy" their wives. The matter stopped there, but some of these young men, who had left to work on plantations, returned several years later with wives they had "bought" with their earnings from the tribes living around these plantations or from the Chimbu or other Highlands groups where payment of bridewealth is traditional and who are always short of money because most of it goes into ceremonial exchanges.

up for competition, which implies that the number of these ranks, titles and positions is well below the number of groups and individuals vying for them (Mauss 1990). The consequence of this relative "scarcity" of "Political Goods" compared with the number of players is that those who want to stay the course and win are socially obliged always to give more than the others or to give objects that are far rarer, far more valuable than those given by the others. Another consequence is the imposition of an oratorical, emphatic ceremonial style on the gestures that accompany the presentation of the gifts and countergifts. But above all, this war of gifts is possible only if the objects given are comparable, even though their value may differ, and if they can, up to a point, be substituted for each other even though they are classified according to rank, the highest of which contains only a few, nearly unique objects, as is often the case with sacred objects.

It now also becomes clear why, in this type of society, it is difficult or even impossible for the majority of individuals and groups *not to get drawn into* the game of gift and countergift, or to quit the game. The only ones who are partially exempted are those whose elevated rank raises them well above the fray or those whose inferior, servile status excludes them from below. For the rest, to avoid giving is to forfeit one's honor and that of the group one represents.[7] To refuse to give or not to give in return becomes impossible. Thus the act of giving contains a violence which is not only that of the individual, since it springs from beyond the individual, from the social relations which imply that the struggle for power and fame is to be waged by means of wealth. Gift-giving contains this violence in both senses of the term: it carries the violence within itself, and it keeps it within certain bounds, while allowing it to be manifested publicly, politically.[8]

Thus we have come back to Mauss and his text, with its mine of ethnographic information on Melanesia, Polynesia, North America drawn from Boas, Swanton, Thurnwald, Malinowski, and analyzed in order to construct his essay on the gift. We can now survey the ground that has been covered.

---

7. "As may be seen, the notion of honour, which expresses itself violently in Polynesia and is always present in Melanesia, is in this case [North America], really destructive...The Polynesian word *mana* itself symbolizes, not only the magical force in every creature, but also his honour, and one of the best translations of the word is 'authority,' 'wealth'" (Mauss, 1990: 37–38).

8. "Everything is based upon the principles of antagonism and rivalry. The political status of the individuals in the brotherhoods and clans, and ranks of all kinds, are gained in a 'war of prosperity,' just as they are in real war, or through chance, inheritance, alliance and marriage. Yet everything is conceived of as if it were a 'struggle of wealth'" (Mauss, 1990: 37). And also "The potlatch is a war. Among the Tlingit, it bears the name of 'War Dance'" (*Ibid.*: 113, n. 114).

But before we do, we will pause over an example from Melanesia, because it illustrates how an object of trade can become a gift-object or a sacred object.

Concerning the Metamorphosis of an Object of Trade into a Gift-Object or a Sacred Object

It is to Michel Panoff that we owe a very fine analysis of this process, which he observed among the Maenge of New Britain. The Maenge live on the southern coast of the island; they used to buy, from the mountain tribes of the interior, rings (*page*) cut from giant clam (Tridacna) shells and strings of beads (*tali*) made from seashells. These they purchased with dogs and coconuts, and used them in different kinds of exchange, as brideprice, as bloodprice or stored them away in the clan treasure. The Maenge were unaware of the origin of these shells, which the mountain tribes themselves bought from the Nakanai people on the island's north coast. The Nakanai procured them by organizing seagoing expeditions to buy the *page* on New Hanover Island and the *tali* on New Ireland, in other words, hundreds of kilometers from New Britain (Panoff, 1980: 5–38). It was only around 1914, when a number of men were recruited among the Maenge and other tribes in the south of the island to work on the big German plantations in the northeast, that the Maenge learned the true origin of these objects. Until then they had believed them to be the work of supernatural beings who kept them in a mysterious place before giving them out to humans. These objects had not been distributed to the Maenge's ancestors, however, but to those of the other tribes from whom their own ancestors had bought them.

We see here in what contexts and through what social mechanisms objects of no practical everyday use, useless when it comes to society's subsistence, have gained entry into society without ceremony, but as commodities, and little by little take on human attributes or those of persons more powerful than humans — gods, nature spirits, mythic ancestors — once they enter the areas of social life in which their use is *necessary*, in which they are *depended upon*. Like human or supernatural beings, they acquire a name, an identity, a history and powers. The bulk of these trade items, originally characterized by mysterious origins and possessing an exchange value, will circulate as substitutes for persons, living (brideprice) or dead (bloodprice), or serve as instruments of the reproduction of the social, kinship or power relations entertained *among the clans* that comprise Maenge society, which would be unable to reproduce themselves without such exchanges.

But these exchanges are not the only condition for the perpetuation of the clans. There is another, which is just as indispensable; however it is less visible because it does not have the public and even ostentatious character of the exchanges of goods, but remains in the background. I am talking about the relations each clan must entertain *with itself*: the gestures, the ceremonies, the efforts by which each reproduces its identity, ensures its continuity, maintains a constant connection with its origins. It is when the object of exchange achieves this, when it enters the domain, no longer of exchanges between the living, but between the living and their dead, and between the living and their gods, that the trade object *becomes sacred*. Already set apart because it has no use in daily life, because it is ascribed supernatural origins, and because it already possesses a universally recognized value, the object of trade ceases to circulate and comes to rest at an essential spot in society: at those places to which each clan feels obliged to return periodically because it comes to encounter itself, to confirm its being, its identity, its substance, preserved from time and conserved in time. In short, it comes to confront its origins.

To sum up: it is when the trade object enters this place and is used to reactivate the imaginary and symbolic relationship with the origin that it becomes sacred and acquires even greater value still for having moved into the sacred area of power.[9] For the sacred—contrary to the views of Durkheim, who made too sharp a separation between the religious and the political— always has to do with power insofar as *the sacred is a certain relationship with the origin* and insofar as the origin of individuals and of groups has a bearing on the positions they occupy within a social and a cosmic order. It is with reference to the origin of each person and each group that the *actual relations* between the individuals and the groups that comprise a society are compared with the order that *should* reign in the universe and in society, and are judged to be *legitimate or illegitimate by right*, and therefore acceptable or unacceptable. It is therefore not the objects which sacralize all or some of people's relations with each other and with the surrounding universe; it is the reverse.

In the Maenge example, we see clearly how people *project* onto things and *embody* in the matter and form of these objects the *imaginary cores* and the *symbols* of the real relations they entertain with each other and with the world around them. This entire social process is at the same time a mental process which involves both parts of thought and, above and beyond thought, the two parts of the human mind, the conscious and the unconscious. For people are not aware of projecting and reifying the realities that comprise their social being. They are confronted with things which have a name, a soul, force, powers, things which come from themselves, but which

---

9. See also Gregory, 1980, 1982.

they regard and treat as something different from themselves, as having come from somewhere else. Or more accurately, they find themselves face to face with person-things that are both alien and familiar. Familiar because, in a certain sense, people *see themselves in* the exchange objects and the sacred objects, but alien because although they see they do not *recognize* themselves. In other words, people generate duplicate selves, but do not recognize themselves in their replicas, which, once they are detached, stand before them as persons who are at once familiar and alien. In fact, it is not the replicas who stand before people as aliens, it is people themselves, who, by generating replicas of themselves, have become in part strangers to themselves, alienated to these other beings who are nonetheless part of themselves, though they do not know it.

II. The Dis-enchanted Gift

Listening to Mauss and Choosing the Right Trail

In reality, all we are doing here is following Mauss' own theoretical indications: when the Baruya exchange women in order to produce their kinship relations, they are practicing, at least in this area of their social life, a form of total prestation. And for Mauss, total prestations are the starting point for understanding the agonistic prestations that define the potlatch. Potlatch, he writes, is an "evolved form" of total prestation in which "the principles of rivalry and hostility dominate." (Mauss, 1990: 6) Prestations are "total" when it is not individuals but groups, clans, tribes, families, legal entities that put each other under reciprocal obligation; when what they exchange is not solely property and wealth, but "acts of politeness, banquets, rituals, military services, women, children," and they do this in "a somewhat voluntary form...although in the final analysis they are strictly compulsory" (*Ibid.*: 5).

The purest type of such prestations for Mauss, was "the alliance of two phratries in Australian or North American tribes in general" (*Ibid.*: 6). In short, for Mauss, potlatch societies were evolved societies which had arrived at this stage after a series of *sociological* and historical *transformations* that had modified the structures characterizing them at earlier periods in their history. The model Mauss had in mind, when he imagined the starting point of this evolution, was that of Australian societies divided into two halves which exchanged women, property, children and played distinct but complementary roles in fertility rites, initiations, Australian societies which Durkheim, before Mauss, had analyzed at length.[10]

___

10. "But in every possible form of society it is in the nature of a gift to impose an obligatory time limit.... The notion of a time limit is thus logically involved when there is a ques-

The Baruya, with their kinship relations resting on direct exchange of women between two lineages, are thus a "weakened" example of this ideal starting point. The way their society operates, as among the Australian aboriginal peoples, leaves no, or almost no room for gifts and countergifts of an "agonistic kind." Mauss thus seems to have indicated the right starting place, but to get from societies practicing total prestations to potlatch societies, *there was a piece missing* from Mauss' reasoning, and this hole stemmed from the fact that he had *not* analyzed the forms and meanings of the gift when it *did not serve* social and political rivalries and antagonisms. If it is not used in these interests, it is because there is no basis, no room for this kind of gift in this type of society.[11] For when "everything is complementary and presumes cooperation between the two halves of the tribe" (*Ibid.*: 6), there is little room left for competition, and the exchanges become part of a complementary relationship between two halves of a whole, each of equivalent status, or if this whole is ranked, one being of higher or lower status than the other, either permanently or merely in certain social contexts.

Because Mauss did not analyze non-agonistic gift-exchanges, he lacked the sociological keys that would have enabled him to unlock the precise nature of the transformations required for a society based on non-agonistic gift-exchange to become a society economically and morally predicated on potlatch. Since these transformations gave rise to these differences, the latter needed to be understood in order to take the measure of the former. The problem was to isolate the principal difference between the two kinds of gift-exchange: non-agonistic and agonistic. In the first case, one gives so that the other person will give something equivalent; in the second case, one gives so that the other person *cannot give* something equivalent in turn. In the first case, after each exchange of gifts, the giver is temporarily superior to the receiver; but in the end, at the level of society as a whole, all lineages and all individuals have received, if not an equal share, at least an equivalent share of women, rituals, and so forth. In the second case, following

---

tion of returning... Current economic and juridical history is largely mistaken in this matter. Imbued with modern ideas, it forms *a priori* ideas of development... In fact, the point of departure lies elsewhere. It is provided in a category of rights that excludes the jurists and economists, who are not interested in it. This is the gift, a complex phenomenon, *particularly in its most ancient form*, that of total services, with which we do not deal in this monograph. Now, the gift necessarily entails the notion of credit. The evolution in economic law has not been from barter to sale, and from cash sale to credit sale" (Mauss, 1990: 35–36; italics added).

11. Only once did Mauss suggest, on the basis of Baldwin Spencer's material on the Northern Australian Kakadu, that intertribal competition might once have existed in Australia, but he went no further (*Ibid.*: 85, n. 9).

the social logic of gifts and countergifts of wealth, at the level of society as a whole, only certain clans, and certain lineages and the individuals who represent them appropriate the titles, ranks, positions of power and prestige open to this competition, after having temporarily succeeded in outgiving all their rivals. To be sure, both cases feature gifts and countergifts, and in both cases the gift establishes a double relationship between giver and receiver: on the one hand a relationship characterized by sharing and solidarity; on the other, a relationship characterized by superiority and distance. But beyond this common feature, beyond this core-structure present in both kinds of gift-giving, the underlying social logics are not only different, they are opposed.

The example of the Baruya practice of direct exchange of women, *ginamare*, which entails a whole series of additional reciprocal services over at least a generation, is very helpful for understanding this difference. Here we have the example of a *social* mechanism which obliges a person to reciprocate, to give again after having received, which is not the same as giving back the same as one has received. Now Mauss presented the mechanism of gift-exchange as a concatenation of three obligations: the obligation to give, the obligation to receive, and the obligation to reciprocate or to give in turn. This approach tended to present the third obligation, that of reciprocating, as an enigma, as the one that *posed the most difficult theoretical problem*, the one that most required explaining.[12] And that is where Mauss' analysis went wrong, for he believed he had found his explanation in Polynesian religious representations, in their belief that things were endowed with a soul, with a spirit that made the receiver "give back" what he had received.

> The most important features among these spiritual mechanisms is clearly one that obliges a person to reciprocate the present that he has received. Now, the moral and religious reason for this constraint is nowhere more apparent than in Polynesia. Let us study it in greater detail, and we will plainly see what force impels one to reciprocate the thing received... (Mauss, 1990: 6).

This explains Mauss' long analyses of the Polynesian concept of *hau*, the spirit of a thing, and of *mana*, the wealth, force and power contained in persons and in things.

> Concerning the hau, the spirit of things... Tamati Ranaipiri... gives us, completely by chance, and entirely without prejudice, *the key to*

---

12. For example: "Concerning the *main* subject of our analysis, the *obligation to reciprocate*, we must acknowledge that we have found few facts in Hindu law" (*Ibid.*: 146, n. 61; italics added).

the problem...What imposes obligation in the present received and exchanged, is the fact that the thing received is not inactive. Even when it has been abandoned by the giver, it still possesses something of him. Through it the giver has a hold over the beneficiary...*In reality, it is the hau that wishes to return to its birthplace*, to the sanctuary of the forest and the clan, and to the owner...in Maori law, the legal tie, a tie occurring through things, is one between souls, because the thing itself possesses a soul...Invested with life, often possessing individuality, *it seeks to return* to its "place of origin," *or to produce*, on behalf of the clan and the native soil from which it sprang, *an equivalent to replace it* (*Ibid.*: 11–13; italics added).

Between the Explanation for Giving and the Explanation for Reciprocating, a Hole in Mauss' Reasoning and Two Theories that Come Down to One

There seems to be a piece missing from the theory Mauss has constructed. On the one hand, he advances what we will call "social" reasons in explanation of the first two obligations: the obligation to give (to put others under obligation, to reciprocate within a time limit, to serve one's own interests by demonstrating disinterest, etc. (*Ibid.*: 13) and the obligation to receive (to refuse would be tantamount to losing face or declaring war, etc.) (*Ibid.*: 19–20, 41–42). But he advances what we will call "religious" explanations for the third obligation, the "obligation to reciprocate," which "constitutes the essence of the potlatch" (*Ibid.*: 42). It is as though, between the two analyses of the two sides of exchange, there were a hole in the theory, which he plugs with an exemplary explanation, an indigenous theory based on the belief in a soul or a spirit that makes things want to return to their owner, a belief which, although it actually exists, is clearly not the final explanation. Thus, on one side, there were social reasons which make a man give a thing that belongs to him, and on the other, religious reasons which make the recipient reciprocate. On one side, in giving and receiving, men act; on the other, in reciprocating, they are acted upon. Furthermore, this "religious" reason itself combines two reasons: one is not "mystical," but social and psychological: the thing given is believed to take with it something of the giver. The phenomenon is universal and it is what creates the bond between giver and receiver the world over. The other reason is if, as the Polynesians believe, what the thing takes with it is the soul of the giver's clan, then it is this soul which makes the receiver return the thing to the original owners or reciprocate with "an equivalent to take its place." This presents a paradox, however, since the soul of a clan or a person cannot have an equivalent, properly speaking, unless one says one person equals another person, but in this case there is no longer any need to give back the *same* thing or the *same* person. The equivalent is enough. But if equivalence is enough, the theory explaining that things are returned because their soul makes them want to go back to their place of origin is useless, superfluous. Everything is mixed in the theory on the pretext that everything is mixed in reality.

Souls are mixed with things; things with souls. Lives are mingled together, and this is how, among persons and things so intermingled, each emerges from their own sphere and mixes together. This is precisely what contract and exchange are (*Ibid.*: 20).

The paradox is that, when the souls mixed with the things are not human souls, but those of gods, nature spirits or mythic ancestors, these things become "sacred"; *instead of being given, they are carefully stored away*, instead of being exchanged, they are kept out of exchange. And without further explanation of these different fates of souls and things, Mauss comments, "it might be difficult for it to be otherwise."[13] In sum, Mauss fails to explain both the obligation to *reciprocate* "animate" things when they are received from humans and the obligation *not to give them away* when they have been received from the ancestors and the gods because they are inhabited by an even more sacred soul, and by non-human, supernatural forces and powers.

Finally it seems to me that it should be possible to assess the place of potlatch societies in history. Of course the history we are talking about here is not the specific history of each of these societies. It is the history that gradually takes shape when, through these many histories, parallel developments begin to emerge which make sense because they suppose irreversibilities which are no longer singular and accidental but structural and necessary. Now these parallel irreversibilities, which are linked to convergent structural transformations, occur in societies which have never had any contact with each other and which quite often do not even belong to the same time period.

This means that history entails development. Not that there are laws for the evolution of human history which are inscribed in nature or in the mind

---

13. Mauss, *Id.*: 134, n. 245. "These pieces of property are *sacra*" (p. 43). "The sum total of these precious things constitutes the magical dower . . . [which is] always, and in every tribe, spiritual in origin and of a spiritual nature" (p. 44). "It would seem that among the Kwakiutl there were two kinds of copper objects: the more important ones that do not go out of the family and that can only be broken to be recast and certain others that circulate intact, that are of less value, and that seem to serve as satellites for the first kind" (p. 134, n. 245). "The copper objects are often identical with the spirits" (p. 135, n. 252).

of God, laws which would precede History and predispose societies to move in one direction or another. Nor is History driven by history. It is human beings themselves that do the driving: it is they who cause things to change, they who modify their relations among themselves and with nature. But not everything is possible. One thing cannot be exchanged for no matter what other thing, and at any one time in any one society, the number of transformations open to it is always very small. It is impossible—sociologically, mentally, materially and therefore historically—for a Neolithic society organized more or less along the lines of the Baruya society before 1951 to have transformed itself directly into a society organized by market-economy principles, governed by a centralized State and having mastered several sources of energy, including nuclear power. Simply raising this possibility is enough to show that *it is absurd.* Therefore, somewhere and at some time, some societies must have gone through *several stages* for such transformations to have come about in one or several local societies and for others to have access to the same results *without having to go through* the same stages themselves. This necessity of clearing certain stages is what is called "the conditions of evolution" or "historical necessity." No society is exempt: if some seem to be, it is because others have gone through these stages for them. All existing societies result from transformations of societies which have gone before and which sometimes continue to exist alongside the new forms. All existing social structures are transformations of other structures which characterized the same or other societies that went before in the same places. Transformation means both the conservation and the destruction of certain components of the old structures, not only the preservation of former components but also the emergence of new ones, which combine with the old and give them new meaning and new functions.

In this perspective, and after having taken these many theoretical precautions, we broadly espouse Mauss' conclusion, namely: that those societies which have developed an economy and a moral dominated by potlatch, agonistic gift-giving, correspond to

> a regime that must have been shared by a very large part of humanity during a very long *transitional* phase, one that moreover, still subsists among the peoples [of the Pacific and northwest America]...this principle of the exchange-gift must have been that of societies that had gone beyond the phase of "total prestations," from clan to clan, and from family to family, but have not yet reached that of purely individual contract, of the market where money circulates, of sale proper, and above all of the notion of price reckoned in coinage weighed and stamped with its value (Mauss, 1990: 20).

Of course one must make reservations about certain claims, such as the absence of "individual" contracts or sale proper in these societies, but the overall picture is valid and would not be invalidated by the new material with which Mauss could be confronted today. Between the economic structures of societies based on "total prestations" and

> the individualistic and purely self-interested economy that our own societies have experienced at least in part, as soon as it was discovered by the Semitic and Greek peoples...there is an entire and immensely gradated series of institutions and economic events, and this series is not governed by the economic rationalism whose theory we are so willing to propound (*Ibid.*: 76).

For Mauss, then, all we can expect to find in the past history or in the present-day workings of Western societies are fragments of this gift-based economy[14] or forms of gift-giving present in other areas of the economy and which are not necessarily vestiges.[15]

But other societies followed evolutions that did not lead to a market economy and restricted the room for a potlatch economy. The emergence of centralized States which deduct a large portion of their subjects' labor and wealth in the form of *corvées* and tribute curtailed the practice of potlatch to local or regional competitions insofar as, at these levels, outside the sphere governed by State power, there were still positions of power to be gained by accumulating and giving out wealth. At the level of State power, there was no more room for potlatch. The products taken by the State were sometimes redistributed as a token of the generosity and solicitude of those embodying the State, while another portion normally went to maintain a political and administrative élite that did not produce any wealth of its own, but did accumulate and consume wealth. Mauss was aware of this other direction open to societies based on gift-giving: he had noted that the basic components of the potlatch existed in Polynesia even though the institution was not found in its entirety. And, after having advanced the suggestion that the potlatch may have existed at some earlier time in Polynesia, he added this note which, for once, alludes to the nature of the political structure of potlatch societies:

---

14. "This ethics and this economy still function in our own societies, constantly and, so to speak, hidden below the surface" (Mauss, *Id.*: 4). Mauss' method was first to scour the legal systems in search of economic and moral forms of gift-giving. All he found in the ancient codes of the Greek, Roman and Jewish peoples were vestiges, but he did discover a vigorous presence in the Old Germanic system, which he believed could be explained, in accordance with nineteenth-century *idées reçues*, by the fact that "Germanic civilisation was itself a long time without markets" (p. 60). This did not mean, as he stressed, that the Germanic peoples lived in a "natural economy."

15. Mauss says: "In that separate existence that constitutes our social life" (*Ibid.*: 65), and goes on to list, pell-mell, rules of hospitality, popular attitudes and customs, and so on.

Indeed there is a reason for its [the institution of potlatch in its entire-
ty] having disappeared from part of this area. It is because the clans
have definitively become hierarchized in almost all the islands and
have even been concentrated around a monarchy. Thus there is missing one of the main conditions for the potlatch, namely the instability of a hierarchy that rivalry between chiefs has precisely the aim of
temporarily stabilizing (*Ibid.*: 97, n. 79).

So what explains that, among the Baruya of Melanesia, who have no
aristocracy or kings, and in Polynesian societies, which have both, the practice of potlatch did not develop, whereas all of these societies abound in gift-
exchanges? In my opinion it is the fact that, in these societies, however different they may be from one another, the political-religious hierarchy among
kin groups and local groups tends *to appear* as a framework, a rigid structure, immutable, inherited but also hereditary. The foundation of potlatch
societies is therefore the presence, but also the absence, of certain social
structures: absence of a rigid political hierarchy, presence of kinship relations entailing the transfer of goods and wealth. It is in these structures that
the explanation of their workings is to be found, not in "the soul of things."
   But these two conditions are not of the same nature and they do not operate on the same level. For kinship relations alone do not make a society. A
society exists only if it forms a totality, and somewhere it must be present
and represented as such, at a level on which the interests of the kin-groups
or the other constituent groups are also represented, but *subordinated to
the reproduction of this society as a whole.* However at both these levels,
that of society (the whole) as well as that of its parts (families, clans and
even castes or classes), there are two opposing principles which must always
be combined: exchanging (and changing) in order to subsist, and subsist-
ing in order to exchange (and to change). In every society, therefore, alongside those things which circulate, there must be stable, fixed points, social
relations and identities, which stand outside the sphere of exchange and at
the same time enable it to exist, which found the practice of exchange and
at the same time set its limits, its boundaries.

Translated by Nora Scott

Chapter 4

Women and Wealth in New Guinea*

Pierre Lemonnier

Although it grew out of his general investigation into the transformation of economic and social formations down through history, Maurice
Godelier's model of Great-Men societies has also fuelled comparative reflection on forms of power in Melanesia, and in particular gave rise to the
debates published in the collective volume, *Big Men, Great Men*, which
he edited in collaboration with Marilyn Strathern (1991).

Earlier, in his *Making of Great Men*, first published in French in 1982 —
and initially in the field study begun in 1967 — Godelier had observed that
the Baruya either lacked or relegated to second place a number of social
institutions and practices typical of so-called Big-Men societies, which at
the time were the most-studied groups in the New Guinea Highlands (e.g.,
A. Strathern 1971). While it was the practice of the ethnographic literature to show societies obsessed with ceremonial exchanges of pigs and shells,
with rivalry between the Big Men who organized these exchanges, and with
the raising of the pigs that were given on any number of occasions, the
Baruya themselves do not have ceremonial exchanges. Furthermore, pigs
play only a modest role in social relations, particularly in marriage. The
focus of group attention in a Great-Men society like the Baruya is war and
male initiations. These two events articulate the three main hierarchies struc-
turing the life of the society: the ranking of Great Men with respect to
each other (masters of initiations and great warriors, in some cases great

* First published as "Femmes et richesses en Nouvelle-Guinée," in P. Descola, J. Hamel
and P. Lemonnier (eds.) *La Production du social. Autour de Maurice Godelier*. Paris, Fayard,
1999: 315–332. "La Production du Social" by Colloque de Cerisy © Librairie Arthème Fayard
1999.

103

shamans); the subordination of all women to men as a group; and the authority of the older men over first-stage initiates.

It is this striking contrast between two types of social logic that is brought
out in Godelier's analysis, using a model that establishes a connection between
the initiation ceremonies and all-pervasive male domination, the marginal
role in social life of exchanges of wealth and the form of these exchanges
characterized by the equivalence of their terms in both kind and quantity
(1986 [1982]: 171). In the forefront of these perfectly symmetrical prestations specific to Great-Men systems is marriage by sister-exchange.

Both this theoretical model and this outlook guided my fieldwork among
other Anga groups as well as my comparative research on New Guinea. But
in terms of the ethnography presently available on the Anga, what cries out
for our attention, as much as the contrast between "sister-exchange" and
brideprice, or the coexistence of the two types of marriage within the same
society (Godelier, 1990a: 78), is the place of wealth in marriage in general,
including on the fringes or even at the heart of sister-exchange itself. We
will see that, while the issue of the equivalence between women and wealth
in New Guinea loses nothing of its pertinence or its heuristic value—Godelier emphasized its radical consequences for Highland societies—it is clear
today that the relation between women and wealth does not take the form
in all Anga groups that was announced in *The Making of Great Men*. This
being the case, there is reason to look into the strategies developed by some
societies in this island for maintaining a certain distance between women
and wealth, while pursuing the ideal of sister-exchange at all costs, and to
attempt to measure the consequences of such strategies.

* * *

The many ethnographic studies conducted among the Anga[1] have made
it possible to confront the Great-Men society model, which Godelier built
using his Baruya material, with information gathered in other Anga groups.
The model emerges largely unscathed. From one Anga language group to
the next, the links between political order, gender relations, war and initiations are those described by Godelier. In all cases, political power is held
by the men responsible for a complex of institutions in which are tightly
interwoven war and the machinery of the initiations by which men preserve
and reproduce their fighting powers while keeping women (and to a lesser
degree young initiates) in a position of inferiority. In all groups, too, at the
heart of this system of institutions and social relations, resides the idea that
female sexual physiology is detrimental to men, that it threatens their fight-

---

1. In particular, Fischer, 1968; Herdt, 1987, 1994; Mimica, 1981, 1991a, 1991b; Lory,
1981–82; Bonnemère, 1996; Lemonnier, 1997.

ing spirit and consequently jeopardizes the survival of the group as a whole. The initiations endow men with their physical and moral strength; and it is within this framework that the practical knowledge which will enable them to attenuate this dangerous state of affairs is transmitted. Furthermore the rituals simultaneously found and reaffirm male domination.

In each Anga tribe, then, we find the basic components of this core of relations whose centrality, coherence and social "logic" were first shown by Godelier. In particular, the variations encountered here and there have not stopped people regularly designating male initiations as a crucial institution which has always ensured the two main functions highlighted in *The Making of Great Men*: to "mold all of the men into a collective force, each generation forming a bloc which transcends their divisions," but also with respect to women, presented as a "constant source of danger for men, and especially a danger for the reproduction of society itself" (Godelier 1992: 19–20).

Comparative Anga ethnography also confirms the absence of another pillar of the Big-Men complex, which is the foundation of political power on the manipulation of wealth. Exchanges of wealth within or between groups are strictly limited. The only collective prestations are feasts at which a whole tribe or local group presents itself with cooked vegetables and game as it honors its new initiates. The prominent men are those who, owing to their birth in a particular lineage (masters of the initiations) or to their personal skills (great hunters and shamans), distinguish themselves by the responsibilities exercise or by the role they play in initiations or in war.

However, another hypothesis advanced by Godelier (1990a: 86; 1992: 19–20), that of a link between initiations and marriage by sister-exchange without bridewealth, must no doubt be abandoned.[2] While all Anga groups do indeed have Great Men corresponding to the Baruya prototype, while they all rank male initiations at the head of their collective events and while all are unfamiliar with large-scale exchanges of wealth, the bulk of these groups practice a form of marriage involving the mandatory transfer of wealth to the wife-givers, notably in the form of bridewealth, with no emphasis on the exchange of sisters.

In other words, while the Anga situation is a counter-example showing that, without generalized circulation of wealth, there is no place for Big Men (Godelier, 1986 [1982]; Modjeska, 1982; A. Strathern, 1982), it also demonstrates that marriage with brideprice in the totality of cases is by no means incompatible with a Great-Men system. Male initiations in themselves, in

---

2. "It was then that I suggested that there could be an internal link, a close connection between the existence of kinship systems based on direct exchange of women and the existence of male initiation systems relying on inherited ritual powers" (Godelier, 1990b: 13).

the general form they take among the Anga, do not appear to be linked with a particular type of marriage.

Given this conclusion, one might expect that male initiations nevertheless have a tendency to be associated with sister-exchange and consider, along with Godelier, that "there where, in New Guinea, bridewealth is the *dominant* rule of marriage exchange, one does not *generally* find *highly elaborate* initiation ceremonies" (Godelier, 1992: 19, author's italics). But such a proposition is not substantiated by the facts. In the majority of Anga groups, we find both marriage with brideprice and male initiations every bit as elaborate as those of the Northern Anga (Baruya, Sambia).[3] In the case of the Ankave, it can even be said that marriage with brideprice is not merely the "dominant rule," it is the *only* form practiced and commented on (Bonnemère, 1996: 79–89). It would therefore be better to try to draw our conclusions from a counter-example that is all the more significant for bearing on a society relatively like the Baruya, and to ask ourselves how it alters our understanding of the role of marriage in the logic of Great-Men societies, and more particularly our understanding of the role of wealth in marriage exchanges.

* * *

Ankave ethnography points us first of all in the direction of a more nuanced definition of the causal link between initiation and kinship. In Godelier's work, male domination forms the backdrop for such reasoning; this is made explicit, for example, in his article "Sociétés à Big Men, Sociétés à Grands Hommes":

> For the Baruya, the direct exchange of women among men supposes the direct ideological and social coercion of women. This would seem to me to impose a collective male force which stands behind each man, especially when he must exchange women under his direct control (sisters or daughters). This collective force created by the male initiations builds a solidarity among the men that transcends any differences or oppositions that may exist between their lineages or villages. (1990a: 86)

In another article, Godelier advances the hypothesis

---

3. Having attended both the Baruya and the Ankave ceremonies, I can say that Ankave initiations are neither more nor less elaborate than those of the Northern Anga groups, either as a crucial moment in the life of the group, or in dramatic intensity, grandiose staging, duration or involvement of everyone in a key-event in the reproduction of the social order. Only the violence of the initiates' break with the world of women is relatively attenuated among the Ankave.

...that the link between kinship and initiation systems, by way of the requirements of warfare, may have been the existence of an ideology in which women were seen as a constant source of danger for men, and especially a danger for the reproduction of society itself, because of their flow of menstrual blood at regular intervals. It is this representation of female pollution which legitimizes the segregation of the two sexes, particularly that of boys, and which gives rise to the systematic denigration of women, the "theft" of their powers, and so on. (Godelier, 1992: 20)

Comparing this situation with what can be seen among the Ankave reveals the importance of denigration. As Pascale Bonnemère points out (1996: 121–22), Ankave women, too, are a "source of danger" for men, whom they are said to weaken, and for society, since by sapping the warriors' strength, they jeopardize the survival of the whole group. Once again it is their physiology that makes them dangerous, but, unlike Northern Angans, the Ankave by no means stress women's responsibility for men's weaknesses: they merely note the incompatibility between the presence of women and the male fighting spirit. However absence of denigration[4] as well as the additional existence of women's discourses which differ on this point from those of Ankave men show that the men's intensely negative discourse on women and the fact that women and men share these representations — which is characteristic of the Baruya situation (Godelier, 1986 [1982]: 148–49) — correlate strongly with the relative violence of the men's domination (Bonnemère, 1996: 382–83).

Lastly, the Ankave case shows that, even in the absence of marriage by direct sister-exchange, women are held responsible — although less responsible perhaps than among the Baruya — for the misfortunes of the male half of society. There is assuredly a parallel to be drawn between the segregation established and reproduced by male initiations and female pollution, but — and this is where I would recast Godelier's hypothesis — women's responsibility for the male condition is emphasized only there where men control the fate of their sisters and daughters, in other words, there where marriage is carried out by sister-exchange, which raises another question: for what reason(s) should women be held to be more *responsible* for men's weaknesses (but not more dangerous) when the dominant form of marriage is sister-exchange?

One avenue of investigation is suggested by Godelier's hypothesis (1986 [1982]: 180) that there is a logical link between the relatively high status of

---

4. And of female initiations in which the women are led to share the men's discourse on women.

Photo 14: Betrothal among the Ankave: A man, his daughter on his back, receives the piece of pig meat and fat given by his future in-laws to "set aside" the girl whom they wish to marry to one of their sons (Photo P. Lemonnier, Ankave, Ikundi village, 1988).

women in Big-Men societies, on the one hand, and their twin roles as producers of wealth (pigs) to be used in ceremonial exchanges and essential link between exchange groups, often affines, on the other.[5] If we turn this reasoning around, it points to the fact that, in Great-Men societies—which have warriors and masters of initiations but no manipulators of wealth—women do not take part in major collective events.[6] The corollary is that their status (which can be assessed from their right to speak their mind, the blows they receive or give and husband-wife relations) seems to be less elevated than in Big-Men societies. In particular, it is likely that in this case men act with less restraint in exercising the "collective force" Godelier talks about (1990b: 14) on their daughters and sisters. However this hypothesis about the non-recognition of women's positive role and their denigration does not mention any form of marriage. And above all, it does not account

5. Confirmed by Feil (1978).

6. Or at least their participation is not recognized, for male initiations draw heavily on female powers, which the men dissimulate for the occasion (Godelier, 1986: 63–76; Bonnemère, 1996: 356–58). Furthermore, Bonnemère (forthcoming) has shown that, although they are kept apart from the *mai* ritual places, the mothers and sisters of the novices play a key role in the latters' physical transformation.

for the sharp contrasts in the intensity and forms of male domination within Great-Men societies themselves (Bonnemère, 1996: 369–71).

Perhaps we should look instead into the initiation machinery itself, into the various forms and contents, for elements that might be bound up with sister-exchange. The Ankave-Baruya comparison suggests one such correlation. In Ankave male ceremonies, the "rebirth" of the initiates and the fashioning of their adult body use a surrogate of the substance to which local procreation theories attribute fetal growth: women's blood.[7] In Northern Anga groups, on the other hand, this growth is attributed to semen, and it is owing to the ingestion of semen in the course of homosexual rituals that the initiates grow into full adults and warriors (Godelier, 1986 [1982]: 51–55; Herdt, 1981: 232–36). In addition to the presence or absence of denigration and of female initiations, which are directly linked with the former, ritualized homosexual practices are thus another component of the initiations which seems to vary with the status accorded women (Bonnemère, 1996: 380–83). One might therefore wonder whether that particularity of Northern Anga (Baruya, Sambia) initiations known as "boy-inseminating practices" (Herdt, 1993: ix) might not in one way or another be connected with the prevailing form of marriage in these societies, sister-exchange. Unfortunately, Knauft (1993: 61, 244) has already indicated a number of counter-examples to this hypothesis, advanced elsewhere by Weiner (1982: 29), Feil (1987: 178) and Lindenbaum (1984: 39), of a link between homosexual rituals and marriage by direct exchange.

To sum up: sister-exchange is not a necessary component of the social logics that found the originality of Great-Men systems.[8] Although there may be some specificity in the Baruya case which was Godelier's departure point, it remains to be identified. It is clear that denigration (here, emphasis on women's imaginary responsibility for men's condition) and homosexual practices in the initiation setting are two features which distinguish Northern Angans from other Anga groups, and that the first practice sister-exchange while the second favor brideprice. But there is no satisfying explanatory system that links the four elements together. However, as we are going to see, there is some new ethnographic material that shows a use of wealth in Baruya marriage which permits a better characterization of its role in Great-Men societies in general and, secondarily, perhaps even greater relativization of the place of marriage by sister-exchange in these societies. Finally and above all, this reflection gives us an opportunity to explore new impli-

---

7. Even if this blood is "defeminized" for the occasion (Bonnemère, 1994: 30, 1996: 356–58).

8. My "internal" criticism concurs here with the comments made by Whitehouse (1992: 111), who similarly challenged the "centrality" of sister-exchange in Godelier's model, adducing counter-examples from other New Guinea ethnies.

cations of the relationship between women and wealth in New Guinea. Finally, it is not the absolute presence of wealth in the marriage sphere that matters, then, but rather where and in what conditions wealth is used.

Wealth on the Fringes of Sister-Exchange

Godelier tells us that, among the Baruya, where direct exchange is the most prevalent form of marriage, bridewealth is not entirely absent, but it is reserved for marriage outside the tribe (1986 [1982]: 22). There is, however, another practice, every bit as rare, which introduces wealth into the exchange of women itself: a long time (two or three generations) after a marriage for which a woman has ultimately not been given in return, even though many daughters and granddaughters have resulted from the union, the descendants of the maternal and paternal kin of the woman originally given require a gift of wealth from the wife-takers, as compensation. A capital point here: an identical payment—of cowry strings, vegetable salt, barkcloth capes and today PNG currency, but never pork—must be made when, following a marriage by "sister-exchange," one of the women gives birth to many more children than the other. In other words, even in an Anga group where sister-exchange is central to their social practices, wealth plays a role in marriage, a fringe role, perhaps, but one that is nevertheless clearly defined.

The Baruya thus appear as a society which pursues the exchange of women, which considers that several kinds of exchanges contributing to harmonious relations—working together, sharing food—can compensate a lack of women or of children born of a marriage, but that, in the end, a gift of wealth re-instates a balance in terms of people, labor, food and so on. The long lapse of time before such gifts are demanded shows that people wait as long as possible before bringing wealth into the exchange of women.[9]

---

9. According to Koumain and his wife, Urumianac, who had the patience to drum into me what I was not ready to hear, this is a traditional practice, as confirmed by the fact that it has a name. This payment is called *min'ni ngwiye*, or "head payment," *minyaginya* meaning "head," and *nigwia*, "cowries, shell money" (Lloyd, 1992: 570, 615). This etymology was pointed out to me by Koumain, who explained why (at first incomprehensible to me) he had had to make a payment to the family of the mother of his father-in-law, Warineu, in place of his own deceased brothers-in-law. Warineu was no doubt over 75 at the time of his death in 1993, which says a lot about the date of his own mother's death, which was the object of the regularization. Juillerat reminded me that the expression "head payment" exists in a non-Anga group, the Gimi, where it designates a mandatory recruitment payment made to the bride's parents upon the birth of a son. Unlike the Baruya case, this "head payment" is not meant to re-establish a balance or to minimize the consequences of an uncompleted exchange

Godelier's suggestion (1986 [1982]: 173) that "because the production of relations of kinship does not depend directly on the accumulation of material wealth, there is little incentive to produce such wealth, pigs in particular," is still fundamental, but one point must be modified: in Great-Men societies, the production of kinship relations has *little* to do with the accumulation of wealth; what remains to be done is to define this "little" and to grasp its implications for the island as a whole.

The ethnography shows that, in this area, the manipulation of wealth entails both an effect of scale or threshold involving the respective *quantities* of wealth manipulated in Big-Men and Great-Men societies, and a phenomenon of *quality*: the very way of using wealth here is crucial. Godelier stressed the possibility of various forms of marriage existing side by side within the same society, notably marriage by direct exchange of women and marriage with bridewealth (Godelier, 1990a: 78). In the present case, there is reason to look into the condition in which sister-exchange too can be accompanied by a limited use of wealth. What is wealth doing hovering on the fringes of sister-exchange? What kinds of relations does it point to? What is implied by the use of wealth in the context or on the occasion of a marriage by the exchange of women, especially in the wake of the failure or impossibility of direct exchange?

The Baruya's exceptional use of wealth around the edges of sister-exchange is only a variant of practices observed in other New Guinea societies that have neither Big Men nor Great Men, but which relentlessly pursue the ideal of marriage through the direct exchange of women. This used to be the case in particular on the southern coast of the island, on either side of the present border between what is now West Papua and Papua New Guinea. Williams writes (1936: 128, 139) that, in the absence of a female relative to exchange, the Keraki give valuables (axes, knives, seed necklaces, tobacco, but not pork) to acquire the "sister" they need to be able to take a wife. The Jaqaj, too, give their affines wealth when they do not have a "sister" to give in turn, but this gift is not regarded as compensation, or brideprice: it is seen as a temporary payment until a woman can be found to return. The wealth given as a sort of security deposit is then given back. The same Jaqaj also use wealth when a widow remarries. In this case, the payment compensates the deceased's kin for the sister they gave in exchange for this wife (Boelaars, 1981: 36–37). The Kimam (or Kolopom), from the same

though, it is a complement of the brideprice, also mandatory, even though the marriage is carried out by sister-exchange (Gillison, 1993: 53–61). In addition to the danger of the affines demanding that the boys be given back, people fear the maternal uncle will curse them. It would be useful to undertake a systematic study of such payments designed to protect children from dangers stemming from their maternal kin, especially because they appear to be largely unconnected with the form of marriage.

region, used to pay an exceptional marriage compensation when, for some reason or other, the woman initially promised in exchange for a wife was not given in the end (Serpenti, 1977: 129–30); this wealth can be seen as compensation for "breaking the contract." One last example: alongside sister-exchange between men from the same "men's club house," the Asmat also had a form of marriage with compensation between members of different men's houses. In the latter case, if the young man could not get together the requisite payment, he could go to work for his in-laws, which implies an equivalence between brideprice and labor (Zegwaard and Boelaars, 1955: 277–301, quoted by Knauft, 1993: 80; Sowada, 1961: 84).[10]

All the above cases show wealth being forced out to the periphery of sister-exchange and underscore a same tension: pursuing marriage by the exchange of women without brideprice even when a woman cannot be found to give in turn. The indirect or temporary equating of women and wealth is thus a device used to repair the snags in the fabric of direct woman-exchange. There is yet another tactic, the giving of human beings, which is often presented as an alternative to the use of wealth. The co-existence of these two forms of compensation—wealth and human beings—is remarkable in itself.

For instance, among the Ilahita Arapesh, who marry by the simultaneous exchange of women (the ideal) or by deferred exchange when a wife cannot be provided, it is possible to give a child born of that union: either a boy, who goes to live definitively with his maternal kin, or a girl, who is not given as a wife but as a woman to be in turn exchanged in the context of a marriage with a third lineage. If, and only if, one of these procedures does not work, the wife-takers pay a high compensation (Tuzin, 1976: 100). Similarly, among the Maring, when sister-exchange is "technically" impossible and when there has been no temporary bridewealth, a girl born of that union goes to live with her maternal uncle, however, once again, not to marry into her mother's group, but so that this uncle may obtain, for his own use, the brideprice paid for the young girl by yet another group (Rappaport, 1969: 123; LiPuma, 1988: 168). A parallel must be drawn between these human gifts and the Gebusi's solution to imbalances in marriage by sister-exchange, which is the only form they practice. Although they do not have any form of compensation, they "tolerate" failure to reciprocate in nearly half of the marriages in each generation. The ideal of harmonious

---

10. I would like to thank Bruce Knauft for having availed me of several texts on the Asmat which were hard to find in France. Eide (1966: 203) writes that, even in the case of sister-exchange, gifts of wealth must also be made to the affines as long as one lives, in return for access to the stands of sago-palm belonging to the wife's people. In the case of sister-exchange, these prestations are reciprocal. Trenkenschuh (1982: 21) stresses the same link between access to palm trees and bridewealth.

relations and sharing between brothers-in-law is maintained for their life-time, but at the cost of affines accusing each other of sorcery, which inevitably[11] leads to the killing and cannibal consumption of the alleged sorcerers (Knauft, 1985: 178, 183).

As McDowell has already pointed out (1978) in the case of the Sepik Bun, sister-exchange is a norm which everyone seeks to respect by drawing on a whole arsenal of ruses and exceptional procedures: by playing on the category of "sister" or juggling with time, or by introducing the possibility of indirect or temporary compensation into the marriage sphere. Such procedures are designed to oil the cogs of "sister"-exchange, the ideal of perfect reciprocity which often goes hand in hand with cooperation between affines and what Knauft (1985) calls "good company."

Substitution and the Paradoxes of the Pursuit of Parity

Such artifices are only one aspect of what is almost an obsession with parity in all areas of exchange: mutually inflicting the same number of deaths in war and sometimes the same types of wounds or victims; compelling the other couple formed in an exchange to divorce in case of a mismatch; giving a sorcerer who lifts a spell a "payment" identical to the one he received for bespelling his victim; exchanging wives for the night, and so forth (Lemonnier, 1993: 140).

Maring marriage is a good illustration of this passion for equivalence since it applies this rule to the very "qualities" of the women exchanged. Direct sister-exchange, their ideal marriage, accounts for only fifteen per cent of Maring marriages. Most unions take the form of a deferred exchange, sometimes at a distance of several generations, in which any subclan of the wife-takers can give back a wife to the giver subclan. These marriages include a brideprice (in pigs, cassowaries, money, feathers, etc.), even in the case of sister-exchange, for "the value of each woman is still unknown, and hence there is no way to determine whether the exchange is equivalent" (LiPuma, 1988: 150ff).[12]

Substitution — giving back something other than a woman — has a

---

11. Affines and maternal kin account for over 50% of those accused of death by sorcery, and these accusations result in the murder and cannibal consumption of the presumed guilty party in over 60% of cases (Knauft, 1985: 96, 183).

12. This "value" whose acquisition is compensated reciprocally refers to "female substance and fertility." It is also pointed out that some women work harder and bear more children than others (LiPuma, 1988: 154, 165).

Photo 15: Women's work: the wife's tasks, here the confection of her husband's kilt, is one of the services taken into account in the context of matrimonial exchanges, as well as sexuality, procreation and economic cooperation between affines (Photo P. Lemonnier, Ankave, Ikundi village, 1994).

special place among the strategies for coming to terms with ill-balanced marriages in a fraught context of equality. It takes two forms, which are often combined: deciding that the relation between wife-givers and wife-takers is balanced *when at least some* of the "attributes" or qualities of a woman given in marriage are compensated by a gift of the same kind as one of these attributes (a child, labor, "good company," etc.); or establishing an equivalence between certain typical female characteristics and goods of a different nature, in other words, replacing them with wealth.

The Baruya or the Maring highlight an equivalence "in kind" between two women exchanged in marriage by introducing a partial non-equivalence in the terms of the exchange, specifying that the wealth offsets an (actual or potential) imbalance between the "services" provided by the women. A first important point is that this wealth can be set against a whole range of social realities. For instance, the Baruya consider that compensation in wealth is due not only for failure to reciprocate a wife, but for an imbalance in the number of children born from a sister-exchange or a lack of cooperation between affines, as working together is itself inseparable from sharing food and good company. This equivalence is implicitly established in the commentaries that accompany and justify payment of the *min'ni ngwiye*. If there is no way to return a woman or to make up the difference in the number of children born of the two unions, a lot of shared work, shared food or good times together will do.[13]

But it must also be said that these equivalences imply a *conceptual dissection* of what "makes up" a wife. In the exchange of women without brideprice, which is extremely rare in New Guinea, the wife given or received is regarded as the inseparable set of "services" and powers given to the takers by and through her: labor, children, sexual pleasure, rights to the children. Alternatively, establishing an actual or theoretical equivalence between women and wealth means dissecting the woman into what M. Strathern calls "values generated by certain relationships," all or some of which can be compensated by wealth.[14] To introduce wealth into the equation is to accept that part of what is exchanged in marriage *exits* the sphere of reciprocity in kind, including by differentiating it explicitly from the exchange of a woman for a woman, properly speaking. This is what various New Guinea societies (and their anthropologists) are doing when they discuss the institution of bridewealth or the exchange of women, when they oppose exchanges made for the woman herself and those made for her procreative powers, for access to her sexual services, for the affiliation of her children, and so on.[15]

Use of wealth on the fringes of the exchange of women thus produces a paradox. Whether compensation is designed to establish a parity that was impossible because there was no "sister" to give in turn, to prepare

---

13. A similar equivalency of heterogeneous social realities could be found on the island's southern coast. Among the Kiwai, the kinsman who provided a "sisterless" man with a woman to exchange in marriage was indemnified by periodical gifts of food. Another possibility was to promise to "give back" a girl when she was old enough to marry. Marriage with bridewealth, on the other hand, was reserved for those marrying outside the tribe. A man whose wife bore many children would present his in-laws with gifts of wealth "by way of acknowledging the benefits she has brought his 'blood'" (Landtman, 1927: 244–45).

14. M. Strathern 1984:63. My thinking obviously runs parallel to that of M. Strathern on the "partibility" of persons and on "multiple social identity" (M. Strathern, 1984, 1988). With the exception of one nuance: I analyze this phenomenon and its consequences in groups where bridewealth does not exist. Alternatively, I do explore the contexts in which these qualities are conceived as being "detachable" from the persons concerned (M. Strathern 1992). In a neighboring area, see too E. Goody's remarks (1982) on the multiplicity and acknowledgment of "parental roles."

15. For example, for the Mendi, bridewealth is not the purchase price of a woman but payment for her services to come (Ryan, 1969: 167); the Mekeo do not pay for the bride or buy her, they acquire rights over her children (Mosko, 1985: 138). The same is true of the Dani, the Etoro, and the Telefolmin (Craig, 1969: 189, n.14; Jorgensen, 1993: 62–63; Kelly, 1977: 214; O'Brien, 1969).

As Kelly remarks about the Etoro, " The exchange of women is governed by balanced reciprocity which can only be achieved by giving women in return for those received. Brideprice is irrelevant in this sphere . . . Marriage payments . . . are essentially compensatory and reciprocity is thus inappropriate to the nature of the transaction"(1977: 221–22).

the future parity of an exchange of women, or to correct an imbalance which has appeared over time or even generations (in the Baruya case), it corresponds to a constant pursuit of equality in the area of marriage, in accordance with the general form of exchanges in the societies under discussion. In every instance, the use of wealth in a general atmosphere of exchange of women is explicitly designed to reinstate a strict equivalence between the women themselves: it is because they are not of the exact same value that it is necessary to top up the exchange with gifts of wealth. But the use of wealth is also by definition a necessary condition of the institution of bridewealth, which is characterized by non-equivalence of the nature of the terms of exchange (a woman, on the one hand, objects, on the other); with it often goes inequality between the exchanging parties (wife-takers and givers are in an asymmetrical relationship), or even between the terms of exchange: a woman can never be compensated "correctly" by wealth, and a continual stream of gifts will have to be made to the in-laws or to the children's maternal kin.

The passionate pursuit of equality paves the way for less egalitarian or even frankly non-egalitarian social systems. These are only a few "thresholds" away, whether they be quantitative—like the absence of incentive to produce great amounts of wealth among the Baruya, as indicated by Godelier, or qualitative. In this case, the form of the exchanges becomes pertinent, that is to say, both the nature of the terms involved in the exchange (the range of exchangeable items and the way they are combined) as well as the nature of the relations between the exchanging parties themselves, in this case, their segregation or their inclusion in a single sphere. Big-Men systems have long been characterized by the existence of all manner of transactions, and particularly by the payment of brideprice within a "single exchange sphere" involving goods of the same kind (A. Strathern, 1978; Modjeska, 1982; Godelier, 1982). Here I propose to define the particular ways wealth is used in a context of "sister"-exchange, and at the same time to identify the conditions in which this type of marriage can turn into a bridewealth system.

Segregation of Exchanges in Great-Men Societies and in General

When the possibility of partial substitution is introduced into sister-exchange, the use of wealth dilutes the necessity of returning a woman with other exchanges. Instead of being perfectly balanced by the equivalent services of another woman, some of a wife's qualities and capacities, which have been conceptually dissected, are compensated with goods. This process results in distinguishing—and therefore segregating—marriage-related areas which are inextricably intertwined in strict sister-exchange. This is the case among the Anga, who in the majority do not have sister-exchange but instead practice a form of marriage with brideprice. The Ankave, for example, present this compensation (*abaXa' nungwa'*, literally: "money for the woman/wife") as indemnification for the bride's body, for the work she will provide, the children she will bear; the emphasis falls on the (relative) break that ensues with her paternal kin and on affiliation of her children to her husband's group (Bonnemère, 1996: 170). Again we find, within the practice of brideprice itself, the non-differentiation of the wife's qualities already seen among the Baruya. Alternatively, the Ankave differ from the Baruya in that they pay a brideprice for each marriage as well as making other mandatory gifts of shells at a boy's initiation and following a death.[16]

These gifts (to which must be added homicide compensation) all occur in extremely precise contexts and usually involve specific kinds of shells. The *samoe'* gift that a maternal uncle receives from his nephew for having borne the blows with him at the time of the boy's initiation has to be a whole (slaughtered) pig, and the uncle's countergift to his nephew must be a pearl-shell. Likewise, the brideprice is paid to the young woman's paternal relatives in the form of cowry strings, which are inevitably draped over the haunches of pork presented to her maternal relatives. The compensation for an enemy warrior killed in battle must be composed of an assortment of shells but can never include game or pork. Gifts of pork are reserved for marriages. In each case, the circumstances of the prestation, *the direction of the gift and the nature of the object given are very clearly defined.*

Lastly, the Anga use wealth in two ways. In groups like the Baruya, where sister-exchange is the most prevalent form of marriage, wealth is the means of compensating killings and making peace and, in rare cases, of minimizing the various imbalances arising in marriages. There is no real segregation of the exchanges involving wealth which occur in the life-cycle; it is the scarcity of such exchanges that is significant. However, in those groups where wealth is given at several points in the life-cycle, its circulation is characterized by the extremely clear-cut segregation of these exchanges in which wealth is used. Unlike Big-Men societies, where pork is a sort of universal equivalent used in a host of gifts and transactions, many "objects" are exchanged among the Anga and in the majority of cases they cannot be substituted for each other: a game-gift cannot be replaced by a shell-gift, and a shell cannot replace a piece of pork.

At first glance, the situation on the south coast of the island appears to be of a different order, where exchanges were characterized by the

---

16. The Baruya and other Northern Angans are also familiar with gifts of shells and wealth (vegetable salt, barkcloth) outside marriage, particularly as compensation for homicide (e.g., Godelier, 1986 [1982]: 150). To be noted here are the generality and the systematic character of the phenomenon.

variety of the "things" given and by the fact that they could appear on both sides of the transaction. For instance, a woman's (wife's) sexual services were commonly offered as compensation in various contexts involving ordinary services and wrongs. By lending his wife, a Kolopom, a Kiwai or a Marind-anim could indemnify someone from whom he had stolen, pay for the services of a killer, a magician or a sorcerer, and even compensate help received with a job or the loan of a tool (Landtman, 1927: 250; Serpenti, 1977: 184; van Baal, 1966: 164, 813). But a woman could also be given as a wife to an enemy group in compensation for a warrior killed in battle, with the explicit idea that she would bear a warrior to replace the dead man (Landtman, 1927: 165–66). In other words, in the south of the island, women could be used in a variety of compensations outside marriage. Alternatively, except in a temporary and indirect manner, wealth was not exchanged for a woman. As terms of exchange, labor and children also appeared at times as something to be compensated and at times as means of compensation.[17] Murder is another area where humans either compensate or are compensated: one compensates a group that has suffered a loss by giving wealth (or a wife or a child), but a death in one's own group can and must also be balanced by the death of an enemy. What emerges from this ethnography, then, is the diversity of the contexts in which compensation occurs and the interchangeability of the means used.

There was one nuanced exception, however, for compensation was practiced in two separate spheres: the first, in which wealth was used, concerned life and death, people's fate (marriage, killing). Human beings could also be given here. The second, characterized by the non-reciprocal lending of a sexual partner, had to do with all manner of services and wrongs, except marriage and homicide compensation. So, on the south-

---

17. Work can be indemnified (by labor returned at another time, by the loan of a woman for her sexual services, etc.), but it is also used as compensation (e.g., a young man unable to get together a brideprice will work "as a son-in-law" for his affines). In the case of children, their birth often entails payments to their maternal kin: the compensation is for the children. But children can also be used to replace a warrior killed in battle or a woman; in the latter case they are sent to live with their mother's group. In passing, it is worth mentioning that, if the generalized use of wealth as the equivalent of principles of life and death characteristic of Big-Men societies is tantamount to "converting [the terms of the gift and countergift] into varied forms of wealth and, in the last analysis, into varied forms and quantities of human labor" (Godelier, 1986 [1982]: 185), direct equivalence between these principles and work "already" exists wherever equivalent realities (in kind and quantity) are exchanged. The use of wealth merely extends the chain of equivalences (and introduces the possibility of dissimulating the exploitation of the labor of others; cf. e.g., Modjeska, 1982: 95; Josephides, 1985).

Photo 16: Eel traps. For the Ankave, smoked eels, one of the proper offerings to make to a distant cross-cousin of a deceased person, when his soul is ritually driven out of the hamlet. The decoration and display of the traps are part of the magic insuring their efficacity (Photo P. Lemonnier, 1988).

ern coast of New Guinea, there turns out to be a segregation of exchange practices just as fraught with consequences as the separation discovered among the Anga, even if it did not take the same form. Here it is not so much the various life-cycle prestations that are segregated as two areas of exchange and social life: on the one hand, the fate of persons and, on the other, the various prestations connected with the work, the objects and the wrongs of daily life. It is not indifferent that this separation is translated by a distance maintained between women and wealth in marriage. Exchanged as a means of pleasure, women replaced wealth in an area where the use of riches was restricted. In parallel, sister-exchange was the norm, and the use of wealth was relegated to the fringes of marriage practice.

With respect to a society like the Baruya, Big-Men societies are characterized, as I have said after many others, by a single sphere of exchange, in which both marriage and numerous compensation procedures involve the giving of wealth. But compared to those Anga groups which exchange wealth for women, or to the societies on the southern coast, the world of Big Men is distinguished only by a desegregation of exchanges: a single type of goods— or items that can be immediately substituted for each other (pigs and shells)— is used without distinction for a great variety of gifts. The things given and the circumstances of the gifts are clearly defined and even named, but the gifts are overwhelmingly comprised of a single item of wealth, pigs (Strathern, 1980: 53, 57).[18]

The use of specific items of wealth for well-defined compensations (as among the Ankave), the distance maintained between women and wealth (as in the southern part of the island) and the very noticeable absence of domestic pigs among those things used for homicide compensation all serve to check the incorporation of exchanges of wealth into one single sphere and its exchange on a large scale. This is firstly because these societies have less reason to prolong peace-making by peaceful rivalry based on the competitive exchange of pigs (Lemonnier, 1990, 1991); and secondly because the limited role of pigs in exchanges goes hand in hand with minimum recourse to "finance," which A. Strathern (1969) showed to be central to the intermingling of prestations and to Big Men's sociopolitical strategies.

In what conditions do these constraints disappear? No one seems to know. Representations of life, of women, of pigs, and of the fertility of everything all play a part, entering into combinations which have not yet yielded up their secret. One thing is certain though: that the question of equating women and wealth raised by Godelier is one of the avenues that could lead us to a better understanding of this complexity, of which we are now able to define not only the quantitative but also the qualitative thresholds. The irony is that it was, paradoxically, with the aim of maintaining, providing or reestablishing strict parity between individuals and groups that the New Guinea societies practicing sister-exchange introduced, in the form of substitution, the very instruments which, in other

---

18. Going somewhat against the current of contemporary historical anthropology (although I appreciate the warnings and the problematic as long as one recognizes that some South Pacific societies were less disrupted and at a later date than others by colonization; e.g., Biersack, 1991; Carrier, 1992; Thomas, 1989), my reasoning obviously concerns the logic of hypothetical social transformations occurring in "traditional" Melanesian societies. Nevertheless a similar process of desegregation is illustrated by the recent history of marriage in Telefolmin society, documented in detail by Jorgensen (1993). Whereas marriage formerly took place by sister-exchange accompanied by reciprocal gifts of shells for pork, today the money earned working for mining companies has replaced shells for marriage payments. At the same time, sister-exchange and endogamy are now only a memory, and marriage has (almost) become just another way of making money. With the changeover from shell money to national currency, the bridewealth is now used to buy all sorts of consumer goods and no longer goes into new marriage or funeral payments.
On the segregation of kinds of exchange, see Rodman (1981) who shows the many obstacles to convertibility between exchange objects (pigs and mats) and the episodic connections between two types of ceremonial prestations (marriage and obtaining a rank) in the island of East Aoba (Vanuatu).

parts of the island, have laid the foundations of inequality between people.

Translated by Nora Scott

Chapter 5

The Spectacle of Things

A Melanesian Perspective on the Person and the Self[*]

Stéphane Breton

Every society entertains a special relation with the objects it displays. Melanesia, which produces all sorts of ceremonial objects, seems to make its destiny depend on their ongoing, ritual circulation. It is not very different in this respect from Western society, which justifies its legitimacy and grounds its reproduction in the exchange of commodities, however paradoxical their reality may be when it is reduced to that of a simple image. In Melanesian symbolic exchange, just as in what Guy Debord (1971) calls the society of the spectacle, that is, the extreme form of social commodification represented by the market economy, consumption of the object tends

[*] This is a revised version of "Le spectacle des choses : Considérations mélanésiennes sur la personne," *L'Homme* 149: 83–112 (Breton, 1999a). The material pertaining to the Wodani of West Papua was collected during twenty-eight months of field work, from 1995 to 2000. Research was initially organized in collaboration with the Lembaga Ilmu Pengetahuan Indonesia and the Irian Jaya research group at Leiden University (The Netherlands). It was funded by the Fyssen Foundation, Paris, and the French Ministry of Foreign Affairs. My special thanks go to E.K.M. Masinambow and Roosmalawati Rusman, as well as to Wim Stokhof, Jacob Vredenbregt and Jelle Miedema. Marc Augé, Daniel de Coppet, Maurice Godelier and Bernard Juillerat offered their advice and encouragement, for which I am most grateful. The part dealing with Wodani shell money as a representation of society and as a symbolic description of personhood was later expanded and published as Breton 1999e. For another perspective on the same question, see Breton (forthcoming). The Wodani live in the Paniai regency of the western highlands of West Papua. Fieldwork was conducted entirely in the vernacular language, without the help of interpreters.

to be confused with and dissolved into its display. In both instances, society is grounded in the spectacle of a typical object. It is that object that maintains, and in a way establishes, the prevailing societal fiction.

What is involved here is much more than an economy: it is an aesthetic attempt, based on the construction of an external object, to define personhood by things that are separate from the self. Georg Simmel, in *The Philosophy of Money* (1978) suggests that "it is the fact that things stand at a distance from us that should bring them to us." He goes on to point out that Plato defines love as the state intermediate between having and not having. Nothing brings one closer to oneself than the spectacle of things. The quest for objects is a phenomenon of no scant importance, and one should recall that our relations with those objects are conditioned by the myth of lost wholeness: definitely so in the West, and perhaps in Melanesia as well.

The purpose of the present essay is to ponder on how human societies strive to invent separate objects, to display them and to make them desirable, much as if the stake is what a person is to be in his or her own eyes, and also, how society undertakes to institute personhood. To do so, I will compare the head-hunting tradition of the Marind of West Papua, as described by Jan van Baal (1966) in his monumental monograph, *Dema*, with my own work on shell money and the system of compensation of the Highland Wodani, who also live in the western part of the island of New Guinea, now, regrettably, an Indonesian province.

Heads

As every observer was well aware, but no-one has ever taken literally, the Marind used to cut heads to give a name to their children. Each year, during the rainy season, this necessity sent them on drawn-out expeditions that took them hundreds of kilometers from their home (van Baal, 1966: 706, 713). They had no doubt that those alien tribes with a language and totemic organization completely different from their own existed for the sole purpose of giving them the names they needed (*Ibid.*: 696). Head-hunting within the confederation was in fact prohibited (*Ibid.*: 691). Only outsiders were in a position to offer what they were looking for.

Marind women snatched up any children they could find: these were spared and taken home to be raised normally (*Ibid.*: 710, 717). In the meanwhile the men, using bamboo knives, beheaded anyone who crossed their path, after having asked what the victim's name was. Executioner and victim were obviously incapable of understanding each other, but the last sounds uttered by the latter, patiently awaited so that he could be decapitated, were reputed to be his name (*Ibid.*: 745). If hunters returned home with a head whose name they had been unable to learn, they simply invented one. On other occasions, wiles were used to learn the name beforehand: for instance, on the arrival in Marind territory of a journeying foreigner who believed he could trust his hosts (van der Kroef, 1952: 225).

Head-hunting, then, was an opportunity to capture a sound, perhaps no more than a death rattle or a sigh, to which the murderer gave some consistency when he reproduced it in his own language. The salient point here is the fictitious nature of the name collected, and the awareness of that fact by the Marind themselves (van Baal, 1966: 403, 745). For the murderer, what was important was not so much what the victim said as what he himself said. It is as if the head-hunter, when taking possession of a head, did not listen to it but rather, spoke. The victim simply served as a mirror. Women actually acted in a somewhat similar fashion: they snatched up children in order to become their mother; in other words, so that those children would become part of them. Only "ripe coconuts" were to be cut (*Ibid.*: 754); that is to say, only adults could be beheaded. Irrespective of whether the object was sought by men or by women, of whether it was a word or a child, its capture was an act of repossession. It is as if it appeared as a detached part of the person who subsequently seized hold of it.

Once they had returned home, the Marind exhibited the heads in a ceremonial house. First skinned, then covered with the skin once it was dried, they were carefully arrayed and given headdress (*Ibid.*: 746–747). Speech, and speech only, was strictly prohibited during contemplation of the trophies (*Ibid.*: 721). Like the silence that reigned within the realm of the Eumenides, this was a most telling silence: over and beyond the exhibition of the heads, what mattered was the enhancement of the value of their names. This was followed by a ceremony during which the role of each hunter was publicly proclaimed, and the property of the names officialized (*Ibid.*: 750). Those who had distinguished themselves during the expeditions were honored, and became "big men" (*Ibid.*: 751). If several hunters had participated in a beheading all were entitled to take possession of the name accompanying the head. This explains why several children might bear the same name (*Ibid.*: 709). The great warriors had a large number of names in reserve, waiting to be transmitted (*Ibid.*: 710). Head names (*pa-igiz*) were worthless unless they were given, and it was inconceivable to keep a name for oneself.

At birth each child, boy or girl, had to be given a *pa-igiz*; this was an obligation, attached to parentage in the same way as the obligation to initiate the child or to provide him or her with a spouse. A child without a head name would be incomplete, so to speak. When the colonial administration prohibited head-hunting, names even came to be transmitted hereditarily (van der Kroef, 1952: 223). We will never know what the Marind found lacking in a child without a head name, but we do know that he or she was the laughing stock (*Ibid.*: 222). Perhaps this flaw in our knowledge is due to the fact that at the time, observers' interest in this exotic practice was confined to mild curiosity and did not exert ethnographic rigor. But I tend to think that the Marind never formulated a theory of the head name, because such a theory would be objectless. The name does not correspond to a positive quality, but rather to an absence; as we shall see, it is the fact that what is involved is not designated that makes the *pa-igiz* significant.

Once the name had been given, the skull was no longer of any consequence, and it was occasionally disposed of, whereas such was never the case for the jaw, which was carefully preserved and even worn as an ornament by elderly women (van Baal, 1966: 751). Perhaps, as sometimes happens in New Guinea, it was viewed as the organ of speech. Children occasionally wore the jaw to which they owed their name around their neck (van der Kroef: 222–223). Van Baal (1966: 718, 720) expresses surprise at the fact that the *pa-igiz* were not of any special utility, and had no supernatural meaning or magic powers. Actually, the transmission to the child of a name is what it is all about. What is involved is nothing but the power to name: it pertains to the order of the signifier.

It was the father's duty to transmit the *pa-igiz* to his child. But he might not have a name available at that particular time, in which case he could turn that duty over to one of the child's relatives. Nothing prevented the father from fulfilling his role later on (*Ibid.*: 717). Consequently, a child might receive several *pa-igiz* from different people (*Ibid.*: 135, 718). The bestowing of the name was not accompanied by any special ritual. In the case of a first-born child, the name passed through the mother, who became its receptacle, so to speak. When a woman married, before her child was even conceived, she was given a teknonym designating her as "mother of x," x being the head name intended for her child (*Ibid.*: 130). The names—both the *pa-igiz* and the teknonym—were to be transmitted in the order of successive generations.

Immediately after she had received her name as a spouse, the young woman was handed over to the men of her husband's clan or phratry for a ritual orgy, even before her husband was allowed to have intercourse with her (*Ibid.*: 130, 163, 819). Such debauchery was a regular part of the Marind's ritual activities (*Ibid.*: 807–821). The participants themselves were quite weary of it, and partook in it only because it was called for by a higher necessity (*Ibid.*: 816–820). The Marind viewed semen as the fertile substance par excellence, one which, in their myths, gave birth to many creatures all by itself (*Ibid.*: 817), but it was apparently believed to be effective only in the form of a mixture produced by having all the men of a given totemic group deposit it in a woman during intercourse. Ritual orgies, affording opportunities to collect semen for many purposes, both magical and dietary, were repeated for the benefit of sterile or recently married women, in order to stimulate their fecundity.

The Marind, like the Highland Gimi (Gillison, 1993: 201), seem to have conceived the woman's role in conception as confined to that of a receptacle, and to have refused the idea that she contributed any substance to the child's body (van Baal, 1966: 817). If so, this would not be the only instance in which the characteristically substantialist New Guinean theories of procreation viewed the power to conceive as confined to only one of the sexes: the Trobrianders thought that the father played a strictly mechanical role in opening the passage for birth, since the mother was fertilized by the spirits of her clan, whereas an exactly opposite theory prevails among the Wiru—despite their patrilineal organization—with the mother as the exclusive giver of substance to the child (Clark, 1991: 312). Once the future mother had been designated through the teknonym as carrier of the *pa-igiz*, she could then become the receptacle for the substance of her husband's clan, to which she had nothing to add.

The interpretation I am formulating here is both hypothetical and original. In every probability, what is involved here is a belief in the *exclusive*, and at the same time *collective*, nature of the male function in procreation (an ethnographic precedent to such a belief has been documented among the Canela of South America (Crocker & Crocker, 1994)). The Marind no doubt represented impregnation as an act requiring that the male substance and mystical being of the totemic community be reunited. This is evidenced, in my opinion, by the fact that a baby born to an unwed woman, and conceived during a ritual orgy, was said to be the child of the spirit of the totem personified in the rites, and was immediately put to death (van Baal, 1966: 496, 528), as opposed to a child born to a married woman, whose husband then retained full rights over the child. This points to several conclusions. Firstly, that a supernatural intervention is believed to be involved in the production of a child during collective copulation, and secondly, that the individual action of a legitimate father is not sufficient for the conception of the child, but last, that it is nonetheless necessary to avoid the fathering of the child by a spirit only.

The transmission of the *pa-igiz* by the father, or in his name, becomes meaningful in this hypothesis. Indeed, it may be viewed as grounding the particular legitimacy of the father's rights over the child, or as putting a final touch on a collective but incomplete conception. It would correspond to a principle of individuation. In response to the question raised earlier, it may be that what a child without a head name was lacking was quite simply a father. So that perhaps the child fathered by a spirit was killed because no one had the obligation to give it a name. In a way, the *pa-igiz* is the father's name, and the father gives it only so as to authorize himself to have a name, as father. There are in fact a number of instances, in Marind mythology, of parents who give their own name to their children (*Ibid.*: 271, 398).

The vivifying power of semen was also cited as justification for the initiation rites in which novices were sodomized by their mother's brother (*Ibid.*: 147, 479, 493–494). As in many New Guinea societies, the Marind viewed male individuals as incomplete. Only the rites—that is, society—could complete what nature had simply outlined. What was needed to turn a creature brought into the world by a woman into a full male was the addition of substance. For the Marind, then, to produce a boy some male substance had to be contributed, first by the father's clan at the time of conception, then by the mother's clan at the time of initiation. The gift of the *pa-igiz* should therefore be interpreted as parallel to the gift of sperm.

In this context, head-hunting had a very precise function: it concluded the initiation rites during which the novices were taught the esoteric names of spirits and totems and during which, like new-born babes who had not yet learned to speak, they were reintroduced, step by step, to the various techniques and everyday gestures (*Ibid.*: 544–547). They were taught, as though this was something new to them, to use bows and arrows, to climb coconut palm trees and to chew betel nuts, and were only given ordinary food again once it had been ritually mixed with semen (*Ibid.*: 548). There was nothing new to be found in the initiation, other than the repetition of what was already known, with the addition of mythological significations (*Ibid.*: 544). When initiation was outlawed by the colonial administration, the elderly complained that the younger generations would lose the use of the world and of its objects, once and for all. Immediately following the initiation, once they had received a bull-roarer (*Ibid.*: 487–489), a phallic symbol vouching for their new condition as men in a position to beget offspring, the initiates went off head-hunting. They had been prepared for the hunt by learning names, and they were to return from it with names.

The Marind's passionate interest in esoteric names is not a passion for secrecy. As curious as this may seem, given their extremely rich totemic terminology, resistance to secrecy is, according to van Baal, one of the salient cultural features of this people (*Ibid.*: 792). Their mythological names fit together, one inside the other, onion-skin like, in a sort of esotericism through which a ritual name may, in turn, be overshadowed by a name of a higher order. This all corresponds to the quest for what they call the "true name" (the *pa-igiz* is also a "true name"). The truth of names is fused with the mythological origin of things and is expressed by a word designating the female genitals (*Ibid.*: 930). Names point to the source, the matrix. But the giving of a head name is not simply an act attesting the bond with the origins, it is also an act of begetting. Children are given a name just as they are fed male substance.

When the men go head-hunting, they go looking for a name—needed for the true establishment of filiation—but not just for any name. They need a name that can be wrenched from another person. It is missing, and does not offer itself up voluntarily. To obtain it, then, one must seize it. It is both detachable and the object of transmission. What is brought back is a fiction, a completely incomprehensible sound, a pure, empty signifier that is given whatever meaning is desired. There is something here that is so alien to the Judeo-Christian relationship to the signifier that it is worth a brief digression. According to the biblical myth, the Law—the founding signifier in the Western tradition—is the Word, first received and then written in stone, on the forehead of man and on the lintel of his door. The idea that it may not be anything more than a sound would not occur to anyone: the signifier is a revealed truth. The head-hunter, on the other hand, knows that the single word he covets is meaningless. It will only become meaningful inasmuch as he offers it as a gift. It is simply the empty vehicle allowing him to transmit what he has to transmit. The head name does not denote anything worthy of consideration, but as a sign it connotes the fact that its bearer has been granted a social *persona*. What, then, does the head name mean? What does the child need, that is lacking in the father and which the father must find elsewhere in order to give it? What is it that one does not possess, that no-one possesses exclusively, except the other inasmuch as it may be taken away from him, and which nonetheless must be transmitted to you in the form of a fiction, as a consequence of the fact of having been born?

The difficulty resides in the fact that head-hunting has two facets: first, the search for the head itself, and secondly, the transmission of the name. Its signification resides in the actor's dual perspective. The gift to the child involves the transmission of a male, paternal "identity" to the child, as we have seen. The other facet, the beheading, seems to be a sort of castration inflicted on the other. To be in possession of what he has to transmit, the father must have taken it from someone else. Only then can he offer it as a gift; that is, achieve fatherhood. What is it then, that he takes and gives? Is it a sign of his own capability as a male? Could it be the *penis* (the actual organ), or perhaps the *phallus* (the symbol of its detachability)? The symbolism of castration seems to pervade the whole institution of Marind head-hunting, and one author (J.F. Weiner, 1995), in an otherwise stimulating book, has concentrated his efforts on showing that it had to do with the representation of a sort of ontological "caducity" constitutive of both the self and the social *persona*. I wish, however, to argue that in this case this notion is improperly understood as the caducity of an imaginary appendix (the penis), in the form of a picturesque castration, and that on the contrary, to be faithful both to Jacques Lacan's formulation and to the Marind perspective, it should be described as the symbolic transmission of a part that has been missing from the start (the phallus). The truth of head-hunting lies not in the cutting off of an object, but in the original absence of the object that is constitutive of the person, and that triggers the dynamics of the quest. Head-hunting, once again, is not about severing heads but about finding and giving names. Caducity is simply the imaginary form taken by the symbolic experience of missing parts.

Before being asked his or her name, and then being beheaded, the victim must necessarily be clobbered over the head with a sort of cudgel composed of a stone disc sliding on a stick crowned with an ornamented sculpted part which must be broken by the blow (van Baal, 1966: 725–745, 758). The stone disc and the stick along which it slides represent a couple copulating. Once broken the sculpted part is left behind, as if in exchange for the decapitated head, and it is out of the question to return empty-handed from a hunting party with an unbroken cudgel (*Ibid.*: 726). The Boadzi, who are neighbors of the Marind and have many cultural features in common with them, use the term for penis to designate that club (*Ibid.*: 729). This points to the fact that the hunter has to part with something in order to obtain what he wants. So that head-hunting deals with a double castration: that of the severed head, and that of the duly broken phallic club. The Marind myth of Yugil relates the adventures of a totem spirit with a penis so long that he carried it on his shoulder like a head-hunting club, and had it cut off by an old woman when he was about to use it to molest her daughter (*Ibid.*: 311, 763). Whence the conclusion that breaking that implement on the head of the victim has the same meaning as aggressing a woman with a penis (*Ibid.*: 758), and that head-hunting is a form of "military copulation" (Knauft, 1993: 210) in which, in exchange for castration—for being subjected to, or inflicting castration—one cherishes the hope of obtaining something. But what?

The decapitated head is such a rich symbol that one sometimes wonders by which ear it should be grasped. The Boadzi myth of the origin of beheading suggests a helpful path (van Baal, 1966: 729). Upon the death of one of his sons, on whose tomb coconuts are seen to sprout, Aneseke, a totem spirit, offers a head-hunting club to his last remaining son and demands to be decapitated by him. The son immediately gives in, and religiously follows the detailed instructions that the head continues to deliver following the beheading, enumerating the rules to be followed to prepare it to be exhibited. As a consequence worms begin to crawl out of the head, and soon turn into human beings. This tale—reminiscent of *The Facts in the Case of Mr. Valdemar*, in which Edgar Poe stages a man hypnotized during his agony, and whose corpse will then testify by speech to the condition to which he has been reduced—describes the emergence of the first human beings through a gift from father to son—mere words—that nonetheless embody the very meaning of filiation. However, the words pronounced by the father only become meaningful once he has been beheaded by his son. That is to say, the only object of his mutilation was the act of transmission, a transmission that has to do with the capacity to engender.

This myth points to an all-important equation: the equation between the decapitated head and the coconut, which sprouts and produces off-spring. The Marind plant a coconut when a child is born, and cut a coconut palm tree when someone dies (*Ibid*.: 461). They also say that the birth of a child is the outcome of a head-hunt (*Ibid*.: 754). That is, when a head is removed, it may be symbolically planted, and made to produce something through the rule of fissiparity that pervades Marind myths, in which we are told of a child born of the blood coming from a cut on a foot (*Ibid*.: 327), of all sorts of beings generated from bones, (*Ibid*.: 396) or from pieces of flesh that the hero cut off from his own body and cooked, after having mixed them with his own semen (*Ibid*.: 299). All this concurs with the fact that mythical offspring often bear the names of their own genitors. The same may be born of the same, provided a mutilation takes place. What a man transmits when he "cuts" a name for his son is simply his own word.

The invention of head-hunting is attributed to Sobra, an old woman whose genitals are represented by the stone ring of the club, and who is present in the tale of the origins of the birth of the first human beings (*Ibid*.: 211). When the totemic spirits of the clan journeyed back from some festivities in which they had participated in a westward region, they traveled along an underground path leading them eastward, followed by the totemic Dog spirit, which had walked above the ground. The dog then dug a hole, from which sprung unfinished human creatures, whose shape was suggestive of a bull-roarer; that is, a penis. A fire was lit, and into the fire were thrown pieces of bamboo, and it was the explosion of these that gave the creatures their natural body orifices. Their limbs were then fashioned using a bamboo knife. Sobra was the first to appear, and she fashioned those who came out after her. Some light is shed on this myth by the myth of Geb, the primordial totemic spirit who travels from east to west during the day and returns eastward at night by an underground route, and whose decapitated head is said to be the sun itself, the masculine celestial body (*Ibid*.: 221, 226). This astral journey is described in the adventures of Uaba, an avatar of Geb (*Ibid*.: 243). The totemic spirit decides to participate in an initiation ceremony, and takes along a woman whom he intends to take to the ritual orgy. Unhappy with her fate, she runs away to the west. The totemic spirit catches up with her and fornicates with her. They are discovered, prisoners of their copulation, and carried back eastward on a litter, still stuck together, covered by a mat. They are finally separated, and this wrenching apart gives birth to fire, which is none other than sunrise, just as the eastward journey was the nocturnal copulation of the sun and the earth, in the obscurity under the mat, by which humans were conceived. In turn, the sun's course to the west describes the deadly movement that will carry humans to the westerly land of the dead. Human destiny reproduces the sun's journey as described by the myth. The life of individuals is strictly subsumed in this socio-cosmic order. Head-hunting and initiation rites are the locuses in which society displays itself as a cosmic totality.

The theme of the amputated object is consistently accompanied by the theme of procreation, via an all-devouring copulation—in other words, by the theme of the regeneration of life through death. Van Baal emphasizes the fact that for the Marind, the penis is both a death-dealing weapon, perfectly illustrated by their head-hunting clubs, and a life-giving instrument, since men believe it provides them with control over procreation (*Ibid.*: 758). Through the equivalence between the decapitated head, the coconut and the sun, a parallel is established between sexual reproduction, plant fertility and the cosmic cycle. Head-hunting is a socio-cosmic operation that helps to maintain fertility, in the same way as the initiation rite of which it is the last act, and which involves both the relearning of the names of all things, and the replaying of the mythological scene in which the first human beings were engendered (*Ibid.*: 550). There is nothing fortuitous about this. To be the son of man and to be the subject of the verb are the two sides of the same coin. To be constituted as the likes of the verb means, at the same time, that one is prey to an irreparable absence; let us say, to the absence of a signifier that one knows is fictitious, but that one would like to be definitive—a *pa-igiz.*

This is why the theme of castration, in the picturesque form it takes in the myths, is secondary in comparison to its symbolic meaning, which is not that of a penis cut to pieces, but of the quest for a name. In the myths, the episodes containing the trope of mutilation are much less frequent than the scenes where the hero is faced with a separation or a loss. There are those passengers on a canoe who are left behind, one after another (*Ibid.*: 312), the husband and wife who are separated (*Ibid.*: 299), or the mother parted from her child (*Ibid.*: 295). Or again, there is the kidnapping of a boy who takes revenge by copulating with his foster mother and is punished by beheading (*Ibid.*: 248), the vain attempts to retrieve a son who is being sucked into the mud and transformed into a tiny fish (*Ibid.*: 342), or to find a spear that disappeared mysteriously after having been thrown into a bush (*Ibid.*: 286, 331), the pursuit of a bird that causes the hunter to suffer three injuries to his foot (*Ibid.*: 326–327), or the necessity for the hero to be hunted down before death turns him into a totemic spirit (*Ibid.*: 284). The examples abound. Castration occurs in the context of the quest for an object. This is not where the main theme resides, then, but rather, in the symbolic loss of the object, or its essential absence. Castration appears as the narrative consequence, not as the precondition for the absence. It is just an illustration of the explanatory principle. The penis, which may easily be cut off, should not be confused with the object that is lacking by definition, and in search of which the myth is launched, in the belief that it may be found elsewhere, in an other, whence its unreality.

The masculine, paternal "identity" sought out and then given, is not a natural organ, then, or a positive object, but the sign of an absence that must be transmitted. Lacan would call it the phallus. The proximity between this purely symbolic aspect and the notion of the "true name" designated in Marind thinking by the female genitals, is characteristic. Behind the reification of the penis and of its mythological substitutes, in the form of detached appendices, lurks, concealed, the terror caused by woman's apparent castration (Freud 1953c). This is why an essential distinction must be made between the *penis* and the *phallus*, the latter designating something that is conspicuous by its absence and is erected in the place of a void, but that each man must display if he wishes to procreate. This is where the violence displayed in head-hunting can bear some meaning. The head, as what is left after something was made to disappear, is the remains of a presence that has been written off. Murder is the first semiotic act: the corpse stands, in true Saussurian terms, as the sign of an absence.

The Marind view the person as defined by a missing part. There is no chance of that part completing the person (supposing that is at all possible) unless its purely symbolic character is doubly attested: by the fact, firstly, that it is only a name, and secondly, that it cannot be kept for oneself but must be transmitted.

Shells

Compared with the prolific mythical production of the Marind, the practices of the Highland Wodani, who circulate shell money commonly known as cowry (*kipe*) in all sorts of corporate and economic transactions, may seem quite subdued. The origin of the *kipe* is a mystery for these people. It is the only object in their universe that can only be found in the hands of men, and yet it is not a human creation. There is no trace of it in nature, and nothing is known about where it comes from, since the existence of the sea is unknown. The Wodani claim that the *kipe* arrived at the same time as men, that neither can exist without the other. Of all of the objects known to them, this is the only one with a strictly social existence.

The *kipe* is described as having a human anatomy. It possesses a "nose," an "anus," "thighs," a "skin," which is the enamel on the surface of which darker, accidentally chipped spots form "eyes" and also a "mouth," a tooth-edged opening cut in the bulging part of the shell, through which the convoluted spine known as the "backbone" is visible. The first of the three numeral classifiers applied specifically to shell money means "skin." One essential attribute is lacking in this body, however: that is, genitals. Between the nose and the anus, all one finds is a very large "mouth," suggestive of the cloaca-like organ typical of infantile sexual theories. The more valuable shells are given a name. They are so truly living beings, it is said, that it is prohibited to re-cut a shell through the "mouth" to increase its value. This is as inconceivable as it would be to slash someone's lips using a bamboo knife.

Inasmuch as it is a "person," this money is an adequate means of payment in matrimonial or homicide compensations (see Breton, 1999b, 1999d). Whenever a clan is diminished by the loss of one of its members—a daughter who is married away, or a murdered son—, shell money is offered in compensation by the clan of the husband or of the killer, as if the social group viewed its unity as a finite, quantifiable and negotiable substance.

The Wodani practice sister-exchange, which dispenses them of paying bridewealth. Marriage with payment, although incomparably more frequent, is not conceptually different since a shell, or metaphoric person, is offered in exchange for a real wife. I am tempted to reverse the alliance theory, for which marriage by payment is a transformation of marriage by exchange, and to claim that from the Wodani viewpoint, the exchange of sisters is an offshoot of marriage by payment, a liberty occasionally consented by the rule of monetary compensation. For them, every filiation shows the mark of shell money. The genealogy of an individual is never the outcome of an unending succession of exchanges of sisters. There can be no reproduction without *kipe*.

Just as corporate groups are composed of negotiable bodies, the body of a person is composed of parts. Shell money enumerates these in matrimonial or homicide compensations: the whole it represents then replaces the parts of the bride's or the victim's body, symbolically divided, just as a pig is carved up according to the ritual rule. This relation between the symbolic body of the shell and the body parts of the person is as much a metonymy as a fractal representation, as Roy Wagner (1991) puts it: the monetary homunculus describes the constituent elements of the person by a simple reduction of scale. Payment applies on a part-for-part basis to the different organs, beginning with the head and continuing in the order of decreasing importance from the mandible, the heart, eyes and kidneys on to the rest of the body, arms, legs and hair included, without going into the details for the lesser parts. Several *kipe* may be needed to pay for each part. One shell may be said to "cut off" the bride's head, to "dislocate" her jaw or to "chop up" her body. These same terms are used when carving up a pig. A very valuable shell which may be used to pay for the head is said to "kill" the bride.

Paying for the wife is a way of killing her and cutting her up. The most precious body parts, those paid for by valuable shells, are those which the local theory of procreation ascribes to the doings of the father: the skull, jaw, heart, eyes and kidneys. The heart and the eyes are the seat of the person's spiritual component, the source of dream life which, like the *larva* of the Latins, leaves the body at death and forms the ghost of the dead person, with which relatives will continue to entertain exchanges. This aspect of the person, a combination of an unconscious and of an immortal soul, is the reflection of the person as seen in the eyes of other people.

Monetary payment describes the person according to his or her socio-corporeal architecture, with emphasis on body parts that belong to the patrilineal clan. Strikingly, there is no formal payment for the female parts of the bride; that is, for those organs that were produced by her mother, although it is asserted that every part of the bride has been paid for. Just as a shell is a body without a sex, the bride, when she is broken down by payment into several pieces, also appears sexless. In homicide compensation, which functions on the same principle of payment part by part, the paternal organs of the victim are enumerated first, but the genitals are never mentioned. Monetary detotalization therefore describes an incomplete body, in which an essential aspect is lacking. Only under this condition is compensation feasible. In this monetary evaluation no attempt is made to distinguish the person's individual or sexual features; to the contrary, what is described is the body's collective, generic form. The emphasis on the paternal components allows the beneficiaries of a payment to each take their share of their married sister or their murdered brother as if they were shares in the clan's capital, or better yet, shares of their own substance. What the monetary compensations do, then, is recycle within the clan the impersonal male aspects of a person's identity and reproductive agency. It is just as if shell money was the means of designating, preserving and transmitting—that is to say, reproducing—a masculine, paternal substance specific to the clan.

No-one is obliged to contribute to a marriage compensation. The basis of the payment is the clan or the residence-based community, but a clan-brother may very well shirk this formal obligation. Since all of these payments take the form of an interest-free loan, reimbursable in identical terms upon the marriage of a daughter born to the original couple, anyone who does not contribute to it cannot transmit the corresponding matrimonial credit to his son. Conversely, a man whose mother was paid for by his father thanks to the contribution of matrimonial creditors does not have to pay them back from his own pocket; but at the occasion of his sister's marriage, the wife takers will reimburse them directly. These payments are an integral part of bridewealth. It is not men who are security for matrimonial debts, then, but daughters.

Men readily slip into other men's marriage expenditures, to generate a credit that is reimbursable a generation later. This is a sort of long-term savings plan based on the principle of clan solidarity. The latter is actually no more than an accumulation of debts, as all matrimonial credits are taken into account, even those between members of the same clan. It is the creditors of the father's marriage, or their sons, who are entitled to bridewealth for the daughter. It is out of the question for a father to receive payment for

Photo 17: The Wodani of West Papua (Photo S. Breton, 1996).

his daughter. He must not "eat" the shells given for her, it is said, and he will even refuse to comment on the transaction. He remains in the background, and it is the son who is in the foreground. The same taboo exists in compensation for a murder: the members of the victim's clan are excluded from the benefit of the payment, which they distribute to their affines (for a detailed analysis of murder compensation, see Breton, 1999d).

The system of matrimonial credit has major consequences for a person's identity. An immigrant who contributes regularly to the matrimonial payments of the men of the host clan will be reaffiliated into it rapidly. In exchange for his contribution, he will receive part of the marriage payments for the daughters of that clan, he will "eat" those payments, and have his bodily identity transformed in the same way as when he eats the food grown on the host clan's land. Sharing money is equivalent to sharing bodily identity. This equivalence is corroborated by the rule of legal paternity. A child's father is his mother's legitimate husband, the man who has entirely "bought" her. If, for instance, a woman has been made pregnant by a man who fails to pay for the union, and she is finally married to another man who fulfills his matrimonial obligations normally, the latter is considered the father of the child. This man is said to bestow his organs—head, jaw, etc.—on the child. This is so because according to the Wodani, conception requires repeated inseminations. The latecomer inseminator is authenticated as father by the shells he has paid. The only body parts of the child that are said to have been produced by the mother's original husband are the heart and the eyes, the first organs produced in conception. But the rest of the body is the result, it is said, of transfers of both semen and shells by the regular husband. One rarely encounters an individual among the Wodani whose genealogy does not include a change of clan affiliation. Such modifications of social and bodily identity are prompted by a monetary transfer of substance. Although this transformation may not be complete, every trace of the original affiliation is gradually erased by the accumulation of subsequent compensations given or received in the name of the host clan.

The shells given in matrimonial or murder compensation form a monetary homonculus of the person. The body of the victim or the wife is composed of a number of shells, and conversely, a shell is composed of pieces of the body of several people previously "paid for." The same is true for the begetting of each individual. People are the product of the sum total of payments given and received in the name of all those members of the group who went before them, and of whom they are the outcome — like those Arcimboldo-style mannerist portraits, made of an accumulation of objects (as J.F. Weiner [1995] convincingly suggests). Rather than being confined to the narrow perspective of transactions assigning a value to each part of the wife, the metonymic and fractal function of shell money may also be viewed as applying comprehensively to the social groups involved. Each child fathered bears traces of previous marriages, and that trace takes the form of money. This is what the Wodani express in the saying that money is "the only person who never dies." We are reminded here of Kantorowicz' analyses (1957: 302–313) on the Two Bodies of the king and the immortality of the mystic body in which the mediaeval community conceived the principle of its continuity and of its transcendence. Inasmuch as the clan is a corporate whole, a composite body that survives the physical disappearance of its members and reproduces itself in the unending recycling of monetary fragments of past compensations, it is a precipitate of monetary transactions. Shell money, a true *corpus mysticum*, is the effigy of the person just as it is the substance of the social body. The fact that it is offered in compensation for the departure of married sisters or murdered brothers indicates that it represents the identifying principle of the clan in its corporeal, but transmittable form. It is the locus in which the clan appears as a whole, as a pool of patrilineal organs. This is what makes shell money a *res publica*. Thus, Wodani society may be viewed as composed of two sorts of beings: mortals, who are born, marry and die; and shell money, fictitious persons without which human reproduction could not take place. Begetting is an act that does not engage the carnal human body only, but the social and perpetual body of shell money as well.

Aside from its generalized use for purchasing commodities, which we will not deal with here, *kipe* is the object of exchanges in a separate system very suggestive of the stamp-collection market, in which people show incredible voracity as they barter and trade—or rather, "pull out," as it is said—their pieces. *Kipe* is not only the universal currency, it is also the most coveted and most often exchanged item. It is an infinitely more fluid valuable than wives or pigs, and it "travels" with disconcerting speed. There is nothing unusual about seeing a shell that was given for a wife being immediately exchanged by its new owner, and following a complicated circuit involving a number of individuals, coming into the hands of another wife-taker, who offers it, that very same day, during the same marriage payment, to another of the bride's entitled parties. There reigns an atmosphere conducive to deceit, similar to the atmosphere encountered on the art market, which incites owners of *kipe* to lie about the name, class and real value of their shell to abuse the gullible individuals desirous of obtaining them. This is made possible by the fact that a shell is not valued on the basis of its class, as determined by subtle morphological criteria, but also according to aesthetic considerations, often of a personal nature and open to endless debate. While the evaluation of shell money is an interpretative art, its exchange is a game, in which the speculative element is limited by the fact that the *kipe* to be obtained in exchange for one's own shells is known beforehand, the only difficulty simply residing in estimating its value properly.

To understand what real admiration is, one must have seen the Wodani sitting in a circle, commenting shells and passing them around from hand to hand. They view the aesthetic experience as calling for contemplation rather than for poïetic acts. For them, the aesthetic realm is entirely coextensive with the realm of shell money. A beautiful *kipe* is said to be "ripe." The older and the more worn it is, the more it is prized. Its value comes from its resemblance to a body that has had offspring. One removes a shell from its sheath "head" first, in a downward movement suggestive of a birth. Freud (1955a) points out that in works of art, satisfaction is essentially narcissistic, the outcome of the illusory action of the ego taking itself and its fantasies as the object of its libido. Reality disappears behind the mirror-like contemplation of the ego. Money, as an object of representation and of aesthetic pleasure, inhabits that "transitional space" (Winnicott, 1971) in which it is no longer quite the naked self and not yet a real object. It is irresistibly beautiful only because it is a part of the self, simultaneously infinitely close and infinitely distant. This is aesthetics in its nascent state, based less on positive representation than on an act of projection.

What is interesting here is the compulsive character of shell money collection, tending towards an increasingly rapid pace of exchanges reflecting both the desire and the dissatisfaction of the collector. When two individuals trade shells, they may be seen to hesitate until the last minute. The sentimental attachment to a *kipe* can only be overcome by the pleasure of novelty. Sometimes one of the partners returns the following day to cancel, acrimoniously, a deal he regrets and in which he feels he has been cheated, often because some third party made fun of him. What encourages a person to part with a *kipe* that he already misses is that the other person is also parting regretfully with his. The first party is anxious to conclude the exchange before the other man changes his mind and thus invalidates what makes the former's shell so desirable; but if the other party accepts too quickly, then his own shell is worthless. It is not surprising that some highly coveted *kipe* are temporarily withheld by their possessors, who feel somewhat sentimental about them, as if they were unique works of art, thereby attracting numerous, assiduous claimants anxious to purchase them. This is reminiscent of Duclos' licentious novel, *Les confessions du comte de * * **, in which a witty *libertin* upbraids his more successful rival in the following terms: I have allowed you to enjoy the favors of this lady for some time now; if you are a true gentleman, put her back in circulation. A person who is unable to part with his shells will be treated somewhat disdainfully, and will meet with the same reproaches as someone who commits the unpardonable impropriety of eating alone in front of others.

Shell money is not an object that can be innocently hoarded. There is something fundamentally disappointing about it that necessarily leads its holder, like the stamp collector, to exchange it. In fact, an implicit rule obliges the holder to trade his *kipe* if a reasonable offer is made. As soon as the possessor of a particular shell exhibits it or makes the fact known, he exposes himself to the necessity of trading it off. Anyone who gets a glimpse of an object acquires a right to it. To stroll through a garden is equivalent to demanding some of its fruit. A person who sees you eating a sweet potato takes it from your hands, and you have no right to protest. Often, spectators to a bridewealth payment are given a share, however small, as a matter of form. The verb "to see" means "to find again," but it also expresses the notion of making something dependent, or affecting it by one's action. To say that a fruit is "seen" by the sun means that it has been spoiled by it. The compounds of the verb "to see" express an incipient action: "to touch" is, literally, "to see with the hand." A person who is unsuccessful both in acquiring money and in hunting game will claim that he does not "see" them. A valuable shell, one that "travels" openly and conspicuously, and the history of which is known to all, is said to be "visible." When its involvement in a transaction has just been decided—when, for instance, it will soon be used to pay for a bride's head—its owner will refuse to satisfy any gratuitous curiosity, to the point where he may lie to the insistent meddler, and claim that he has already traded it, to avoid having to exhibit it at such an untimely moment. "To see" is a bit more than to see, it includes a degree of possession. There is a whole art of exhibiting or concealing a shell at the right time, then, since the act of displaying it or making it public is the first step toward losing it. Such a sophisticated strategy for seduction, heavily charged with meaning, is reminiscent of the œdipal situation of a

Photo 18: The Wodani of West Papua (Photo S. Breton, 1996).

person who has lost his sight, as if by castration. The compulsion to indulge in calculated display is suggestive of a constituent absence, and of a doubt that one strives to obliterate. What more do we need to draw the conclusion that money is the object of an absence?

During what psychoanalysis calls the "oral stage," the first phase in libidinal development linked to the primacy of eating in the child's life, the drive to incorporate may be satisfied in a different form, through sight, for instance, as illustrated by the expression "to devour with one's eyes." A similar movement may be seen here. A *kipe* that is changing hands is said by the Wodani to be "eaten," and during the transaction it "dies." When it is bought on credit, and the last installment, payable in pigs or shells, has not been paid, it remains "alive" and cannot be disposed of and exchanged with a third party under any circumstances. Conversely, once the final payment has been made the shell is said to be "dead." This death only refers to the transaction at hand, however, since *kipe* are constantly being exchanged and dying again, so to speak. "To eat" a *kipe* also refers to the idea that one puts an end to its possession in a sacrificial manner, by killing the pig that it purchased, and whose "image" will be "eaten" by the spirits. "To eat" a valuable shell, to convert it into pork, with all of the disdain required by the occasion, means that you are greater than the people who envy your possession of it, or than the circumstances through which you acquired it. The same vocabulary is used for homicide payments. People who pay for a homicide are said to be "cooking" the victim in an earthen oven, like a pig, and the people who receive the payment are said to "eat" it.

To acquire a shell, be it in the context of a marriage or a murder compensation, then, always amounts to "eating" it. The destiny of shell money is located in the belly, and to begin with, in the belly of the parturient wife for whom it constitutes payment. Shells, brides and pigs are interchangeable valuables. Inasmuch as shells form a corporeal representation of a group, in which future marriages are composed of fragments of previous marriages, and in which one "eats" past wives by cutting up the present bride, I would argue that monetary transactions engender one another through a series of successive ingestions. None of the substance of the clan is lost, nothing is created, everything is transformed. Human reproduction is based on the redistribution of monetary representations of traded daughters and murdered sons. It is a metaphoric reingurgitation—by people who are horrified by cannibalism—the purpose of which is the transmission and the recycling of the male substance of the clan. This substance takes two forms: first, the sperm of the fathers, and secondly, the shells offered in compensation for its expenditure in the daughters and sons who have left the clan. But in this claim that money is the substance of the social body, one further point must be clarified. The clan does not possess any monetary treasure. The shells given and received in compensation for the loss of its members are not the same pieces. Money derives its symbolic reality exclusively from its circulation; this reality is not so much substantial as it is an expression of social relations.

The rule presiding over the collection and bartering of shells prescribes exchanges on a five-item basis: a *kipe* of a particularly valuable class is exchanged for four shells of lower categories designated as male or female— although the shell has no genitals—, plus a whole pig or a side of pork. The shell that is divided into several pieces is the "mother"; those used to purchase it are her "children." But while the *kipe* used in this exchange is divided up like the bride, it is not carved in the same fashion as a pig. The metaphor used is the carving of a marsupial. Pigs may be carved into as many pieces as desired, but a marsupial can only be cut into four quarters. It is thus said to be having "children," as though the carving had generated some additional value. This is a division that produces a symbolic increment. The second numeral classifier used for the *kipe* also designates the quarters of a marsupial: from the beginning, shells are construed as the outcome of a division. Just as matrimonial payment "kills" the wife, when a shell is exchanged for another one it is "killed" and divided into four parts. The pieces given in compensation are quarters, which is to say, "children." This is how the fiction of the reproductive capacity of shells and of the constant increase of wealth through exchange is maintained.

Significantly, the semantic field of monetary transactions revolves around delivering death, cutting up bodies, eating, and the symbolic multiplication of objects through exchange, when in reality what happens is just a monetary division. Despite the frequent portrayal of transactions in terms of sexual reproduction, the ultimate explanation of monetary wealth does not refer to those female activities that generate a real increment, such as child-bearing or gifts of food. If *kipe* beget children, they do so according to the masculine rule of division. The specific nature of their symbolic multiplication is expressed in the opposition between two modes of symbolic production: that of pigs, fattened by women, which will breed young, and that of marsupials, killed by men and consumed outside of the domestic sphere, and which will be split up. In this way, the power to kill coincides with the fantasy of male parthenogenesis, of the begetting of the same, freed from dependency on women.

This same element is found in the symbolism of the trophies that decorate shell money pouches. These include the tail or scrotum of certain marsupials, which women are not allowed to consume lest they jeopardize their fertility, both agricultural and sexual. At the same time, these male hunting emblems, positively linked to the multiplication of shell money through financial operations, are worn by women as necklaces. Women and shells hold equivalent positions as symbols, since both are marked, for different reasons, with the signs of male agency. To simplify, we may say that women make children, while shells make women and men make shells.

The third numeral classifier that applies to *kipe* designates the planks used to build garden fences and walls of houses. These objects operate a separation—fundamental to Wodani thinking—between inside and outside, the garden and the forest, the domestic sphere and the hunting sphere. But at the same time this classifier applies to those tools—bows, axes and bush-knives—made by men and designed to wreak destruction or to break things into pieces. Moreover, the head of the bow and the money sheath are both decorated by the tail of the same marsupial.

The three classifiers used for shell money provide an accurate description of its symbolism. The first means "skin"—the *kipe* is a person; the second designates a quarter of a marsupial—the shell is the product of a division; the third stands for a plank, bow or sharp tool—the shell is an instrument for separating, demarcating and killing. The latter two aspects are particularly striking, inasmuch as in one the shell is conceived as the outcome of the operation it performs in the other. It is both that which separates and that which is separated, that which does the killing and that which is killed.

This is reminiscent of a similar theme observed in the Marind case. The club used in head-hunting had first to be broken on the head of the victim, and the piece broken off had to be left behind. This head-breaking cudgel was described as a penis, and we came to the conclusion that the symbolic function attributed to the male organ was ambivalent; it is instrumental both in giving life and in taking it. It is the separated object par excellence, but at the same time the object that induces the mutilation. The same thing applies to the head name: on the one hand, it is cut off, but on the other hand it operates a separation, since it differentiates individuals.

This detotalizing function of shell money is of course accounted for by the fact that, in true metonymic fashion, *kipe* both splits objects and at the same time is split by the exchange. But a deeper meaning may be perceived here, particularly if we take a look at the Tolai of New Britain (Epstein, 1979: 164–166) and the Mono-Alu of the Solomon Islands (Monnerie, 1996: 49–51, 55). In one case shell money is spoken of as "taboo," while in the other, the word for "taboo" designates the value of shell money. For the Tolai, the taboo acts as indicator of a property and of conceptual limits that must not be exceeded. For example, it is taboo for a pregnant woman to go to a coastal area where bonita is being fished. The proximity of the two, both gorged with blood, would cause a dangerous confusion between their respective cosmic and symbolic domains. The taboo, or interdiction, is a separating principle, a normative, classificatory tool. It is even more: a means of organizing the universe through the use of signs. Inter-diction, according to the Latin etymology, means the placing of words between things, the cutting up of things using words. To call shell money "taboo," or "interdiction" is indicative of an amazing intuition regarding the detotalizing function of money; that is, of its function of separating things with words. The ancient Greeks had a similar conception. The term *nomisma*, "money," derives from *nómos*, which took on the meaning of "law" and belonged to the register of division, since it originally designated "distribution," or "legal attribution," for instance on the occasion of sacrificial offerings (Will, 1954: 211, note 2, 226–230). The notions of prohibition and thus of law semantically derive from the notions of cutting up and sharing. Among the Melanesian islanders, money is often used as an offering or payment connected with the termination of periodic taboos, compensation for transgressions, or the establishment or crossing of limits in time and space.

The Wodani do not correlate shell money directly with the notion of the taboo, but they do link the latter with the principle of separation, since the word for "taboo" in their language is the stem of the verb "to cut." Now, money cuts people up, distributes the pieces among groups, and in doing so defines the latter and at the same time determines the identity of individuals as the outcome of splitting and mixing. Further, it is the instrument of the paternal continuity of the clan, constantly ripped out of the body of married sisters and murdered brothers to be recycled, preserved and transmitted. Money is the social organ of male reproduction.

The Missing Part

Although dissimilar, the two objects described—the head and the shell—are symmetrical. My intention, in choosing objects as different as possible, is to make a connection between them and to show that their meaning is comparable. First of all, if we look at how they function semantically, both express duality. The head is the metonym for the spoken word, the only thing that counts. But this word is turned into a name, a metaphor for the identity of the person who receives it, and also a metonym of the person who gives it, just like the sperm with which he has parted. As for shell money, it is a metaphoric person, but it is only equivalent to parts of the body, and may therefore be said to represent the person metonymically, or fractally, so to speak.

Both of these objects are constructed around a subtle tension between these two aspects of their identity. They are simultaneously the image of and a part of the person, an ideal representation just as much as a constituent element. They inspire hopes that their possession will elevate the person and enable him to achieve the status of a totality, and at the same time act as a reminder that they are simply one more piece, and consequently, that the person will always have something missing. Head-hunting involves cutting something off of someone, a stranger about whom one knows nothing, to complete a person. Shell money in turn divides the person in order to show that he or she is constructed with social substance. What is at stake in this interplay between the part and the whole is not so much the object as the subject, and the way in which he is constituted in his relation to the object. The object is a piece detached from the subject. The object defines the subject. The opposition between the two, a typically Western view of things, becomes meaningless. It is this reversal that I wish to examine here.

This will give me the opportunity to deal in a roundabout way with the relationship between the person, that is, the subject as socially informed and constituted, and the self, that is, the subject with an awareness and representation of his or her own existence and agency. The self must be carefully distinguished from the ego of psychoanalytical theory in that the self refers to the subject as experiencing himself, while the ego refers to an aspect of the structured subject, about which impersonal generalizations can be made (in Freud's second theory of the psychic apparatus (1955c), the ego is an *Instanz* of the personality, in the same way as the super-ego, the ego ideal and the id). Moreover, the ego contains unconscious, repressed aspects that cannot be recognized by the self as parts of itself. The person and the self are not the truth of the subject, because the person, on the one hand, is a social and ideological construct while the self, on the other hand, is built on the moving sands of the failure to recognize one's inner personality. I wish to argue that the socially organized hunt for the object triggers and feeds on a disposition to incompleteness on the part of the self. The spectacle of things is an exercise in self-enlargement. But that is possible only because, at the root, the subject is child of its own finite and divided nature. Freud defines such a split as taking place within the ego. My main purpose is to show, while avoiding the meanders of a psychology of the ego or of the self, how a Freudian perspective on the division of the subject can shed light on the interplay between the person and the self. The self is not free of the external constraints weighing on the social *persona*, any more than the person is a pure fiction unrelated to the subject's own understanding of himself. According to Freud, the subject is fundamentally divided and lacking something, and this is not without consequences with regard to the social quest that shapes him and to the representation he forms of his own agency. By the same token, I would like to argue that Marilyn Strathern's seminal formulation of the Melanesian "partible" personality (1988), with which the present paper concurs, could be enriched by a broader understanding of psychoanalytical views on the relationship between subject and object, and in particular by Donald Winnicott's description (1971) of the self as taking form while experiencing its objects, in what he calls the "transitional space" which stands in between subjectivity and objectivity.

Let us return to the facts. In Marind society, the subject is someone who is lacking something—a name. A person's identity is not something that belongs to him or her, but something that is missing. The person is essentially unfinished. To whatever small extent he achieves completeness, it is by taking on a name that has been stolen from someone else. To receive a head name is not enough, however. If one is a father, one must also give the name; that is, transmit the sign of the male continuity of the social group, an act of the same meaning and consequences as procreation itself.

For the Wodani, the subject is the object of a monetary division through which the agnatic identity is transmitted and thus preserved. The person, be it a sister from whom one is severed by her marriage or a brother of whom one is deprived by murder, is carved up metaphorically like a pig, and distributed among clan mates. In this way, the substance of the group is recycled, "eaten" in an ongoing round of transactions which will result in other marriages and the begetting of other children, so that the specific identity of every person born within the clan appears as an admixture of the social substance of the clan.

This has a number of consequences. First, in both cases, the subject is not conceived as a whole, but as always lacking something, as always being somewhat short of real completion. The missing part, which is the defining element of the subject, is only perceived as such because its quest is constantly encouraged. Wholeness, then, is outside of the person. By transmitting sperm, a name, pieces of sisters and brothers, the person fits into a socio-cosmic order and reproduces the whole of which he is a constituent part. This makes the person the result of social authentication, in Pierre Legendre's acceptation of the term (1994: 105); that is, the result of an act that designates him as having been socially begotten. Head-hunting and the exchange of shell money give subjects a *raison d'être*, a social rationale.

This is a capital point: the ability to beget and to reproduce the social whole is linked to possession of an object. The social reproductive capacity is reified in the object. Without a head name or without shell money, a person cannot transmit what must be transmitted. The subject is therefore deprived of access to the means of reproduction. He is dependent on society for this. Conversely, society is essentially constituted by the formal conditions of its reproduction—in the present case, these are the rules governing transmission of the symbolic object.

Authentication of the subject can only take place in the framework of socio-cosmic reproduction. What makes him a subject of society is not the peculiar tasks he undertakes, but rather, his contribution to the social act of begetting. Heads and shells are the object of a passionate quest, since they are the instruments of perpetuation, which the person acknowledges as his main social aim, and which he turns into a subjective goal, tied in with his own self-definition. The subject is not conceived as standing alone or as constituting a finality unto himself, but as a means in a process of succession. Accordingly, the person and society are not heterogeneous in magnitude, related as a unit is to an aggregate, rather, they are homothetic, with a simple change of scale (Wagner, 1991). This is obviously worlds away from the Western way of thinking, in which the self is both the atom and the ultimate end of society. In Marind and Wodani society, the person is authenticated by the act of incorporating the other in himself.

The need to be identified and authenticated operates within the framework of the subject's submission to otherness in the broadest sense of the term. The head must be taken from someone, shell money describes the person as a mixture composed of pieces coming from other sources. What we discover here is a conception in which the subject's identity is composed of relationships. The subject is both a "dividual" entity and a "social microcosm" (Strathern, 1988). The Western vocabulary referring to substance is inadequate here, and has only been used to indicate that the relationship is reified in a thing—a head name, a shell, semen. At the same time, that thing is the sign of a gift, a handing over. As in a relay race, one must not focus one's attention on the stick, but rather on the way it passes from one person to the next, establishing a connection between two distinct temporal realms.

Moreover, going after a name the way the Marind do places the other on center stage in such a striking manner as to be significant in itself. To name someone is in fact paramount to constituting him or her as a subject to be looked at and spoken to by the other. The name is "the image of an other person's speech" (Legendre, 1994: 47). Indeed, the name that is given, that *pa-igiz* that authenticates the person, can only do so because it comes from elsewhere, from someone else's mouth, someone who is so much an other as to be an alien whose language is incomprehensible; and further-more, the name has to be given away by the person who seized it—given away to someone else, son or daughter, in the name of the father. The name that the Marind give to a child is the image of an other person's speech in two respects: first, because it is a name that has been wrenched from an anonymous victim, and secondly, because a name is of no value when pro-nounced by the person to whom it belongs, but receives its value from being pronounced by someone else. A name only really belongs to a person inas-much as it is used by those who speak to him or her. The subject does not call himself by his name, any more than he says "you" to himself. Only a person who speaks to me is in a position to address me as someone else. "I is an other," as Rimbaud said, only because I am not alone. My name, then, is that part of me that does not belong to me, since it makes me an other. The name attached to me is my image in the eyes of others. Thus, to name someone is tantamount to considering him as real only inasmuch as he exists, first, for an other.

The inscription, in the subject, of the relation to the other is described as an absence, resulting in a quest for the object, and in the case of the Marind and Wodani, this quest is compulsive. What the Western world des-ignates as an absence constitutes the meaningfulness of the relationship in Melanesia. Every subject has a missing part. One might almost claim that a person is made of missing pieces. And that missing part is not represent-ed positively, even in the case of shell money, as something that would enable the person to achieve wholeness, were he to seize it. The object represents an absence. It seems to me that this explains why the Marind could not have a positive theory of head names. It also explains why the Wodani indulge in vain, collector-like exchanges, the underlying motivation of which can-not be anything other than disappointment. Through the symbolic object, acting as something that must belong to the subject and at the same time something other than the subject, the person does not achieve completion, but rather is confronted with his or her incompleteness. In both cases this constituent absence is doubly stressed for women, since they are not allowed to deal with the symbolic object. Its transmission is a male enterprise. The missing part is essentially masculine, and women are essentially deprived of it.

What is involved for both genders, then, is not the object as a piece detached from a previously complete person who attempts to retrieve that wholeness, but rather, the subject as being unable to conceive of his or her identity as other than fundamentally split into pieces. In New Guinean mythology, the theme of the incomplete person who is gradually differentiated, sometimes through the workings of a bamboo knife that shapes his or her limbs and genitals, is quite frequent. To put it in Freudian terms, the consequence of the erection of the object in the self is to stress that: you are the subject of an absence, you are the subject of a relationship, you are not an island unto yourself, the other is within you.

Head-hunting and monetary payment are not so much aimed at dismantling the other, even when a victim is decapitated or a bride cut into pieces, as at placing the subject in the clutches of the other. The subject is alienated in the other, so to speak, just as people in these societies are alienated from their means of reproduction rather than from their means of production. The other has that missing piece of us in his pocket. The not-me constitutes the truth of me. The person bears the mark of separation: separation from an other who, by definition, is constituent of the person, separation from the self, since he or she is always short of unity. Strikingly, the image used is one of cutting up: both the Marind and the Wodani require a massacre, literal or figurative, to put the person to a test.

The subject goes searching for, cuts off, wrests away, or picks—to use the terms employed by the Marind and the Wodani—but also gives, transmits and exchanges what he is lacking. It would be a total misconception, however, to think that what is lacking is some definite object, or that the subject lacks the object sought. The object involved is nothing but the representation of an absence. This explains why we have not been able to learn the meaning of head names. Since the symbolic object is both something that must belong to the self and something other than the self, it does not serve to achieve fulfillment, but rather, to confront subjects with their incompleteness.

The dismembering and castration enacted in head-hunting and the circulation of shell money should be interpreted as the expression of this lack rather than as its cause. What is involved here is not a detached part of a previously complete self, but a self that is unable to conceive its unity in any form other than that of an imaginary state of division. We must bear in mind that what we refer to as castration does not refer to any actual body part that might be removed, but to something that no-one actually possesses, and which both sexes lack, in different ways: men, in whom it is missing, and women, who are deprived of it. The object is not something real, literally speaking. It has an heuristic function in that it sets the rules for searching and discovering. It is a signifier.

Incompleteness is the measure imposed on the subject by the displaying of the symbolic object. But the fact that each culture imagines and develops the forms it takes in its own particular way does not imply that the theme itself is arbitrary. Suffice it to recall, firstly, that it is simply the expression of the ontological position of the subject with respect to the objective world. Psychoanalysis shows that this is a dialectic position. The self and the object come into existence correlatively (Winnicott, 1971), and it is out of the question to view the two as given in advance, independently constituted, and simply called upon to meet. In this perspective—an extension of Hegel's intuition—the me is subordinate to the not-me.

The first object encountered by the human child is a partial object: the mother's breast. But it is only because it goes away that the breast takes on an objective character. Before the breast vanishes, the child experiences it as undifferentiated from himself (Winnicott, 1971). Thereafter, the representation of the object is irremediably associated, once and for all, with its loss. With this experience, which marks the subject for his entire lifetime, "to find the object" is actually "to retrieve it" (Freud, 1953b). This takes the form of an unceasing, unsatisfactory quest, in which the object appears, paradoxically, as something inexorably contingent, susceptible of taking an infinite variety of forms (Freud, 1957c): "The subject is bound to the lost object by nostalgia, which informs all efforts to find it. It is nostalgia that places reunion with the object under the sign of an impossible repetition, since, precisely, the object is not and cannot be the original one" (Lacan, 1994: 15).

As Lacan points out, this produces an ontological position in which the being is defined by what it is lacking (*Ibid.*: 214). One cannot help thinking, then, that playing at "leaving and returning," as in the *Fort-Da* by which the child flings a toy away and then recovers it (Freud, 1955c), is the prototype not only of symbolic activity in general, by which the object is subjected to the law of permutation according to which it is alternately present and absent, and which is the very principle of language (Lacan, 1994: 67–68), but also of ceremonial exchange. The latter are frequently encountered in Melanesia in a variety of forms, all of which comply with the conception of the object as something whose value resides in its vanishing, in being given, only to be returned, lost and then retrieved. The unending quest, along with the illusion of completion, and the essentially disappointing character of exchanging, which is nonetheless just as mandatory as the law to which the subject must submit in order to achieve existence: all of these elements are present in both the Wodani and the Marind. The object relationship intrinsically leads to multiplication—multiplication of the object, on the one hand, and of attempts to possess it, on the other hand: "We have learnt from psycho-analysis in other examples that the notion of something irreplaceable, when it is active in the unconscious, frequently appears as broken up into an endless series: endless for the reason that every surrogate nevertheless fails to provide the desired satisfaction" (Freud, 1957a).

When the maternal object is first lost, the subject does not yet have a complete representation of him or herself, and only exists through anarchic partial drives which derive satisfaction from one part or another of the body, in an auto-eroticism oblivious of any external object. This is the phase of the divided representation of the ego. The object only begins to take shape through a gradual unification process, resulting from the fact that the subject takes himself as a libidinal object (Freud, 1958a). At the outset, the object is simply the narcissistic expression of a nascent ego. According to Lacan (1966), the ego first starts to develop when the child apprehends the image of the other, or his or her own image, as a unified whole, intuits its sameness with himself, but is incapable of perceiving it otherwise than through an imaginary identification. It is in the aftermath of this fragile epiphany of the ego, according to Lacan (1966), that the fantasy of the dismembered body appears, and not, as Freud would have it, prior to its subsequent synthesis. The ego develops through identification with the other, through gradual sedimentation, and is nothing but the image of its objects and its universe. Conversely, the complete object that it will eventually form, and that will be the target of the genital drive—that is, the other as such—"is never devoid of narcissistic implications; it is constitutionally formed more by a sort of coalescing of a number of partial objects into a shape modeled after the ego than by a harmonious synthesis of those objects" (Laplanche & Pontalis, 1967: 293).

The ego beholds itself in its objects. The object is not the other, it is the mutilated ego. It is that from which the subject parted in order to come into being as such (Lacan, 1973: 60, 95). Similarly, in ceremonial exchange, the self gives a part of himself to the other so as to define that other as being outside the self. There is a narcissistic dimension in giving, which is echoed in the fundamentally aggressive nature of the object relation. The fiction according to which the object belongs to the other and must be wrenched from him simply reflects the subject's wounded narcissism.

It is in the light of these remarks that castration takes on its symbolic dimension. As we know, the presence or absence of a given organ (viz. the genital organ) plays a decisive role in the child's representation of his own identity at the precise point at which that identity is more like a puzzle, when he remains particularly sensitive to the fear of withdrawal of the object (Freud, 1961c). Some might question Freud's (1961b) assertion that girls are subjected, just as boys are, to the primacy of the phallus. There should however be agreement on the idea that the Œdipus complex produces a new order in that it makes the desired object, or the object whose loss is feared, the stake of a pact, a gift and a prohibition.

Girls know that they do not have a phallus, but they do not know that this is the rule. Boys are afraid of losing it or not having it, but do not know that they will eventually be entitled to it. In the girl's case, the castration complex leads her to desire the father (Freud, 1961d). She will subsequently obtain what she is deprived of, but in the form of a partial, external object: a child, and this will lead her from narcissistic love to object love (Freud, 1957b: 89–90); a penis, to which its bearer is, conveniently, appended (Freud, 1955b; 1961d). In the boy's case, his desire for his mother is put to an end by his rivalry with his father, which makes him fear castration and enunciates the prohibition, but also teaches him that he, in turn, will bear the phallus (Freud, 1961d). For both boys and girls, the question of possessing or not possessing the object lies outside the realm of plain reality, to take on a symbolic meaning tied to the law—the law of the incest taboo and of transmission. Thus, the object of an absence becomes the object of a gift, such as the gift of a head name, or of the right to procreate, represented by a shell. For the boy, this gift is underwritten by his identification with his father, who is introjected, so to speak, in the ego and becomes an independent "object" within it: the superego (Freud, 1961a). The Œdipus complex amounts to the fact that for the first time in the subject's relation to the object, an impossibility arises. It is not a painful, chance mishap, then, as is commonly believed, but an absolute necessity through which the child enters the social order.

The object of castration has an essentially symbolic signification, and is not restricted to the penis, its image. To repeat an earlier assertion, what is involved is not a part detached from a previously complete self, but a self that is unable to conceive its unity in any form other than that of an imaginary division which must be overcome. The object may therefore be withdrawn, returned, awarded and lost: it is the sign of everything that confronts the subject with his or her incompleteness. It is characterized by the fact that it is detachable and susceptible of circulating from one person to another (Laplanche & Pontalis, 1967: 311). It is an object that is removable and replaceable: in other words, an object of exchange.

As we have seen, that object—in the present case a head name or a shell valuable—through a singular condensation, is both a separating instrument and a separated object, a fact that becomes fully significant in this context. It is the same operation seen once from the actor's viewpoint, and once from the patient's viewpoint. The point is simply for the subject to take from the other, or to receive from him, or again, to give him, what that very same subject is lacking; to do to the other what is done to oneself. In doing so, what is expressed is very precisely the œdipal logic of transmission.

We began by noting the considerable efforts made by both of the societies investigated here to define the position of a detached object. However distant, and however improbable it is that it would ever afford satisfaction, this object was found to exert an extraordinary constraint, and to be tied to the subject by the bond of the quest and of gift-giving. The subject necessarily perceives himself as incomplete and fundamentally lacking something. From a psychoanalytic perspective, the following remarks were added: the object is lost, and lacking, by definition, like the first object encountered, the mother's breast; to find the object is to retrieve it, so to speak, as if one had always expected it to return; the self is necessarily constructed through identification with the other; this frail synthesis creates awareness of the divided nature of the subject; the only representation of the object, for the self, is that of a piecing together of parts, modeled after its own uncertain wholeness; the Œdipus complex, by setting a rule and establishing filiation, affords the necessary transition, for the subject, from the absence of the symbolic object to the possibility of transmitting it.

To the Freudian way of thinking, the formation of the self is not based on the belief that the self is everything while the object is no more than an extension of the self as an undifferentiated whole. That, rather, is the fate of Narcissus. To the contrary, the apprenticeship of one's humanity is the defeat of that illusion. The self rises out of the revelation that if there is a me, it is because there is also a not-me, an irretrievably lacking part within me. By creating an object, then, a subject is created. In his work, to which I am much indebted, Pierre Legendre attempts to show that each society is embodied in an arrangement by which the subject is instituted through the introduction of an internal split. The subject views himself or herself as deficient, then, as lacking something, and at the same time as dependent on society, which stages this absence through the spectacle of things and the instructions as to how to search for and make proper use of the symbolic object.

Thus, a twofold separation is operated. The first, as we have seen, takes place within the subject, and constitutes his subjugation to a lacuna that precedes him ontologically. This takes the objective form of what I am tempted to call a social game; for example, the quest for a name or the exchanging of shells. The subject perceives himself as incomplete because he lacks something which the social spectacle both displays for his benefit and inscribes in him as necessary. This is a game in that it leads to a form of satisfaction in which there is no object other than one's self. The second split is external to the subject, but it too is representable by him. It is the separation from a reality that is not his own, corresponding to the authority, the rule of this game he has not invented—from society, the Third party guaranteeing the symbolic order. This explains why the actors view it as transcendent, as Durkheim observed.

Now, this symbolic order is only visible in the spectacle it stages of itself, in the way it puts the object on display. This is an essential point. Society cannot be exhibited as an institutional arrangement producing authentication, bestowing meaning and value on human undertakings, unless it stages a representation of itself as the manifestation of the whole separate from the subject. For this to occur the social game puts some distance between the subject and his objects—through the theater of the quest and of gift-giving. Society only appears as a separate authority inasmuch as it separates the subject from himself. But it is the fact that the subject is originally split that enables society to enter the scene. At the very same time as it exhibits itself as an articulated whole, distinct from the subject, offering the spectacle of its splendid wholeness, it inflicts a narcissistic wound on the subject, who experiences his insufficiency. From then on, the person bears the mark of that socially instituted incompleteness, of an absence that is constituent of social life. Conversely, it is only through the spectacle of the person's own incompleteness that he or she is introduced to the notion of the authenticating Third Party, gaining access, at this point, to a level at which that incompleteness takes on a meaning that otherwise escaped him—a social meaning.

There can be no quest for the symbolic object without the backing of the Third Party, both as "rule of the game" and "directions for use," which Third Party is the abstract spectator who bestows meaning on the duel of exchange. Actual exchanges are too limited to be meaningful in themselves. Society, as the authenticating authority, is external to social commerce, which is dependent on the guarantee of an instituted meaning beyond its control. Like the gift given, this instituted meaning is a truth offered to the subjects so that they may find their bearings.

This is where we encounter what Pierre Legendre calls the "parental function of the State" and of society as an institution. The institution, looming most discernibly over the subject like a monument, designates the place reserved for truth and legitimate discourse. The fact that this truth is a fiction, just as arbitrary a rule of the game as head-hunting or the monetary convention, does not make it any less indispensable, precisely as every game must have its rules. As the scholiast, Alciat puts it, it is a "false truth." The only thing that matters is the existence of a designated place for such a truth, and its demarcation of the distance between the level of individual action and the level to which this action must refer to become meaningful.

The social institution is linked to the narcissistic structure of the person, as Legendre stresses. This explains why it is so powerful, and why the person relates to it in the same way as to the object, be it a head or a shell, those mirrors of the self. The Third Party is not a repressive apparatus that imposes its rule on the subject from without. It is through this social dimension of identification that the human subject acquires an existence and finds a singular identity. It is only because human beings have already been divided by language (Legendre, 1998) that the Third Party seems to separate the subject from himself. Speech gives humans a representation of themselves as other, it plunges the sword of the question into the crux of their being, and demands that the place of the truth be defined so that words may circulate.

At this point, I would like to avoid a misunderstanding. The assertion that society separates the subject from himself in that it provides him with an object may give the illusion that I picture society as some sort of divine being, or some superior plane of reality with a will and concrete goals of its

own. This is of course not so. Society is nothing but a whole as represented by persons. But without that representation, there could be no social life.
Inasmuch as human beings are endowed with speech and live and communicate with their fellow creatures, society necessarily takes on a transcendent nature, precisely because it is fictitious, as Durkheim understood
so well. This does not imply that society has an existence of its own over
and beyond the persons that compose it, even though the existence of the
latter depends on their believing the opposite. Their need to be socially
authenticated—the fruit of man's innate tendency to identify with others—
should be understood as both the cause and the effect of life in society. The
fact that the latter is a fictitious being does not exempt us—all to the contrary—from the need to discover why and above all how it displays itself
as divine; that is, as a separate object.

This distancing process is in fact precisely the same as that operated by
myths. In their attempt to account for the consistently identical nature of society, they stage the spectacle of its origin and refer to a process of differentiation and distance-taking. So that when traditional society claims—or rather
when we believe we hear it claim—that it is commanded by tradition, which
is to say, continuity, we are deluding ourselves. It is commanded by a split,
which makes transmission possible. The idea of a myth that would justify
the present state of affairs by pointing to the fact that things have always been
that way is inconceivable: it would have no motivating force. Rather, the myth
is based on the postulate that the present order was established at some point.
This temporal disunion echoes the disunion in space, in the path taken by
the ritualized object. One may very well imagine a discourse on the origins
based on a separation in space. This is precisely what we find in ancient Rome,
as Yan Thomas (1991) has so remarkably shown, with the cult of the Penates,
those household divinities linked with the Romans' ancestral origins. These
divinities are usually worshipped near the hearth, the most intimate place in
the family dwelling. They are the epitome of household gods. Interestingly
enough, in the case of the civic Penates belonging to the city and the people
of Rome as a whole, they were not worshipped within the heart of the City.
The cult was celebrated outside of Rome, in Lavinium, where their idols were
housed in a symbolic, purely fictive city, uninhabited and ruled by a nominal
magistracy that did not officiate where its duties supposedly called it. It was
in Lavinium, according to the legend, that Aeneus, upon his arrival from Troy,
founded the first settlement that was later to become Rome. The interesting
point here is that in Roman legal thinking, to transfer the Penates to the City
would have meant that the City emancipated itself from its origins, and broke
with its foundations. To represent its own filiation Rome needed to refer to
distancing and separation. What was internal was placed outside. The heart
of Rome was outside of Rome. Thanks to this fiction, the city was able to
view itself as an instituted totality.

Why does every society necessarily produce a representation of itself? Sociology has hardly addressed this question since Durkheim, perhaps because the need to which it refers is general, and therefore too vague. Durkheim posits that emblems are inevitably sacralized whenever a symbolic representation of society exists. He raises two questions: first, what makes a society choose a given emblem? Secondly, why is that emblem taken from the natural world? As we know, in his critique of totemism Claude Lévi-Strauss (1962b: 142) answers the second question by turning the "why" into "how," and by postulating an order of constraint that is not a "reflection of the concrete organization of society" but lies in the realm of language. Rather than attempting to comprehend the need, either because it is self evident or because it is not worthy of sociological investigation, he concerns himself with grasping its modus operandi. Durkheim (1968: II, chap. 5, v) explains this need as follows: the emblem symbolizes the sentiment a society has of itself for the simple reason that it contributed to the formation of that sentiment; the emblem must be present in order for society to become conscious of itself, and it is equally important in ensuring the "continuity" of that consciousness; its objective nature provides a palpable form of "externality"—as he himself puts it—of society; last, there can be no society unless it is represented.

Durkheim's analysis, in my opinion (Breton 1999c), has been discounted far too quickly, most probably because it was dressed in unsuitable psychological clothing. If we take his analysis further—that is, if we accept the idea that totemism is a specific application, and not simply a poorly defined object, of the underlying principle according to which no society can do without a representation of itself, with all of the forthcoming implications as to the definition of the subject as a divided being, the awareness he has of himself and his constituent identifications—it becomes clear that the social authentication of a missing object is a contributive factor in making society an external totality. This has the same sense as the authentication of the emblem. For even in so-called totemism, what is at issue is not the representation of a segment of society as opposed to other segments, but rather, society itself as the Third Party instituting the subject. In symbolic exchanges, this representation of the social sphere does not take the form of an emblem, it is a process. In its own idiosyncratic way, Melanesian society gives existence to subjects by lending existence to separate objects. But isn't that what every society does?

Any theory of social anthropology willing to take Freud's discovery of the unconscious into account should be committed to addressing this essential interrogation: what is society for the subject? In the present instance, so instructive that its lessons extend far beyond the shores of New Guinea, society takes the form of an institutional arrangement for the objective authentication of the subject, barring which he would be nothing in his own eyes. It inscribes the absence in him and enjoins him to make it an object of social commerce. It amounts to the same thing to say that the subject is split, or that social life results in a split within the subject. The unconscious is not solipsistic, it is entirely social.

Translated by Helen Arnold

Chapter 6

The Other Side of the Gift: From Desire to Taboo

Representations of Exchange and Œdipal Symbolism Among the Yafar, Papua New Guinea*

Bernard Juillerat

> One of the first groups of beings with which men had to enter into contract, and who, by definition, were there to make a contract with them, were above all the spirits of both the dead and of the gods. Indeed, it is they who are the true owners of the things and possessions of this world.
>
> M. Mauss, *The Gift* (1990: 16)

> The central object-relation, the one which is dynamically creative, is that of lack.
>
> J. Lacan, Séminaire IV, "La Relation d'objet" (1994: 51)

With Marcel Mauss (1923–24), and even before, with Richard Thurnwald (1910, 1912), the main focus of the sociology of the gift was the

---

* First published as " L'envers du don : du désir à l'interdit. Représentations de l'échange et structure œdipienne dans une société mélanésienne ," *Social Anthropology* 5 (1), 1996 : 1–20.

question of reciprocity, which led to including gift-giving under the heading of exchange. Based on his fieldwork in the south of Bougainville in 1908 and a few years later among the Banaro of the Sepik, Thurnwald noted cases of debt, credit or security, but he also described the principle of agonistic ceremonial exchanges among the Buin of Bougainville, and went on to compare Buin and Banaro forms of marriage: with the Buin principle of brideprice and their use of shell money, he contrasted the Banaro prinicple of "a woman for a woman" (but also the Buin rule of a slave for a slave, a death for a death ...), and, more generally opposed deferred exchange and direct exchange. Whereas he reported negative forms of reciprocity in feuding or, on the contrary, in making peace by paying a bloodprice, in Bougainville, for the Banaro he observed and analyzed rigorously symmetrical forms of partnership. In 1936 he gathered all his ideas on the principle of reciprocity into a theoretical article.

In his essay, *The Gift*, Mauss pays homage to the Austro-German ethnographer, but chooses even more telling illustrations, which became available after the publication of Thurnwald's *Forschungen*: these were essentially the exchanges of men's and women's goods in Samoa, reciprocity according to the Maori theory of the *hau* as reported by E. Best, Malinowski's analysis of *kula*, and above all the Kwakiutl potlatch found in British Columbia. To these he added some examples from Antiquity as a preamble to a few considerations on oblatory or disinterested gift-giving in our own contemporary societies.

Both Mauss and Thurnwald were still heavily influenced by the juridical sciences and the late-nineteenth-century interest in comparative legal systems, one of the wellsprings of theories on the development of different forms of society. They also concurred in the importance they attributed to religion as an influence on law. But while Thurnwald relied heavily on psychology, seeing in the obligation to reciprocate, a "bio-psychic" reflex, Mauss chose to speak in terms of ethics and honor, or to espouse in a certain fashion the theory of the *hau*.

The two anthropologists diverged in their respective evolutionist reconstructions as well. Mauss was content with evoking a juridical evolution of gift-exchange, which he saw as going from the gift of "total service" between groups to more individual prestations, ending finally in exchange based on a convertible value; whereas Thurnwald, on the contrary, saw the origin of the reciprocity principle as residing in economic cooperation within the couple.

In beginning with this brief comparison between the two authors, I wanted first of all to recall the place Thurnwald had come to occupy in exchange theory by 1910 and then to emphasize that, from the outset, the gift was interpreted as calling for a counter-gift, and that it was this reciprocity, more than the unilateral gift, which came under study. It has been only more recently that some studies[1] inspired by Mauss' work, have argued that the oblatory gift is a social act in itself and should be distinguished from exchange. In effect, Mauss' essay, *The Gift*—while continuing to focus on reciprocity—from the first pages tended to break the exchange into three steps, which he distinguished as the obligation to give, the obligation to receive and the obligation to reciprocate. Though I agree with Mauss' distinction, in order to introduce the material I will be presenting, I feel I must nonetheless both attenuate the systematic character of these three stages as well as challenge their association with the notion of "obligation."[2]

This is all the more necessary as the ethnographic examples presented below have nothing to do with agonistic exchanges; instead we will be dealing chiefly with relations between humans and the spirits of the dead or the totemic gods.[3] Of course, religious rites can be seen as a form of obligation, but they are also a matter of free *choice* on the part of the individual or the group, which can be motivated by an economic and social *need* but also by a *desire*. In the collective representation, choice and desire can be imputed as much to the gods and spirits as they can to humans. Choice in turn implies *negation*, the refusal to give, to receive or to reciprocate. Mauss' triad thus becomes: desiring to receive/receiving or not receiving/reciprocating or not reciprocating; or it could be desiring to receive/giving or not giving/receiving or not receiving, and so on. Such chains often form a cycle, but they can start with receiving without having given. The negative option has the further advantage of introducing into the psychological as well as the sociological dimension the possibility of the gift failing, of the exchange aborting together with the consequences this can entail for the human/spirit relationship or that between humans themselves, for instance when there is a desire to exchange but no available partner. The social strategy of exchange engenders a "negative of the gift," comprised of challenges, calculations, frustration, renunciation or repression, the same processes and feelings being projected onto the spiritual entities. The present text also deals with another notion of Mauss', the *expectations* humans have of nature and of the gods. These expectations may well remain passive or even be regressive, and be expressed by a request or a prayer not accompanied by a gift.

The following ethnographic examples are drawn from my field notes

---

1. For instance those published in first the *Bulletin* and then the *Revue du MAUSS* (Mouvement anti-utilitariste en sciences sociales).

2. In competitive exchanges the first gift is never obligatory; furthermore, it can be refused by the designated receiver.

3. It is hardly important that gifts from the gods are only an illusion, since what we are trying to understand is not only how the society practices gift-giving, but more generally how it represents or even fantacizes gift-giving.

on the Yafar of Papua New Guinea, a small group of hunter-gardeners.[4] I will first analyze a rite addressed to the primordial totemic mother, which expresses the desire to receive without giving either before or afterwards; next I will show how a cargo cult has appropriated this search for maternal fecundity, this time on the œdipal plane; then the exchange contract with the forest spirits will be shown to be the logical extension of the free gift from the mother; and finally I will attempt to explain why the exchange of gifts between humans is absent there where one would expect to find it.

Receiving Without Giving: Semen and Milk

During the long period (8–9 months) needed to prepare the totemic Yangis rite,[5] which is marked by various prohibitions, the Yafar go through a number of economic, technical and ritual processes; these are not public and are restricted to men, divided into the two moieties of the society. On this occasion, economic needs (amassing the food to be distributed to kinsmen who come from other villages to attend the public ceremony) are closely associated with the invocations to the primordial divine couple. Even before the universe came to be, these somewhat abstract gods, never consulted or even named aloud, were incarnated in the two totemic plant species, the paternal sago palm and the maternal coconut palm. The so-called "male" moiety of society belongs to the father's side, the "female" moiety, to the mother's; but each moiety partakes of both the father and the mother by virtue of two different sago clones and two pseudo varieties of coconut palm ("black" nut and "red" nut). The men will therefore address specimens of these species when opening respectively a period of intensive sago-working and a no-less-active hunting period, the latter at the very heart of the cynegetic prohibition covering the entire preliminary phase of the public rite.

The period devoted to working and storing huge amounts of sago opens with the ritual felling of two sago palms, belonging respectively to the two totemic varieties of the moietes: each group of men works the variety identified with the other moiety. The sago quickly exploited by the men (whereas this is normally women's work) is stored in the forest until the public rite; but a small amount is first consumed in the form of sago jelly by the men of each moiety (women and children are not allowed at this meal), once again with the men ingesting the sago starch of the other moiety. As sago is explicitly given as the vegetal incarnation of the divine paternal semen, this meal can be seen as an act of totemic communion with consumption

---

4. West Sepik province, Amanab district. Cf. Juillerat, 1986 (1996).

5. This is the Yafar equivalent of the neighboring Umeda Ida cult (Gell, 1975); for more on the Yangis cult, see Juillerat 1992, and 1995.

of the sago of one's own moiety being prohibited. A bit of the two varieties of sago that have been stored will be used, at dawn of the first day of the ceremony, in making the (non-consumed) sacred jelly which represents the conception of the two totemic sons (one for each moiety), called "primordial men" (*ifegê*), who will appear in the anonymous guise of two masked actors at the end of the divine pregnancy, at the close of the public rite.[6] Although I did not manage to collect all the spells uttered when the totemic sagos were felled,[7] it is clear that the purpose was to gather the primordial paternal semen, to identify with it by incorporation, to store and finally to use it in a symbolic act of fecundation. In *L'Avènement du père*, I showed that this anticipated "patricide" allows the biological and social functions of the father to be separated. The sacrifice of the totemic father is thus a "gift of semen," which takes place in the absence of the mother.

Let us now move on to the reactivation of the primordial mother's nurturing function (and implicitly that of her fecundity), constituted by the "prayer to the coconut palm." Shortly after the sagos have been felled and while the women continue to work great quantities of sago for the household to redistribute, it comes time to open the intensive hunting period, thus breaking the cynegetic prohibition that is in force. The adult males of each moiety[8] gather in separate groups at the foot of two coconut palms, one with "black" nuts for the "male" side of the village, the other with "red" nuts for the "female" side, once again respecting the reciprocal exchange of totemic identities. These men, led by the ritual master of their respective moieties,[9] include, for each moiety, those who will embody the *êri*,[10] the *yis*,[11] and the *ifegê* in the public rite; anticipating their role, they summarily paint their bodies. Beneath each of the two coconut palms, the men first kindle a fire and cook the meat of small game, after having set aside the heart and the blood. The meat is eaten with ordinary sago jelly. Then, dec-

---

6. The rite stages, successively, intercourse by the divine couple, loss of the hymenal blood, conception, gestation, announcement of the birth, the birth, the search for the breast, the appropriation and loss of the breast, identification with the social father.

7. With the exception of the usual spells evoking access to the *hoofuk*, to the fertile marrow enclosed in the sheath of the trunk (*roofuk*). If we look at the prayer to the mother-coconut palm analyzed below, we can suppose that the primordial father, too, is invoked.

8. The women and children have been sent off to carry out some task in the forest.

9. Respectively, the Master of the Sky (male-paternal moiety) and the Master of the Earth (female-maternal moiety).

10. Literally "The people": each is the incarnation of the primordial parental couple; they are also called "mothers" and dance throughout the first night of the public rite (the primordial coupling).

11. Literally: "Sago jelly": in the public rite, these two masks dance at dawn, while the ritual jelly is being prepared by the Masters of the moieties (figuration of conception by the male and female totems).

Photo 19: Ritual personification of the Great Mother or Father (*êri*) in the Yangis ceremony, Punda village (Photo D. Niles, Institute of Papua New Guinea Studies, 1986).

orated with the fruits of *Rejoua aurantiacia*[12] and their bodies painted with red ochre,[13] the *ifegê* climb their respective coconut trees, repeating first of all three words: *Naya, ka fay!* "Mother, give me (/-us)!" And then, "Mother give me a pig, give me a cassowary," and so on. The rest of the men cluster around the base of the tree, their heads bowed and their raised hands cupped above their heads. When he reaches the top, the *ifegê* cuts the spathe of a flower cluster while reciting a spell for the reproduction of the animals

12. This bright orange inedible fruit symbolizes ripening and caducity.
13. Symbol of the blood of their mythic mother's who died in giving them birth.

of the forest: "Bring forth[14] young of the possum, bring forth young of the cassowary..." and so on. Then he shakes the inflorescence and showers the blooms on to the men, who are forbidden to look up. Those who receive flowers in their hands will feel fulfilled by the totemic mother and will say they are in "Mother's carrying bag"[15]; alternatively, those who receive nothing (the great majority) will say they have been "abandoned by Mother." Coconut flowers are the conventional symbol of mother's milk and are normally forbidden to eat. Indeed, when the flowers fall from their stem, the *ifegê* says: "Mother's milk is acting, the children of the cassowary (and other animals he names) fall with it, the children of the *ogomô*[16] spirits (which he names) fall with it...," and so forth. Once back on the ground, the *ifegê* receives a welcome from the men, who touch him, saying the word *tot* ("breast," "milk"), while the *êri* and the *yis* mix, in a bark container, the blood and the hearts that were set aside with the hunting-magic plants and the coconut flowers received by the fortunate elect. All gather around the container and stir the ingredients with sticks, saying: "Mother's milk! Cassowary milk! Wild pig milk! Possum milk!...Cassowary blood! Wild pig blood!..."[17] Finally everyone takes a taste of the mixture and says: "Eating the blood from Mother's milk." Each man takes a small amount home for his dogs. Afterwards they hunt intensively for one or two months until enough smoked meat has been laid in. At the close of this period of production, during a simplified rite, the two *ifegê* once more climb their respective coconut trees to tie back up the cut spathe of the inflorecence, reciting spells such as: "Tie up (close) the young of the possum (naming other animals as well)..." The mother that had been opened must be closed back up. The rite in this case works two kinds of magic: one for momentarily reinstating the primordial object (M. Klein) before relegating it to its rank of object lost for ever; the other for transmuting baby food into adult-male food. In the Yangis myth, the newborn children emerging from their mother's spilled blood are given a bow and arrow by their mythic father, with which they immediately set out "in search of the breast." Breast and game are virtually fused in the hunters' line of sight...

When he decided not to include the mother/child relationship in his atom

---

14. I translate the word *tekya*, meaning "to open suddenly, to burst" by "bring forth"; it refers in many chants to giving birth (similar to the breaking open of seeds).

15. A womb symbol.

16. Dangerous spirits responsible for the growth of sago palms and embodying the phallic principle active in fetal growth; they appear at the public rite in the shape of actors painted with charcoal body paint and wearing their clan masks. Each of the main clans has its own *ogomô* and an emblem that represents it (painted on the masks).

17. These statements are followed with the onomatopoea *totototototo* (*tot*), evoking things that run.

of kinship, Lévi-Strauss[18] justified his choice saying that he had no need for a bond not standardized by the rules of society, adding that, sociologically speaking, the mother/child relationship "is defined in function of the fact that the mother represents the giver group." In the organization of the group, the mother can, according to this author, be nothing other than the object given, and her founding role in filiation is thus rejected by the primacy of the alliance theory. Yafar culture, on the contrary, is careful ritually to re-enact in separate episodes (at least at this point in the ritual) the father's gift of semen and the mother's gift of milk, the child being represented in both cases by adult men from the group and, implicitly, from the whole society. The "patricide" reduces the biological father to his semen (sago) alone, while the *ifegê* climbing towards the coconut's breast anticipates the moment when he will shoot his arrow at the sun at the close of the public rite with the aim of getting the sun-breast. The myth tells that the mother died of a hemorrhage while giving birth, and her body was dismembered by her divine companion, thus creating the universe: her single, central breast was hung in the sky by the divine father, where it became the sun. It should be said from the outset that the regression to the breast-feeding mother seems to avoid the possibility of an even riskier regression to the womb; this is unambiguously indicated by the allusion to the reproduction of game as well as by the Yafar commentaries which mention a temporary restitution of the "umbilical cord" between the mother and the group.[19] Just as the mother was absent when the sagos were felled, the father is absent at the time of the prayer to the coconut palm.

To sum up: In each moiety (whose respective signifiers are the male and the female, more specifically the father and the mother), the men address both totems, the father *and* the mother, one after the other. The keynote of both rites is orality, which founds the object-relation: the paternal semen transmuted into sago, as well as the milk symbolized by the flowers and mingled with animal blood, are ritually ingested.[20] From the standpoint of the gift, both substances are received and consumed without compensation. Humans do not give the divine couple anything. The meat eaten together at the opening of the coconut-palm rite is not seen as a gift that carries a request or a sacrifice offered to the mother, but more simply as an act of communion among hunters. The *ifegê* is the incarnation of the mythic son

---

18. Cf. the discussion following André Green's contribution (1977) to Lévi-Strauss' seminar on identity. See also Juillerat, 2001.

19. The link is temporary because definitive regression to one's source is out of the question; it would be tantamount to dying.

20. Nevertheless, it should be noted that the paternal totem yields an edible food (sago) while semen is not a food; inversely, the coconut flowers are not a food, while milk is. In other contexts, however, the breast is represented by milk-filled coconuts.

and acts on behalf of all the men gathered there and of the group as a whole. His prayer is made directly to the totemic mother, without intercession; the first phrase is comprised of the three essential words of any prayer; the *request*, or what Lacan terms the *appel* (appeal, call) "Mother" (a vocative calling upon the donor)—"to me" (the recipient of the gift)—"give" (imperative); then the gift-object is stated: not milk (fantasy) but the game animals of the forest (reality). The Yafar say that "everything (in the world) comes from the mother," all of nature *is* or comes from the mother's body. The mother's gift-object is therefore potentially the world, the mother gives her dismembered body in the form of a universe, but the mother/child bond remains founded essentially on orality, hence the cosmologically privileged status of the breast (sun) as the first (oral) cathectic object. The diurnal heat of the sun alternating with the night does not fail to evoke the mother's presence/absence and the child's gratification/frustration.[21] The prayer proper is followed by the spells which formulate its fulfillment. First the milk flows with the flowers, then the milk is transubstantiated into "the young of game animals" and into "blood"; the milk becomes the forest animals' blood, "milk" and blood mingling in the last meal when the men "eat the blood of Mother's milk."

Through this milky manna that falls upon the heads of these mature men, gathered like children beneath the prolific breast, the mother appears more powerful than generous: only some will be elected by her, but the gift unequally given will later be shared by all: the solidarity of the sons repairs the omissions of the mother. The child's own mother has been replaced by the group's totemic mother, given from the outset as present/absent. Yet each participant in the rite seems to ask himself: "Who am I for the mother? Does she recognize me as her son?" In terms of reality, desire is confused with need (meat), but symbolically, there is the desire for the breast as gift, or rather the desire to be loved or recognized by the mother, in other words the desire for the mother's desire. As André Brusset notes in his commentary on Lacan: "Desire does not attach itself to an object but to a fantasy" (Brusset 1988: 30). It is a relation with the (fantacized) object rather than an object-relation, which would suppose the reality of the object as another subject (Brusset 1988; Lacan 1994). A recurrent theme of Yafar symbolic thinking emerges here: the ambivalence of the mother's goodness, now giving everything, now on the contrary giving nothing: it is the "law of all or nothing"[22] characteristic of the pre-oedipal phase. In this logic of the gift,

---

21. In Lacanian terms: *deprivation* of milk leads, in children, to frustration of the mother's gift and of her love.

22. "What is at stake here is life or death, that is the presence or the absence of the Object, frustration or gratification…This archaism is determined by the particularities of the oral phase: the Breast is there, or it is not there when it is wanted" (Mendel, 1972: 290). See also

she who is capable of giving everything is also capable of giving nothing, or of taking everything back (including her own child) because there is no possibility of exchange: *one can not give the mother anything, one can only receive or not receive from her.*[23] That is why the desire to receive is here inseparable from the anxiety of not receiving, both being dominated by lack. This would suggest that the rite addressed to the coconut palm is more than a device for improving the hunting which makes use of maternal symbols, and the ritual of the totemic sago palms is more than a rite for multiplying sago by invoking the fecundity of the divine semen. The totemic palms "represent" the mother or the father, but in the rite, what they reactualize (this is more particularly true for the mother totem) is his/her loss: the totem is a formal sign of absence, an *absence consacrée* (Green 1995: 86). The rite, as a re-enactment of the lack, seeks to avoid total loss of the object, but its dramatization and its consecration actually reactivate the feeling of loss. Insofar as the found object is nothing more than an object found after having been lost (Freud, 1953b; Brusset, 1988; Lacan, 1994), it is clear that the game animals that will be shot are bound up with the mother's breast through the agency of the blood and the flowers consumed.

Submitting to the Law in Order to Receive: Gratification and Guilt

Moving on to the next "stage" in the elaboration of the Yafar representation of exchange, I will briefly set out the logic of the "desire to receive" as it features in the millenarian cult introduced into the region from West Papua (Indonesian Irian Jaya) at the end of the 1970s and which peaked among the Yafar in 1981.[24] As we will see, the father is here restored to his prohibiting function, thus taking us from a pre-œdipal structure to a fully fledged œdipal representation.

This cult was in no way associated with Yangis, but the Yafar did interpret some of the symbolic material, which they brought back from their affines in West Papua (a day's walk away), using some of their old myths. There are two, complementary, levels to this cult. The first was finding the

---

Brusset, 1988; Lacan, 1994; Green, 1995. See myth B in Juillerat, 1995 (chap. 1), in which the mother cassowary, who causes the alternation of abundance and scarcity is stoned to death and her body shared out by the people.

23. This remark can be associated with the prohibition on exchange (matrimonial or other) characteristic of relations between the Umeda (Gell, 1975) and the Yafar, mythically related as mother/daughter.

24. For more details, see Juillerat, 1991: 75–81 and 1996: 534–544.

Wes, a huge underground (womb-like) chamber located somewhere west of the Indonesian border. In the longer term, the goal was to gain entry to this place, but only after having passed a certain number of tests. The successful Yafar men (women, here again, were not admitted to the cult or even, at least in the beginning, supposed to have access to the Wes) would be reunited with their dead—the true manufacturers of Western commodities—and above all would have unlimited access to the *cargo* (the inexhaustible totality of industrial goods) which the Whites had appropriated for their own benefit; cargo was thus given as a lost object which needed to be reappropriated. The millenarian quest also partakes of the loss, and not only the lack, of an imaginary object. Once all the Yafar men had made contact, a great two-lane road (a lane for each moiety) was supposed to open up between the cavern and the village, like an "umbilical cord" (the term used by my informants), along which the eternally renewed abundance would arrive. But—and this is where the second level comes in, which is missing from the rite to the coconut tree—this right of access to the Wes depended on a certain number of conditions that each man had first to fulfill. What were these conditions? It turns out that all involved some form of examination or appearance before some kind of judge. The candidate had, for instance, to undergo combat training in special "schools,"[25] to appear before an awe-inspiring man after having meticulously examined his own conscience and purified himself of any female contamination, he had to confront armed men surrounding the cavern and, last of all, inside the Wes itself, to gain the favor of a guardian, covered in blood like the dead.

This configuration reveals, first, that the cavern is a huge maternal womb prepared to bring forth cargo,[26] and, second, that the tests are connected with the father's law, and therefore with the superego's defenses which are projected into an imaginary space-time. Hoping to finesse the father's assent would be suicidal, not only for the individual but for all the Yafar, thus making the individual feel responsible for the group. It is immediately clear that a step has been taken with respect to the ritual devoted to the father-sago palms and the mother-coconut palms, beings which were still separate and which could be united only by the performance of the public part of Yangis. In the cargo cult, on the other hand, one can return to the mother only by first submitting to the father's law; but—another striking dif-

---

25. An image probably arising from the Melanesian guerilla camps in Irian Jaya training fighters to combat the Indonesian military power.

26. The many fantasy elements, the reference to ancient myths and other secret commentaries that I collected in 1981 but do not have room to include here confirm this unambiguously. The chthonian womb containing the wealth corresponds notably to the Yafar myth of the origin of game which, kept in a secret underground cavern, was the monopoly of an abusive father who refused his son's filiation: (Juillerat, 1991: chap 1; 1995: 45; 1996: 183–184).

ference—in this case, one will accede directly to the eternally fecund maternal womb, and not simply to her nurturing breast, to her *hoofuk*[27] and not only to her milk. Furthermore, we no longer have here a chain of signifiers (flowers-milk-blood-game), as in the totemic rite; what is sought in the cargo cult is a reality in the image of the fantasy, which avoids the need for the symbol. But at the same time, in both cases, regression has a utilitarian and momentary function, since the mother must be "closed back up" once the gift has been received: tying up the coconut inflorescence or returning to the village after the descent into the maternal "hell" are two modalities of social re-aggregation (in Van Gennep's sense of the word), and in the second case a form of rebirth as well—perhaps even salvation—in a new individual and collective identity. In both cases, the idea of a periodical re-establishment of the "umbilical cord" is necessary for the renewal of the gift, but also for maintaining sufficient physical distance to preserve the psychic separation from the forbidden mother.

Unlike the mother-totem's gift of milk and the father-totem's gift of semen, the gift of total wealth does not come free of charge; one must first give. Not pay in advance some material price, but give of oneself, become good and pure, show bravery in combat, indifference to the charms of the lascivious women who will rise up along the initiation path, take the risk of becoming the victim of the anger of a "terrifying father" who forever banishes those who fail and even conjures up the threat of the end of the world, which my informants described, unbeknown to them, in the imagery of the Book of Revelations.[28] In short, one would have to go through a veritable initiation, the gratification being not, as in initiation rites properly speaking, to renounce the mother for the sake of entering the male community, but here to return to the maternal womb (the men will descend into the Wes "as naked as newborn babes"), to re-emerge cleansed of every stain and forever gratified. Success can be guaranteed only by submitting to the father. All the ingredients for an initiation are present, but the "liminal phase" (Turner) is not only a new gestation, it is the act of the pre-social mother delivering wholesale all of the products of her fecundity, under the control of the father. The only thing she can give, however, is renewable wealth,[29] she can do nothing about a new identity, which can only be vouchsafed by the consenting father. The mother's gifts are first and foremost material things, which partake of having, whereas only submission to the Law guarantees moral and social

---

27. The substance and principle of fertility.

28. The Yafar had not yet been Christianized.

29. The cargo contains things that people know about or have seen, but as an indivisible totality, it is a global hallucinated object. One is reminded of Melanie Klein's thesis (1957) according to which the body of the archaic mother contains every imaginable object (see also Lacan, 1994: 185).

enrichment, which partake of being. That said, once these tests have been passed and absolute abundance is flowing freely into the village itself, it was indeed in terms of an eternal dependence that the Yafar fantacized their radiant future, ultimately forever subject, no longer to the Law, which was merely a preliminary test, but to that state of passive regression from which lack itself would be lacking: a pre-Fall Garden of Eden, endowed with every modern technological device. The guilt of transgression would be redeemed in advance through the tests and particularly the moral appearance before the almighty judge, while the homecoming laden with the signs of election (cargo, military uniforms and guns, paternal blessing, new identity...) would reinstate the geo-psychical distance that safeguards the reintegration into society. After the attempt at a non-mediated return to the mother's breast, we find ourselves steeped in œdipal logic, where total gratification is the result of merit, but where the father is ultimately dismissed. Behind the image of the terrifying father lurks a complicit father who is so weak as to allow the return to the womb. Such seems to have been the unconscious desire of the Yafar at the time. But whoever sets out in search of the total object, finds himself plunged into in total lack.

To Give/to Receive or Not to Receive: The Exchange Contract

The prayer to the coconut tree and the search for the cargo, each in its own way, evokes a state of crisis: a privileged point in the ritual, in the first case, millenarian imagery in the context of historical transition, in the second. I am now going to outline the structure of gift-giving and exchange between the forest spirits and society in the course of Yafar *daily life*. We will see that direct relations with the primordial father and mother gods disappear, replaced by a socialized relationship with the *nabasa* forest spirits, some of which are non-human but most of which are spirits of the deceased. At regular intervals, however, an exception recalls the "petition to the mother": in principle once a year, just before the onset of the rainy season, a specialist from each founding clan performs a secret rite on a hilltop (chthonian gestation) located on his ancestral land; alone or accompanied by an assistant, he thus ensures the *reproduction* of the game animals or, according to the myth, their being loosed into the forest from the maternal-terrestrial womb, represented by a cavern,[30] which no doubt served as a model for the millenarian Wes cult.

---

30. Having been unable to obtain sufficient information on this secret rite, I do not know if the request is addressed directly to the mother or if it appeals to a mediating father figure;

Throughout the year however, relations with the spirit world, whether individual or collective, concern the *nabasa* and them alone. If only the cynegetic rites are considered, these relations take the form of offerings left at the tree-dwelling of one of the spirits of the hunter's lineage land or hung on the mask of a certain *nabasa* during a variety of collective rites, or an offering of food, tobacco and betel to the mediums possessed by a spirit. What people expect of the spirits is not the animals' reproduction, but simply the *gift* of game, which the *nabasa* is supposed to push into the hunter's path. The mother-earth thus brings forth the animals, the secret rites of the founding clans free them from her control, and the *nabasa* make them *visible* to the hunters in the framework of a tacit contract.[31] In addition to gifts, men also exchange words with the spirits, in conversations with entranced mediums and in a particularly convivial collective setting (usually in the evening, after a successful hunt, when the men are gathered on the village grounds).[32] In the case of individuals—including the hunter's close female kin—the *nabasa*'s messages are received in dreams.[33] In this case, the dreamer does not converse with the spirit; he or she merely receives the message and interprets it on waking. The dream-message itself is rarely verbal: rather, it takes the form of a gift. But the dreamed gift is not game,[34] it can be anything (most often food, tobacco, betel, but any other ordinary object, too), which will be interpreted as a *sign* of the spirit's desire to give the dreamer a big animal, in principle the next morning: that is why the favored dreamers go hunting at dawn. These gifts and countergifts do not alternate in a rigorous manner, though, and here, too, as in the prayer to the totemic mother, man still depends on the spirits' good will. Nevertheless, he can improve his chances by gifts of solicitation.

In *Children of the Blood*, I discussed Yafar dreams and the basic rule for their interpretation, which follows a logic of receiving/not receiving. The negative option is every bit as significant as the positive: dreaming about a figure conversing with him without giving anything, or dreaming he has lost

---

whatever the case, it is not addressed to the *nabasa*, and, I was told, it evokes the myth of the birth of game through their escape from the mother-earth's womb (cf. note 26 above).

31. This contract concerns mainly hunting (to which I will restrict my discussion), but extends to the felling of trees for clearing gardens, sickness and healing, or the protection of domestic pigs lost in the forest.

32. Cf. Juillerat, 1975.

33. Anyone encountered in a dream is in principle a *nabasa*, or its female counterpart (*sawangô*). Nevertheless, a dream figure who not only gives nothing but does not speak to the dreamer will be identified as an *ogomô* spirit (chthonian growth spirit) or a ghost (*ifaaf*, as opposed to the spirit of a dead person or *nabasa*). In either case it is a bad omen.

34. Dreaming of killing a wild pig is an omen that someone close will die.

or forgotten something will dissuade the hunter from going out the next day. The prolonged absence of any gift (received) is a sign of rejection or even (at least temporary) abandonment by the *nabasa*, which the hunter will seek to interpret ("What did I do to deserve such treatment?"). Here we recognize the feeling of abandonment and therefore guilt that we identified with the rite to the mother-coconut tree and in the millenarian imagery. Conversely, and in another context, whoever reveals cultural secrets to the anthropologist never fails to announce that now he runs the risk of no longer *seeing* game, the revelation itself carrying a compensation represented by the anthropologist's gratitude and generosity.[35]

It would be apposite here to add a few words on the connection between the logic of the gift in the context of Yafar hunting, on the one hand, and the role of scopic capture in exchange, on the other. Elsewhere, I stressed an analogical relationship between seeing game and then shooting it, and seeing a woman's genitalia (a condition for the arousal of desire according to the Yafar) before having sexual intercourse. In both cases, the sight arouses the desire; in both cases the desire is fulfilled by a phallic act. Scopic capture of the object is thus the condition of its physical appropriation; at the same time, however, one has the impression that it is the object which, *by allowing itself to be seen*, captures the subject's gaze and attention; in the case of the animal, it is in fact the *nabasa* which manifests itself without allowing itself to be seen, for it is seen, in disguise, only in dreams. Conversely, visual relations between humans and spirits take the form of reiterated attempts at (quasi homosexual) seduction on the part of the hunter. The adolescent is introduced, not to hunting proper, but to the cynegetic contract, by minor rites in which the red ochre, the betel juice, the fragrant rhizomes that are rubbed on his body, and the decorations placed on him by his initiator are there so that he may be "seen" and "loved" (two terms that feature in the ritual chants) by the forest spirits.[36] The hunter allows himself to be seen by the *nabasa* without this enabling him to see them, whereas he will see the game they send to him with clearer vision. The experienced hunter also seeks to seduce the *nabasa* by rubbing his body with rhizomes and strong-smelling possum "musk" before going hunting; at the same time this masks the man's natural odor so that he will not frighten the game. The hunter's dog, too, is subjected to rites so that the *nabasa* will notice it and improve its sense of smell. The exchange therefore involves, prior to the material gift, an unequal,

---

35. In this sense the valuable information given the anthropologist is a gift that anticipates a both material and affective countergift. The anthropologist "replaces" the *nabasa*, as it were, by substituting for the latter's game gifts reminiscent in certain respects of the Wes cargo.

36. The initiation songs express the *nabasa*'s thoughts as he catches sight of the young hunter: "as beautiful as a butterfly" or "as a Lorius parrot." Cf. Juillerat, 1978.

Photo 20: A successful pig hunter, Wamuru village (Photo B. Juillerat, 1971).

deferred exchange of gazes, odors and desires. We are dealing with a reshuffling of signifiers arranged in a triangle of spirit-man-game, in which the seduction dialogue, as it were, fans the flame of the gift-exchange. But the hunter also gives food, in addition to giving himself to see (to love), without claiming to harbor similar feelings for the forest spirit, in particular because of its anonymity.[37] Furthermore, the *nabasa* receives little and (may) give much in return, for man is on the side of shortage, subjected to the test of

---

37. The Yafar never speak of their love or their affection for the *nabasa*; rather, they treat them as purveyors of meat, whose favors must be courted and with whom negotiations are carried out in the course of medium seances. The spirits of the dead never take on a personal identity in possession; their original social identity remains of secondary importance.

reality; the spirits are on the side of plenty, governed by the pleasure principle characteristic of the imaginary. This Freudian conceptual opposition is perfectly suited to the psychic mechanism underlying millenarian cults in general. The contrast is even more flagrant in this case because the pleasure principle is connected with the relation to the mother, while the father, by severing this fusional tie, imposes the test of reality (Freud, 1958b). The cynegetic contract is thus based on unequal reciprocity, in which man gives what he can in the hope of receiving much (an areca nut for a wild boar!), a hope which betrays a trace of expectation, the hope of the mother's oblatory gift; for it is she who is the source of the game. Indeed, the Yafar hunter finds himself back in the same situation of uncertainty that governed his nonmediated relation with the totemic mother (the coconut palm), a "relation" elaborated on the very loss of the mother. It is this risk of not receiving — the implicit rupture of the contract by the spirits — which creates the negative, hidden face of the Yafar ideology of the gift. The consistently unlucky hunter describes himself as "blind"[38]; an imaginary "fog" veils the game and shrouds the forest thus breaking the visual exchange between *nabasa* and hunter, and therefore between hunter and game. The empty-handed hunter will ask himself why he is undeserving to receive (from the *nabasa*, but also from the now inaccessible mother), somewhat like the members of the cargo cult who, conscious that man is unworthy, restore themselves to a deculpabilizing state of virginity. All this brings us back to the prototypical relation to the breast in Yangis, where, to the men standing with closed eyes under the totemic flowers showering down on them, corresponds, in the finale of the public part of the ceremony, first the visual then the phallic capture of the breast-sun (an identification attested by the Yangis myth) on which the *ifegê* fix their gaze while uttering the word *tot* ("breast") and then shooting their arrow.

In *Children of the Blood*, I showed the extent to which hunting in Yafar culture was marked by secrecy and in a certain fashion regarded as sacred. The hunter leaves the village without being seen if possible, no one speaks to him nor does anyone comment on his success when he returns with a possum carefully wrapped in leaves; when a pig or a cassowary has been killed, the hunter or hunters keep the secret (the women in particular must know nothing about it) until it is cut up and shared out. For the time required to

---

38. In the context of hunting, he will also use the specific term, *mabiyik*, which can be translated as "unsuccessful in hunting": *kam mabiyik feg*, lit. "to me/*mabiyik*/it does," where the impersonal verb *feg* (like the English *does*) and the (implicit) neuter grammatical subject clearly express the hunter's passive situation as victim of an action the doer of which is not clearly identified. The notion of "fog" refers not only to visual obstruction, but also to the idea of *roofuk*, in other words to the "skin" which acts as both protection for the regeneration of the *hoofuk* (fecundity/fertility) and an obstacle to its access.

integrate the game-gift into the social network, the gift is denied, just as the newborn child is denied until it is introduced into the family (see below).

The quest for the object is based on lack, and its phallic capture at the same time partakes of orality. Yet it is one thing to receive a gift and another to consume it. Nearly all hunting societies forbid consuming the product of one's own hunt. The young Yafar man consumes nothing of the first ten or fifteen pigs and other game he kills, and abstains for life when it comes to cassowary. Violating this prohibition would, here too, make him go "blind" and would break the contract with the spirits. Elsewhere I analyzed the identificatory reasons (mediation of the hunter's arrow and sexualization of the act of shooting) which can be associated with this prohibition.[39] Since the animal given by the *nabasa* comes in fact from the mother, the prohibition must also have something to do with keeping her at a distance, so as to avoid any misuse of fertility. But might there not also be, in the social elaboration of the representation, an ostentatious but non-agonistic way of winning prestige in the eyes of those who, as non-recipients of the gift, will consume it? "To be in the *hoofuk*," in other words to have access to the source of abundance, means more to receive game than to eat it. To receive from nature-mother or her representatives, the *nabasa*, enables a man to show generosity to others and them to show gratitude.[40] The gift is no sooner received than it is, not given back, but redistributed within the community, in other words it is socialized, just as the "milk" arbitrarily dispensed from the maternal coconut palm is shared in the totemic meal. If he loses the spirits' trust, the unfruitful hunter at the same time loses that of the group; if he is fulfilled, it is by abstaining from consuming the game he has hunted that he ensures that both the gift and the social recognition will be renewed. The Yafar hunter's gratification has two sides, and he himself becomes an intermediary between the *nabasa* and the group, yet another link in the chain running from the primordial mother to the consumer.

But failure to receive does not always result from a dysfunction of the three-party contract. A fourth element may enter in: I mean the desire to do harm on the part of some member of the society. This is an individual act of evil (called *mwaywey*) consisting, through the use of magical plants carrying the signifier "closure" and through explicit spells, in "covering" the forest animals and the victim's eyes with "fog." Having been "blinded," the

---

39. Similar prohibitions apply to the fruits forbidden to the person who planted the tree and who gives the future harvest to a close relative in his own generation or the one following.

40. Potlatch societies and those with competitive exchanges have taught us the extent to which social prestige can be acquired through generosity or even abnegation.

latter becomes impotent as a hunter, "castrated;"[41] all he now has to rely on (like the non-initiated pre-contractual individual he used to be) is his luck. When, despite gifts and rites, the entire local community continues to consider itself abandoned by the spirits, the men can exceptionally avenge themselves by banishing them for a time: the magical plants normally used to communicate with the spirits (and which, according to one myth, humans received from them) are burned at the foot of their tree dwellings. After a lapse of time during which hunting is neglected, since it has become only a matter of chance, the men can decide to recall the *nabasa* by means of a ritual inviting them back to the village through medium possession.

In exchange with the gods and the spirits, the Other is introjected (constructed by the subject); this is what makes it possible to represent exchange situations not produced in social life. In the light of the above, let us now see what can be said about exchange within the society.

To Exchange/Not to Exchange Between Humans

Rupture of the cynegetic contract, the unlucky hunter's feelings of abandonment, the attributions of sorcery that may arise from it, but also the preference for marriage by direct "sister" exchange and the fact that a lapse of time between the gift and countergift of a woman is tolerated only among kin, the absence of agonistic exchanges between individuals and groups, asking the anthropologist on-the-spot payment for any food given, all point to a fear of deferred reciprocation insofar as it may generate conflict. To put off reciprocating is regarded as a "bad custom" by the Yafar; always paying off all debts, alternatively, is a guarantee of social peace. Debt or unequal allotment of food is a source of not only economic but also social frustration, and therefore of revenge; most attributions of lethal sorcery (*aysiri*) follow the death of a person who had "forgotten" some relative in a distribution of meat and consequently implicate the victim of the omission. For the Yafar, the ideal society is one in which no one owes anyone anything, and where the social bond is founded on convivial sharing.

The only acceptable delay between gift and countergift is when, inevitably, time must be allowed for a transformation before it is possible to reciprocate. This is the case notably of the haunches of pork that must be given the mother's brother in return for the maternal care received by the hunter as a child. These can be seen as payment for the milk in the shape of the "meat" into which the totemic coconut "milk" has been transmuted. I have often recalled the Yafar saying: "the mother's brother is the breast." The

---

41. As a cancellation of the scopic instinct, blindness refers us back to the fear of castration.

redirection of the countergift from the mother to the uncle confirms that the mother cannot be the direct recipient; that would void the gratuitous nature of her gift and block the social extension of the exchange.[42] However, the mother is allowed to receive a portion of the meat through her brother. The mother's brother/sister's son relation here results from a shift of the mother/son relationship towards the social sphere. The order of filiation has in Yafar culture symbolic primacy over that of alliance; the notions of wife-givers and wife-takers remain vague, never explicitly stated, since the modest matrimonial gifts and countergifts (which do not constitute "bridewealth") quickly balance out, even in the event of a unilateral marriage (always the case among kin or co-residents). Nevertheless, marriage by direct exchange (Thurnwald's "a woman for a woman") cannot be compared to a death for a death or an exchange of identical items, since what is given or exchanged in marriage is the woman's *future* fecundity. The symmetry of marriage by direct exchange is therefore only momentary; it must subsequently be confirmed by the birth of the children of the two couples and the stability of their unions. As a consequence, one would expect a system of compensations that would secure the symmetry of the exchange at the birth of the first child or at the death of a spouse or a child; more generally, one would also expect, as happens in other patrilineal societies in New Guinea, a gift to the mother's people on the occasion of birth or death, or an active claim on the part of the maternals on a sister's child. But there is nothing of the like: instead, among the Yafar such occasions are characterized by a total absence of exchange, by the uselessness (if not the prohibition) of gifts of any kind.

What accounts for this apparent paradox? There are two explanations: one sociological, the other symbolic. The first, mentioned above, has to do with the fact that the ideology of exchange predicated on debt-avoidance entails a weakening of the opposition between wife-givers and wife-takers as well as between paternal and maternal sides. On the other hand, it seems to me that the symbolic explanation resides in the fact that Yafar culture regards the main biological processes as not being amenable to socialization. This is the case more particularly of sexuality—sexual relations are relegated to the forest, and the inaugural rite for the new couple's first intercourse identifies the woman or the yet-to-be conceived child with game—but also of death and of sickness when the latter heralds the approach of the end. The prolonged separation of the newly delivered woman and her

---

42. That is no doubt what made Lévi-Strauss say, in reply to André Green, that he did not need the mother/child relationship to explain collective behaviors (Green, 1977; Tahon, 1995; Juillerat, 2001). From a strictly sociological standpoint, the maternal function is in reality the "blind spot" that articulates all exchanges. The sister becomes a wife, the wife, a mother: only then can the system reproduce itself.

child, their contaminating nature, the physical distance maintained between the child and its father in the first months, the banishing of the sick person to the forest to die, the almost total absence of funeral rites, all indicate that phenomena not subject to human control are socially repressed. This apparent indifference, which ill conceals a major anxiety, takes the more specific form of silence and secrecy: one does not talk about a woman's pregnancy, one does not mention the new mother or the child during their isolation, the father goes about his usual activities without a word and is never questioned. Young people betrothed in an arranged marriage ignore each other and formally deny the betrothal when asked about their future spouse; the bride's change of residence is not marked by any rite or public ceremony and is carried out on the sly. Someone who is sick, especially when their physical appearance (weight loss, dehydration) associates them with *roofuk* (sterile skin, sheath, corpse...), hides away and does not receive any visits, and no one inquires about their health. Finally, the dead are promptly removed to an abandoned garden where they are laid[43] and where a few members of the family, away from the rest of the community, keep a fire burning for the five days of discreet mourning; no object circulates between the families at this time; people avoid speaking of the deceased in the village and, generally speaking, the dead are not commemorated. The *nabasa* are the spirits of the deceased fathers and ancestors, but they are anonymous; the spirit "riding" the medium does not introduce itself, with the exception of the first time, when it is supposed to reveal the site of its forest dwelling where it will thereafter receive the food-gifts left by its relatives.

Where there is no exchange of words, how could there be an exchange of goods? Where the birth of a child is initially seen as something to be "ashamed" of, where its very name (assuming it has already received one) goes unspoken and where people feign ignorance of its sex, how could there be a place for gift-giving? One might suppose that gifts appear once the prohibitions have been surmounted, once the child is taken into the community, at the close of the mourning period and so on. In reality, after these liminal periods, normal social life resumes as discreetly as possible, not marked in any particular way: if the liminal phase is blocked out, the moment of reinsertion will be as well. In all events, it is the symbolic weight of natural fecundity, of the cycle of life and death, which impedes their social processing.[44] The society therefore decides not to know, not to see, and waits for it to pass.

---

43. The body wrapped in a sheath of blackpalm is suspended beneath a tree or buried in the ground.

44. The absence of initiation rites among the Yafar and their neighbors could be explained by the same incapacity to socially integrate the renunciation of the mother and the splitting

Mother's Gift, Father's Gift

In the above examples, the desired gift is imaginarily expected to come from the divine parental couple and, in the last instance, from the mother. In this case the father is absent when the desired object is symbolized by that which every mother, by her very nature, gives (her milk) without the father's law interposing itself (the rite to the coconut palm); alternatively, the gift is mediated by prohibiting father figures when it is not symbolized by the mother's milk or her love, but by the fecundity of the womb, which belongs to the father (the cargo cult). It is clear that, when the men pray to the totemic coconut tree to receive the primordial mother's milk in the form of flowers, these are merely the desired sign that the broken tie is restored and that the mother-earth consents to bring forth game; similarly, the object received from a stranger in a dream is the sign that the spirit wants to give the dreamer a wild pig in exchange. Inasmuch as the breast is the first object cathected in the course of ontogenetic development, it represents the missing object, an indelible loss: "The object of œdipal desire is an object lost forever, and not simply one that is unattainable for external reasons, on the one hand, and for super-egoistic reasons, on the other, but also for reasons of inadequacy to the object of desire due to the discrepancy between somatic and psychic maturity" (Luquet-Parat, quoted by Green, 1995: 78). Furthermore, the breast is not only the symbol of the source of food or the satisfaction of hunger. Freud (1953b) with his notion of anaclisis, showed that hunger strictly speaking gives rise to the pleasure of suckling, as a libidinal satisfaction. André Green on the other hand relegates developmental phases to the background, and instead sees the interest of the theory of the breast as prototype in the fact that "orality is what provides all instincts with their appetitivity and their objectal quest," thus placing it "at the heart of sexuality" (1995: 31). But this is all quite alien to our hunters' appetite and duty of hospitality. It must not be forgotten that the human mother feeds her child more from love than from instinct, and that what the words of the rite express are indeed maternal love, or its lack ("To be in Mother's netbag"/"To be abandoned by Mother"). It is therefore the mother as a person, both loving and all powerful (able to give or not give), that we glimpse in the rite more than the breast as pre-œdipal part-object. And yet the relation as structured in the prayer to the coconut palm remains typically pre-œdipal. It is useful here to distinguish between the breast as object of satisfaction and the breast as gift-object (Lacan, 1994: 68). If we are clearly dealing with the order of orality and loss here, the nostalgia pervading the

---

of the procreating and socializing parental imagos which Yangis, a symbolic initiation played out as a ritual drama, expresses in its esoteric language.

prayer to the totemic mother does not refer back specifically to archaic hunger or libidinal satisfaction, but to the lost relation in its entirety and more specifically to the all-encompassing character of its affective dimension. We have gone from the (outgrown) drive to the (perpetuated) affect, since the first with respect to the breast-object is no longer appropriate in the adult. The symbol of the lost object can do no more than rekindle emotions, which have been transformed but which had been attached to the breast and refer back to the all-powerful mother. This remembering nevertheless comes at a cost, which is the simultaneous establishment of a renewed dependence. Evidence of such affective residues is clear in the emphasis placed in the rite on the ambivalent good mother/bad mother (presence/absence), that is on the simultaneous maintenance of desire and lack which characterizes all love-relations.[45] In this case the function of the rite is to place at the service of an immediate need (hunting) the fictive restitution of a basic affective tie associated with a vanished oral drive.[46]

The same is not true of the quest for cargo. In this case, the fantasy is given more rein, since it goes as far as to lend credibility to a chthonian womb that produces every kind of wealth, especially that which cult-followers never possessed but which millenarian mythology raises to the rank of lost-object-to-be-recovered. A shift occurs here from the reactivation of the sentiment of having lost a former real object (the breast) to the activation of the lack of a fantacized object whose arrival is projected into the future. The mother is still a central figure, but she is no longer men's "interlocutrix": she has become merely the stake of the negotiations now undertaken with the father alone. The move from the dual register of the prayer to the coconut palm to the ternary register of the millenarian cult transforms the quest for cargo into a typically œdipal fantasmagoria, in which the stake is no longer the mother's love but the total gift, the hallucination of which arises from her cosmic fecundity, on the one hand, and from recognition by the father, on the other. The maternal womb (the Wes cavern) brings forth every kind of wealth, but the act of giving will come from the father, just as the game brought forth by the mother-earth is given the hunter by the *nabasa*.[47] And yet this father-with-the-many-faces is not given as the procreator of the cargo or the game but rather as the giver of

---

45. See Luquet-Parat quoted by Green, 1995: 77.

46. Historically speaking, it is probable that the rite arose from this breakthrough of the repressed material associated with immediate economic needs, but that later it was the instituted rite that gave rise (to a different extent depending on the individuals) to the same breakthrough of the affects.

47. Except that in the first case, the imaginary and not socialized negotiation takes place in a particularly conflictual psychic climate, whereas with the *nabasa* the "bargaining," which is part and parcel of daily relations, is good natured and without risk.

laws, the absolute master of the parthenogenetic product of the mother-earth. It has already been said that the inexhaustible store of riches found in the Wes is supposed to have been diverted by the European conquerors for their own use, to the detriment of the Melanesians, whose ancestors are supposed to have been the sole manufacturers of this wealth. During the active phase of the cult, the primordial *hoofuk* was located in Melanesia, and not in alleged "factories"[48] in Europe. White people are identified not so much with the bad father in the myth of the origin of game and the jealous custodian of the mother's fecundity[49] as with a false father, an impostor. Thus negotiation is possible only with the former reinstated in his legitimate position. The demand for unconditional filial submission, the state of physical and moral purity come from the superego, for the real negotiation is intrapsychic and takes place between an adult male community endowed with reason—but living a crucial moment of their history—and their projected, reactivated œdipal imagos.

When we switch from these moments of "crisis" and symbolic re-elaboration to the everyday relation described above between hunters and spirits of the dead (*nabasa*), we see an implicit renunciation of total wealth and a return to game as a reality-object: desire flows back once again, as it were, into the mold of need. While the image of the all-powerful chthonian mother fades away, the father's symbolic authority is weakened to the same extent, as is the severity of the superego (as the introjected father's law); the totalitarian figures of the Wes thus give way to the spirits of those who have recently died, figures of socialized ancestrality, in other words reduced to human proportions. Although they refer back to generations past, the *nabasa* look more like peers, almost otherworldly comrades with whom speech and exchange are liberated on both sides. We even see a hierarchical inversion in the sense that the man in charge of the worship of a *nabasa* living on his lands refers to himself as its "father" (*awaag*), meaning in this case someone who is responsible for the cult or is its celebrant. Here we have an œdipal structure that is no longer "in crisis," but which has become instituted; or at least when all goes well, in other words when the contractual relationship between hunters and forest spirits is sufficiently well balanced. This is not the case when the hunter or the men of a local group declare themselves "blind." Such a fate is usually accepted with passivity and a certain fatalism, even though individual magical rites are available for trying to remedy the sit-

---

48. The notion of *pabrik* (an Indonesian term translating the Dutch *fabriek*) was not used by the Yafar, but it has become a key word in the cargo cults recently reactivated in Irian Jaya by the local political situation (Giay and Godschalk, 1993).

49. According to the myth cited: above note 26.

uation.[50] People say that "cynegetic blindness" is experienced as a punishment inflicted by the spirits themselves or as the result of an intentional human act. In the first case, the unlucky hunter feels guilty, in the second, he is simply a victim. The notion of guilt brings us back to the crisis and, eventually, to the œdipal triangle and the demands of the superego, whereas self-victimization can, in some cases, reactivate a paranoid defense which can result in social conflict. The *nabasa*'s punishment may be a response to abusive hunting, to the violation of a secret connected with the esoteric representations concerning fertility, or again to the felling of a tree inhabited by a powerful spirit (although in this case, the usual sanction is a non-fatal illness). The forest spirit thus intervenes as a paternal agent, putting an end to the dangerous proximity with the primordial *hoofuk* by castrating the guilty hunter both of the mother and of his own cynegetic potency, the sexual connotations of which no longer need demonstrating. Then the forest vanishes into the "fog," the hunter's vision grows dim, the hunter himself is no longer visible to the *nabasa*, his dog's sense of smell is dulled, his arrow is useless... All he can do is wait, and then seek to win back the *nabasa*'s love. But if a Yangis rite is in preparation, the hunter will not fail to bow his head and stretch his cupped hands towards the milky inflorescence of the totemic coconut palm.

The Yafar economy has two staple foods which are complementary: one, sago, is abundant; the other, game, is in short supply. Eaten together, they constitute the ideal dish. The first, symbol of male semen, is (normally) produced and shared out primarily by women; alternatively, the hunting of a product brought forth by the mother-earth is reserved exclusively for men. Whereas the ritual hunt in the Yangis cult opens with the search for the breast, sago production is inaugurated by the symbolic tapping of the ancestral semen. Father and mother here contribute separately, but are united in the exchange in which the father figures appear and regulate the asymmetrical dual relationship between men and the primordial mother. The breast has become the sign-object of nature-mother's free gift of food. But its status as prototypical object and, more generally, the founding function of the maternal bond will serve as a sign for other gifts better suited to adult needs, whose uterine origin will have to be mediated. The father thus appears as the *mediating pole, initiator of exchange* in the non-exchanging relation with the mother, which thereby fades away. As A. Petitat notes: "The unilateral gift can be said to be the symbolic operator of exchanges because, with its extravagance, it founds the properly human imaginary space of exchange" (1995: 26).

---

50. That is, not by calling upon the spirits but by formulating something using signifiers organized according to the principles of analogy or opposition.

"Everything comes from the mother," the Yafar say. In this cosmological vision, the mother is no longer, as she was in the prayer to the coconut
palm, "my mother": she is fantacized as the incarnation of the cosmicized
female capacity to produce all of the things of which the world is made,
things that only the father god will be capable of organizing in space. The
father is not given as the procreator of the world but as the one who builds
it out of the mother's body-parts. And when we turn to the millenarian
imagery, the natural world acquires the machines and the wealth of the
White world brought home to the primordial womb and thus naturalized.
The loving mother who gives for nothing has become a sort of monster capable of producing everything but whose willingness to give is subjected to
the law of the father, who imposes himself as the sole interlocutor in the
exchange he inaugurates. He becomes a father by setting his law between
humans and the world that arose from the dismembered body of the mother (according to the cosmogonic myth). While relativized by the possibility
of negotiating, the prohibition on returning to the womb, in the millenarian cult, makes it clear that the primordial womb is also a place where all
transgressors will be annihilated. Furthermore, the Wes also contains the
deceased whom the cult is supposed to restore to life. This calls to mind
Freud's "Theme of the Three Caskets" in which he reminds us that death
is a return to the mother-earth, in other words to the prenatal fusional state,
before the dual relation with the nurturing mother: a return without the
father, it must be added. Or a return negotiated with the father, in the case
of the cargo cult, or a return instigated by the father as punishment for incest
(filicide).[51] In these circumstances, it is not surprising that death, like
birth, is the object of social denial.

The foregoing remarks on Yafar gift-exchange deal with only one specific register: that of relations between humans, and the spirits and gods,
in other words between the individual and his/her own unconscious, whose
representations projected into the outside world become the objects man
desires or to which he forbids access. These symbolic exchanges can be
regarded as part and parcel of what Mauss calls "total service or total prestations."

Although at the time, Mauss' essay, *The Gift*, focused on phenomena
that had not yet caught the interest of anthropology, it must be recognized
that today its value is essentially historical, that of a ground-breaking work,
but which can no longer be considered an obligatory reference, in spite of
the well-deserved homages it continues to receive. In the light of the ethnographic knowledge and theoretical reflection produced in recent years, I
believe I am justified in addressing two critical remarks to his essay, inde-

---

51. See note 26.

pendently of the fact (which aroused Lévi-Strauss' interest in 1950) that Mauss never returned to his plan to develop his analysis of the gift, whose deficiencies he himself pointed out. As I announced at the beginning of this article, my reservation bears not only on the forms of gift-giving that may have been "forgotten" by Mauss, but also on his essentially juridical approach as well as on his omission of the negative dimension, which is of capital sociological and psychical importance. We saw that, behind need lurk both desire and seduction; and that desire itself is grounded in the loss of the loved object, which engenders nostalgia (a brief reminder of a never totally resorbed bereavement); that the feeling of abandonment gives rise to the fear of castration and to guilt; that the object lost and sought again and again is part of the fantacized relation to the Other, more specifically to the split parental imagos restored in the dynamic of the œdipal structure, as well as in the variable reactivation of the superego as an agent of prohibition or moderation...The signifiers in the ritual call up repressed material even as they disguise it, economic necessity attracts forgotten affects that the rite brings to life in a transitional space-time where gift-giving and exchange are carried out between the imaginary and reality. Alternatively, the rite as a liminal phase opens onto the re-aggregation and the assumption of the reality principal by the production of food and the organization of society.

Finally, the example of Yafar gift-exchange and its religious forms, together with the unconscious representations and psychical mechanisms to which it refers us, prompt me to propose, first of all, that we should pursue the unshackling of gift-giving from exchange, to which Lévi-Strauss' theory bound it,[52] and, secondly, that we should also liberate it from an exclusively sociological analysis.

Translated by Nora Scott

---

52. See also Godbout, 1992.

Chapter 7

To Help and To "Hold"

Forms of Cooperation Among the Sulka, New Britain*

Monique Jeudy-Ballini

The Sulka people, who live in the eastern part of New Britain (Papua New Guinea), are split into three main geographical groups. Sometimes attributed to the need to escape murderous enemy raids, sometimes blamed on forced recruitment of labor for colonial plantations, according to today's Sulka, this late nineteenth-century division continues to exist. While the bulk of the population still lives in the original territory, along the Wide Bay coast, south of Gazelle Peninsula, most of the remainder fanned out over the northeastern part of the peninsula, in the Mope and Lat regions.

The strong cultural homogeneity between these groups living some two-day's walk from each other can no doubt be explained by the constant stream of visits back and forth. While a simple penchant for mobility—a taste for tourism as it were—is a non-negligible aspect of Sulka sociology, it seems that the frequency of these trips is linked primarily with the vitality of the ceremonial exchanges conducted within these communities. The necessity for any protagonist of an exchange to appeal to others for material support in assembling the requisite quantity of goods to put into circulation, the diversified origin of this support, and its often

* Revised version of "Les Formes de la coopération chez les Sulka de Nouvelle-Bretagne," *Anthropologie et sociétés* 19 (1–2), Université de Laval, Québec 1995: 207–28.The ethnographic material presented in this article was gathered over the course of four stays with the Sulka, between 1980 and 1994, with the financial support of the French Centre National de la Recherche Scientifique.

obligatory character are, for any ceremony touching on the life of a group member, all factors contributing to a general participation.

In many villages in the Mope, Lat or Wide Bay areas, the presence of individuals from a distant location is often justified by the fact that they have come to help prepare a ritual. The length of these preparations, which can go on for years, would suggest—insofar as the distinction has any meaning for the Sulka—that daily activities are no more than a pause in the continuum of ceremonial activities.

However this may be, because of the need for identity that it satisfies in the separated communities, cooperation provides a vehicle for important social issues. The present paper describes the forms taken by this cooperation and the ways it is accomplished. Although it has often been treated in the ethnographic literature on New Guinea societies (e.g., reviews by Feil, 1987 and Lemonnier, 1990), the ever-problematic question of the nature of the groups involved in exchanges will be addressed once more here. In the course of this analysis, I will explain the conditions which not only enable the protagonists to assemble the requisite quantities of goods they will give, but also authorize the very movement of these goods. For the main threat hanging over a Sulka ceremonial exchange seems to be not so much the shortage of resources as the presence of an impediment that would immobilize the gift circuit. In effect, this circulation does not function automatically, and, as we will see, ensuring that these goods are able to change hands calls for the same kind of know-how that exchange partners need for managing the assistance they receive.

"Following Roads"

The aid a person may give or receive in view of a feast is of two specific kinds and depends on the type of social relationship activated between the giver and the receiver. It is the nature of the connection linking the two which defines, and opposes in terms of value, a durable form of assistance called *mokpom* and a more temporary form of help called *turang*. Depending on the circumstances, and according to the availabilities and strategies of the moment, a person can request or provide one type of support or the other. Although their material content is generally the same, the underlying social presuppositions and implications are very different.

The obligation of solidarity which dictates that several individuals see themselves as being bound up with each other is called *mokpom*. This obligation, actualized at the time of the ceremonies, consists in cooperating in the preparations by providing a share of the tubers, pigs, valuables (shell money) and national currency that will circulate in the exchanges.

Photo 21: Sulka women dancing near a pile of food to be exchanged during a wedding ceremony (Photo M. Jeudy-Ballini, 1988).

Those who are thus duty-bound to lend their support in preparing a ceremony are called "spears" (*mus*) or are designated as the "army," "fighting group" (*humevek*). They are said to stand "behind" the person they help, but they are also his "shield."

In many ways reminiscent of what Panoff (1976) wrote concerning the *galiau* institution of the Sulka's near neighbors, the Maenge (Mengen), the "armies" thus mobilized, which number between five and fifteen individuals, are never defined as corporate groups. They are more like networks which form for the duration of the ceremony and then dissolve to form again with variations around the man known as the "father of the feast" (*a pnes ka tet*), to whom it next falls to organize a ceremony.

The vernacular term *mokpom* is a reflexive verb meaning literally "to hold," "to have a hold on each other" or "to hold hands." The notion is approximated in Pidgin by circumlocutions evoking the idea of solidarity and mutual assistance. Some English-speaking Sulka translate *mokpom* as "relationship," without further qualification, a word which does not refer directly to these concepts.

Even if the help extended in preparing a celebration can be seen as a way of paying back help received at an earlier time, neither the support nor the act motivated by the duty to reciprocate, according to the Sulka, adequately describes the *mokpom* relationship. It is defined first of all by its enduring character, by which it suggests transmission, and by its continuity or in local parlance, the "road." Although the Sulka have a matrilineal descent system, such a road can be transmitted by either the father or the mother.

The Sulka say that, in contrast to the *mokpom* relationship, all *turang* help exchanged between people who have no inherited duty of mutual assistance creates a creditor-debtor relationship.

> *Mokpom* means to follow your mother and to follow your father. Suppose you want to follow a new road, that now means debt. Whoever helps you or you help, your mother and your father don't know him. You both are doing as you desire, like a new road. Suppose he helps you with a pig, you know he isn't working at the *mokpom* custom; you need to know that this pig is now your debt. When he gives a feast he will ask you for it, and you will have to give it back right away. You won't even be able to wait until the feast; you will have to give it back before, whenever he wants it. (Matthew Magil, Milim village 1988)

> Everything has to have a beginning...Father's road, mother's road, everything must follow. All we do is follow roads...*Turang* is different: you help somebody, that's your desire or his desire, if he asked [your help]. Helping is only your own desire or his desire. But *mokpom* isn't that. It's following the road, the ancestor's road... *turang* help has an end, it always has an end. If somebody helps me, then I help him and it's finished. Suppose I don't help him, he can get mad and say: "You give me back that thing." And I must give it back. Afterwards he will forget me and I will forget him, too. And it will be finished. *Mokpom* is different. Everything goes to die. Nobody can ask me for anything: If I can, I help; if I can't, nobody can say anything, I will help another time. Nobody can get cross because that, *mokpom*, is made to go on for ever and ever. (John Sakle, Ploresel village, 1988)

The commentaries present *turang* help as something like a "loan" or "credit," *a tol*. The help given is assimilated to a debt or to repayment of a debt. From this standpoint, *turang* seems so devoid of any social content that it looks suspiciously un-Sulka.

> Today people follow their desire, but it is the desire of the Whites. The Whites came and they wanted to bind us together. "Friends" is their idea, not our ancestors' idea. Before, there were no "friends." The ancestors followed the straight road. Somebody couldn't ask somebody else to help him with pigs or food. He had to follow the road.

Suppose somebody doesn't follow the road, then afterwards it is like a debt.[1] (John Sakle, Ploresel village 1988)

When contrasting the two kinds of cooperation, the Sulka constantly stress the fact that, in one case (*turang*), the help is expressly requested, while in the other case (*mokpom*), it must be offered spontaneously as soon as the news of an upcoming feast runs through the villages. The usual phrasing of the commentaries opposes those who request help to those who "come" to help without being asked, and who, literally "do according to their knowledge" (*a papat*, "knowledge-thought-memory," in Sulka), who "go of their own accord to stand with/to hold [the "father of the feast"] for his work."

"Fighting" and "Going to Die"

Every Sulka ceremonial exchange has two categories of gifts, both of the same kind. One requires simultaneous identical countergifts, unlike the other, which is given with nothing expected in return. Identical balanced prestations are said "to confront each other," to "combat each other," to "fight" (*momgu* or *momhu*), from a term commonly used for any physical confrontation, between two men or two dogs, for example. In the context of the exchanges carried out at marriage or mourning ceremonies, the goods which "fight" are termed "hot" (*kopet*), as opposed to "cold" (*roro*) goods, which are not reciprocated and which are said to "go to die" with the one who receives them. "To go to die" (*ta mek iur*) describes the movement of the gifts presented as marriage or funeral (*kek*) payments. The sum of pigs, tubers and monies comprising this "payment" therefore do not "fight" with any other analogous set of gifts.

To say that the prestations provided in the context of *mokpom* cooperation "go to die" with the person one helps means that the assistance provided is not motivated by any expectation of a return. "Holding" each other (*mokpom*) would thus define a relationship actualized by contributions seen less as help that would "fight" with reciprocal help than as a "payment," in its local sense of a one-way contribution. The *mokpom* relationship recognized between individuals is in sum the "road" that connects all "payments": the "payments" honored by the ascendants and those taken over by their successors. "To pay," *srim*, or as the Sulka would say, "to

---

1. This way of looking at things is strikingly different from what is said about the role of "friendship" in cooperation among the Chimbu, the Melpa, the Enga or the Mendi of New Guinea, for example (see Feil, 1987: 260–61).

correct," "to rectify," does not "pay off" anything: it does not cancel the support received on the occasion of a previous ceremony or discharge the obligation to "pay" again if the preparation of another ritual demands it.

Conversely, in the context of *turang* help, aid on request implies compensation on demand, compensation in identical terms, which brings the relationship to a close. The assistance in this case comes down to a finalized act, entirely directed to its own end, which is equilibrium, the fulfillment of reciprocity; in a sense, "forgetting" the very act. Repaying the help one has received allows one to forget it afterwards, and to act as though nothing had happened. A relationship of the *turang* type avoids being caught up for life, being "held" forever and makes it possible to owe nothing to anyone. "*Turang* help has an end, it always has an end", one of my informants observed.

If such a connection between creditor and debtor is the opposite of the *mokpom* relationship, as the Sulka commentaries stress, it is because *mokpom* solidarity transcends the mechanical application of the rules of reciprocity, thereby excluding the possibility of squaring any debt, of freeing oneself of the obligation to pay back—of returning help received or even merely anticipated. In a way, because it is said to be inherited, and because inheritance always places the living in the debt of the dead, the *mokpom* bond can be interpreted for those who "hold" each other as the mutual recognition of a common debt, but one that is ongoing, indelible, which accounts for their solidarity as well as for the fact that this debt is never "paid off." While there is always an end to *turang* help, the *mokpom* relationship, in which the prestations provided are supposed to "go to die," is a lasting one. Furthermore, the fact that the aid "goes to die" can by no means be understood as an ending.

There is nothing obligatory about *turang* assistance, the Sulka say, since all it does is "follow a person's desire." Once given, however, it must be counterbalanced, or it may give rise to recriminations and disputes. In the *mokpom* relationship, on the other hand, the fact that one is not supposed to ask for help avoids the risk of open refusal, in other words a response that might jeopardize the relationship. To obtain nothing when one has asked for nothing does not endanger the relationship, or at least not as much as not obtaining what one has expressly requested. The absence of a request leaves the relationship intact. The fact that the bond is not actualized does not mean that it is broken; a non-actualized helping relationship is not dead or void, it is simply on standby, waiting to be activated. The absence of an expressed request is thus linked with the lasting quality attributed to the *mokpom* relationship—"made to go on forever," one man said—as though everything must be done to ensure it could not be said to have ended.

This principle of cooperation, which anticipates and includes the possibility it will not be applied, "euphemizes," as it were, its failures by voiding them of any negative social significance. On the contrary, it tends to optimize the social import of any assistance by classifying it as a non-obligatory act, a gift freely given, a manifestation of pure solidarity.

In the *mokpom* relationship, help given on the occasion of a celebration is something like a transfer of rights. When one gives tubers or pigs to a person in charge of a ritual, one puts at his disposal that upon which "his name is [thereafter] placed." From the moment a man establishes himself as "father of the feast," he becomes, within his own *mokpom* network, "father" of the pigs he has not raised, "father" of the gardens he has not cultivated, "father" of everything that has no way of circulating other than by taking the "road" that now runs through him.[2] Insofar as they themselves do not have the responsibility of a ceremony in the same period, those who have raised these pigs and grown these tubers are no longer free to dispose of them as they wish. The *mokpom* bond dictates that they owe these goods to the man among them who now has his "name on them," as though the ritual created a "paternity" which temporarily transcends all others. Still, conflicts of loyalties sometimes arise which, as we shall see, justify failure to cooperate.

Group Composition

It is said of the *mokpom* relationship that it "follows two roads," the father's road" and "the mother's road." For a given Ego, following these roads means recognizing one's duty to help the people (and the descendants of the people) with whom one's father and one's mother commonly cooperated. There would be members of their clans and of their matrimonial moieties, but also members of their father's clan and members of the clans of the men who in previous generations married into Ego's clan.[3] The "roads" in question bring into virtual relation representatives of all the groups that make up Sulka society. A diversity of relationships thus intersects within the *mokpom* relationship, none of which, in isolation, is a decisive criterion of belonging since people "holding" each other are consanguines as well

---

2. Among the Sulka, anyone who grows plants or raises animals is considered to entertain a relationship of nominal paternity or maternity with what he or she cares for. Depending on the person's sex, people will speak of the poultry's, pigs' or tubers' "father" or "mother," for instance.

3. The clan of the men who have married women from the other clan is said to be related as "father" to the latter. Panoff (1976) describes a similar relationship also implying a duty of solidarity among the Mengen. In this respect, the question of the "operational" meaning that can be assigned to the notion of matriliny, raised by Panoff in the Mengen case, similarly arises with regard to the Sulka material.

as affines, members of the same clan as well as members of opposite moieties, co-residents as well as members of far-flung villages. From this strict point of view, there are no specific features which distinguish those bound together in the *mokpom* relationship from those on the outside, and at the same time, it seems that the parents, children, siblings, cousins or affines who "hold" each other could just as easily be bound up with others.

The "armies" mustered on the basis of a *mokpom* relationship are not corporate groups and have no visible existence outside ceremonial occasions. The members are geographically dispersed and have no shared activity, even if those living in close proximity occasionally help each other in building a house or making a new garden. This dispersion—but also the relative flexibility—of their functioning accounts for the difficulty of circumscribing these "armies." At the time of the festivities, those who have lent aid are never all present in person. Furthermore, the contributions that flow in to the "father of the feast" often represent only a fraction of what could have been assembled had all those who "hold" each other been mobilized. There is in effect nothing automatic about *mokpom* support, since from one ceremony to the next it may not be given or be given by different people. The "armies" in question are thus not monolithic blocs, as is indicated by another observation which I will now discuss: the constant overlapping between the *mokpom* relationship and other relationships of the same or of different kind.

For those bound together in *mokpom*, the fact that they "hold" each other does not exclude the possibility of being in the same relationship with others as well. By a cumulative effect, the support given the "father of the feast" draws indirectly on the support that each of the members of his "army" has received from their own respective "armies." So a ceremonial exchange, as LeRoy (1979) observed for example, commenting on the Kewa of New Guinea, always appears as a constellation of ego-centered exchange networks. Between these networks, although the commonly held discourse tends to deny or make light of it, relations seem to be imbued with a certain competitiveness, which can sometimes also be detected in relations between members of the same network.

When envisaging a feast, for example—plans are usually laid several years in advance—those who will stand "behind" the "father of the feast" begin clearing new gardens in the forest and setting aside pigs for the ceremony. In the context of these preparations, they may in turn receive (in the form of pigs, tubers and/or help with the garden) aid from people who do not have *mokpom* ties with the "father of the feast" but with whom they are in an individual "holding" relationship.

The cumulative effect of the interplay between several *mokpom* networks is further amplified by the relations of *turang* assistance at work. If they do not have pigs that would enable them to cooperate with the "father of the feast," the people of his "army" can effectively call on those indebted to them for previous aid or to whom they will be indebted afterwards.

When it is thus motivated by the preparation of a ceremony, *turang* help assumes a rather peculiar form, insofar as it is organized essentially in terms of local belonging. In preparing a ceremony, the "father of the feast" now turns, not to isolated individuals, but to the group of his co-residents. The latter clear and cultivate gardens, a share of the produce of which will be given him as aid later to be reciprocated. To this will be added the pigs the villagers are able to advance.

When the two principal representatives of the exchanging groups live far apart, the bulk of the aid comes from their respective localities. Participation is not restricted to their co-residents but can extend to the inhabitants of neighboring localities. In this case, the exclusive aid given one or the other of the exchanging parties is organized in terms of greatest spatial proximity.

If the principal exchanging parties live in the same village, the help they receive from their co-residents will follow the division of the village into two "sides," or *maksin*, each of which will reserve its support for one of the parties. The dividing line may, but need not, be decided by topography; for instance, it can run along a path, or a river flowing through the locality and separating the sea side from the land side, or the southwest side from the northeast side. These "sides," which cannot be represented as a spatial projection of the two marriage moieties of the society, are not designated with reference to their geographical orientation but with respect to the house of the person receiving the support. Thus people speak of "So-and-so's *maksin*." The dividing line changes place and modifies the distribution of the aid if, for some later ceremony, the principal exchange partners change.

The term *maksin*, which here designates one part of the residential unit, can sometimes cover the entire unit. Depending on the context, a *maksin* can be one village as opposed to another, a section of this village as opposed to one or several other sections, or even one house as opposed to the other houses in a hamlet.

Those who have lent their material aid are indemnified at the close of the ceremonial exchange by an equivalent gift. The relation of *turang* assistance is then over. It can be reiterated between co-villagers on the occasion of other feasts, or, on the contrary, may cease altogether if one partner moves far away. In this case, unlike the *mokpom* relationship, the *turang* tie between former co-residents does not survive the move. For the person who has left his village, it is now to the inhabitants of his new residential village that he will have to lend aid or turn for help.

In the *mokpom* relationship, the importance of the spatial dimension gives way to the importance of the temporal dimension. Because it extends over time, no longer village time but the time of the rituals carried out by the ancestors, *mokpom* forms a "road" which "holds" together the dead and the living, a chain running through generations, kinship groups and localities, which has no identifiable beginning. Nevertheless, although the relationship is inherited, history (a shallow genealogical memory) and propriety make it impossible to say how far back it extends or how long it will last. Breaks in the chain are not called by their name. Furthermore, to say that "all we do is follow roads," as one man put it, means that it is not up to the living to make new ones, to set themselves up as the initiators of something that could be on the order of "holding" each other. Yet the vitality of the system clearly depends on the possibility individuals have of developing new ties, adapting or transforming already existing ones, as I have already shown elsewhere (Jeudy-Ballini, 1995: 215–16).

The Rules of Solidarity

Actualized through the solidarity arising during the preparation of ceremonies or when carrying out ordinary large-scale jobs, the *mokpom* relationship is governed by two prohibitions imposed on all those who "hold" each other: the prohibition on eating the pigs or the tubers provided by each other and the prohibition on marrying each other.

The Food Prohibition

This prohibition prescribes that *one cannot eat that which comes from oneself* or *that which comes from oneself cannot return to oneself.* The vernacular for the object of this prohibition is *knen*, and many people compare it explicitly and repeatedly to incest, *kuis*, defined as marrying someone "who has come from oneself." Everything that comes from those who "hold" each other or who share a bond of co-residence is considered to "come from oneself." The prohibition covers the goods which, at the close of an exchange, are redistributed and shared out by the "father of the feast" between those from whom he received the help (*turang*) and those with whom he shares a more lasting relationship of solidarity (*mokpom*). By virtue of this prohibition, the people of his village cannot accept the pigs or the tubers initially given to the exchange partner of the "father of the feast" by people with whom they are linked by co-residence or *mokpom*. To say that they cannot accept them on pain of violating the *knen* prohibition means that they can neither consume the slightest morsel themselves nor even act as intermediaries, accepting them and passing them on to others.

To break the food prohibition and commit *knen*, people say, would be

Photo 22: Circulation of a batch of cloth during ritual exchanges in a Sulka wedding ceremony. In the forefront: tubers and pieces of cooked pork (Photo M. JeudyBallini, 1980).

"like stabbing yourself in the neck with a spear" — "spear," like the term for the person who lends support. It is striking that the only consequence associated with such a violation is a social one. The Sulka never mention the harm that might come to the transgressor's body from eating a prohibited food.

By the very fact that it applies to those linked by co-residence and therefore led to "help each other" (*moturang*), the *knen* prohibition is not peculiar to the *mokpom* relationship. Nor is it specific to ceremonial exchanges, since it also covers food that circulates between villagers in the ordinary course of life.

Every day, for example, the quantity of tubers women bring back from their gardens well exceeds the needs of their household. These tubers are divided up and shared out, and may even be sub-divided again by those who receive a portion. While nothing forbids a villager consuming or receiving food directly given by a co-resident, alternatively, the prohibition applies to all food that returns in any form whatsoever to the initial donor. It is forbidden to return cooked tubers to the person whose name is on the garden from which the raw tubers were taken. To accept them would be tantamount to breaking the *knen* prohibition, whether he were to eat them or to take them to give to a third party. The same rule applies to anyone other than the initial donor of the tubers through whose hands they have passed.

This prohibition, which is valid for cultivated foods and domestic pig meat, also holds for the products of hunting and fishing.

The preceding example of sharing among villagers can be diagrammed as follows:

A —— B —— C (allowed)
A —— B —— A (forbidden, *knen*)
A —— B —— A —— C (forbidden, *knen*)
A —— B —— C —— B (forbidden, *knen*)
A —— B —— C —— A (forbidden, *knen*)

In the case of sharing food outside the boundaries of the residential unit, an analogous rule operates, which brings into play not only the nominal relationship with the garden, but the more encompassing criterion of local-group membership. This can be illustrated by a diagram identical to the preceding one, except that, instead of designating co-residents, A, B, and C stand for distinct localities. In this case, the prohibition pertains to all food returning to the village or to an inhabitant of the village in which the food-giver lives. This implies that a man's residential membership is taken into account even when he is living temporarily in another locality. If, for example, village B receives food from village A, no visiting member of A can accept the least bit of this food, either to eat or to circulate.

However, in a non-ritual context of food circulation, nothing forbids a villager receiving a portion of the pig or the tubers from a person who lives in another village and with whom he has a *mokpom* relationship. In the case of ceremonial exchanges, on the other hand, it is out of the question to accept any part of the food initially coming from somebody one "holds," independently of whether or not one has personally taken part in the ceremonial preparations. The same rule applies to a co-resident. The co-residence criterion here means the fact of belonging to the same unit known as *maksin*—a living unit which, as we have said, can, depending on the circumstances, coincide with either the village or part of the village.

As we saw above, the existence and continuity of a *mokpom* relationship does not imply systematic cooperation. The rule that giving help to one of the main protagonists of the exchange necessarily excludes giving any help to the other can entail conflicts of loyalty and thus explains the decision in this case not to cooperate with anyone. Such abstention can be decided by someone bound up in a *mokpom* relationship with both the "father of the feast" and the latter's principal exchange partner. In such a case, the support given one of the parties would, when the time came to exchange, place the other in a situation of transgression (*knen*). This would, in order to avoid such a transgression, place the latter in the situation of refusing the pigs given and thus blocking the circulation of the goods.

The Art of Consultation

The know-how of the "father of the feast" consists precisely in enabling the exchange to proceed; in other words, it ensures that the things given in the name of *turang* help or *mokpom* solidarity are able to move in the direction of their recipients. This kind of skill, regarded as inseparable from the old rank of chief or "father of the village" (*taven*), is described by the Sulka as a "labor." Well in advance of the actual ceremony, the "father of the feast" is supposed to hold numerous consultations with his exchange partners; these consultations are designed to assess the prestations that will be circulating on either side. In the framework of exchanges, everything is done, in effect, to ensure that there will be no surplus. The same rule applies to unbalanced prestations, those involving a "payment," as in marriage or mourning ceremonies; it is important to avoid an imbalance that would crush the party receiving more than it gave. For any excess in the discrepancy might be interpreted as a desire to belittle and humiliate the exchange partner. In the course of the pre-ceremony consultations, the "father of the feast" inquires of his partners as to how many pigs in all they will be putting into circulation and, of these, how many will have a "tail." In exchanges, pigs with a "tail" are those that require the immediate return of a pig of identical size.[4] The Sulka classify these among the gifts that are said to "fight," as opposed to the pigs "without a tail," which are said to "go to die."

In these preliminary consultations, the "father of the feast" must also learn the precise origin of the pigs he will receive, not only from his partners in exchange, but also from those, co-residents or *mokpom* relations, who are lending him their support. Using this knowledge, which affords him an overview of everything that will go into circulation, his task, his "labor" will be to enable these prestations to move, to avoid their being blocked by the *knen* prohibition. He must therefore assure himself that, by accepting the pigs offered out of *mokpom* solidarity or *turang* aid, he will not be violating a prohibition (thereby leading their future recipients to transgress as well), nor be wronging a recipient who has priority. In other words, he must ascertain that the origin of the pigs is compatible with their destination.

Insufficient consultation can sometimes lead to a paralysis of the system and places the organizer of the feast in the position of being unable to ensure the circulation of the pigs he has obtained from his principal exchange partners. This happened at one ceremony I observed in 1984, in which several

---

4. When it comes to exchange, equivalence is taken literally, since the pigs are measured (and subsequently compared) using a piece of string.

potential recipients sounded out by the "father of the feast" refused the pigs
he had received and which he was offering them. One of them commented:

> He didn't sit down to talk [i.e. consult us] about his work. He
> thought: "I'm the only big man of this feast. I'm an orphan, I don't
> have anyone." He wanted to raise himself up on his own! He thought:
> "I have a name and I have many pigs, I alone am going to call the
> people, I'm going to give them food." And he called out: "Hey, [here's]
> your pig." He did that with ignorant people, with stupid people who
> don't know the custom, and who are itching to eat some pork and
> who answered: "That's right, bring it on." But people who know
> the custom are not itching to eat pork. You've got to talk it over first,
> and you've got to find out where the pigs came from, how they came,
> what road they followed . . . But not a word was spoken . . . And
> then the people he had called began thinking: "Wait a minute, he
> never talked to us about that!" And when he called some men, "Hey,
> here's your pig!," one of them answered: "I'm not hungry," and he
> tried another: "Hey, here's your pig!," "No, I'm not hungry, eat it
> yourself!" Just like that . . . He hadn't talked about his own work,
> and now he was throwing this work to us. It was his food, let him
> eat it himself! The road was blocked, he no longer had a road for his
> pigs, so he killed them himself and made a sort of new road of his
> own. Because he hadn't talked about this work, he had done things
> according to his own desire, all alone. (John Sakle, Ploresel village
> 1984)

The word "orphan," *tumrek*, like *karhop* (Pidgin *rabis*, English "rub-
bish-man"), are among those one can use only when humbling oneself.
When applied to others, they are an insult. In a ceremonial context, the
speaker's allusion to his situation as an "orphan" is a rhetorical device cus-
tomarily used by every "father of the feast" at the start of the festivities. It
is unambiguously understood as an act of pseudo-humility, consisting in
declaring one's purported destitution as a man with no family and consequently lacking any material support and having only paltry gifts to offer.
In the context of the conflict alluded to above, this self-deprecation is pur-
posely interpreted on the contrary as a mark of presumption, the expression of an arrogant claim to self-sufficiency.

The incident is typical of the kind of sanction that can follow on the
fact or the fear of violating the *knen* prohibition. It is plausible that the reference to the prohibition implicit in the uncertainty as to the origin of the
pigs serves here as a handy rationalization for avoiding mention of other
reasons for dispute. However the fact remains that it is incumbent upon

anyone taking on the position of "father of the feast" to forestall the possibility of someone having recourse to such arguments.

It thus falls to the "father of the feast" and well in advance—as soon as the new gardens are begun in view of the feast—to take every precaution to ensure that the pigs he assembles will later be able to "fight" or to "go to die" in the exchanges. To make sure that the circulation of these goods will not be hampered by the *knen* prohibition, he must make the "roads clear," "straight" or "clean": these notions in this context are all rendered by the term *roro*, which describes the state of something being literally "cold."

In Rossel, where according to Berde (1973) the length of the preparations for a ritual varies with one's social rank, the speed with which a person calls in the goods to be exchanged from those helping him is a gauge of his prestige and credibility. The same could not quite be said of Sulka preparations, for the length of the "labor" seems to depend more on the care taken to ensure that everything that needs to be is "cold."

Redistribution

Of the pigs received by the "father of the feast" at the time of the exchanges and redistributed by him, one cannot accept those raised by a co-resident (a person from the same *maksin*), or by somebody one "holds" without breaking the rule. So that these pigs are not immobilized in his hands, the "father of the feast" can choose to replace them with other pigs from his own herd or with those he calls in from old debts. This substitution, by which forbidden pigs are, as it were, turned into neutral or "cold" pigs, makes it possible to circumvent the dangers of transgression and thus enables the prestations to move.

Pigs regarded as "coming from oneself" are not necessarily those raised by someone with whom one acknowledges a particular tie. This also applies to pigs one has caught while hunting and given to someone else. The piglet taken from a wild litter and given to someone (co-resident or not) who raises it to full maturity cannot, at the close of the exchange, be given back either as a live pig or in the form of cooked meat to the person who caught it: "He didn't raise it," it was explained to me, "but he held it." Whereas persons having raised different pigs are allowed to exchange them directly, the circulation of the same pig raised by one and given back to the person who caught it is forbidden. Inversely, the circulation of this pig is perfectly admissible in the context of a helping relationship if it is to assist the original holder of the animal in getting together the necessary resources for an exchange.

In the consultations prior to the festivities, the "father of the feast" agrees with the members of the other exchanging parties on the number of live pigs to be put into circulation and the number of pigs to go in as pieces of cooked meat. He also discusses these details with those from whom he has received aid and who, if they are not involved in contributions to an upcoming ceremony, can accept a pig that has been cooked and cut up in compensation for the live pig they gave.

Of all the food laid out on the village grounds in view of the exchanges, a certain amount is supposed to have been cooked so that all those attending the feast receive a share, whether or not they have contributed support. The live pigs stemming from the exchanges and redistributed by the "father of the feast" can be put back into circulation for a future ceremony. The same applies to the pieces of cooked meat, providing this other ceremony takes place rapidly (before the meat can spoil).

The "father of the feast," together with his wife, his children (including those living in a different village) and the other members of his household, must abstain from any food from the exchanges. People commonly say that the "father of the feast" "eats" the food given by his exchange partners; this means that he is the original recipient, but it is understood that "it is only his name that eats [the food]."

The "father of the feast" is charged with allocating the food to those he "called" specially to the ceremony (relatives or homonyms, for example[5]), those whom he asked for aid and eventually those he "holds"; he cries out these names one by one on the village grounds ("So-and-so, here's your pig!" "So-and-so, your food!"). Pigs and tubers are taken home or temporarily set aside by the people called, who will then circulate them among those they themselves have sounded out, who can in turn circulate what they have received. Thus passed from hand to hand and even from village to village, the living pigs received in the exchanges may accomplish a fairly long circuit before reaching their final destination. This observation is expressed by the saying: "The pig is like the possum" — the latter being reputed to be ever on the move and always from somewhere other than where it is seen. It is also said that the circuit is sometimes so long that the pigs finally arrive in such a thin and wasted state that it gives rise to complaints from those who expected to be compensated by an animal of the same size as the one they had provided.

The "father of the feast" does not personally, that is with his own hands, distribute the cooked food. For this task he designates someone to be responsible for dividing the tubers and pieces of pork into roughly equal heaps. But first of all, he sets aside this person's share, usually including the head

---

5. Homonymy, as defined by the Sulka, is one of the most important relationships — however the simple fact of carrying the same name is not a necessary or even sufficient condition for recognizing such a relationship, as I have shown elsewhere (Jeudy-Ballini 1999a).

of a pig, regarded as a less valuable piece not fit to give someone else. This is done discreetly, almost secretly, and no one is supposed to know about it or at least to mention it. When one asks whether the person who divides the food can eat any, the answer is always no. It seems that any allusion in public (by the anthropologist) to the portion set aside and taken into a house is inappropriate and each time occasions discomfort and perhaps shame.

It is the *knen* prohibition which here accounts for the fact that the person who does the sharing out cannot include himself in the distribution on pain of putting himself in the impossible situation ("stabbing oneself in the neck with a spear") of eating that which he gives to others. This prohibition on the food he has "held" applies equally to the food the later recipients will "hold" if the tubers and pieces of pork are again shared out by those who receive them.

Like the breaking of any prohibition, the violation known as *knen* is punished by "shame" and in the past could spark anger, exposing the violators to retaliatory killings. The meaning of this prohibition seems inseparable from the notion of "incest" (*kuis*), and thus must be understood with reference to Sulka marriage rules.

Marriage Prohibitions

The Sulka marriage system, which consists entirely of negative rules, regards as incestuous any union with a member of the same moiety (*a ngausie*, "vine") or with a member of the same matrilineal group (*a ngausie ka kha*, "fork in the vine"). It further outlaws any union with a first-degree cross-cousin, that is to say, for a man, marriage with a "sister" (MBD or FZD), and for a woman, marriage with a "brother" (MBS or FZS).[6]

Alongside these prohibitions, there are others which take into account more particularly relations induced by the circulation of food. For example those forbidding marriage between adopted children and adoptive parents, or marriage within the *mokpom* solidarity network.

In Sulka society and whether or not they belong to opposite moieties, persons having been breastfed or weaned by the same woman cannot marry, and the prohibition extends to their children.[7] In addition to the proscription of marriage between adoptive siblings, unions between individuals hav-

---

6. When the speaker is a man, Iroquois terminology is used for male cousins and Hawaiian for female cousins. For a female speaker, the terminology is inverted: Hawaiian for male cousins, Iroquois for female cousins.

7. A mother will often entrust the weaning of her child to another woman. At the end of a period which may last from several days to several weeks the child is given back to its parents, but weaning also often ends in adoption (on the representations underpinning this practice among the Sulka, see Jeudy-Ballini, 1992, 1998a).

ing been adopted into the same household are also forbidden, even when they are not related by blood, belong to different moieties and the adoption was of short duration. Furthermore, the temporary help one woman receives from another in the form of small, informal gifts of food or child-care when the mother is in the garden, for example, explains why the children of these women are not allowed to marry each other, even if there is no recognized tie of kinship or adoption.

In all events, people explicitly refer to sharing one food (mother's milk or garden produce) to explain that, were such a marriage to take place, it would be assimilated to "incest" (*kuis*). The Sulka connection between *knen* and incest appears not only in the fact that both of these prohibitions can be stated in analogous terms ("that which comes from oneself cannot return to oneself"), but also in the fact that "whatever comes" through food cannot "return" through marriage. Food from the same garden, like milk from the same woman, when shared, creates a bond such that it precludes any sexual or matrimonial union between these children ever after. Later we will see that the same kind of consideration accounts for the prohibition on marriage between persons sharing the same tradition of solidarity (*mokpom*).

The Ways of the Cassowary

When incest does occur, it is denounced by the subverted use of kinship terminology, which implies, along with the "shame" felt by the family circle, the confusion of relationships. For instance, the terms *kohal mang kosnerip*, "my son-in-law of a son" (or *kohal kar kosnerip*, "my son-and-son-in-law") and *kokwek mang kovla*, "my daughter-in-law of a daughter" (or *kokwek kar kovla*, "my daughter-and-daughter-in-law"), which make just about as much (non)sense as would the expression "blood son-in-law" or "blood daughter-in-law" in our society. Such particularly offensive terms must not be used openly. The only time I ever heard anything of this sort uttered out loud in a village it was proffered by a man who was drunk.

Designated by a verbal form, *kuis*, incest is also evoked in everyday language by two expressions, both of which refer to the cassowary: *tkaem a mrap*, "to eat *mrap*," the vernacular name of a tree whose fruit is this animal's favorite food; and *ta kerer a wong*, "to hunt cassowary," a formula explained as the fact of "following its ways."

What the Sulka retain about the cassowary are several features having to do notably with sexuality and food. They credit this bird with a frightful temper which makes it dangerous to hunt. People say that it disembowels its assailants, men or dogs, with the razor-sharp middle toe, or "spear" (*ka mus*) on each of its feet. Its touchiness is exacerbated during the mating season, when it flies into rages, venting its destructive fury on everything around and transforming certain parts of the forest into veritable clearings. Those Sulka who have seen *kung fu* movies do not fail to compare the practices.

People claim that cassowaries mate with their conspecifics without distinction between relatives and non-relatives, but this is a practice they recognize as being shared with other animals, like the dog or the pig. The propensity for incest is therefore not confined to the cassowary.

The Sulka also attribute this bird with the peculiarity of using its body as a water trap. Its cunning consists in squatting in water holes with its wings outspread so that little fish or crustaceans will enter the feathers to feed on parasites. They are rewarded for their greediness by being eaten in turn when the cassowary, hopping out of the water, shakes itself and gobbles them up as they fall to the ground. Another of its peculiarities, that of moving from one place to another like humans, on foot beneath the trees instead of flying, designates it as the only bird that can die like the wild pig: pierced by men's spears or strangled in a spring trap.

But its chief characteristic, with respect to other animals, has to do, for the Sulka, with yet another observation: the fact that this gluttonous bird eats like it defecates: abundantly and leaving the food intact. In the cassowary, which distinguishes itself by its ability to ingurgitate its food whole and to expel it likewise in its excreta, the ingestion-defecation cycle is therefore theoretically meaningless. It could just as well eat what it defecates, since its excreta is still food—fruits and vegetables that remain edible and which, one supposes, could be eaten by a human after a good washing. The cassowary's food and its excreta are virtually one and the same thing. With respect to the *knen* prohibition, stated as the fact that "one cannot eat that which comes from oneself" or "that which comes from oneself cannot return to oneself," the scandal of the cassowary or someone who "follows its ways" resides precisely in the fact that they eat that which comes from themselves or that which comes from themselves returns to themselves. This scandal was already illustrated by the fact that the cassowary, using its own body as a trap, eats the small fish and crustaceans that had previously fed on it.

To say that the ingestion-defecation cycle becomes theoretically meaningless is also to say that, in a certain fashion, there is no longer any distinction between what is taken and what is given, between what comes from elsewhere and what comes from oneself. With the cassowary as well as with the incestuous human who "follows its ways," the taker and the giver become one, and this confusion negates all relations with others.

Incest Through Food

According to Sulka tradition, marriage is also prohibited between those who "hold" each other, the *mokpom* "army" being defined theoretically as an exogamous unit. Independently of genealogical considerations, the existence of a *mokpom* relationship also creates a distinction among people of the opposite moiety between those who are "near" (*kanmok*) and those who are "far" (*hagenmok*), in other words between forbidden spouses and allowed spouses. The idea of marriage between those who "hold" each other shows the impossibility of assembling or receiving the marriage "payment" without breaking the *knen* prohibition, since one would put oneself in the inconceivable position of standing "behind" the people who are standing "behind" oneself, of both giving and receiving the same prestations. By committing such a senseless act, in the case of such a marriage, one man explained in substance, no one in the *mokpom* army could still "stay inside" or, as a consequence, cooperate in preparing the ceremonial exchanges. If they did, he concluded, they would be committing "incest through food." When asked how to translate the vernacular expression, "incest through food," which he had formulated in Pidgin as "*kulis long kaikai*," he answered that one would say *knen*. He added that one could also use the expression *ta kuis pum klol*, which corresponds literally to the Pidgin.

In the context of *mokpom*, marriage is indicted less with reference to incest (*kuis*)—a notion reserved for violations of the clan and moiety exogamy rule—than with reference to the ceremonial exchanges whose movement it distorts or paralyzes. If a man and a woman both of whom one "holds" marry, no prestation can "go to die" because those who would have been responsible for assembling the marriage payment can no longer be distinguished from those who would have been supposed to receive it.

> How can we receive it now? Now this payment is stopped among us. Because a payment, once it is gotten together, must go round. But there, it can't! There is no more direction now and the payment for the woman isn't a payment now. There is no more payment to sit down on. All the labor has gone wrong. There is no more payment to hold. He [the person who should have received this payment] will die like that, without holding any money or pigs. The *mokpom* is all messed up. (Simon Mut, Milim village 1988)

When it occurs within a *mokpom* "army," violation of the marriage prohibition threatens to spoil relations between the "spears." This disruption is designated in Sulka by the verbal expression, *mukrur*, and is described as the appearance of discord and the impossibility thereafter to "hold" each other or to "remain connected by food."

As we saw above, each of those bound together in mutual solidarity by the *mokpom* relationship can also entertain the same kind of relationship with another network relatively independent from the first, that is not bound to it by any recognized duty of solidarity. By lending support in the framework of a ceremony involving one of his networks, a person can thus call on the help of another.

Those whom a man or a woman "holds" reciprocally are not necessarily connected by *mokpom*. This raises the question of whether these people (their siblings or their children) are allowed to intermarry. Views diverge. Some say that, provided the fiancés are not "one blood," such unions are the epitome of a "good marriage": one which eliminates the danger of rivalry and disputes, while at the same time preserving, in the event one of the couple dies, access rights to the land of the surviving spouse. Others, on the contrary, deem that the primacy given to considerations of land is the result of a vision skewed by today's concern with cash crop growing:

This isn't the right way to think. This thinking follows business, like Whites' thinking. It follows coconuts, cacao trees…all these things. But the ancestors' thinking didn't follow business. It followed *mokpom*. It is only today that all people say to themselves: "What if somebody other than my people were to come and hold my coconuts, my cacao trees and all the things I planted…So too bad, we'll marry among ourselves!" And the thinking follows business…

Only now do people mix up everything when they follow business, when they follow money, when they follow coconuts, cacao trees, but not before. Before it was the father and the mother who showed the road, the road that went through…(John Sakle, Ploresel village 1988)

According to this point of view, marriage between those who do not "hold" each other while they "hold" a third party justifies the latter's refusal to cooperate with either one. For those who disapprove of such marriages, the refusal to validate the *mokpom* relationship, in other words to participate in the ceremony, can translate into the refusal either to help assemble the marriage payment or to receive it. The threat of declining to participate, when made by someone (homonym, maternal uncle) who had been invited — "called to hold the food" (= to take part in the exchanges) —, in the initiation of one of the fiancés concerned sometimes creates so much pressure that the couple calls off the marriage. In effect, the prestations put into circulation for an initiation ceremony are said to "show the road" to be taken by the ceremonial exchanges to come. The person "called" by the parents of the initiate is the same person who will be "called" to provide or receive the greater part of the marriage compensation when the child marries. Therefore any reprobation on the part of this person is rarely taken lightly.

It is said that a disagreement between those who "hold" each other can cause them to break off the *mokpom* relationship. Nevertheless, in the few

cases where the defection of one or several "spears" was explicitly attributed to discord of the sort, the concerned parties did not see the relationship as being broken off, but merely suspended until it could be reactivated on the occasion of later ceremonies:

> The anger could not last forever, otherwise where would you get
> your strength? (Barbara Koklekning, Ploresel village 1988)

> If you no longer have an army and you find yourself isolated, you
> don't have any more strength. (Paul Anis, Kilalum village 1988)

An individual is only as strong as his group. This "strength," *ka selpak*
(the same term is used for "muscles"), the capacity to fulfill a ritual duty
by calling on the support of an "army," today seems more endangered by
such circumstances as emigration linked with intermarriage, or with membership in fundamentalist Churches which, without necessarily excluding
mokpom relationships altogether, at least promotes a certain deterioration
of this bond.

"Strength," "armies," "fighting groups," "spears," "shields," movement
of goods destined to "fight each other," or to "go to die": the vocabulary
of cooperation and the circulation of wealth would suggest further investigation, of the kind P. Lemonnier (1990) has carried out on New Guinea
Highlands societies, into the relation between war and ceremonial exchanges.
As such an analysis is beyond the scope of the present paper, I will merely
mention the existence of a Sulka practice designed to turn certain conflictual relationships into helping ones.

One Form of Non-voluntary Cooperation

Domestic animals are usually given a name by the "father" or the "mother" who raises them. These names are drawn from a common pool fed by
mythology, local anecdotes, a physical peculiarity of the animal, elements
of the natural environment, imported objects, brand names, Christian names.
For instance, a pup or a piglet will be dubbed "Basket" because that was
how he was brought back to the village, "Five kinas" referring to his purchase price, "Tomato" for the tinned mackerel in tomato sauce, "Two-moth-
ers" because two women took care of him, "Bakardi" for a brand of whisky,
"Sinsios" like the name of one of the Provincial administration boats, "Drunk-
en man" alluding to its odd walk, "Mokpelpel" from the name of a mythic ogress who devoured everything in her way, "Panguna" after the copper
mine in Bougainville, "He follows me everywhere," "Jail," "Lemon," "Trac-
tor," and so on.

With the exception of dogs' names, which are utilitarian, used for example when calling the dogs to go hunting, animal nicknames have a chiefly ornamental value. A person calls a pig by grunting, never by using its name, which is almost never pronounced during the animal's lifetime. Some of the nicknames given pigs seem to stem from the same sources as those for dogs, but present, in the case of more emotionally charged names, the exclusive particularity of establishing homonymy between humans and these animals. Several kinds of circumstances lend themselves to this invention, motivated at times by affliction, at times by a sense of derision or at times by the desire to actualize a particular emotional tie.

The anecdotal character of the pig names may thus refer to an insult, a grievance or a snub experienced by the owner. Names like "He's scared of water" (= he is dirty because he does not wash), "Smokes alone" (= stingy with his tobacco), "Hollow head," "He's mad," "Lazybones," "Drunk," attest to some such event and make the pig a sort of living and walking reminder of the offense. Mocked by a villager for her poor health, one woman decided, for example, to call one of her piglets "Always sick." By letting this particular villager know about the name, she indicated to him that she had given him the animal as his "homonym" (*kiok*). Similar resentment prompted the leader of a messianic movement to dub one of his pigs "Cargo Cult" because he felt it an insult that some co-residents adopted this derogatory term used by the Church and the local administration for his religious activities.[8]

Whatever the tone—affectionate, ironic, vindictive, commemorative or other—the nickname chosen for a piglet not yet born or not yet named is charged with a particular inter-personal meaning. It usually establishes a homonymic association between the pig and the human referant who inspired the name.

The offender is considered to have put "his name on" this animal, which is also said to be named "after him," thereby becoming the pig's homonym (*kiok*). This homonymy gives him first claim to the animal, and its "father" or "mother" can no longer give it to anyone else. To fail in this obligation would be to commit an offense by making the original offender (the pig's homonym) feel he had been despoiled. In the past, people say, such an act would have meant death: that of the person offended and then offending, or failing that, the death of a close relative or of the undeserving receiver. Nowadays whoever (the original offender) was scandalized by the "homonymous" pig being given to someone else would simply receive a monetary compensation from the animal's "father" or "mother."

But although he is obligated to the offender of the nicknamed pig, the one who is offended turns around and makes the creditor into a debtor,

---

8. For details on these activities, see Jeudy-Ballini 1997 and in press.

since, obliged to reciprocate as soon as he has received his "homonym," the latter must immediately or at a later time, as the offended party wishes, give back a pig of the same size. When these rules are followed, the nicknamed pig, a living reminder of the offense, is transformed, as it were, into a neutral pig, and the conflict between individuals is absorbed, transcended by the wider circle of exchanges.

Thus the obligations that "friendship," disparaged in the previous quotation as a White invention or value, would be ineffectual to develop, could be given shape by hostile relations. In matters of mutual assistance, to simplify the Sulka point of view somewhat, offenders would have the advantage over "friends" of always being able to be counted on, at least in the case of minor offenses, not in that of insults implicating the reputation of a group. When the nickname conjures up an affront to a clan or a group of co-residents, the person raising the pig gives it not to the offender but to a representative of the slandered group.

The same rule holds when an animal's nickname implies an accusation of murder. When, for example, someone gives a pig named "Mot" or "Momot" to someone in mourning, they are associating themselves with the interpretation of this death as having been caused by a particular brand of sorcery called *kolmot*. Names like "Nothing wrong," "Without fault" or "Without being sick" have the same accusatory note when they are prompted by an unexpected death. A death that cannot be attributed to imprudence on the part of the deceased or to an illness that is expected to end in death suggests sorcery. The nickname which, by allusion, constitutes an accusation of murder and creates a posthumous relation of homonymy with the deceased, means that the pig must be given to one of his relatives— there being no limit on the number of such "homonyms" he may thus receive. People say that the accusation carried in a nickname must be expressed in a shortened, oblique, coded or euphemistic form, so as not to arouse the suspicion of the one who ordered the murder and to ensure that he remains unaware of any reprisals in the offing.

It is probable, though we do not have the means to verify it, that giving a pig to the group of someone presumed to have been assassinated used to be one way of indicating one's solidarity and of willingness to rally to their aid in the event of open conflict. Today the pig is given as a spontaneous contribution in the context of a ceremony in which the victim's group is involved and which it will be obliged to reciprocate with an identical present.

Like an offense or a presumption of murder, affliction can prompt the naming of a pig. The nickname in this instance may refer to the death of a loved one or to an event in the period preceding the deceased's disappearance ("He no longer speaks," "She got up," "It was raining"). As a "homonym" of the deceased, the pig is destined first of all for a member of the deceased's group — a member or a fitting representative of his or her clan.

Homonymy between people and pigs shows that the process of cooperation thus includes other considerations than those associated purely with the risks of "incest through food" (residence, clan affiliation), and with motivations other than the benevolent desire to demonstrate one's solidarity.

Translated by Nora Scott

Photo 23: Young girl anxiously waiting for the nose piercing ritual; she is decorated with shell money (ring and necklace) (Photo M. Jeudy-Ballini, 1984).

Chapter 8

Copy Rights for Objects of Worship, Land Tenure and Filiation in New Ireland*

Brigitte Derlon

The northern half of the island of New Ireland and the small adjacent islands of Papua New Guinea formerly possessed a class of funerary effigies known as *malanggan*, with countless types and subtypes, subjected to copy rights. Only specific individuals who had previously been duly given the right to exploit or reproduce the pattern of a particular *malanggan* were allowed to order the crafting of one or several specimens of a subtype of that object and to stage a ritual in which it was displayed. In addition to describing these copy rights, which circulated between individuals and groups and included a number of prerogatives and obligations of various sorts depending on the clauses enumerated in the agreement and the nature of the partners, the purpose of the present article is to show the connections between these practices and the laws governing land tenure in the same region, and to focus on some aspects of matrilineal society and dual organization in New Ireland, through the investigation of the social strategies underlying these. In doing so, it focuses on the social symbolism of the *malanggan*.[1]

The findings discussed in this paper were recorded in 1983–1984 in the only mountain population still in existence on the island, the Mandak of the Lelet plateau (450 people living in four villages) at the eastern limit of

---

* First published as "Droits de reproduction des objets de culte, tenure foncière et filiation en Nouvelle-Irlande," *L'Homme* 130, 1994: 31–58.

1. For a discussion of other aspects of the *malanggan* system and of the corresponding objects, see Derlon, 1990–1991, 1997b, 1997c, and 1998.

the distribution of *malanggan* objects, which formerly covered ten linguistic zones counting approximately thirty-six thousand people.[2] The investigation took place nearly thirty years after the people in this linguistic subgroup had ceased to practice their ceremonies, and therefore did not unable us to reconstitute all of the subtleties involved in the transfer of *malanggan* rights. We have therefore confined our discussion to the most salient aspects. There are tens of thousands of *malanggan* objects in museum collections throughout the world, but none whatsoever left in New Ireland. Strikingly, these objects are extremely heterogeneous, both in appearance and in their frame of reference. Most are rounded sculptures carved in wood (*Alstonia villosa*), while others may be of basketwork. They may be life-sized statues or dummies, several human figures piled up column-like, or again sorts of friezes or bas-reliefs (depending on how they were exhibited against a leafy wall backdrop) predominantly representing animals or composed of abstract designs. Viewed as effigies, they covered the entire range of traditional New Ireland supernatural beings, referring to everything from death and its embodiments to the solar and lunar beings that created the world at its origins, and including various categories of spiritual forces.

Each type of *malanggan* differed distinctly from the others in form and in its main design, and was accompanied by a complete corpus of specific rites governing the making, exhibition and destruction of its specimens. Each of the subtypes, easily recognizable by some specific designs, also displayed some distinctive ceremonial peculiarities. Inasmuch as the types and subtypes of *malanggan* were connected to specific social units, as will be shown below, each linguistic group or subgroup only disposed of a limited number of types of *malanggan*, and these were necessarily heterogeneous. Rather than being ascribable to any regional particularism, the heterogeneity of these objects and of their specific rites was an underlying characteristic of the *malanggan* institution itself.

These objects were exhibited during ceremonies designated by the same name, usually connected with funerary rites. The ceremonies, performed two to three years after the death of an adult of either sex, were often collective, in that they were dedicated simultaneously to several individuals who had died within a short lapse of time, provided all had been buried on the same burial site, located in the courtyard of a men's house in the hamlet. They were organized by the local segment of the clan or lineage in charge of that particular site, on which, according to tradition, the remains of all of its deceased members were to rest. In those exceptional cases where the deceased admitted to the burial site belonged to more than one group, the

---

2. For information on rights formerly prevailing in the Kara area in connection with rituals and land tenure, see the writings of Küchler (1987, 1988 and 1992 in particular).

rites were co-organized by several different clans. The ceremonies, which lasted several months and attracted countless visitors to the hamlet for the festivities, revolved around the long, secret process of making and the brief public exhibiting of one or more *malanggan* objects, which were subsequently destroyed or discarded. Although occasionally a single object might be used for the collective celebration of several deaths within a same clan, as a rule a single piece was produced and exhibited for each death. Each object, made by a craftsman, was ordered by a close relative of the deceased person, generally on the maternal side, often a politically influential figure and the financier and organizer of the ceremony, as a way of partially fulfilling his obligations towards the dead person. It made no difference what type of object was made; what counted was the symbolic benefit of the ceremony. By virtue of the copyright system applied to the making of those objects, the only person habilitated to finance a specimen of *malanggan* was the man who was in possession of the right to exploit the pattern of that particular subtype, or one who acted in the name of the woman owner of that right.[3] For women, like men, did own copy rights, in spite of the strict, typically Melanesian prohibition on their seeing *malanggan* objects, or at least the vast majority of types of them, which is to say that they were even supposed to feign ignorance of the physical nature of what was being made and handled by the men behind the high palisade specially put up for the occasion along the surrounding wall of the men's house.

The men who possessed such rights were extremely knowledgeable in a vast customary realm, an exclusively male preserve. Their knowledge generally included precise expertise on the pattern, which is to say, the mental representation of all those specific designs, with their names, that had to be present on each of the specimens made to prove that they belonged to a given group and subgroup, knowledge of the myths connected with the pattern, any technical or magic procedures connected with the crafting of the specimens, and last, knowledge of the specific rites connected with the production and ritual manipulation of the latter. When in possession of all of this knowledge, the person was then capable of directing a *malanggan* ceremony and assisting the professional craftsman in his secret work, either to make sure that he respected the pattern in its ultimate details or to teach him the specifics as the work progressed, if he had never before had an opportunity to sculpt or weave an object of that type.

The only knowledge open to women, on the other hand, was attached to the specifically female rites (dances, food distribution rites, etc.) con-

---

3. A copyright system was also applied to the masks which, in the coastal areas—but never on the Lelet plateau—played a role in the men's dances performed at the same time as the *malanggan* were exhibited (cf. Billings and Peterson, 1967: 27; Lewis, 1969: 130–133; Gunn, 1987: 83).

nected with the subtype of *malanggan* for which they had the copy right. The right was exploited in the woman's name by a close male matrilineal relative, generally a brother (assisted by members of his group with knowledge of the pattern when he himself did not have the right to reproduce it). Although women could not be cognizant of the nature of that copy right, its possession enabled them, like men, to meet some of their social obligations.

For men, the copy rights of patterns of subtypes of *malanggan* were inseparable from a vast body of knowledge, of an essentially technical nature. Rights were frequently transferred from one individual to another, and could only be transmitted during ceremonies in which at least one specimen was displayed, and which were generally staged once the male recipient or recipients of those rights had undergone a number of rituals, including the most secret of all, to acquire the necessary concrete knowledge. The object was exhibited for three days at most to a vast public of male visitors before being destroyed or discarded. During that period, the man who had ordered it to be made and was in the role of *lunkak* (parting with his copy right) made a speech in which he told of how, in the past, the right to exploit the pattern had been transmitted to him personally (or to the woman in whose name he had exploited it), and proclaimed the identity of the *lunpanga* (the person to whom he (or she) was giving it).

Copy Rights and Control of the *Malanggan*

There were mainly two ways for an individual on the Lelet plateau of the Mandak area to obtain a copy right for a *malanggan*. First, during childhood, it could be received from a close matrilineal or patrilineal relative just one generation older; secondly, an adult might acquire it by passing a contract with an adult member of another clan.

Between the approximate ages of 5 and 16, an individual of either sex might receive a copy right for several *malanggan* patterns, transmitted by representatives of his or her own clan or paternal clan (by a maternal uncle or the father's father, mother or sister respectively) during ceremonies in which the latter play the role of the person ordering the making of the objects. The acquisition of a copy right was a highly ritualized occasion, marked by the bestowing of a ritual name, linked to the subtype of the object and the sex of the recipient. The person who was parting with the right (or her representative in the case of a woman) whispered the name into the child's ear and then placed a limestone mark on his or her forehead or shoulder. This ritual name, termed the "*malanggan* name," reflected a sort of symbolic identification between the *malanggan* and the child, who then entered a period of seclusion and had to conform to numerous prohibitions. In the case of boys, this symbolic identification was reinforced by their physical contact with the object that had been exhibited, the scent of which[4] they are said to carry. The boy was initiated to the secrets of a subtype of *malanggan* by an elder who allowed him to accompany him during certain phases of the making of the objects and taught him some of his knowledge during the period of seclusion. But when, having reached adulthood, he had an occasion to order and display a specimen of the pattern, he had to rely on the help of an adult already in possession of the same copy right and the same knowledge (his initiator, if he was still alive), since he had been too young at the time to assimilate all of the details completely.

An adult who had given away all of the copy rights received during childhood or, exceptionally, who had never been given any such rights through that process, could ask someone who was about to order an object for a forthcoming *malanggan* ceremony but who did not belong to his own clan to take that opportunity to transmit to him the copy right for the pattern, along with the knowledge attached to it. Unlike the child who received a right, the person on the receiving end here was not given the "*malanggan* name," with which he was not symbolically identified and for which he had never gone through any ritual contact. This is a major difference. He simply assisted the organizer of the ceremony and the craftsman in most of their tasks, so as to learn the role he would soon be allowed to play on his own.

Each clan traditionally claimed to be affiliated with at least one subtype of *malanggan*, generally created, originally, by one of the group's ancestors. This bound the possessors of the right to exploit a pattern directly associated with their social group to two obligations. They had to exercise that right, by ordering the production of one or several specimens of the pattern, and secondly, they were obliged to transfer the copy right on to one or several young members of the group, so as to pass the tradition on to the next generation.

Copy rights were given to children free of charge, with the understanding that it was a sort of heritage of a possession—the pattern and the corresponding knowledge—intimately tied to their group. In transferring the right to the child, the giver (the maternal uncle or the mother) relinquished his or her own right, and from then on was no longer allowed to make specimens of the pattern. The child was the complete owner of the copy right, said to include the "bone" (or skeleton) of the *malanggan* (*lissimalanggan*),

---

4. The smell of *Evodia anisodora*, a bush exuding an extremely heady anise-like fragrance, the sap of which was mixed with red ochre and coconut milk to form the mixture used at the time by men to paint their body during initiation, and the leaves of which were placed on corpses when they were exhibited because they were an element of the materialization of the dead, to which all *malanggan* objects referred, in the last analysis (Derlon, 1990–1991).

meaning that theoretically, once grown up, he (or she) could make as many specimens of the model as he or she desired. "Theoretically," because the existence of close matrilineal relatives of age to be initiated to the secrets of the pattern, along with the pressure of the influential male members of the group including their own initiator in person, obliged them to pass the right on. The latter was actually rarely used during more than two ceremonies, but several specimens of the pattern could of course be ordered for each ceremony. By passing the right on to a number of youthful members of his clan during a single ceremony, as was frequently the case, the possessor made sure that the survival of the pattern was not threatened by the death of one or several recipients, who might not have had time to exploit and transmit their own rights. At the same time, the fact that some would inevitably die prematurely avoided the exponential increase in the number of owners of copy rights for the same model, which would end in having all members of the clan having the same copy right, in the long run (as opposed to only a few of them).

The individual who possessed the right to exploit a pattern associated with his clan, and could not neglect his duty to the clan to transmit it to representatives of the younger generation, was also allowed to transfer the copy right for the same pattern to a member of another clan—either a child or an adult—subject to a number of restrictions. In that case, the transaction was anything but free, and was necessarily attended by the gift of a large-sized pig. Moreover, the giver retained his own copy right, which he could pass on, either later or during the same ceremony, to young members of his own clan. Last, the copy right obtained by the new holder was said to exclude the "*malanggan* bone," meaning that not only was reproduction of the pattern confined to a single specimen, but it was not transmissible within his own kinship group and had necessarily to be given back to a child from the clan that was originally associated with the pattern (only a non-adult could be given the right to exploit a pattern linked to his own social unit). The child who recovered, for his clan's benefit, a copy right temporarily transferred to a member of another clan, obtained full rights for the reproduction of an unlimited number of specimens, like any other possessor of a copy right for a pattern associated with his own clan.

In most cases of transfer of limited copy rights of this sort—the only kind of rights allowed to circulate between members of different clans— the partners involved were father and child, and almost always father and son. The father thus took the responsibility of alienating, to another clan, an exploitation right for something associated with his own social unit. It was up to him, then, to make sure that once his son reached adulthood he would be in a position to initiate a youthful member of his paternal clan during the ceremony for which he would make his one and only specimen,

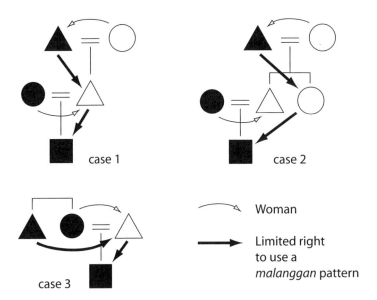

case 1

case 2

Woman

Limited right
to use a
malanggan pattern

case 3

Figure 1: Three typical ways ot giving and returning a limited right to use a *malanggan* pattern.

and to give his right to exploit it back to that boy. This was a way for the father to exert his authority over the son to whom he had given one of his group's "*malanggan* names," so that he would take wife within that clan[5], a marriage which he had in fact promised since the boy's infancy (it is the father who gives bridewealth payment for his son's marriage). By doing so, he would improve the chances of having the right returned to the clan from which it came. Thanks to his wife, the son would have children who would belong to the father's clan, and would be happy to give his exploitation right to one of them (see Fig. 1, case 1). When a man had no male children, or when his sons were too young to be initiated, he transmitted his copy right to a daughter, but he always managed, subsequently, to arrange to have a younger son or a classificatory son marry a woman from his own

5. With the exception of his crossed patrilateral cousins, as is frequently the case in matrilineal societies. Marriage between crossed cousins is strictly forbidden here, and only individuals with a distant classificatory kinship relationship may marry, provided the girl does not belong to the boy's father's subclan. Marriage between crossed cousins was prohibited throughout most of the linguistic areas of the northern half of New Ireland (cf. Chinnery, 1929: 15–16), but was an accepted practice in the Tabar islands (Groves, 1934–1935: 353), while in the Kara area, marriage with the crossed patrilateral cousin was in fact the preferred form of alliance (Küchler, 1983: 73).

clan, and one of their children then became the recipient of the daughter's right (Fig. 1, case 2). Moreover, when a man agreed to transmit a limited copy right to an adult, the new holder was necessarily a man to whom his clan had previously given a bride (as a rule, his sister's husband), and who had already fathered children with that woman (Fig. 1, case 3).[6]

Another, original kind of *malanggan* known as *uli* or *lulilom* was extensively used on the Lelet plateau. Specimens of the latter were intended to last and instead of being destroyed following a ceremony they were washed, repainted or otherwise repaired for further use. Their existence does not contradict the spirit of the rules described above, since only members of the clan linked to such a *malanggan* could be given the right to make new specimens, whereas in the case of transfer of limited rights between members of different clans, it was the specimen itself (rather than the right to order the making of a specimen) that was transferred for a single instance of use, and it had to be given back to a young member of the clan with which the pattern was associated.

One gathers from this description that there would be considerable ambiguity in designating the close bond with a *malanggan* pattern claimed by a given clan in terms of a claim to "property." Never, at any point in time, did clan members dispose of an exclusive right to reproduce a particular pattern, or of exclusive access to the knowledge required to display its specimens properly, and there were always other individuals, belonging to clans to which they were linked by intermarriages, who shared that right and that knowledge. By restricting the copy rights given to members of other clans (limited to the right to make a single specimen of the *malanggan*, and the necessity to give the right back to a youthful member of the clan of origin at the next generation), the clan made sure it maintained "control" over the pattern. This control consisted mainly in the collective right to continue to exploit the pattern generation after generation, through certain co-opted members of the clan (co-responsible for the control or the "bone" of the *malanggan*), and to prohibit or conversely, to permit the use, by members of other clans, of a limited copy right on the same pattern, and last,

---

6. On the Tabar islands, considered by oral New Ireland tradition as the birthplace of the *malanggan* custom, the rules governing transfer of copy rights were comparable but different in many respects. From the observations of Gunn (1987) it may be inferred that only copy rights for patterns considered by the clan as minor could be given to members of another clan, and that the new holder of the right was not initiated into the secrets of the making of the object, or allowed to be present when it was made. But, similarly to the Lelet plateau practice, the controlling clan preserved its own right to reproduce that particular pattern, and the right to use, often passed on from father to son, had to be returned to the clan in which it originated at the following generation, through another marriage between members of the two clans involved.

the right to alienate the pattern to another clan which then gained control of it.

There are in fact some instances of a contract between two individuals belonging to different clans and acting on behalf of their respective groups, stipulating the giving away, once and for all, of control of a pattern; which is to say, the handing over of the "bone" of the *malanggan*. Three types of compensation, closely dependent on the context in which the transaction took place, might be offered to the clan in an attempt to persuade all those of its members who possessed copy rights for the pattern to relinquish their claim to use them.

Under the responsibility of a man who assumed leadership, a clan that no longer had any female members of child-bearing age but wished to make sure that its dead would receive the proper honors could transfer its control of a *malanggan* pattern to another clan in exchange for its promise to organize burial ceremonies for the remaining men and women, when the time came. If faced with more than one candidature, that doomed clan would give priority to the clan whose members included children of one of its last surviving men. When the near-extinct clan organized its last *malanggan* ceremony with one or several specimens of the pattern it was giving up, it transmitted the concomitant knowledge to several members of the receiving clan, chosen by the leader of their own group, and declared them officially co-responsible for the "bone"—for the control, in other words—of the subtype of *malanggan*, while the "*malanggan* name" was ritually given to the youngest clan members. Henceforth, all of these new possessors of the copy right that would from then on be associated with their clan were obliged to pay their share of the financial burden (in pigs and shell money) of the *malanggan* ceremonies they would perform for the members of the dying clan.

There are also some instances in which a clan, through the agency of its leader, accepted to hand over its control of a *malanggan* pattern in exchange for the payment of a large sum in shell money necklaces—the equivalent, according to my informants, of approximately thirty pigs[7]. There is every reason to believe that only a great penury of possessions, and consequently, the prospect of being unable to honor its dead properly, could motivate an act of this sort. The oral tradition ascribes the disappearance, at an early date, of two *malanggan* patterns that originated on the Lelet plateau (the *lamalom* and *lavatindi*) to the sale of their control to clans from now extinct villages formerly located on the eastern and western foothills of the plateau. Those individuals who had managed to put together the sum needed for

---

7. A transaction of this type has been described by Powdermaker (1933: 210–233) in the Notsi area.

acquiring control of the *malanggan* were proclaimed the new possessors of the copy rights on its pattern, and the sum was divided up, as compensation payment, among all those copy right possessors in the clan that was selling, who had all accepted to forego their rights simultaneously. Theoretically, sale of the control of a subtype of *malanggan* could be reversed. In principle, the "father of the *malanggan*" (*tamak at lamalanggan*), which is to say the clan originally associated with the pattern created by one of its ancestors, had simply to return the shell money necklaces received. The buyer clan was then obliged to relinquish its recently acquired control.

Finally, until the turn of the century, when both the German colonial administrators and the missionaries banned these practices, a clan could in all probability obtain the control of a subtype of *malanggan* originally possessed by another clan by offering it the remains of one of its members—a woman or a child—specially sacrificed for that purpose. Although none of my informants ever mentioned this custom to me, I have inferred its existence from at least two indications. One of the stories traditionally narrated by the Kara, another linguistic group in the *malanggan* area (Küchler, 1983: 73), relates the tale of a man who secretly transmitted his knowledge about a *malanggan* pattern, free of charge, to his children. When he died, the children's clan group decided to kill one of its own women—in fact, the dead man's own wife—to appease the righteous anger of the outraged clan, and in compensation for the lost knowledge. The act most probably brought them control of that particular pattern. Secondly, I have been told by my informants on the Lelet plateau of how, at the turn of the century, a Mandak clan from a west coast village (Mesi) celebrated the "cargo cult" and sacrificed several of its infants, in vain, in the hopes that its members would become "the new holders of a copy right (*lunpanga*) for one of the White man's *malanggan*": in this case, a shark loaded down with goods and books, coming from the subterranean world of the dead, and diverted from its true destination—the Mandak—by the White men.[8] What I had first taken for rumors about cargo cult worshippers was probably actually a traditional way of achieving control of a *malanggan* pattern belonging to an alien group, converted into a way of obtaining Western commodities.

Despite the existence of these transfers from one clan to another, which were probably relatively exceptional before groups were obliged, by acculturation and the disappearance of many *malanggan*, to "portion out" the remaining patterns through a series of transactions, the *malanggan* (which varied considerably in appearance, and were accompanied by specific ceremonies) were unquestionably expressions of the specificity and identity of

---

8. See Derlon, 1997a.

the clan. Inasmuch as the copy rights given away by a clan were limited to a single specimen and had subsequently to be given back to the original clan, only a group that controlled a *malanggan* pattern could order the crafting of a great many specimens over a period spanning many lifetimes. Its name thus remained historically tied to a *malanggan*, clearly defined as different from the others by its form and its ritual display, and which was often decorated with designs showing its animal emblem. Moreover, Wilkinson (1978: 238) reports that in 1970, in the Tabar islands, the birthplace of the *malanggan* custom, several clans claimed to be the "owner" of a same "family" of *malanggan* (probably because the rules governing the management of the patterns were out of kilter by then). Each of these had modified, omitted or embroidered on some of its designs so that it could continue to express the "clan's individuality" through its particular treatment of that "family" it nonetheless shared with others.

Although it is no longer possible at present to obtain information about the origins of *malanggan* patterns, there is good reason to believe that they were often linked to the creation of new social units. A lineage or group of lineages that split off from the original clan because it had become too large, and sought to constitute an independent clan, needed to quickly acquire the means to express its new-found individuality through objects and rites of its own, and therefore invented a pattern of a new type or subtype of *malanggan*.

Land Rights: Use and Control

In the same way as it is improper, in my opinion, to use the term "property" to describe a clan's rights with respect to the *malanggan* pattern, and I believe the term "control" should be preferred, the expression "land ownership," ambiguous in itself, was rejected long ago by a number of specialists in their attempts to describe rights pertaining to land in most non-Western societies. As Jessep (1977: 128), taking the same course as Crocombe (1974), so rightly remarked, land tenure in most Papua New Guinea societies may be characterized by the distinction between two broad categories of rights: "use rights," usually exercised by individuals (with the exception of usage rights pertaining to a men's enclosure or to ceremonial grounds, for instance) and "rights of control," generally wielded by groups (local groups, kinship groups, etc.).

Jessep conducted research on land tenure among the Barok of New Ireland, the southerly neighbors of the Mandak, but never did any work on the *malanggan*, which had never taken hold in that particular region. Furthermore, he formulated a very clear definition of control of land, writing that it includes the following rights for the lineage that exerts such control:

"the right to exclude outsiders (or conversely, to allow outsiders to enter and make use of the land), the right to decide how the land and things on the land are to be used by existing members [...], and the right to alienate the land (i.e., to transfer the 'control' elsewhere)" (*Ibid.*: 145).

What I would like to show in the present discussion of land tenure is the very definite parallel between the "rights of control" and the "use rights," or "rights to exploit" (or to copy) as they applied to the land and to the *malanggan* in New Ireland. This parallel does not stop at the simple fact that in both cases the former were exerted by social units and the latter by individuals, any more than the fact that "control" included similar managerial rights in the two instances. In fact, there is a distinct analogy between some characteristics of these rights, the way they were acquired and the very objects to which they applied: land and the *malanggan*.

While the *malanggan* were an important element in the expression of the specificity of the clan, land was unquestionably the main symbol of the clan's identity, through the sacred site and the being which justified control over it.

Among the Mandak of the Lelet plateau, as in every known region where the *malanggan* prevailed, each clan was connected, and still is, to this day, with an animal spirit (bird, pig, dog, fish, etc.) with a name and a sacred site believed to be the place where the latter resides. In the local language the site and the animal are designated by the same term: *masalai* in neo-Melanesian (*laranda* in Mandak). The clan, personified by its first female ancestor, is said to have been born on the land that was the home of the animal which was to become its *masalai*.[9] The presence of the *masalai* site of the clan, bearing witness to the fact that it had emerged there, provides justification of its control on the surrounding land, exploited generation after generation, and on which the hamlets and men's houses administered by it are built. When two clans quarrel over a piece of land, there is always one clan that asks the other: "but where is your *masalai*?" If the clan questioned is unable to prove that its *masalai* is located near that particular plot, the chances of having its claim validated by the community are extremely slim.[10] Not only is the *masalai*, as a specific place, linked with the origins of the clan and its rights to the land, it is, moreover, the place in which the human potential of the clan is rooted, through the existence of invisible

---

9. There is a possibility that the animal-*masalai* was formerly viewed as an ancestor of the clan members. Both Powdermaker (1933: 39) and Jessep (1977: 162) report on villages (located, respectively, in the Notsi and Barok areas), investigated by them, in which one of the social units represented possessed a myth of its origins in which the first woman was born to the group's *masalai* animal.

10. Jessep (1977: 166 ff.) made the same finding for the Barok area *masalai*, which is linked to the lineage group rather than to the clan in this instance.

replicas of each of its living members, who live there with the animal-spirit. Unsurprisingly, then, when the Mandak express the fact that several lineages belong to a same clan, instead of mentioning the name of the clan to which they all belong (the clan name may in some cases be the same as the name of one of its lineages), they prefer to say that they share a same *masalai*, thus linking the clan's identity with that particular place and that intensely meaningful being.[11] It is in fact the *masalai* animal that is sculpted on many *malanggan* objects, to symbolize the clan. Furthermore, this *masalai* is viewed as particularly dangerous for the spouses of members of the clan with which it is associated, which spouses therefore avoid going anywhere near its site, or throwing any refuse (urine, excrements, food that has been in the mouth, spit, hair, etc.) anywhere in the area, since it might be drained onto it by flowing rainwater. In this sense, the *masalai* is probably a reflection of the perception that matrilineality would be endangered by excessively strong ties between husband and wife (see Schneider, 1961), and is the symbolic guardian, so to speak, of the matrilineal identity of the clan.

Let us now take a look at how individual rights to use of the land are established on the Lelet plateau, enabling the beneficiaries to build houses there and to cultivate the land, practicing, to this day, the slash-and-burn method.

In addition to the primordial, inalienable rights to use, acquired by birth on the land of his or her own clan, each individual possesses derived use rights to the land of his father's clan until the death of the latter, as well as to the land of his or her spouse's clan for the duration of their marriage.[12] The last two rights are understood as being comprised in the series of services (care, food, aid, etc.) owed to his children by a father, and by husband and wife, mutually, but for which the beneficiary is indebted, the debt being canceled, upon the death of the father or spouse by giving a pig as an offering for the rite (known as *lararabis*) preceding the end of the funerary cycle, formerly involving *malanggan* ceremonies.

When the Australian government inaugurated its policy of bounding native land in the 1960s, the native population, poorly informed, was under the erroneous impression that its intention was to reform the traditional land tenure system, replacing it by a rigid system based on the simple, strict rule

---

11. The same phenomenon was observed by Clay (1977: 37) in the coastal Mandak village of Pinikindu.

12. When a person dies, the harvests (consisting of taros, yams and bananas) from the gardens located on his or her own clan's land are entirely consumed during the various funerary rites. Inasmuch as trees (banana trees, the only ones that grow on this plateau, at an altitude of 1000 meters) are viewed as belonging to the person who planted them, any trees planted on his wife or children's land are uprooted by them within hours of a man's death.

of matrilinearity,[13] and that all use rights other than the above-mentioned would have to be sanctioned by the duly registered monetary purchase of the plot. Prior to that period, every individual possessed traditional means of obtaining lifelong rights to use the land of another clan. When a member of another clan died, a person could acquire the right to exploit and/or to occupy plots of land belonging to the clan of the deceased member for his entire lifetime, by offering a large pig during the funerary rites (*lararabis* or *malanggan*). This practice, known as *lembokakai* (from *lombo* "pig" and *kakai* "to acquire"), required the prior consent of the clan that controlled the desired piece of land. The clan retained the possibility of returning a same-sized animal to the giver, even years after the original transaction, thus signifying the termination of his rights to use.

Anyone could attempt to obtain use rights on land belonging to another clan by offering a pig, but those who did so most frequently, and with reasonable chances of being successful, were unquestionably the dead man's children, who wished to extend the derived rights to use a plot of land on their father's clan's territory. For one thing, there is not a single instance, in what remains of the oral tradition on the Lelet plateau, of a refusal by the father's clan to grant an extension of these rights, or of their sudden cancellation previous to the death of the beneficiary. Secondly, what angered the Mandak so was the fact that the new land laws introduced in the 1960s would prevent them from obtaining lifelong use of a piece of land from the paternal clan otherwise than by such a crude means as buying it. The other main advocates of this custom were those individuals who resided on the land of their spouse's clan (statistically speaking, there is a slight tendency for couples to live on the husband's territory) and had no desire to leave the hamlet in which they had spent so many years when their spouse died, to return to the territory of their own clan. The reason behind this might be some very strong ties they had developed there, or their immigrant or refugee status. As opposed to the children of the deceased, however, a spouse might not be given lifelong rights to use that land despite the many years he or she had spent with the spouse from that clan. Furthermore, even if a right was granted, there was no guarantee that it would not suddenly be withdrawn, by returning another pig, at the slightest quarrel between his or her clan and that of the deceased spouse.

In the old days, according to one of my elderly informants, this right could be obtained by offering a *malanggan* object rather than a pig. It was possible for an individual to use his personal right to reproduce a *malanggan* pattern to order a specimen which he would display on behalf of the

---

13. See Jessep, 1977: 117–120; 1980: 325.

deceased person's clan, with the prior consent of the latter. The advantage of this formula was that it enabled a clan or lineage to organize *malanggan* ceremonies for a deceased member even if no kin of the latter possessed a copy right for a pattern of a funerary effigy. At the same time, a person possessing a copy right for a *malanggan* was able to use that right and to transmit it to some young kin even if no death had occurred recently among members of his own group. For instance, by presenting a specimen on behalf of the clan of his deceased wife, a man might take advantage of the funerary rites for his wife to transmit a limited copy right for the pattern to one of his children and at the same time earn lifelong use rights to a piece of her clan's land.

Traditional land transactions between clans were not confined to rights to use, however. In some relatively exceptional contexts, a clan might alienate all or part of its territory to another clan.

When a clan died out, the clan that had agreed to perform the funerary rites for its last dead members inherited all of its territory in exchange. The only acceptable candidates for this transaction were—and still are, at present—either the clan of the children of one of the last male members of the near-extinct clan or at worst, a clan living on a territory adjacent to their own. In the former case it was because a child is always indebted to his father's clan, and cannot leave its dead unburied. In the latter, the idea was that as time passed and the *masalai*—or sacred site—of the extinct clan was gradually forgotten, the clan's control over the recently annexed territory would be eternally justified by the proximity of its own sacred, original site.[14]

Moreover, a clan, under the responsibility of its leader, would occasionally agree to give the control of a specific portion of its territory to another in exchange for a large sum of shell money. In an area such as the Lelet plateau where each clan's territories are extensive and quite similar, resourcewise, the main reason for purchasing permanent rights to land originally controlled by another clan was that the clan had fled following a war between villages, to become refugees, or again, the desire of coastland groups to immigrate to that fertile mountainous region.

Finally, although my informants have never mentioned this custom, there was quite probably another less expensive solution for a refugee or immigrant clan in search of land. When the husband of one of its female members died, the woman, or her youngest child, was killed and the remains were offered to the dead man's clan, in exchange for which the latter turned over the control of some pieces of its territory. This hypothesis is supported by a number

---

14. As Jessep (1977: 190) so rightly points out for a similar custom prevailing among the Barok.

of arguments: (1) the existence of this curious way of acquiring land has been reported in some regions touching the Mandak area on either side, including on the Tabar islands, among the Barok, but also among the Kara[15] where, as seen above, the same act—the sacrificing of a woman at her husband's death— could also enable a clan to acquire control of a *malanggan* pattern; (2) the existence of the "cargo cult" among the Mandak, mentioned above, seems to attest that sacrificing infants was in fact a traditional way of gaining control over something belonging to another group, and of a *malanggan* pattern in particular; (3) on the Lelet plateau the other known types of compensation for the transfer of control of land and of *malanggan* patterns—which is to say, the performance of funeral rites for a near-extinct clan and the payment of shell money—are very much equivalent.

In the same way as a "father of a *malanggan*"—a clan originally associated with a pattern—on the Lelet plateau could theoretically repossess itself of that control by simply returning the shell money necklaces it had received in payment, among the neighboring Barok, the clan originally associated with a piece of land (also designated as the "father" of that land) could recover the control of the plots it had given away by restituting whatever compensation it had received in exchange (Jessep, 1977: 147–148). We would not be surprised if the latter rule applied on the Lelet plateau in the case of land as well, with original rights to control overriding those acquired through transactions, as they do for *malanggan* patterns.

Systematic Equivalencies

The management of *malanggan* patterns seems to be very similar to the management of land, then, except for the fact that the right to exploit a *malanggan* pattern was not a birthright, nor did it belong to all members of the controlling clan, but was only transmitted to some individuals within that group.[16]

The analogies between inter-clan transactions for the transfer of control of land and of *malanggan* patterns are so obvious that they call for no comment. The parallels between the rights to exploit these two types of cultural objects are much more subtle, on the other hand.

Firstly, in the case of transfer of these exploitation rights between members of different clans, we note that an individual who had acquired a lim-

---

15. See Groves (1934–1935: 352–353) for Tabar, Linge (1932: 11, 50) and Jessep (1977: 205–214) for the Barok area, and Billings and Peterson (1967: 26) for the Kara area.

16. This has to do with the political function of the rights to exploit *malanggan* as well as with their role as markers of the social distinctions within the clan (see Wilkinson, 1978: 239).

ited copy right for a *malanggan* pattern controlled by another group (his father's clan or the clan of a kin by marriage) could not transmit that right to a member of his own clan, but was obliged to give it back to a young member of the clan controlling the pattern following use. Similarly, a person who had acquired lifelong use rights to a piece of land controlled by another clan (his father's clan or the clan of a kin by marriage) could not transmit them to his descendants but had to turn them over to the controlling clan for exploitation by a member of the younger generation. In other words, in both instances—land and *malanggan* patterns—rights to exploitation transmitted to non-members of the clan were not conceived as permanently acquired by the beneficiary's own group, but rather as strictly individual, temporary rights that should not deprive the younger generations of the controlling clan of the legitimate use of those possessions.

It is clear, moreover, that an understanding of the land tenure system sheds light on many of the otherwise enigmatic specifics of the legal system regulating the *malanggan*.

The first point is that the only individuals habilitated to receive a copy right during childhood and to be symbolically identified with the *malanggan*, were the members of the clan that controlled the pattern and the children of its male members. The reason behind this becomes clear when we look at what happens with land tenure: (1) the only land rights acquired by individuals *at birth* are those attached to their own clan or their father's clan (for the father's lifetime); (2) the right to lifelong use, acquired at the father's death in exchange for a pig, was an extension of the birthright to the land of the father's clan; (3) although this lifelong right to use was neither free nor automatic, it was nonetheless viewed as a child's basic right, since the father's clan could not deny it, nor withdraw it once it had been granted. In other words, children's access to use of a possession controlled by their father's clan—be it to land or to a *malanggan*—was construed as a right, just as legitimate as the use right enjoyed by the young members of that clan.

The land tenure system also throws light on another peculiarity of the rights to exploit *malanggan* patterns. When transfer of a copy right for a *malanggan* took place between members of the controlling clan, the person who gave it up simultaneously relinquished his (or her) own right to copy the pattern, whereas he retained it when that right was transmitted to a person from another clan, the purpose being precisely to maintain the possibility of passing it on to young members of his own social group in the future. This becomes less obscure, in my opinion, if we consider the fact that only at death did an individual lose his inalienable rights to the land of his own clan, which was then turned over to the younger generation of that same group.

Now, if we take a look at the system of equivalencies instituted by the rules regulating both the *malanggan* and land tenure, we can see that it is quite logical for an individual who wishes to obtain a lifetime right to exploit a plot belonging to another clan to offer to display a *malanggan* sculpture for a funeral ceremony, instead of giving a pig. Indeed, not only was there a definite equivalency between a pig and a *malanggan* object (since, in the transmission of copy rights for a pattern between members of different clans, by offering a pig the new holder earned the right to produce a single specimen of that pattern), but also, the lifelong right to cultivate a plot controlled by another clan was effectively construed as the symbolic equivalent of the right to order the production of a *malanggan* specimen, since the same object—a pig—could be offered as a means of acquiring either of those two rights (see Fig. 2). On the basis of this conception, applied to the transfer from one clan to another of rights to control a territory and *malanggan*, both of which may be obtained in the same manner—in exchange for a human life, shell money and/or pigs, depending on the context—it seems probable that a clan may have offered its control over a *malanggan* pattern in exchange for control over a piece of land (see Fig. 3)[17]. Transfer of rights of control and rights to use of land and of *malanggan* patterns was governed by the following equivalencies, then:

$$\frac{1 \text{ pig}}{\substack{1 \text{ human life} \\ \text{or } n \text{ pigs} \\ \text{or } n \text{ shells}}} = \frac{(\text{Right to}) \ 1 \ malanggan \ \text{specimen}}{\text{Control of a pattern}} = \frac{\text{Lifetime use of a plot}}{\text{Control of land}}$$

Furthermore, inasmuch as a *malanggan* specimen was construed as the equivalent of a right to use land, limited to the lifetime of the beneficiary, it is understandable that rights to exploit *malanggan* patterns were not restricted to a single specimen when transfer took place within the clan, as opposed to the rule applying to transmission outside of the clan, since the main characteristic of the former resided in the fact that they were transmissible to the beneficiary's matrilineal descendants.

Now, as for women's access to copy rights on *malanggan*, it is clearly quite logical, since there were no differences between women and men with respect to land tenure.

---

17. The gift of control over land or over a *malanggan* pattern may have served as compensation for a homicide (the taking of a human life). Jessep (1977: 214–226) notes that in the Barok area, compensation for the death of an ally or an enemy might take the form of the gift of a plot of land, at the end of a war. In 1993, during my second stay on the Lelet plateau, I learned that two hostile groups could make peace if the land on which the blood of a homicide victim had been shed was given to that person's clan by the clan that controlled it.

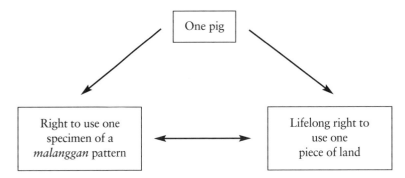

Figure 2: Equivalencies between rights to use land and *malanggan* (case 1).

More generally speaking, in the same way as a *malanggan* pattern controlled by a clan was an abstract image, occasionally concretized by individuals in the form of specimens, land controlled by a clan was a place occasionally worked by individuals in the form of clearings.

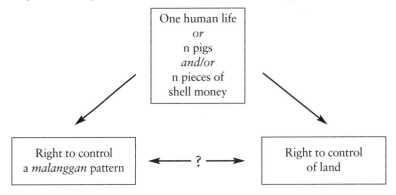

Figure 3: Equivalencies between rights to control land and *malanggan* (case 2).

It must be said that there were probably other analogies between land and *malanggan* patterns. Küchler, who sensed the existence of some such analogies through instances of transfer of *malanggan* rights still related today in the oral tradition of the Kara people of the northern part of the island, establishes one interesting parallel. In this tradition, the production of the *malanggan* object is compared to the cultivating of gardens, both of which took place during the ceremony period, and more specifically, gardening based on the slash-and-burn technique is paralleled with the practice of blowing on incandescent corals applied to the sculpture, so as to obtain delicate indentations in the object, both of which techniques were given to human beings by the same animal entity, according to a Kara myth (Küchler, 1983: 74–75). In addition, there may conceivably have been something, for the *malanggan*, equivalent to the sacred site of the origins of the clan, the *masalai*, whose presence legitimates the clan's control over the surrounding land, which it considers its own, and therefore also justifies the permanent rights wielded by members of that particular clan over the territory. I wonder, too, whether some portion of the wealth of knowledge pertaining to a *malanggan* pattern, including perhaps the myth of its origin, did not fulfill that same function, and consequently was not transmitted exclusively to the members of the clan controlling the pattern. That is to say, in the same way as in disputes over land, an individual claiming rights to use and occupy a piece of land on the basis of an alleged matrilineal right is often asked by the group that questions his rights and asserts its control over the disputed territory to prove its proximity to the *masalai* site of his clan, perhaps an individual claiming possession of an unlimited copy right for a *malanggan* pattern may have been asked, by the clan that challenged the nature of his right and asserted its control over that pattern, to narrate the myth of its origins.

Matriliny, Paternal Filiation and Dualism

How, then, should we interpret this application of the land tenure system to the formulation of a conception of *malanggan* as abstract patterns subjected to rights to reproduction and control?

In my opinion, the first thing to do is to reject any functionalist analysis construing *malanggan* as an institution, mediated by an object and the displaying of that object, aimed at the symbolic reinforcement of fragile land tenure laws. For one thing, there were most probably just as many deviations in the application of the *malanggan* pattern system as in the land tenure system, when applied to the retrocession of limited use rights to the clan of origin. Secondly, in the Barok area, where *malanggan* were unknown, a land tenure system quite similar to the one prevailing on the Lelet plateau has always functioned on the sole strength of its own laws.

Rather, it would be preferable to consider that this overdetermination of the legal system reflected, precisely, its crucial importance to that society. The reasons for the use of the same system for the two primordial possessions of the clan group, both equally linked with its origins and its identity, would then be sought in the very essence of this system, in the social logic conveyed by it, or again, in those aspects highlighted by the specific forms it takes when applied to the *malanggan*.

Considering the matrilineal nature of filiation in New Ireland, one of the main significant points in this legal system definitely resides in the rights received by individuals to exploit the land or *malanggan* of their paternal clan. These rights were similar in the two instances, but differed notably in one respect: where the *malanggan* pattern was concerned, not only was it the father himself, and not his clan when he died, who transferred them personally to his child, but secondly, it was deemed necessary for the son to take wife in his father's clan so that the rights, once used, could be returned to a youthful member of the clan controlling the pattern. When it was land that was transferred this requirement was superfluous inasmuch as the child's usage right automatically ceased at his death and the plots he had exploited until then again became available to the members of the clan controlling the land.[18]

Our first remark is that when a man personally turned the copy right for a *malanggan* pattern over to his male child, he also disclosed the secret knowledge attached to a possession controlled by his clan, thus bringing the boy to participate fully, as a candidate for initiation, in the funeral ceremony organized by his father. This helped to strengthen the emotional bonds between the two. Through a valuable possession transmitted in this way, the son might later hope to achieve the status of "big man," which status was gained by repeatedly organizing *malanggan* ceremonies and depended to a large extent on the child's having inherited—from both the maternal and the paternal sides—rights to exploit patterns of these ceremonial effigies.[19] Last, the father gained considerable ascendancy over his son since it was he who guaranteed that the right he had given to the latter would be returned to a youthful member of his own clan in the future.

This did not mean that in doing so the man let down his matrilineal group, which expected him to transmit both the possession and the knowledge to his sister's child, thus making sure his own clan would remain in possession of its entire heritage over the generations. For although he could give his child the right to reproduce each of those subtypes of *malanggan* controlled by his clan for which he himself had a copy right, he could not rob the clan of those rights, for it was his duty to conserve them so as to give them away, simultaneously or subsequently, to his sister's child. Moreover, to avoid any dangerous confusion between his own child and his sis-

---

18. It should be remembered that whereas land rights were transmitted collectively within the clan controlling the land, rights to the *malanggan* patterns were necessarily transferred from one individual to another, while rights unused by an individual because of his death, leaving for a foreign land or loss interest in the *malanggan* custom (owing to the influence of the missionaries, for instance), were canceled and could not be recovered.

19. It would be well worth finding out whether the "big men" of the Lelet plateau were also great manipulators of land rights, and if they managed to obtain rights to exploit much larger pieces of land than the ordinary people, as Lomas (1979) found to be the case for the Tigak people's "big men." Lomas rightly emphasizes the fact that *malanggan* ceremonies served as a pretense for reexamining land rights, the redefinition of which mostly took place in the context of funerals, as seen above. He believes that this function explains why these ceremonies survived until the 1960s despite the considerable acculturation of the Tigak by that time.

ter's child, the rights transferred to the two kinds of children differed in nature. In the first case the right was a limited one, paid for and necessarily given back, whereas the second was unlimited and was given free of charge. Last, there was no risk that the father's authority would override the authority exerted over the child by his maternal uncle. Not only was it the maternal uncle who made the exploitation right transferable from father to child by providing the latter with the pig without which the transaction could not take place, but again, that same uncle was perfectly free to transfer to the same child his own copy rights to one or several patterns controlled by the clan to which they both belonged. He would then make sure that the boy used those rights later on, and transmitted them in turn to young members of his clan. Again, the maternal uncle who gave the child unlimited copy rights authorizing the production of several specimens of each pattern could be more influential than the father in helping the child to achieve the status of "big man," since a man's prestige depended on the number of *malanggan* ceremonies he organized, and the number of objects exhibited during these.

The subtleties of the rules governing the management of *malanggan* patterns thus enabled the father to satisfy the feelings that prompted him to transmit his possessions and knowledge to his own child, to be instrumental in improving the child's social status and to exert some authority over him without having those feelings constitute a threat to the matrilineal nature of filiation, since they were perfectly channeled. Indeed, as Schneider (1961) has so brilliantly shown, in a demonstration after which I have closely patterned my own discussion, the expression of these feelings is viewed as dangerous by matrilineal societies.

In addition, by leading their sons to marry women from their father's clan, or to be more accurate, by making compulsory what is already the preferred form of marriage (the only observable form, and the only one explicitly acknowledged by the Mandak, along with village endogamy), fathers who transferred exploitation rights for a *malanggan* to their sons and thus caused postponement of the exchange of wives between two clans, which then spanned at least two generations,[20] were thus paradoxically consolidating matrilineal filiation[21] in a society pervaded by strong patrilateral feelings.

---

20. The phenomenon was most probably reiterated from generation to generation, since a man who, having married a woman belonging to his father's clan, transmitted to his own son a copy right for a pattern he had received from his father in a limited form, often also gave that son the right to exploit a pattern controlled by his own clan, and thus obliged him to take wife in his father's clan as well.

21. The advantages, in the matrilineal societies of Melanesia, of having sons marry women from their father's clan, have been pointed out by Nash (1974: 119), in particular, quoted in Jessep (1977: 348) and Panoff (1976: 185).

It is a fact that in New Ireland men's bonds to their children receive symbolic and social recognition in a variety of powerful forms. These are quite unusual in matrilineal societies, but rather similar to what Panoff (1976) evidenced in the Maenge of neighboring New Britain. Far from ignoring or minimizing the role of the father in conception, the Mandak view the father's semen as the substance responsible for shaping the embryo, and confine the mother's role to feeding the child during the embryonic stage. The child is said to be the father's "blood," the "blood" of his father's lineage and clan, and a clan or lineage is said to be the "blood" of another social unit when one of its women had married a man from that social group, in earlier times, and clan members still have matrilineal descendants of that group. Moreover, members of a clan use a special term (*lenat*) to designate the child of one of its male members. There are a great many ways for men to give their possessions to one of their children. For example, the oldest son receives a very valuable shell money necklace at his father's death, bridewealth is provided by the young husband's father, and in the old days when the official "village head" died his oldest son took over his position. Given this context, it was understandably important for sons to marry women from their father's clan. The interest of this operation was reinforced by the *malanggan* custom, thanks to which all of the important possessions transmitted by a father to his son would return to their clan of origin at the very next generation, through the mediation of the grandchild.[22]

The acquisition of individual rights to the land and *malanggan* patterns of the father's clan was only one aspect of a legal system within which the entire range of inter-clan transfers of rights to use and control of land and *malanggan* took place essentially between groups bound by ties of marriage, and for the most part — but not exclusively — in the opposite direction from the circulation of women. To give a woman in marriage to a member of another clan was indeed the surest way for a group to obtain rights to the land and *malanggan* of that particular clan. These might be limited rights to exploitation, transmitted to that woman's child, or include rights to control obtained in exchange for the killing of the woman (or of her infant) when her husband died, or in exchange for the performance of funerary rites when the husband's clan was nearing extinction. Nonetheless, the existence of transfer of rights to exploit a *malanggan* from a man to his sister's husband, like the possibility for a man to obtain lifetime rights to work the land of his wife's clan after her death are indications that the circulation of rights to land and *malanggan* might parallel that of women, at least in the case of rights to use.

---

22. In their kinship terminology, of the Iroquois type, grandfather and grandchild are designated by one and the same term (*tumbuk*, on the Lelet plateau).

At this point, we must raise the question of the logic prevailing in this situation. In a society where clans clamored their specificity assertively, why would a group accept to give an individual belonging to a clan bound to it by a marriage (and most frequently belonging to the clan of the wife of one of its own male members) the right to use a possession—land or *malanggan*—connected with its origins and tied to its identity? Better still, why would it agree to alienate that possession to that other clan, when this meant no less than the renunciation of a way of expressing its own specificity?

Our first remark is that any transfer of a right to land or a *malanggan* was accompanied by cooperation between the individuals or groups bound together by a marriage, inasmuch as the compensations offered for the acquisition of the right to use or control were necessarily displayed at funeral ceremonies for deceased members of the clan that had relinquished the right.

To be precise, it must be said that in the Mandak area, like six of the ten other linguistic areas in which the *malanggan* custom prevailed, including the Tabar islands, believed to be the birthplace of the custom, clans are divided into two exogamous moieties (designated by the names of two birds: *Pandion leucocephalus* and *Haliaëtus leucogaster*) between which exchanges of goods and services abound on all ritual occasions. For instance (and to confine ourselves to the context of funerals), it is always up to the members of the opposite moiety to prepare the corpse for the funeral rite, and during the *malanggan* ceremonies exchanges of equivalent amounts of food and valuables take place repeatedly between individuals representing their respective moieties. In other words, inter-clan transfers of rights to land and *malanggan* take place between two moieties already bound by reciprocal obligations concerning their dead, and further accentuate their cooperation in this domain.

Now, as Wagner (1986: 49; 1987: 58) so accurately put it for the Barok, and as Clay's work on the Mandak area had already indicated, the theories on conception[23] prevailing in these two linguistic areas designate each moiety as the maternal container of its members, and the source of the life of members of the other moiety, who are indebted to them for their "blood." So that an interdependent, perpetually asymmetrically alternating relationship develops between the two groups, each of which claims to have created the other through the male act of procreation of its members.[24]

Perhaps, then, we should consider the possibility that the transmission

---

23. The Barok do not view the father as solely responsible for the embryonic substance, however. His sperm reveals the procreative capacities of the woman by transforming her vaginal secretions into "good blood," as opposed to "bad (menstrual) blood," and the embryo is composed of the woman's blood and the sperm (Wagner, 1986: 62–63).

24. In this case it is not the givers of women who are superior, but the givers of "blood." This is corroborated both by the deference with which people living on the Lelet refer to those

of rights to land and *malanggan* to a group other than the clan controlling them symbolically retraced the path taken by the "blood" transmitted through the paternal line. This would be the case even when these possessions circulated in parallel with women, because in those cases they came from a clan and a moiety which had assumed, in a previous generation, or would necessarily assume, in a future one, the role of taker of wives, and therefore of giver of "blood" to the clan or moiety to which it was giving those rights. "You gave me or will give me wives, I gave you or will give you my 'blood'; therefore I am or will be your origin and the fountain on which your group feeds, and this entitles you to the right to use signs of the origins and identity of my clan." This seems to be the logic of the circulation of rights to land and *malanggan* between individuals and groups united by marriage, and which may therefore be viewed as a recognition of the paternal tie symbolized by the sharing of "blood" and also as a way of expressing the interdependence of the dual groups.[25]

In other words, the *malanggan*, symbolizing the "food" that all individuals receive from their matrilineal group while their rights to a pattern were transmitted, free of charge, from generation to generation within the controlling clan, was a dialectic object that came to symbolize the "blood" transmitted along paternal lines that comes and goes between dual groups. It justified transfers of possessions, subject to reimbursement or retrocession when the rights to a pattern were transferred, against compensation, to a clan united to the controlling clan by marriage. Interdependence does not cancel the specific identity of the groups it binds, and a child, "blood" and substance of his father, is no less a member of his mother's kinship group, and this is why land and *malanggan* patterns had to remain instruments of the expression of the specificity of the clan. The alienation of their control to a group viewed as the "blood" of the controlling clan was only justifiable under exceptional circumstances requiring extraordinary cooperation between clans united by marriage and bound by strong ties of solidarity.

Iconology bears out the idea that the *malanggan*, the patterns of which were under clan control, were conceived as emanations of a dual group, and were linked with the interdependence of the moieties and of the clans bound by marriage.

---

people and groups whose "blood" they claim to be, and by the low bridewealth payments and the fact that these call for valuable counter-gifts.

25. The fact that no such dual organization exists in the extreme northern parts of New Ireland does not contradict the essence of this interpretation. In fact, Chinnery (1929: 14) notes that in some villages, clans said to be "brothers" could not exchange wives and that clans actually were divided into two matrimonial classes. Elsewhere, we may postulate the existence of a tradition of intermarriage between specific clans, which could thereafter mutually consider themselves the "blood" of the other.

Figure 4: *Malanggan* of the *uli* type representing a lunar entity symbolizing one of the dual clan groups (taken from E. Krämer-Bannow, *Bei kunstsinnigen Kannibalen der Südsee: Wanderungen auf Neu-Mecklenburg 1908–1909*, Berlin, Verlag Dietrich Reimer, 1916).

On the Lelet plateau—and in all likelihood throughout New Ireland— the moieties, designated by birds, were also symbolized on the one hand by the male, solar being and on the other by the lunar being represented as female, as the wife of the sun. Through their name and/or what they represented, the *malanggan* types used in this mountainous region referred to the bird or other entity emblematic of the moiety comprising the clans originally controlling their patterns[26].

---

26. The *malanggan* shaped like a movable, bird-like hut evocative of the embodiment of the dead person was designated by the name of the bird (*lamalom*) emblematic of the moi-

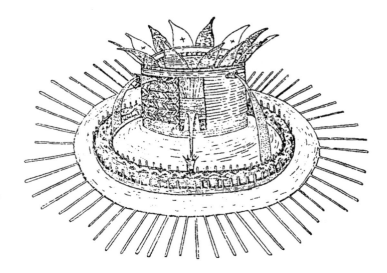

Figure 5: *Malanggan* of the *luara* type representing a solar entity symbolizing one of the dual clan groups (taken from A. Krämer, *Die Malanggane von Tombara*, München, Georg Müller, 1925).

Apparently, in other regions the expression of interdependence of the two moieties may have been an important element in the symbolism of a *malanggan* type controlled by a single clan, through the existence of some subtypes or specimens linked with one of the two groups and others linked with the opposite moiety. According to Küchler (1983), in the Kara area the presence or absence of a circular pectoral ornament on *malanggan* objects representing a figure with a protruding breast served to identify the specimen as male or female, respectively, and as belonging to one of the two moieties.[27] This ornament definitely was not reserved for men only. Because of its form, it certainly symbolized the male solar entity which, in turn, must have represented one of the moieties. Furthermore, according to Küchler, the bird shown on the head and/or feet of the figure was the emblem of

---

ety linked with the moon. The root of the word designating that same bird (*lulilom*—called *uli* elsewhere) was a component of the name of the hermaphrodite-like *malanggan* figure representing the lunar entity with its dual sexual identity. The other type of *malanggan* in widespread use on the plateau, a wicker disc (*luara*), was viewed as representing the sun.

27. Powdermaker (1933: 317), who first mentions the existence of non-anthropomorphic types of *malanggan* in the Notsi area, goes on to say that each *malanggan* object was identified as male or female. If this is the case, it is probably because the sex of the object was purely and simply the emblem of the moiety with which it was identified.

a clan belonging to one of the two dual units, whereas the birds represented on the body of the figure symbolized a clan belonging to the opposite dual group. According to oral tradition, these two clans were linked, precisely, by an exchange of women and of rights to that particular pattern.

I must add that many *malanggan* specimens of every type and from every region display circular or crescent-shaped designs that probably expressed their participation in the moieties symbolized by the sun and the moon, and that other designs may have had the same function, perhaps through a reference to mythic events connected with one or the other of those beings.[28]

New Ireland societies construed sacred *malanggan* objects—perfectly ephemeral and not meant to circulate, since they were doomed to be destroyed—as the concretization of a previously acquired right to their pattern, and that pattern was a symbolic equivalent of the land. Both were equally valuable as exchangeable sources of wealth, similarly linked to the origins and identity of the clan, identically destined to circulate between individuals and groups in the form of rights to use and control. Like land, patterns were exploitable by individuals in the temporary, constantly renewed form of material objects, just as land was exploited in the form of clearings. Through this conception, emphasis was placed on the fact that the only justification of the utilization of things—that is to say, of those possessions that are most prized, both materially and morally, by the clan of whose identity they are the receptacle and the concentrated essence—resides in the law, the primordial, founding principle of the social order. The Mandak did not grant the rights to these possessions restrictively to members of the kinship group that controlled them and for whom they constituted the symbolic equivalent of the food given by a mother to her unborn child. For this people, with their combination of matrilineal filiation and strong patrilateral bonds, those rights that were transmitted beyond the boundaries of the clan were the equivalent of the substance which only the father can give to the child, according to the prevailing theories of conception. This seems to be a way of implicitly acknowledging that the fundamental interdependence which impels exchanges and reciprocity is the interdependence of the sexes in the reproduction of the species: that Sameness must always be nourished by the Other, and that this does not rob it of its identity.

Translated by Helen Arnold

---

28. This conclusion may be drawn from some observations made by Peekel (1927: 22–27), a German missionary who spent more than twenty years in New Ireland. His writings have, wrongly, been overlooked by later students of the *malanggan*, some of whom accused him of being obsessed with the solar and lunar symbolism, the meaning of which has now been considerably clarified.

Chapter 9

Australian Aboriginal Ritual Objects

Or How to Represent the Unrepresentable*

Marika Moisseeff

By definition, a ritual object is a material artifact designed for a specifically ritual purpose. Logically, then, one may suppose that the physical aspect given to it, or for which it was chosen—its sensory properties—is directly related to the role it will be called upon to play in the rites in which it is manipulated. Conversely, the articulation between the physical aspect and the function of these objects may be expected to shed new light on what is at stake in the rite itself, namely, its efficacy: does not the latter derive from the particular representational role such objects are made to play? This question is often evacuated in studies devoted to ritual objects. Some writers view their efficacy as given from the start, and confine themselves to describing their appearance and the way they are used, without establish-

* First published as "Les objets cultuels aborigènes ou comment représenter l'irreprésentable," *Genèse* 17, 1994: 8–32. The study of ritual objects on which the present article is based received support in the form of funding from the Fyssen Foundation (1990–91 research fellowship). It also received encouragement in the form of the comments made during a number of seminars at which I presented some aspects of my work. I wish to express my gratitude to all those who have given me help and suggestions, and more specially to X. Blaisel, R. Boulay, P. Boyer, D. de Coppet, R. Guidieri, J. Hassoun, M. Cartry, M. Coquet, M. Houseman, A. Itéanu, M. Izard, M.-J. and R. Jamous, B. Juillerat, B. Mauzé, C. Rabant, L. Racine and S. Tcherkézoff.

ing any connection between the two (see various examples in Surgy, 1985). Others, those with structuralist leanings, view these objects as conveying meaning, but tend to neglect their specificity by treating such material, non verbal signifiers as though they were linguistic signs. Their material aspect is reduced to phenomena of a discursive nature, such as metaphor and metonymy (Heusch, 1970), proper names (Humphrey, 1993), the opposition between meaningful and "empty" verbal signs (Pouillon, 1970), and so on. For the most part, then, the power of agency of these objects as such remains to be explained.

While the above-mentioned approaches definitely have made interesting contributions, their weak point is their tendency to treat the category of ritual objects as equivalent to that of discursive phenomena. This easily eclipses the distinctive position occupied by these objects as mediators between elements belonging to other semiotic categories (acts, speech) intervening in the ritual. It is all the easier to follow this inclination since local exegeses, when they exist, have the same tendency to account for all ritual phenomena, objects included, in reference to mythical explanations. However, while it is legitimate to establish relations between mythical and ritual symbolisms, it is equally legitimate to suppose that the two are distinct.[1] One pertains to the register of discourse and narration, while the other has to do with representation and action. Rituals do not simply say something, they show and are held to "do" something as well.

The fact that rituals entail the manipulation of material objects immediately locates them in a register other than that to which myths are confined. Such objects are concretely present; their existence cannot be reduced to the discourse surrounding them. Paradoxically, acts of camouflage, as when ritual objects are covered or placed behind a screen, often reinforce their presence. There is a definite connection between the tangible reality of these objects and the invisibility of the agents—spirits, ancestors and the like—held to be brought into play by the rite. As opposed to the process at work in simple narration, these invisible agents, or forces, are convoked by the rite. It is at this level that the specific mediating role of ritual objects intervenes. A special evocative power is ascribed to them. This evocative power, I suggest, is grounded in the unique physical features of these objects, crafted according to special conventions that often lend them a peculiar quality of their own. It is worth remarking, however, that the evocative capacity of such objects is only fully perceptible during their ritual manipulation; that is, when they are handled in a context linking them to other

---

1. This point is stressed by Lévi-Strauss in the "Finale" of *L'homme nu* (1971), in which he reminds us of the need to adopt radically distinct methodologies for the analysis of the formal structure of myths and of rites.

specifically ritual phenomena. When ritual objects are kept after a ceremony is over, their role outside the ritual frame is not the same. They may be used, for instance, to bolster the privileged status of those individuals who have exclusive responsibility for them. The essentially ritual nature of their vocation is all the more patent in the case of objects produced for a particular ritual and discarded or destroyed following its performance.

A whole range of phenomena deployed during ritual activities, including ornaments, body movements, chants, discourse and a variety of objects, are distinct from similar phenomena in use in everyday life. When the ritual is over, these different elements become disentangled, and by the same token lose the distinctive role they had acquired in that unusual context. What distinguishes a ritual act from ordinary acts, then, is not so much the peculiar nature of the various phenomena involved, as their combination in the predetermined space and period of time that define its formal framework. A ritual always brings together phenomena belonging to different semiotic categories — words, acts, objects — entailing different perceptive registers: hearing and sight in particular, but others as well. In this light, to the extent that the efficacy of these objects is to be viewed as one of their essential properties, it becomes fundamental to link the sensory properties of these objects to the way they are used in a ceremonial context, a path first followed by Ellen (1988) and Augé (1988).

This is the approach I propose to adopt in order to reconsider the *tjurunga*,[2] a ritual object of the Aranda. Since the publication of the first anthropological accounts of this Aboriginal group from the central Australian desert (see especially, Strehlow, 1907–1921; Spencer and Gillen, 1899, 1904, 1927; Strehlow, 1968 [1947]), a number of interpretations of *tjurunga* have appeared in the anthropological literature, ranging from *The elementary forms of the religious life* (Durkheim, 1968 [1912] to *The savage mind* (Lévi-Strauss, 1962a), and including those found in Mauss and Roheim, to mention only the great classics. First, the substance of these interpretations will be presented succinctly. As will be seen, it is Durkheim's conceptual framework that has the greatest affinities with the perspective outlined here. In order to develop this perspective further, I will briefly summarize the Aranda cosmology, with its holistic representation of the world in which *tjurunga* play an important role. I will then go on to examine these objects, with particular emphasis on those which may be qualified as prototypical. Next, I will consider their representational properties, whose complexity derives from the fact that the inscriptions that adorn these flat wooden or stone objects are of a special type: neither figurative nor abstract. They are alternately and simultaneously representations of the Aranda's key concept,

---

2. Also written *churinga* after Spencer and Gillen.

the Dreaming, of prodigious beings and of an individual person's singularity. However, as I will show, in the last analysis, the only thing a *tjurunga* refers to is itself. It is, indeed, the self-referential nature of this ritual object—the underpinning of which is its material nature—that makes it so effective in the rites in which it is deployed. A description of one of these rites will be used to illustrate this. Finally, some hypotheses of a more general nature pertaining to ritual objects will be presented.

A Historical Object

In order to put the anthropological interpretations of *tjurunga* into perspective, let us begin with a presentation of the psychoanalytic viewpoint formulated by Roheim (see, in particular, 1970 [1945]). Roheim views the *tjurunga* as a gage given to the man being initiated by his initiators in exchange for his leaving his mother on their demand. It is a phallic object—because of its elongated shape—with a maternal symbol on it—the circle(s) carved on its surface—that enables the novice to overcome his longing for his mother's bosom. At the same time, Roheim sees subincision—an incision made on the under side of the penis—as a way of representing female genitals on the male sexual organ. Causing their subincision opening to bleed during certain rites is interpreted as a way for the initiated men to imitate menstruating women. From this standpoint, the *tjurunga* is related to the subincised penis, in that it is a phallus carrying a female symbol representing the mother. Both are compensations for the loss of the first libidinal object, making it possible to "transfer the libido from the mother to the group of fathers"; both are viewed as cultural means for overcoming the castration complex. Each discipline has its own aims and methods. For a long time, and particularly during the period when Roheim was writing, the primary goal of Freudian psychoanalysis was to uncover childhood sexuality and its metamorphoses in the psychology of adults. In this respect, Roheim's interpretation is not uninteresting. However, it locates the efficacy of the *tjurunga* essentially in its response to the needs of the individual psyche, and therefore diverges somewhat from our own concerns[3].

In Mauss' treatment of *tjurunga* (1969 [1900]), he is carried away by his desire to see any objects that have some value in "the most primitive societies" as objects of exchange, so as to bolster his own conceptions of gift-giving. He takes at face value, so to speak, the description provided by Eylmann, who, in turn, had heard it from native guides "from very distant lands": *tjurunga* were "black people's money" (Vol. 2: 110). Now, native guides are definitely in a position to establish a parallel between the great

---

3. For a new psychoanalytic interpretation of *tjurunga*, see Morton, 1985, 1987.

value ascribed to money by their European employers and the supreme value ascribed to sacred objects in Aboriginal societies. As at once close and distant intermediaries between Whites and Blacks, they are particularly well situated to point to the value *tjurunga* might have as objects of exchange in transactions between these two groups.[4] It is all the easier to make this confusion, since the term *tjurunga* refers to a multitude of objects that do not all have the same function. Some definitely are given away (as a gage of luck in hunting), while others are loaned (those connected with the dead), but no such transaction may be found for those manipulated during fertility rites and initiations, and which are of particular interest to us for that very reason. Unfortunately, Mauss made no attempt to account for the ritual use of these objects, whereas it is the value ascribed to them in this context that is most meaningful. In fact, he reduces their ritual importance to an essentially mythic dimension, on the basis of a somewhat circular reasoning that he ascribes to the Aborigines. Because, in those legendary, bygone days, "it was they [*tjurunga*] that gave birth to the souls of animals and men", and because these species continue to reproduce season after season, the efficacy of *tjurunga* was demonstrated. These objects therefore have both a "mythical" and an "experimental" value, in that they reduce the distance or "at once infinite and historically measured time" separating living persons from that legendary era (Vol. I: 475). This interpretation is somewhat reminiscent of the role ascribed to these objects by Lévi-Strauss: that of restoring diachrony (the historic dimension) within synchrony (the present and ritual celebrations).

For Lévi-Strauss (1969), the *tjurunga* is "the past, materially present" (p. 238) because it represents "the physical body of an ancestor" (p. 86). The phrase is a fine one, and has the advantage of emphasizing the importance of the materiality of the object as the medium for conjuring up the invisible being, namely, the ancestor. Unfortunately, Lévi-Strauss tends to restrict the role of *tjurunga* to this sole function of "giving tangible confirmation of the diachronic essence of diachrony at the very heart of synchrony" (p. 237). This leads him to assimilate *tjurunga* to archival documents, the value of which is derived from their great age (p. 238). From this point of view, then, it is useless "to go as far as Durkheim does, in seeking an explanation for the sacred character of *churinga*" (p. 318). The meaning of the totemic emblem engraved on such objects is on a par with the stamp placed on the documents kept in the National Archives. It simply confirms the fact that their value has been recognized (p. 319). Never, in fact, in the course

---

4. Nicholas Thomas (1991) has provided a particularly cogent analysis of the meaning acquired by exotic objects in relations between the colonized and their colonizers, and of how it is eclipsed in anthropological reports.

of his discussion, aimed at pointing up the relations entertained by diachrony and synchrony in "the savage mind", does Lévi-Strauss directly refer to those rites in which a *tjurunga* is truly displayed. The only ritual he mentions is one involving the examination of the *tjurunga* of the dead, which may indeed be easily compared to the ceremony by which archives are solemnly taken out of the coffers in which they have been locked up. The role of those *tjurunga* linked to the living is played out on a totally different stage, however: that of fertility rites and initiations. It is because he studied these types of rituals that Durkheim (1968 [1912]) tried to discover why *tjurunga* were believed to have a sacred power. The totemic symbol does not represent the totem directly, according to Lévi-Strauss, because "the totem represented is more sacred than the real totem. The individual animal plays the part of the signifier and the sacred character is attached neither to it nor to its icon, but to the signified which either can stand for" (p. 239). Admittedly, the totemic animal held to be represented by the motif engraved upon a *tjurunga* does not exhaust the meaning of this design; the object is not simply a representation of this animal. However, it remains for us to account for the way signifier and signified become indistinct through a particular type of representation, the modalities of which have yet to be explained. This is the approach taken by Durkheim.

As opposed to Mauss and Lévi-Strauss, Durkheim (1968 [1912]) locates the primary meaning of *tjurunga*, their sacred vocation, at the level of the rites in which they are manipulated, rather than at the level of myth, which, in his opinion, intervenes only afterward to account for the respect these objects inspire. He also makes the apposite remark that the term itself, *tjurunga*, refers to ritual action generally, and is employed as a noun when it specifically designates ritual objects. He is nonetheless obliged to acknowledge the fact that there is nothing in the intrinsic form of *tjurunga* that predisposes them to play this role, as they are quite comparable to ordinary pieces of wood or stone. To account for their sacred character, he therefore looks to the images inscribed upon them. According to him, the "ceremonial demonstrations" (p. 174) are addressed to these engraved markings, the proof of this being in the ephemeral nature of these markings which are inscribed upon objects made only for the duration of a ritual: it is only by means of such motifs that the totem to whom the rite is addressed to may be recognized. It is this totemic stamp, then, that makes it possible for the *tjurunga* to materially represent the totem. Durkheim is then faced with the following problem: why don't the Australians attempt to represent the external appearance of their totemic animals accurately, instead of representing them by geometric designs? He attempts to deal with the problem of the indirect link between the animal represented and the design that represents it through a study of the forms taken by this ritualistic representation. This leads him to note as highly significant that the few elements entering into the totemic designs are recurrent, polysemic and apparently chosen at random, the outcome of a conventional meaning known only to members of the particular clan involved. One can only concur with this analysis of the symbolism of central Australian imagery (see Moisseeff, 1989 and 1995), the accuracy of which is particularly remarkable in that it took more than a half-century for it to be reconsidered and completed (see Strehlow, 1964b; Munn, 1964, 1973). Durkheim comes to the conclusion that Australian Aborigines are not trying to draw a portrait of their totem, but rather, they feel the need to represent their idea of it, using a material sign (p. 179). As Lévi-Strauss points out, Durkheim's intention here is to demonstrate the emblematic character of totemism (1966: 239). Viewed in this way, the emblem engraved on a *tjurunga* is postulated to be a material expression of the clan as a social unit, as a collective identity. For this reason, these objects are able to elicit the feeling of belonging to a same community in each participant during a collective ritual.

This is an interesting perspective, in that it considers the object as capable of producing some effect within the ritual. It is imperfect, however, in that *tjurunga* of the type mentioned by Durkheim are in fact a physical medium for *individual* singularity. Moreover, such reasoning can not account for the ritual role played by those *tjurunga* that are unadorned by any such emblems. In the latter case, it is not the engraved markings that make a *tjurunga* valuable, as they may well be lacking. Rather, its value resides in the object itself, in its very material existence. Now, as Durkheim points out, it apparently does not matter what substance is used to make *tjurunga*. Beyond the ritual scene, nothing, *a priori*, predestines these objects to produce meaning, and indeed, as we will see, their efficacy depends on their being accompanied by gestures that spell out that meaning. Even more fundamentally, then, the efficacy of *tjurunga* must be sought in the complementary relationship between their appearance and the bodily movements that enable them to express what their apparently mundane physical reality is unable to convey unaided. From this viewpoint, the more ordinary their appearance, the more it justifies the exceptional representational role they are called upon to play: a stone or a piece of wood is necessarily more significant *within the framework of a ritual* than its immediate appearance would suggest. Within a ritual context, *tjurunga* act as both signifiers and signifieds. The same paradoxical logic applies both to *tjurunga* and to the emblems engraved upon them: by showing something in order to better dissimulate, new meaning is created.

In point of fact, those objects that play a specially important role in rituals seem to be precisely those that are the least expressive. I will have more to say on this subject. However, a connection may be made here with Durkheim's passing observation regarding North American Indians. While they represent their totems in a more realistic fashion than the Australians, the techniques used for this purpose are nonetheless quite crude (p. 178). It is as though the ability of ritual objects to produce meaning depended, fundamentally, on the impossibility of assigning a univocal signification to them. Durkheim situated *tjurunga* in the context in which they are used, and it is to his credit that in doing so he not only recognized the importance of their physical appearance, but also revealed one of the principles underlying their functionality, namely, a specific representational mode. A *tjurunga* is a material artifact used to stand for an idea, or in other words, to represent something that transcends the totemic referent associated with it.

Durkheim was struck by the way *tjurunga* function as "pure" or "unadulterated" signifiers, capable of representing a relationship or concept. A brief look at Aranda cosmology will enable us to specify the principles governing this complex representational role.

A Discursive Object

The Aranda cosmology is the product of a cultural process grounded in three principles. (1) The classification of the various visible elements of the world into three distinct categories: features of the landscape, the human species, and other living species, be they plants or animals. (2) These three categories are articulated such that each element of one category is related to an element of the other two: each human being is linked to a feature of the landscape and to a non-human species (his or her totem). (3) There exists a hierarchical relationship between the two categories of living beings: humans, through their ceremonial activities, are responsible for the fertility of all species. The holistic nature of this cosmology derives from the fact that the Aranda ascribe this ordering of the world to a single, asubstantial, eternal process: *alchera*, a spatial dynamism (Moisseeff, 1995) referred to in contemporary anthropological literature as the Dreaming (see, for example, Elkin, 1961; Munn, 1964; Myers, 1986; Glowczewski, 1991).

According to the Aranda, and other Australian Aborigines as well, everything—the shaping of the environment, the embodiment of living beings, the full range of cultural phenomena including social organization, rites, and so forth—proceeds from the Dreaming. Conversely, the Aborigines perceive their entire surroundings, everything they see, as an indication of the reality of the Dreaming. Consequently, the universe of visible occurrences is also designated as the Dreaming. Observable phenomena are so many partial representatives of it, none of which, taken separately, can pretend to represent it as a whole. In its role as dynamic generator of forms, the

Dreaming differentiates substance, but being asubstantial, it itself remains invisible. The best way to portray the Dreaming, or rather, to suggest it so as to convey the sense of a multidirectional movement and of a shaping process, is to represent changing place or displacement. At the same time, however, in order to convey the transcendental character of the Dreaming, this displacement must be shown to be exceptional. The way in which this is done depends on whether the representation involved takes the form of a discourse, an object or a staged action.

First, let us take a look at the discursive modes of representation of the Dreaming.[5]

On a narrative level, in order to evoke the Dreaming, the Aborigines describe the wanderings of eternal beings whose nature is simultaneously human — they think, dream and behave like human beings — and non-human. They look like and/or are capable of changing into (a) an animal or a plant, which defines their totemic identity, (b) various features of the landscape and (c) ritual objects (*tjurunga*), which are concomitantly associated with that totemic identity. These hybrid entities, or Dreaming beings, are believed to have extraordinary abilities linked to their mobility. They walk, run, fly and burrow their way into the ground. The contours of the Australian landscape are believed to have arisen from their passage and thereby to have been impregnated by eternal, spiritual elements, spirit-children, from which the embodiment of all living beings proceeds.[6] As each Dreaming being travels around, it disseminates a multitude of spirit-children, which are emanations of its body. Some are presently incarnated in the form of human beings (and the individuals concerned are then designated during the narration), or in the form of the other natural species associated with that particular Dreaming being (when this species is named during the narrative it accounts for the totemic identity of the places being mentioned).[7] In fact, the stories about Dreaming beings consist mostly of descriptions of the topography and the toponymy of the territory that account for the totemic identity of the individuals and places involved and the relationships between them.[8]

---

5. For a more complete analysis of the discursive mode of representation of the Dreaming, the reader is referred to Moisseeff, 1995.

6. Reproduction is in fact construed as founded upon two complementary processes, the one carnal, the other spiritual. Spirit-children, it is thought, hover over the entire territory and inject vitality into shapeless matter, thereby causing it to become animated, and producing differentiation into the different forms corresponding to the various species.

7. Many examples of these Aranda narratives are to be found in Spencer and Gillen, 1927 and Strehlow, 1968 and 1971.

8. Lévi-Strauss (1969: 228–229) perceived this essential aspect of narratives of this type very clearly: "The myth establishes that the ancestor appeared at such and such a place, fol-

Moreover, everything attributed to these fabulous beings is credited to the Dreaming. Narrative discourse establishes them as the agents of the multidirectional, eternal and transparent dynamism that orders the world. In order to do this, such narratives make use of a special stylistic device to portray these beings: hybridity combined with exceptional mobility. By means of these two qualities, each aspect of the landscape may be associated simultaneously with human beings and with another natural species. They also provide the means for expressing the eternal and omnipresent nature of the Dreaming, as they allow each of these agents to be present in a multitude of ways in the form of permanent traces (ritual objects, landscape features, spirit-children). These manifold phenomena, identified with the Dreaming beings, are portrayed as so many metamorphoses demonstrating the eternal character of their presence. The invisible thread that ties these scattered representatives together is speech. It is speech that flows from one point in space to another, weaving the fabric of discourse that brings these Dreaming characters to life and confers a semblance of individuality upon them. It is the echo, so to speak, of their ontological transparency, for like the Dreaming itself, the Dreaming beings as unified, individualized entities, remain invisible. Only through narrative discourse can they be perceived as a whole: there is no other way to constitute them as full-fledged subjects in their own terms.

Telling the story of how some hybrid beings move about is thus a particularly adequate way of conjuring up the Dreaming. It establishes these extraordinary beings as the most appropriate discursive props for the representation of this dynamic process that is simultaneously without substance and capable of modifying substances. To a large extent, representations of the Dreaming through the intermediary of these creatures are effective because they make it impossible to grasp this overall dynamic by means of a unified representation. Not only are there any number of Dreaming beings, but again, each of them refers back to phenomena which are multiple as well. The hybrid or composite nature of Dreaming beings thus refers, by paraleipsis, to their essentially spiritual nature: their bodies are composed of an indefinite number of human and non-human spirit-children. It is this spirituality that underlies their transparency as full-fledged

---

lowed such and such a course, performed certain actions in this or that place which mark him out as the originator of geographical features which can still be seen, finally that he stopped or disappeared in a particular spot. Properly speaking, therefore, the myth amounts to the description of an itinerary and adds little or nothing to the remarkable facts which it claims to establish; that a particular course, and the water-points, thickets, or rocks which mark it, are of sacred value for a human group and that this group proclaims its affinity with this or that natural species: caterpillar, ostrich, or kangaroo."

subjects, and it is because of this transparency that they may be associated with representative figures which are both multifarious and heterogeneous. From this viewpoint, the narrative that brings these fantastic beings to life causes them to pass from the status of subject of a discourse on the Dreaming to that of object deriving from the Dreaming itself (see Munn, 1970). Through this verbal alchemy, the spiritual hybridity of Dreaming beings is externalized: it brings disparate phenomena together by providing them with a common origin, thereby transforming them into so many anamorphoses of a same entity. However, unlike this entity from which they are made to proceed, these phenomena remain differentiated as to their nature.

Now, while it is hybridity in motion that underlies the representation of the Dreaming, it remains unclear which of the various phenomena identified with Dreaming beings are susceptible of materially representing the Dreaming in all of its dimensions. Because human beings are both mortal and differentiated from each other and from other species, they would appear to be unsuitable for the representation of such an eternal dynamism. Because of their immobility, features of the landscape, as well as ritual objects of a similar nature, made of wood or stone, seem to be inappropriate as well. Is there some process, equivalent to that at work in the Dreaming stories, whereby such phenomena might be transformed into a concrete yet unified representation of the Dreaming?

A Relational Object

According to Aboriginal people, each and every visible aspect of this world is capable of actualizing the presence of a Dreaming being. Human beings, because of their capacity for movement, are particularly apt to represent change of place. However, before taking a look at the specific procedures through which humans are made to represent the multi-faceted hybridity of Dreaming beings, let us consider those objects to which a similar function is granted, despite their apparent unfitness to suggest the Dreaming's dynamic quality. I am referring to those *tjurunga* that are specifically linked to human spirit-children. It is believed that at the same time as the Dreaming being disseminates human spirit-children, it disseminates the corresponding *tjurunga* as well.[9] Consequently, as each person is viewed as the embod-

---

9. When initiates have to make new personal *tjurunga*, they nevertheless claim that the original *tjurunga* deriving from a Dreaming being still exists, but that it has been lost and they are capable of retrieving it—and therefore of restituting it—through dreams. Indeed, dreaming is by and large viewed as one of the best ways of achieving a direct relationship

iment of a spirit-child, he or she is simultaneously associated with a *tjurunga*.

Such personal *tjurunga* are made from pieces of hard wood or from splinters of rocks. They are flat, often elongated, oval or rectangular in shape, or rounded in some rare instances. They average from 10 to 40 centimeters in length (although some may measure more than one meter) and are between 5 and 20–25 cm. across. While all carry engravings, the content of each *tjurunga* carving is perfectly original. They are in fact supposed to represent the singularity of the individuals with which they are associated, or to be more accurate, the singularity of the spirit-children that infuse these individuals with life. A *tjurunga* is thus the perceptual counterpart of a sprit-child, and as such, reifies the special relationship between an individual and a particular Dreaming being. From this point of view, personal *tjurunga* are prototypes of *tjurunga* objects as a whole. Indeed, according to Strehlow (1968–1971), the term *tjurunga* is composed of two terms: *tju*, referring to something secret or shameful, and *runga*, meaning "one's own." "One's own" denotes a relationship of great intimacy associated, in Aboriginal culture, with the idea of shame (see Myers, 1979). Anything belonging deeply to oneself must be kept secret and ought not to be revealed to anyone else. Taken in full, the complete designation corresponds perfectly to the role played by personal *tjurunga*: inasmuch as the latter presentify the constitutive, inaccessible part of a person and his or her specific bond with a particular Dreaming being, they are indeed "one's own secret". There is nothing surprising, then, in the fact that personal *tjurunga* are subjected to specially strict secrecy. When they are not participating in a ritual situation, they are wrapped in hair-string and hidden in some hollow place (such as a cleft in a rock, a cave or a tree trunk), the access to which is prohibited to non-initiates and to those initiated men who are not directly affiliated with the corresponding totemic center.

The signs engraved on these objects also serve to dissimulate the meaning they are believed to harbor. While these designs are supposed to represent the specific nature of the link between an individual and a particular Dreaming being, they are generally composed of a combination of non-figurative elements such as circles (concentric or spiraling) and/or half-circles (each set inside another) linked together by straight or curved lines, either full or dotted, and animal tracks. The circles refer to the totemic identity of a Dreaming being and/or to the trace presumably left on some place by an event related to that being. This may be the campsite it set up at such or such a place, or the exact location where it disappeared into the ground. But

with the Dreaming, and of recollecting the phenomena connected with it (see Dussart, 1988 and 2000; Poirier, 1996).

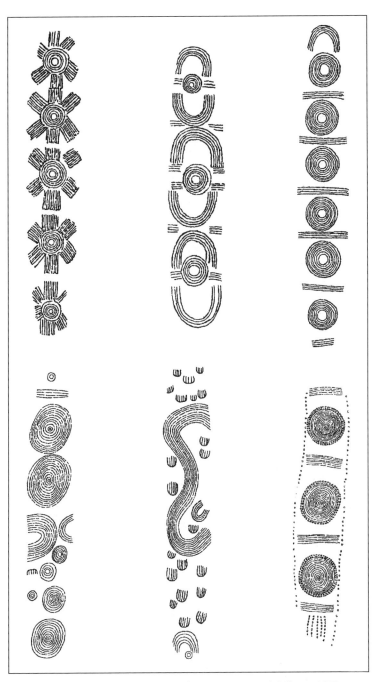

Figure 6a: Engraved designs on *tjurunga* (from Spencer and Gillen, 1927).

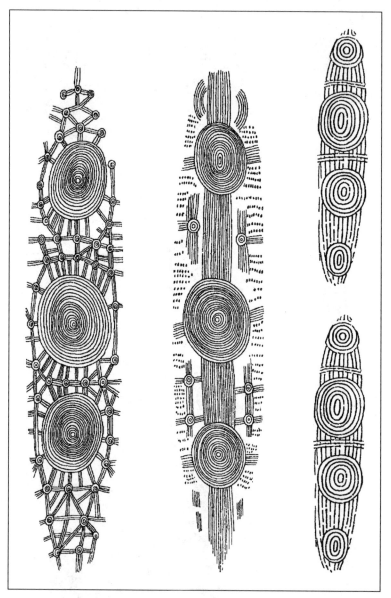

Figure 6b: Engraved designs on *tjurunga* (from Spencer and Gillen, 1927).

again, a circle may be related to all of these different referents at the same time. In this case, it simultaneously represents the totemic being, its camp-site and the rock that is believed to have arisen at the place where it disappeared. A similar circle in another design will refer to a different totemic being and/or to some other geographic feature, and so on. Half-circles represent the human aspect of these personages. Specifically, they refer to the mark left in the sand by a man (or a woman) sitting cross-legged or with spread legs (see Strehlow, 1964a and b; Munn, 1973). As for the lines connecting these different elements, they indicate the paths that link together the various referents (features of the landscape, events, etc.) designated by these elements. They represent a precise, geographically identifiable journey made by the Dreaming being connected with the *tjurunga*'s coming into being. From among the various referents and signifieds these meager pictorial elements may evoke, the initiates select those which are relevant to the establishment of the territorial and totemic identity of the individual to whom the particular *tjurunga* is attributed. By drawing upon the virtual meaningfulness of the design, they actualize its meaning.

Thus, while the engravings carved on the *tjurunga* of different individuals affiliated to a same totemic center all refer to the trajectory and to the stopping-off places of the Dreaming being on the territory of that center, the specific phenomena to which they refer differ from one *tjurunga* to another. This explains why no two *tjurunga* are alike. Their singularity is the product of the choice, the number and the size of the component elements available, on the one hand, and of the way in which they are arranged on the other. In addition to this formal specification, a further particularization derives from the meanings associated both with each of the elements composing the design and with the combination of these component parts. A circle on one *tjurunga* may designate a water hole, whereas on another one it will refer to a frog; two circles on the same object may refer respectively to an emu and a rock, and so forth. The particular arrangement of circles and lines engraved on each *tjurunga* refers to one or another portion of the journey made by one of a number of Dreaming beings.

It is clear, then, that *tjurunga* portray the singularity of individual identities by means of a symbolic yet fundamentally polysemic representation. *Tjurunga* designs do not consist of morphological features of the personages to whom they refer. Rather, they depict the traces supposedly left on the surface of the ground by their travels and the acts they committed. This explains why animal tracks may be a part of such patterns. In this way, these designs are able to indicate the hybrid nature of a Dreaming being. The *tjurunga* on which they are engraved is itself a component of this hybridity, for this object, which traces out a Dreaming being's movements by means of the lines connecting various events or stopping points represented by circles and half-circles, is at the same time held to be a transformation of the being itself. On the level of material objects, such lines take the place of speech which, on the narrative level, weaves together a broad range of disparate phenomena. The transparency of the Dreaming being through which these phenomena may be associated is rendered by the extremely peculiar pictorial mode whereby they are represented. On the one hand, the various elements that compose a design are not sufficiently figurative to be connected, collectively or separately, with a univocal representation. Nor, on the other hand, are these signs sufficiently abstract to provide the basis for a written language or code whose overall meaning can be translated without consulting those who made them. Indeed, in order to determine what is signified by any particular *tjurunga* design as a whole, it is necessary to refer to the discourse that orders its constitutive elements, and that only initiated men belonging to the totemic center where it is located are authorized to deliver.

In their very materiality, *tjurunga* partake in the dissimulation of the meaning they are presumed to exhibit: the polysemic nature of the signs inscribed on them simply corroborates the exceptional, unrepresentable character of the signified which they nonetheless materially represent. The representation of a Dreaming being, be it in discourse or by material means, is thus but a trap laid to perception so as to catch that which is signified by the Dreaming. In other words, it serves to designate something that exists beyond that which it represents. Seen from this angle, a personal *tjurunga* is an ideal material signifier: it is a thing, a piece of landscape which is itself a trace, inscribed with the trace of the movement from which it derives. The recursive process it embodies causes it to signify something other than itself.

At Once Artifact and Concept

Personal *tjurunga* are carried to the ceremonial grounds, where the actors who handle them set them in motion in a way that participates in the representation of a Dreaming being. But over and beyond this function, about which I will have more to say further on, their very nature and existence suggest the dynamism that is latently present in the landscape of which they are a part. The material used to make them (hard wood, unyielding stone) is taken from the natural environment, and once they have been fashioned, they are returned to this environment to be stored in a natural container (a tree-trunk, a cave or fissure in the rock). They are literally pieces of this environment. Furthermore, personal *tjurunga*, their flat surface furrowed with tracks like the central Australian desert itself, represent landscapes on their own, through their engravings and by virtue of their physical independence with respect to any given piece of the land. They are mobile landscapes imprinted with movement.

The Dreaming, as a substance-free spatial dynamism, is held to modify matter without being itself imprisoned by it. Any concrete representation of the Dreaming concept would therefore seem to be impossible. And yet, according to the Aranda, *tjurunga* play that exact role. They are a concept in themselves, to which no definite representation can be appended, barring which they would lose their conceptual character. Let us compare concept and object. In order to be capable of designating the Dreaming in a unified fashion, that which represents it must have the following properties: (i) hybridity, so as to signify and establish relationships between different, visible, worldly phenomena including features of the landscape, as well as human and non-human entities; (ii) tangible permanence associated with spatial eternity; (iii) unquestionable mobility; (iv) a connection with the spirit-children that makes it a fertility-promoting agent.

Tjurunga meet all of these requirements. They are hybrid (while made of wood or stone, they are linked with human beings for which they provide the totemic reference); they are permanent (immutable, they retain their own identity throughout and even beyond the ritual in which they are involved); they are associated with a concrete spatial eternity (they are landscapes in themselves); they are mobile (they travel, and bear the inscription of their own movement). Finally, they are taken to be indicators of the presence of spirit-children whose embodiment is thought to be stimulated by their manipulation. Moreover, while *tjurunga* are posited as being concretizations of the Dreaming, at the same time they subtly evoke the latter's substanceless movement, which is inscribed over their flat surface. If personal *tjurunga* are able to represent the Dreaming in all of its dimensions, it is because the signs which adorn them are neither entirely abstract nor entirely figurative: by denoting a number of different levels of meaning in an essentially polysemic fashion, they suggest rather than rigidly determine the multiplicity of phenomena related to the Dreaming.

Thus, the conditions that enable the *tjurunga* to take on their paradoxical representative function—that of concretizing a concept—arise from the particular physical attributes with which they are endowed. Their highly specific outward form is the result of a very special kind of representational operation which consists in representing the representation of a particular thing, rather than the thing itself. In other words, *tjurunga* do not pretend to represent the world as it is perceived by the Aranda, but rather, the Aranda's conception of the world. They may thus act as the only tangible mediators between phenomena belonging to different registers: human and non-human, animate and inanimate, visible and invisible. Looked at in this way, this artifact is the keystone to the Aranda's holistic worldview.

It should be further noted that the inscriptions engraved on *tjurunga* make them self-referential objects, bearing the conditions of their own emergence. Each one is, indeed, a parcel of landscape upon which is inscribed—as traces—the movement through the landscape of which it is the trace. Through the intermingling of the physical environment on the one hand and the *tjurunga* on the other, a logical telescoping of the macrocosm and the microcosm is obtained. This is similar and complementary to the way the Aranda relate the Dreaming to the human activity of dreaming. Like the Dreaming, *tjurunga* contain everything in the world, in virtual form. They are the part that represents the whole. From this perspective, this microcosm is self-sufficient, meaning-wise, like the Dreaming. But as opposed to the Dreaming, which is "substance-free," the self-sufficiency of *tjurunga* derives from its enduring materiality: it is the very material nature of this artifact that underlies its self-referential nature.

This quality of being a self-referential object is precisely what enables *tjurunga* to act as a special type of signifier, devoid of any ordinary referential relationship. They are "pure" or unadulterated signifiers, for, in the end, they are their own referent. It is worth stressing that it is their very physical materiality that provides the fundamental condition for their being raised to such a status of pure signifier. This is what enables *tjurunga* to play their role as ritual objects. Their manipulation during ceremonies brings to life the presence of the invisible entities which they evoke. In this way, they substantiate the tangible effects (incarnation or initiation for example) whose mechanisms remain invisible.

Let us now take a closer look at the role played by *tjurunga* in one Aranda ritual, the *quabara*.

A Self-referential Artifact

Because human beings are singularized, as attested by the existence of personal *tjurunga*, they are held to be exclusively responsible for maintaining the fertility of all living beings. Each personal *tjurunga* is linked with a number of personal rituals known as *quabara* in which individuals enact the Dreaming being with which they are associated. These rituals are performed during the different phases of initiation, and are held to participate in the production of two concomitant effects: the incarnation of spirit-children and the transformation of novices into initiated men. In the *quabara* presented here, the Dreaming being portrayed is a Frog (Spencer and Gillen, 1927).

The performer's head is adorned by a headpiece composed of a round, flattened bottom made of several meters of hair-string held together by twigs and covered with concentric bands of pink and white down. All around it, fastened to it, are strands of fur string hiding the face, which is further masked by a thick layer of down. A large wooden *tjurunga* about one meter high and measuring about 10 to 15 centimeters across, arranged with tufts of black feathers, is placed vertically in the center of this flattened base. It is wrapped in several meters of hair-string, and this base is entirely covered over with alternating bands of pink and white down, arranged in concentric circles and forming alternating stripes. A tuft of feathers is attached to the upper end of this oblong object. The man's back and chest are completely covered with white spots of various sizes, each of which is encircled by white down. White lines are drawn on the inner side of each thigh.

The rings of down set on the headpiece represent the roots of a tree believed to have appeared at the place where the Frog Dreaming being disappeared into the ground. The Frog being disseminated both frog and human spirit-children near this tree, one of these spirit-children being embodied by the owner of both the *quabara* and the *tjurunga*. The white spots drawn on the body represent the different stages in the metamorphosis of frogs, while the lines on the thighs represent the legs of fully-grown frogs.

Once decorated, the performer squats down in a shallow pit, swaying to and fro. The novices are then encouraged to circle around him, running and shouting, while the initiators swing bull-roarers. The movements of the performer, suggesting those of the Frog, cause the down to fly off, simulating the dissemination of the spirit-children leaving the body of that being. The quality of the performer's movements is considered an essential requisite for the success of the rite.

Three minutes later, one of the novices lays his hands on the shoulders of the performer, who then ceases moving. The ceremony is over; the decorations are removed and disassembled.

The ritual staging of a Dreaming being must conform to the following major directive on which its very efficacy depends: it must preserve, and if possible reinforce, the fundamentally unrepresentable character of the entity it depicts. To conform with this constraint, the ritual representation must meet a number of conditions. It requires:

— the constitution of a flagrantly heterogeneous whole. A construction is thus assembled using paste and ties (blood and string), in which a *tjurunga* placed on a human body adorned with non-human motifs (roots, tadpoles and frogs) is covered with a wide assortment of materials including hair, twigs, down, fur, feathers, and so on.

— a similarly heterogeneous set of ritual roles. The owner of the *quabara*, who belongs to the Frog totem, presides over its organization and supplies the *tjurunga*, but is not the performer. Indeed, the owner, who tangibly embodies the human nature of a Dreaming being, cannot at the same time take on its mobile, non-human aspect, which is acted out by the performer (who, in the case at hand, belongs to the Wildcat totem). The men in charge of setting up the ceremony, who are associated with a number of different totems, prepare the ceremony grounds, paint and attire the performer, and are the only people entitled to provide the ingredients required to transform him into a hybrid entity. The complementary role assumed by such persons is evident throughout, including on the ceremony grounds, where, as active spectators, they sing the song corresponding to the ritual. The novices and bull-roarer carriers contribute to the creation of a noisy, agitated atmosphere, which is also considered indispensable.

— movement, as supplied here by the performer and the novices. Not only can there be no *quabara* without movement, but even more, the presumed efficacy of the rite is believed to depend on the quality of the movement, which in turn depends upon the spectators' singing. Movement causes the down to be blown off, and this is essential to the incarnation of the spirit-children and to the fertilization of the novices.

— evanescence: the performance, which takes five hours to prepare, lasts but three minutes. The heterogeneity involved in this performance is made manifest only when it is set in motion. However, this movement cannot be prolonged, and once this hybridity has been shown and enacted, its various components are immediately taken apart or erased from the bodies that bore them. This need to stress the temporary nature of ceremonial compositions is so important that all of the objects made for a given rite, with the exception of personal *tjurunga*, are always disassembled once the performance is over, even if identical ones are required for upcoming ceremonies. They will never be reused, and other objects will be composed in their stead. A given rite is thus made equivalent to the representation of a particular Dreaming being, and at the same time the ephemeral nature of this representation is emphasized.

— a representation of the spiritual transparency of the Dreaming. Concretely, this is achieved by placing a down mask on the person in charge of animating it. The identity of the actor is hidden, and the ceremonial artifacts employed in different *quabara* are so similar that the only elements that reliably identify the Dreaming being portrayed are the performer's movement and the song that accompanies it. Insofar as ritual representation is concerned, transparency and opacity go hand in hand.

As we see, then, the overall representation of a Dreaming being refers at once to its spiritual hybridity and to its movement. To be effective, however, it must also be instantaneous. It is doomed to dissolve immediately, all the better to translate the ontological transparency of this agent through which the Dreaming is evoked. The necessary conjunction of mobility and evanescence seems to be a particularly appropriate way of suggesting the Dreaming as I have defined it; that is, a subtle dynamism that cannot be pinned down, or rigidified in any unitary representation.

Heterogeneity, while conveying the hybrid nature of a Dreaming being and providing a tangible, comprehensive representation, makes it impossible to situate this entity in any precise fashion. The more varied and numerous the materials and the agents involved in constituting the representation of a Dreaming being, the more elusive this representation becomes. The complementary arrangement of these ingredients gives them a representational ability of which each is obviously incapable in its own right. Only during the brief moment of the ritual act, then, do these disparate components participate in the creation of a definite unitary representation. However, this unitary representation, insofar as it remains irreducible both to the elements that compose it and to the movement that animates it, remains associated with the invisible: when the movement stops, the Dreaming being dissolves into the multiplicity of its components.

The only permanent element present on the ceremony grounds is the *tjurunga*, which will be reused in the Frog totem *quabara* rites belonging to its owner. This object, placed deep down in the composite layerings of the headpiece that signifies its capital importance and at the same time preserves its mystery, is the "hard core" of the ritual representation. It is the *tjurunga* itself which represents the Dreaming being evoked by the ritual, as is evidenced by the fact that the totemic identity being represented is that of the *tjurunga* and not that of the performer. The latter is but one component of the ceremonial apparatus and a vehicle for this object.

The performer, made anonymous by the mass of his variegated trappings, is the bearer of the *tjurunga* which lies at the heart of the performance, the *tjurunga* itself, as we have seen, being the bearer of a representation that is both conceptual and self-referential. The *tjurunga* thus represents a dynamism encompassing all of the signifieds, but at the same time it does not refer to anything other than its own material existence. Seen in this way, a ritual representation of a Dreaming being takes the form of a recursive process of infinite regression: a large number of heterogeneous ingredients assembled into a unified figure constructed around an object whose material existence is self-referential. The outcome is a representation whose very materiality reinforces the unrepresentable character of the being it is held to represent. The paradox clearly resides in the peculiar material nature of the object concerned: in order to represent the invisible, a dynamism or a conception of the world, the object that ensures the visibility of the entity represented refers, in the last analysis, to itself. All in all, the ritual object is a pure signifier, and it is as such that it may be associated with signifieds having no concrete signifiers.

Within the rite, the *tjurunga* may be seen as the signifier whose signified corresponds to the ritual act itself. The latter consists in bringing together at a particular place, the ceremony grounds, and for a limited lapse of time, a number of visual, auditory and gesticulatory phenomena gravitating around a single object. The concrete presence of the *tjurunga* "synergizes" the effects of these phenomena by endowing them with an equivalent degree of meaningfulness. In this sense, this object's signifying value is entailed by the complex of signs brought together in the rite and centered upon an identical signified, signs whose combination within a particular formal structure results in the creation of a unitary, active entity whose presence guarantees the efficacy of the ritual. The *ex nihilo* creation of such an entity is in itself a sufficiently real effect that the production of effects of another order, such as the incarnation of spirit-children or the access of certain individuals to the status of initiated men, may be laid to its account. The formal framework of the rite indicates that ordinary signifying relationships are for a time abolished, whereas the ritual object creatively mediates the new signifying relationships generated within this context by the various phenomena making up the content of the ceremony. When the performance is over, the men have been confirmed in their responsibility for fertility and the *tjurunga* return to their secret hiding place. It is by introducing a pure material signifier with no definite, concrete referent, thereby disturbing the mundane relations between signifiers and signifieds, that the rite is able to generate new meaning.

Are *Tjurunga* Exemplary Ritual Objects?

In the Aranda rites, the representation of an ordinarily invisible power is made possible by the manipulation of *tjurunga* objects. It is by conforming to a set of strict rules that this representation contributes to the efficacy of the ritual. When a rite is performed, a "before" and an "after" are defined, between which something happens which allows the assertion that some extraordinary event has truly taken place. The novices have been transformed into initiated men and the initiators have had their responsibility for fertility confirmed. To our way of thinking, it is, in a very basic fashion, the intervention of the *tjurunga* that is the underlying factor in the effectiveness of these aspects of the ritual (operating a change of status, maintaining fertility). Not only is their presence required, but further, they occupy a central position in the representation enacted by the rite. The logical extension of this hypothesis is a second one that may be formulated as follows: within this specific ceremonial framework, it is the physical characteristics of the *tjurunga* that authorize the claim that an invisible power has intervened, whence the rite's efficacy. While the individual participants in the ceremony are responsible for its performance, the "extra something" — the definition of a "before" and an "after" the rite — must be connected with the manipulation of this particular object. The specific qualities of the *tjurunga* allow it to mediate the relationships between participants such

that through the rite's performance, a new meaning-producing whole is created. The establishment of such a link between the sensory properties of the
tjurunga and its ritual function brings out the importance of its self-referential nature, as a material signifier free of any ordinary relations of signification.

In our opinion, this observation may be extended to ritual objects as a
whole. Those objects assigned a special place in rituals—conglomerates
of heterogeneous ingredients, hardly or not at all figurative, deliberately
grossly-made statuettes, and so forth—are indeed often those which seem
to lend themselves least to a simple representational role. It is as though an
effort is made to obliterate any possibility of connecting them with an
ordinary, univocal meaning, so as to associate them with a more opaque,
and therefore more effective meaningfulness referring to supernatural, immaterial forces. The exceptional potency ascribed to such forces is predicated
on the idea that they are invisible, impossible to portray, and therefore extraordinary: their effects (initiation, reproduction, etc.) may be perceived, but
not their form.

In the everyday world—that is to say, outside of ritual action—these
forces do not, in principle, possess any tangible, univocal representation,
whereas during ritual acts their representation is kept veiled. One might
thus say that meaning-wise, they refer to a floating signified making it
possible for them to be linked to a variety of phenomena.[10] In this perspective, the crafting of a ritual consists in creating its corresponding signifier, which is to say a signifier with no univocal or ordinary signified. If the
rite is to preserve its exceptional character and the forces their putative potency, it is of the greatest importance that their invisibility be safeguarded by
this object. To meet this requirement, the representational capacities of the
particular ritual object must be diminished, so as to avoid, as much as possible, giving rise to any univocal interpretation. Such an object gains in
efficacy what it loses in expressivity. It may then be grasped as a consistent, enigmatic presence, but one whose meaning remains essentially opaque.
This opacity is compounded by its very materiality. Indeed, ideally, to prevent any confusion with an ordinary referent, the referent of such an object
is the object itself. By virtue of its self-referential character, it becomes a pure
signifier, eminently capable of generating meaning.

Such an analysis may also be applied to the case of ritual masks. The
mask replaces the face of the person who wears it, and by hiding his/her
identity, makes him/her anonymous. This prevents any identification of

---

10. The Melanesian *mana*, so elusive that it has attracted any number of anthropological interpretations, comes to mind in connection with the notion designated here by the expression "floating signified." Regarding this point, see Keesing, 1985 and Boyer, 1986.

the signified connected with the ritual act with the person officiating. It is
the performer's movement that becomes the signified, the performer him/her-
self being reduced to acting as a vehicle for this object. Furthermore, the
self-sufficient nature of the mask—it's significance does not rely upon the
identity of the person who animates it—clearly designates it as the true signifier of the ritual act. However, its distinctive appearance indicates that the
signified to which its movement refers lies outside of ordinary norms. It is
precisely because of the presence of this object, with its unique physical features, that it is difficult to ascribe a univocal meaning to the ceremonial act
in which it intervenes. "Neutral" or blank masks are an extreme case of
this, their featureless nature pointing directly to their function, that of a neutral signifier, an object in and of itself. The crude features and/or the composite nature of other masks make the signified to which they are held to
refer even more equivocal. The tangible nature of their presence leads one
to believe that they harbor some secret signified, to be found in the very
matter of which they are made. But this perceptive illusion, prompted by
their "monstrous" appearance, simply serves to conceal their essential empti-
ness as signifiers. In this way, masks may be viewed as magnets, used to
capture the indeterminate signified corresponding to the ceremonial action.
They act as inducers of the movement that testifies to the reality of the intervention of supernatural forces. The potential magnetism of a mask is not
really activated, however, unless it is set in motion and immersed in the
dusky dappled atmosphere of the rite, during which bewitching chants, like
those of the sirens in the Odyssey, incense the participants, causing them
to drift (possibly with the help of drugs that reinforce the perceptive illusion) toward another world hidden from the sight of common mortals. Once
the ceremony is over, the performer and the mask, conjoined for a time, are
separated. The former returns to his/her own identity and therefore loses
his power over the latter, which retrieves its status as object. Outside of the
ceremonial context, performer and mask are cut off from each other. They
can in no way be confused with the force whose intervention for which the
performer was the vector and the mask the catalyst. It is the synergetic effect
produced by their combination within a well-defined, formal space that
leads to the creation of a singular, effective entity.

It would also be well worth applying this perspective to the use of incomprehensible ritual speech, in which the words pronounced cannot be connected with any ordinary meaning, as these signifier-words no longer correspond to any ordinary signifieds (see Bloch, 1974; Sales, 1991). Language
is reified, and the song that conveys it, as well as the gestures accompanying it, by replacing these usual signifieds, hark back to an uncannily strange
presence, suggestive of a world beyond and its presumed power. It does seem
possible, then, to turn discursive phenomena into sounds that are just things,
devoid of any ordinary signified. Indeed, this would be the prerequisite for

having them play a role similar to that played by ritual objects. It seems to be more productive, from this perspective, to view ritual languages as objects rather than considering sacred objects as discursive phenomena. When the physical form of either of the two is altered, a perceptive dissonance is created, producing an undeniably striking effect. This is what makes recourse to special objects, even if they are no more than reified languages, an indispensable aspect of ritual actions.

The representational function of the ritual objects used by Australian Aborigines — who, need it be recalled, were once considered less than human — has led us to identify one of the processes by which our species creates meaning out of things: the invention of a conventional artifact, a paradigmatic signifier, against which the values attributed to all signifieds may be measured. By bringing about a shift in relations between signifiers and signifieds, the introduction of this pure signifier on the ritual scene modifies the usual reference points for the attribution of meaning, and leads to a redefinition or reformulation of the respective positions of the participants. It is this redefinition of positions that lends a degree of truth to the assertion that something really happens between the beginning and the end of a ritual. When all is said and done, an initiation without objects is incapable of producing initiates.

Translated by Helen Arnold

Chapter 10

Culture Cult

Ritual Circulation of Inalienable Objects and Appropriation of Cultural Knowledge (Northwest and Central Australia)

Barbara Glowczewski

Indigenous People are entitled to the recognition of the full ownership, control and protection of their cultural and intellectual property. They have the right to special measures to control, develop
and protect their sciences, technologies and cultural manifestations,
including human and other genetic resources, seeds, medicines,
knowledge of the properties of fauna and flora, oral tradition, liter-
atures, designs and visual and performing arts. (Article 29 of the
Draft Declaration on the Rights of Indigenous Peoples, United
Nations, 1993)

Many Aboriginal cult objects collected in unclear or even unlawful
circumstances have found their way into private collections or museums in Australia and other parts of the world. The South Australian
Museum in Adelaide has set up a pilot program to identify sacred and
secret objects in view of returning them to communities wanting to recover a portion of their heritage. Other museums have followed this initia-

tive of collaborating with Aboriginal peoples.[1] Some groups accept restitution but draw up agreements with museums that the objects be placed in their reserves for safe-keeping. Others prefer to take back the objects but then worry about their protection. Since the 1980s, "safe-keeping places" have sprung up throughout Australia, some in corrugated huts, others in sophisticated buildings. The Aboriginal communities regard them as "living museums" since the traditional cult objects kept there are used in men's and women's rituals. The process of repatriating objects is part of a broader movement to reappropriate indigenous culture and revitalize traditional practices, especially religious ceremonies.

"Safe-keeping places" are increasingly conceived as part of larger structures or of regional culture centers which require more costly technical means for the safe-keeping of objects whose access is restricted to their "ritual custodians." These structures serve as depositories for written, audio and visual archives accessible only to those groups considered to be the owners of this knowledge. Other, everyday objects accompanied by public audio-visual documents are carefully selected for exhibition so as to transmit an image of the culture to the younger generations and to further knowledge of the culture among non-Aboriginal people. Some of these centers also seek to keep tradition alive through the production of crafts, art and all expressions of local culture: audio-visual recording of oral history, dance workshops, bush-food collecting with children of the community, performances and guided visits of the center and its area for schools and tourists, but also the organization of traditional gatherings of Aboriginal groups in places which may or may not be open to the public.

After recalling the international context of the contemporary claims to cultural property, I will explain the concept of inalienability which, in central and northwestern Australia, surrounds the ritual circulation of sacred objects and the cults of which they are a part. Afterwards I will examine the elaboration of a culture center involving the representatives of a dozen Aboriginal languages and organizations based in the coastal town of Broome; this initiative reflects an attempt to control the representation given of these cultures and to reappropriate their objects and knowledge. Finally, I will end with some thoughts on the notion of "keeping-while-giving" (Weiner, 1992).

---

1. Anderson (1990) on exchange-relations between Australian museums and indigenous people; see contributions to Part 2: "Bringing people back into the collections," in Craig, Kernot and Anderson (eds.), 1999. See also Anderson (ed.), 1995; Clarke and Anderson, 1997; Stanton, 1999.

Cultural Property, Inalienable Objects and Knowledge

Objects are repatriated to Australia on behalf of communities led by Aboriginal people who, as citizens, should enjoy moral property rights as defined in the Universal Declaration of Human Rights:

> Everyone has the right to the protection of moral and material interests resulting from any scientific, literary or artistic production of which he is the author. (Tsosie, 1997: 9)

This moral right, conceived as applying to the individual and being limited in time, covers only physically tangible "productions" of an author such as objects, patents or publications. Beyond the period stipulated (usually fifty years), the content of the novel, discovery, musical work or work of art falls into the public domain and is no longer protected by law. This law is clearly not adapted to cultural claims, for it does not recognize traditional property, which by definition dates back more than fifty years, or collective property, since it is shared by a group, often orally, and is therefore intangible. Nevertheless, indigenous people can use incorporated bodies in order to benefit from the repatriation of objects. In the United States, the 1990 *Native American Graves Protection and Repatriation Act* enabled American museums to return more than 80,000 items, including human remains. But such repatriations do not go without conflict when it comes to defining entitled beneficiaries. Zuni, Hopi and Navajo, for example, dispute the ownership of pre-Colombian bones found on one site which all three groups claim as the dwelling-place of their own ancestors.[2] Bones held in museums and laboratories all over the world have also been claimed by Australian Aboriginal people, who are militating against the archeological excavation of sites containing human remains.

> Tangible cultural resources include historic and prehistoric structures and artefacts, as well as cultural objects of importance to contemporary tribes, such as sacred objects and objects of cultural patrimony...property may not be *alienable* outside the group. (Tsosie, 1997: 5,7)

Like sacred objects, sites bearing material indications of the ancestral presence of a culture, but also natural sites (hills, rocks, water holes) held

---

2. *2nd World Water Forum, Home of the Citizen and Water—Water source of culture, traditions and peace.* The Hague, March 2000, Communication by a Hopi/Zuni representative.

to be sacred to the culture, were traditionally inalienable. However, in order to register a land claim in view of restitution, Australian law requires lists of owners, who must demonstrate to the court, for each geographical site concerned, the way ownership of these sites was transmitted—in these cultures without written language. Aboriginal people have often shown judges, who were sworn to secrecy, sacred objects they regarded as their "native title," equivalent of the Western land title. They have also invited them to listen to sacred myths and to visit the sites and attend rites—dances, songs, body painting, and so forth. Aboriginal people consider performance of the rite as proof of their status of "ritual custodians" (*kirda* in Warlpiri) of this body of knowledge, practices and cult objects; they translate this status in English as "owner," to satisfy the Western notion of property and ownership. In the central desert, one is often the "owner" of his/her father's land but he/she is also the "manager" (*kurdungurlu* in Warlpiri) of the mother's or spouse's land, its rites and its objects. In other words, men and women are owners only insofar as they share a certain use and knowledge of their possession with direct kin and affines.

For Aboriginal people, sacred sites and objects materialize culture—which we regard as something non-material, intellectual or intangible—in other words the body of knowledge transmitted via oral or gestual practices, which are therefore also inalienable: languages, stories, songs, dances, medicinal plants and so on. But for Western law, once intangible knowledge is materialized in a medium, it is alienable and comes under copyright law: a work of art, a publication, a sound or a visual recording. The content then becomes the property of the author of the production, the artist, writer, photographer and, of course, anthropologist. Today anthropologists are reproached—as are museums, journalists, collectors, etc.—for appropriating inalienable bodies of knowledge or objects and commercializing them to the detriment of their original cultural owners. Aboriginal people, like other indigenous groups, stress their need to control the distribution of their culture by recording, filming and publishing their own cultural resources. In addition to the contribution of such an approach to the patrimony and to education, the authors' materialization of their knowledge and practices in their chosen media is supposed to protect them from dispossession by others. In many indigenous communities and gatherings, non-Aboriginal people are not allowed to take pictures or make recordings without a permit, which may be refused. Some anthropology students even agree to sign a contract with the communities, promising they will let them read and check their thesis before they publish it, or even submit it to their university. Although many non-Aboriginal consultants are hired by Aboriginal organizations, the material they collect remains the property of their employers and they cannot use it as they wish.

Aboriginal people also claim copyright in recognition of their intellectual ownership of audio-visual productions or publications by non-Aboriginals (Janke, 1998). This position, modeled on the mining royalties which have been in force in Australia for twenty years, was replaced only after numerous discussions with the elders, who were reticent at the idea of drawing income from their lands. Such wariness of commercial alienation has not been overcome among Native Americans either, according to Rosemary Coombe, who objects that "copyright licenses" and other legal solutions to the problem of intellectual property alienate social relations. Indeed, Coombe appears to advocate an ethic for respecting cultural integrity, rather than a legal solution (Coombe, 1997). She advocates the "central importance of shared cultural symbols in defining us and the realities we recognize," which seems to militate in favor of overcoming the strictures imposed by intellectual property law in favor of a free exchange of ideas and expression (Coombe, 1991: 74–96; quoted by Tsosie, 1997: 10).

Several proposals have been made to avoid such alienation of traditional knowledge, including the idea of taking inspiration from "computer software licensing agreements as a potentially fruitful model for indigenous people to adopt as a means for legally protecting their right to just compensation for the acquisition and use of their intellectual products (Stephenson, 1994: 182)" (Tsosie, 1997: 11, note).

Much the same was said to me by young computer specialists and Internet users at a conference at the Cité des Sciences in Paris, where I explained the necessity of recognizing the right of control and distribution imposed by a Central Desert Aboriginal community to whom I restored the written and audio-visual material I had gathered between 1979 and 1998 in the form of an interactive CD-ROM program. After two years of work and consultation with fifty-one Warlpiri artists from the Lajamanu community and a year of trials in their school, the Council and the artists agreed to make it available to the public. At first, some felt that the knowledge should not be commercialized inasmuch as it constituted the very essence of their culture. But after long discussion among themselves, the Council members and the community Warnayaka Arts Centre decided to accept the economic benefits, provided use of the CD-ROM was confined to settings contextualized with respect to the art and teachings of Aboriginal culture, in other words, to museums and universities.

This resistance to open commercialization of their culture was already evident in the same Warlpiri community of Lajamanu immediately following the emergence of the acrylic painting movement among the Pintupi and the Warlpiri of Papunya, their neighbors to the south, who share similar mythic and iconographic elements associated with totemic sites and Eternal Beings (Jukurrpa). The Lajamanu elders decided to take up commercialized painting on canvas only several years after their neighbors' success in art galleries around the world (Myers 1994), and after a delegation of a dozen Lajamanu men had been invited to make a ritual sand-painting at the Museum of Modern Art in Paris.[3] It may be that the success they encountered as painters and dancers reassured them that the elitism of museums and the international art world would protect them against "copy cats." On one official visit to the Australia Room of the Musée National des Arts d'Afrique et d'Océanie in Paris, the twelve elders identified a carved wooden slab as being connected with a secret cult and not supposed to be shown in public (Glowczewski, 1996). The museum withdrew the slab and ensured that it was not displaying any other objects regarded as sacred or secret. In France as well as in the other former colonial countries, where through the agency of national museums the State owns foreign collections, the prospect of repatriation challenges the very principle of national heritage, which has been largely built on the conquest of other peoples. The political issue is far from being resolved, but moral recognition of problems of intellectual property and cultural control has opened the way for protocols which are increasingly respected by museums.

Traveling Cults, History and Secrecy

Sandra Pannell (1994) has very astutely shown the inalienability of sacred slabs, tjurunga (also churinga), and their equivalents in other desert groups. These are abundantly discussed in the literature (see Moisseeff, this vol.) and are still the subject of speculation among collectors. For the Central Desert Arrernte (Aranda), tjurunga are like a spiritual and geographical ID card. Traditionally each person had his or her own slab, which was hidden and handled with the greatest care; it was a sort of spiritual duplicate, linking the person with a specific place and its totemic spirits. Slabs are said to be inhabited by a spiritual force that is animated by the esoteric design carved on the slab. This singular force of the slab is believed to be reactualized from one generation to the next into its new human duplicates. In former times, when someone died, in accordance with the taboo on pronouncing the name of the deceased found in all Aboriginal groups, the name was not mentioned for the duration of the mourning period, which was two years. Similarly, the deceased's slab, his or her material double, was entrusted to a neighboring group until the mourning period was over (Pannell, 1994: 26). In other groups, the slabs are less individualized, but they are still associated with specific places, of which they are the materialization of the life-force, an ancestral and eternal singularity that is also embodied

---

3. Peter Brook's Théâtre des Bouffes du Nord and ARC, Musée d'Art Moderne, as a part of the manifestation *D'un autre continent — L'Australie, le rêve et le réel*, organized for the 1983 Festival d'Automne.

Photo 24: Warlpiri women's ritual slabs *yukurrukurru*, painted with designs corresponding to the Jurntu (Fire Dreaming) and Miya Miya (Seed Dreaming) sites. (Photo B. Glowczewski)

in the group which shares the same totemic name: this singularity, which is named, drawn, sung and danced, dwells in people, places, totemic species and sacred objects; the Warlpiri and their neighbors in the desert call it Jukurrpa: the Dreaming (Glowczewski, 1991).

Other slabs are connected with initiation cults and travel from group to group, often of different languages, when these cults are transmitted over hundreds of kilometers as part of the chain of alliances, which are also manifested by the circulation of everyday goods and by marriage exchanges (Micha, 1970; Ackerman, 1979). After years or even decades of circulating, the rituals acquired new forms of expression and sacred objects which, having been handled by the ritual custodians of each group through which they have passed, are believed to transmit something of the power of the Dreaming. The sacred and secret objects accompanying the initiation cults can by definition be shown only to initiates. Their revelation at the time they are handed over by the initiating group to the new initiates is part and parcel of the symbolic dramatization of the ritual.

The Central Desert Warlpiri immediately recognized the slab in the Paris museum as coming from the Western Desert and as being part of the secret cult that links them with different language groups. As the secret name of the cult must not be pronounced, it is designated by one of the public dances that is part of the cult, Kadranya (Moyle, 1981), on the northwest coast of Broome, or by the expression "Balgo Business" (Myers, n.d.), from the name of the desert community which introduced the cult among the Warlpiri. It took the cult over fifty years to cover the 1,000 kilometers separating the coast from the Central Desert. In 1976, the Balgo elders, who speak Kukat-ja, Walmajarri and Warlpiri, became the "custodians" of the objects, songs and rites that circulate with the cult and in turn passed them on to the east. However, according to these desert groups, the objects remain the spiritual property of those who, at various times, introduced them into the cult, in particular the Yawuru from Broome.

Unlike many traditional initiation cults, which in Australia assign authority to the elders and separate the sexes in view of making the young people into men and women, this cult specifically presents itself as a new mixed Law which enables men and women of some forty years of age to assume a leadership role. It seems to deal symbolically with certain role changes imposed by colonization, the violence of contact, the traumas of imprisonment and forced sedentarization, the economic changes and intermarriage with Europeans and Asians. The secrecy surrounding initiation into the cult excludes — on pain of severe punishment — Aboriginal people who have not yet received the cult, on the one hand, and, on the other, non-Aboriginals, who are not invited to attend. In an earlier article, I defined it as a "cargo cult":

> Aboriginal Law resides in sacred objects (or places) inasmuch as they are metamorphoses of the same "essence" (life-forces) which makes humans, while White Law resides in "wealth," which does not share any essence with human beings (wealth represents a power that people must appropriate). In the new cult, Aboriginal people do not seek to identify with White wealth, or even to integrate it into their traditional system, as they did with the circulation of the early objects from the West. Instead, an absolutely new intention is brought into play: this new power would allow people to affirm a separation from the commodities which mediate matter in the West. (Glowczewski, 1983b: 12)

As symbolic work on "cargo," that is the Western commodity system, this historical cult is highly secret because it provided Aboriginal peoples with their own way of resisting the harmful effects of the colonial system. Many missionaries regarded it as "devil business" on the pretext that it opposed their influence. For Aboriginal people, the accusation was inadmissible: syncretism between Christianity and traditional spirituality is found in only some regions (Kolig, 1979); elsewhere it is above all a case of seeking to create the conditions for a sort of spiritual retreat in which, as in a collective psychodrama or theatrical catharsis, the ritual with its emotional charge enables new initiates to reenact the violence experienced by their mothers and fathers, and to find ways of coping with it.

The Central Desert Warlpiri claim that part of the cult was dreamed in the small town of Broome, on the northwest coast. When I went there in 1980, I was told that the cult dated back to the wreck of the Koombana, which disappeared in 1912 off the coast of Port Hedland, a town further to the south, in the Pilbaras, where a dreamer is said to have received a message from the shipwrecked men.[4] A Broome elder told me about the cult as he had seen it in the 1920s at La Grange Bidyadanga (100 km south of Broome): he added that he was a Nyikina, raised by the Karajarri, and that he had been made the spiritual custodian of the region north of Broome which belonged to the Jabirr Jabirr, who, he claimed, had died out without descendants (see map). When I returned to Broome in 1991, I found that this monopoly of the custody of the land and the ritual was contested by some Jabirr Jabirr families and above all by the groups speaking the traditional language of Broome, the Yawuru-Jugun. Those local groups intermarried heavily with Europeans and Asians, but had constituted a Yawuru Aboriginal Corporation and had resumed initiation of their young men in the 1980s. The secret cult, including a dance relating the Japanese bombing of Broome during the Second World War, was probably added onto an older Yawuru initiation ritual. In the 1970s, a Yawuru elder, custodian of

---

4. Swain (1993) reported a connection between this cult and the Aboriginal resistance movement in the 1940s, in which a certain Coffin, from the Port Hedland region, persuaded the Aborigines to walk off all the cattle stations in the Pilbara. I have shown (Glowczewski, 1983b) that it was also a certain Coffin from the same region who, according to the Warlpiri, dreamed part of this cult. The strike movement was extraordinarily well organized thanks to another Aboriginal man, who made the rounds of the cattle-stations distributing little pieces of paper divided into squares and asking the Aborigines who did not know how to read or write to cross out a square every morning until the day they were to leave their workplace. The cult reported in three regions includes several points at which little papers are exchanged: it is my hypothesis that this now-ritual act is related specifically to this historical event which, by the Aboriginal people's refusal to go on being treated as slaves, threatened the whole cattle-station system in Western Australia.

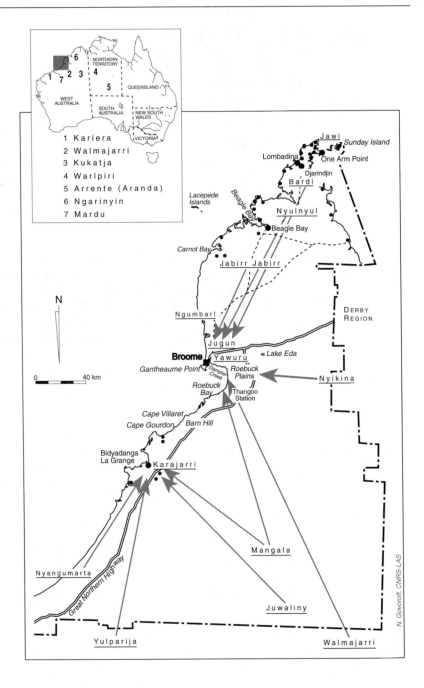

Map 2: Some Aboriginal language groups and migrations in Northwestern Australia.

the initiations in the region, transmitted a new version of the secret cult to some groups living 500 kilometers to the east, around the town of Fitzroy Crossing, who themselves adapted it in the form seen by Kolig (1979) and later transmitted these rites, together with the sacred objects they had received from the Yawuru, to the desert groups.

The Kimberley Aboriginal groups differ in geography, culture, social organization and language (McGregor, 1988), but also in their colonial history and its consequences on contemporary politics (Glowczewski, 1988a). However an exchange network, known as *Wunan*, already linked the coastal groups with the river and desert groups before colonization: these exchanges involved everyday objects (shields, spears, tobacco, food, red ochre and kaolin), cult objects (pearl-shells, sacred objects, hair strings, stone circumcision knives, objects used in love magic), and rites and their attendant myths. Phyllis Kaberry (1939) demonstrated that some of these circulations occurred in her time as chains linking together homonyms of the same sex (*narrugu*). These gendered exchange chains tied together individuals having the same first name or having only the same classificatory "skin" name. It was then necessary for groups with different languages and social organizations (with two, four or eight skins or sub-sections) to deduce equivalences between the different (skin) names: in this way, Aboriginal kinship systems informed and ultimately transformed each other through alliances between their respective owners. In all events, individual members of the same chain, because they bore the same name, were considered as exchange "brothers," or "sisters," which is remarkable inasmuch as the notion of exchange usually suggests alliance rather than siblingship or filiation.

There are other kinds of exchanges as well between same- or opposite-sex affines or kin, ranging from restricted family or marriage exchanges, notably with real or potential affines, to the large-scale ceremonies marking the entry of young people into the adult world or of the dead into the spirit world. Initiation, like death, entails ritual gatherings which require the presence and therefore the travel of allies from other linguistic groups: in both cases hair strings circulate, often between men through their sisters. Ackerman (1979) has mapped the circulation of traditional objects from Western Australia, showing that the circuit extended far into the Northern Territory — which includes Central Desert groups such as the Warlpiri — and progressively integrated spear heads cut in glass from bottles or telegraph-pole insulators, fabric and money. I too witnessed the replacement of traditional artifacts by introduced materials, notably hair strings by fabrics, clothing or blankets, not to mention the acacia-seed cakes, replaced by impressive quantities of cans of flour, sugar, tea and even cellophane-wrapped loaves of bread. The arrival of new, highly prized goods, such as video machines and four-wheel drive vehicles brought these, too, into the gift-exchange circuit. At the domestic level, it should be noted that it is still unusual for Aboriginal people who carry on ritual exchanges to hoard consumer goods for their personal use.

With the advent of pioneer pastoralism in the nineteenth century, many men and women were taken onto cattle stations as itinerant stockmen who ranged over hundreds of kilometers in the Kimberley, the Pilbaras, the Northern Territory and Queensland. Alliances between tribes intensified and expanded owing to new encounters in the course of these travels and to an apparently tacit resistance to the ill treatment suffered by all (Micha 1970). Two hundred kilometers to the north of Broome, the Beagle Bay mission, created in 1890, was used as a receiving center for Aboriginal children forcibly taken away from their families throughout the Kimberley. Trained as domestic help, they were placed with the white pearlers of Broome, and many local women contracted unions with Asian workers, despite the prohibition on interracial cohabitation. It was against this backdrop of unlawful mixed unions and solidarity with the "chain gangs" — prisoners chained together by the neck — that certain secret cults with their sacred objects (Worms and Petri, 1968) spread from group to group: symbolic attempts to mobilize ancestral powers against the upheavals introduced by European domination.

After the 1967 referendum, which obliged cattle-station owners to pay Aboriginal workers a wage, the latter were driven off the stations and took refuge in the fringe camps around the towns. At this time, the young people around Broome were initiated among their various neighbors, who had managed to preserve their ritual life better than had the Yawuru, who had been hard hit by the pearling industry and the missions since the 1880s. Marriages bolstered the ritual alliances and gave responsibilities to members of groups from outside the region: thus, in the 1970s, it was a Karajarri man married to a Yawuru woman who was custodian of the sacred objects in Broome, which had been given back by eastern communities (like Looma) and were kept at the Broome initiation ground. These objects were stolen by a young part Aboriginal man, though some were later located in an art circuit dealing in traditional objects. The case sparked numerous disputes among local Aboriginal people, but after the culprit's release from prison, the affair was considered closed. In the 1990s, the Bardi of One Arm Point and Djarindjin, the Karajarri of Bidyadanga, the Nyikina, Mangala and Walmajarri of Looma, and other groups that initiated young Yawuru men or had received the secret cult from Broome, such as the Kukatja of Balgo, rallied to support the Yawuru when they resumed their own initiations and rituals on their traditional ground. These groups also formed a corporation which is striving to protect the sacred and secret aspects of their culture, in particular with the movement to repatriate cult objects as well as anthropological and historical archives: the Kimberley Aboriginal Law and Culture Centre, initially based in Broome and then transferred to Fitzroy Crossing, home of the Nyikina and the Bunaba, but also of many Walmajarri refugees from the Western Desert.

In 1980, when Noonkanbah, a community in this region, opposed exploratory mining in order to protect a sacred place, it received support not only from the Labor Party, the unions and the churches, but also from distant Aboriginal groups who, like the Warlpiri, had exchanged boys for initiation and marriage, and sacred objects (Glowczewski, 1996; Kolig, 1981). These exchanges followed the desert groups' adoption of the secret cult from the coast, transmitted via Fitzroy Crossing, and gathered strength in the 1990s, when the Warlpiri gave the communities of this town a fire ceremony for the resolution of conflicts between allies, a ceremony connected with the *Ngatijirri* Budgerigar Dreaming and the *Puluwanti* Owl Dreaming (Peterson, 1970; Glowczewski, 1991). Circulation of Aboriginal rites and objects thus continues to be closely connected with the political situation of a region.

The Kimberley example shows that the circulation of cult objects through the transmission of initiation-related cults is a veritable machine for producing culture(s), first by regenerating local specificities and second by asserting a common procedure which, beyond language differences, enables exchange to take place over thousands of kilometers. Each local group's identity is strengthened by this ritual nomadism, which is enriched by new religious forms wherein local variants of what Aboriginal people call their respective Laws nurture those of their neighbors. This is true of men's rituals (Wedlock, 1992) as well as women's (Poirier, 1992b), for both help create these exchanges which reinforce the bond between each group and its sacred places, and the inalienable possession of its sacred objects. Similar identity-building can also be seen in the interregional gatherings for traditional mixed dancing, commonly called "corroborees."[5]

---

5. Today Australian football culture provides a stage for this affirmation of identity through travel: every Aboriginal community has its team which travels several months of the year to compete in tournaments; the players' families often follow them in great numbers. This activity is particularly valorized in eastern Victoria, where the Brambuk culture center displays both the traditional history and the sporting history of the region's Aboriginal groups (Largy Healy, 2001).

The Bugarrigarra Nyurdany Culture Centre in Broome

When the government launched its watchwords, "self-determination" and "self-management," most of the language groups of the Kimberley formed Aboriginal corporations, several of which have their headquarters or an annex in Broome: the Yawuru and the Jugun, natives of this land, the Nyul Nyul originally from around Beagle Bay, the Bardi from the northern Dampier peninsula, and the Karajarri from the south (see map). Some families also established themselves as incorporated associations in order to be allowed to build outstations on the land opened to them by the State, the region or the missions. After passage of the 1993 *Native Title Act*, which established one land-claim procedure for the whole of Australia, a new organization, Rubibi, regrouped the families of the region to help them press their Native Title applications in the face of Broome's developing tourist industry. The federation of Aboriginal groups sought to define strategies using Western law to protect traditional law, notably in the area of property rights on land and the cult objects associated with it. But this institutional centralization of the local groups also gave rise to internal and external segmentation, against a backdrop of "retribalisation"[6] and creolization, which were not without their tensions and disputes, especially concerning the growing influx of Aboriginal and non-Aboriginal migrants to the towns and of tourists to the outback (Glowczewski, 1998b, ed. n.d.).

Various development plans showed the local desire to create an Aboriginal culture center that would at the same time support traditional activities and promote creation, make jobs for the Aboriginal people and protect the local communities and their natural environment (RMIT, 1995; Jackson, 1996). The shire and the Broome Media Aboriginal Corporation each hired an Aboriginal consultant, who put together a working party made up of delegates from Aboriginal organizations in the town as well as from two more distant communities, Bidyadanga and Djarindjin (see map). Numerous meetings were held to draw up a list of the activities people wanted the center to undertake and how it was to be managed. One expert of Tamil origin, invited to speak on his experience with culture centers in North America and Southern Australia, advised first creating the center as a network of cultural exchanges even before constructing the building, putting

---

6. Although the term "tribe" has been rejected for some ten years by Australian anthropologists and Aboriginal militants, who complain that it lends a false connotation to the regional, linguistic and traditional political groups, it is still often used by Aboriginal people, who distinguish themselves as "tribes" or "clans" to accentuate their cultural and social differences.

the argument for "virtual museums" which would use the Internet or CD-ROMs to give back the culture and its objects without the constraints of storage, preservation and security, which are extremely costly, especially in a tropical climate.

As an anthropologist married to a Yawuru man,[7] I was asked to co-ordinate a survey with three Aboriginal representatives. The Working Party wanted to gain a general overview, with statements from people and data that could be presented in a quantified way to the people and to the funding bodies. The main issue was: what is culture for people and what is a culture center supposed to do in relation to different statements about culture? We had to be careful to have a representative sample of people. All the languages of the Broome region had to be represented, and we interviewed some people in their home communities away from town: one third of the 135 people in the sample identified as Jugun and/or Yawuru (42), another third as Bardi (40), whose traditional land lies 200 kilometers to the north, and the rest split between other coastal groups, Karajarri (23), Nyul Nyul (24), Jabirr Jabirr (11) and inland groups: Nyangumarta (7), Yulbarija (6), Mangala (4), Yamatji, Bunaba, Miriwong, Jaru, Walmajarri, Nyigina (17); three people did not identify by a language group. Some people identified to two or more languages, this is why the sum of the figures is higher than the number of people interviewed. The balance between genders was 73 women versus 62 men, and between ages: 54 over fifty, 59 between fifty and twenty, 22 under twenty. Each question listed several answers to choose from, but when, as it often happens, people answered spontaneously, the answer was written down and analyzed to fit into one or the other of the categories so as to allow statistical calculations (Glowczewski ed., 1996). Here are some of the questions discussed in the interviews.

What is Aboriginal Culture for You?

Most people defined culture as language (92), ceremonies, song and dance (91), land, attachment to place (85), old people and family (80), hunting, fishing, living in the bush (79); for less then half it was oral history (71), art and artifacts (69) and less then a third chose the common Western sense of the term "culture" as a cumulative and creative process, expressing Aboriginality with new media (39). All people felt a "loss" of culture and were worried by the fact that local languages are not spoken enough, even if there

---

7. Wayne Barker Jowandi, composer-musician, and film-maker, author of *Milli Milli*, documentary, 53 min., distributed by Ronin Films, Sydney and Jane Balfour, London.

are some lessons in the Broome primary schools and the community schools of Bidyadanga, One Arm Point and Djarindjin.

Asked about what culture is, most old people referred to traditional practices and knowledge: stories about the relation to land, bush medicine identification and use, techniques of hunting, fishing and bush-food gathering, the body of ceremonial Law including dancing and painting. Many stressed that culture is what you eat and how you eat—by a campfire—, your living style, your identity; others insisted on kinship and pleasure: "Going to corroboree was like today people get excited for a new movie; and all the competition between the guys for dancing!" One Yawuru Karajarri woman elder identified culture with *Kunyurrung*, a traditional ritual custom common to all the Kimberley groups through the *Wunan* exchange system, where men with the same name and women with the same name can exchange goods in gendered chains (Glowczewski ed., n.d.). (When a Karajarri child is about to be named, at around the age of four or five, an older person is chosen as his or her namesake and exchange partner. During the naming ritual, the families of the two namesakes share goods.) Other elders insisted on the fact that culture creates unity because of sharing and respecting different ceremonial Laws which connect people from different language groups: "Law spread out and they don't jealous each other because they share. And they should *share* together."

What Does an Aboriginal Culture Center Mean to You?

The majority stressed: respect of men Law and women Law (78), exchange between Aboriginal people (78), resources and exhibitions (78). Less than half chose: place where generations meet (72), place where culture is maintained and alive (72), training and development of skills (71), people with cultural knowledge (68), shows, concerts and festivals (63). In their comments, people insisted on the idea that a center was a place for activities (dance, song, crafts, teaching children) aimed at both Aboriginal children and a non-Aboriginal audience. Many elders stressed the necessity of involving different language groups, sharing culture with other regional Aboriginal groups, including Torres Strait Islanders (who have come to work in pearling), making the wider community understand about cultural differences. While the elders of the remote communities agreed on the need for a big "sharing" center in Broome, they also wanted to decentralize by having "keeping-places" and "culture-teaching places" in their local communities.

Men and women of different ages expressed concern that storage of cultural items in town might represent a spiritual danger and people would get sick. It should be noted that one culture center in Alice Springs, which has a storage place containing sacred objects, is avoided by the local Aboriginal people, who do not want to go near them for fear of transgressing the Law that forbids approaching such objects outside the appropriate ritual context.[8] Showing culture and repatriation are all right so long as secret things are kept at a distance: they have to be protected, but people have to be protected from them as well. The same applies to sacred places.

What Should the Center Do to Support Language and Culture in the Community?

For half of the people, protecting places of cultural heritage, (72) was as important as recording, protecting, teaching knowledge and language (74); other considerations were, give resources for crafts and art (70), give cultural awareness to Aborigines and others (66), provide shop and marketing for artists (61), create programs to develop skills (58), organize exchange with other indigenous people (53); less then a third saw a priority in facilitating creation (art, music, theatre, dance) (42). The need to market arts and create language-teaching resources was presented as a double movement to help communities develop resources themselves and to have a structure in town to host the culture custodians and organize relations with outsiders (art buyers, tourists, schools, etc.).

The protection of culture through the protection of country was expressed as the need to create a network of rangers who would be organized through the center: a model of decentralized cultural/natural management. Protection of country is seen as a mix of prevention of tourist vandalism or other abuses of the land : horses, boats, cars on the beach which erode the banks of the creeks and make the salt-water resources scarce. But the museum rangers also need to protect main tribal areas, secret sites, burial grounds, carved stones, places of spirit related to the reproduction of species: "*gumbali gumbali* (place of spirit), Bugarrigarra (Dreaming). Sometimes they dig it [the ground] and say special word, for snake, lizard, for *yarangal* (spirit) and there is plenty of them then." Not doing this ritual "cleaning" hampers or even blocks the renewal of that species, animal, or seafood, as can be already observed with the scarcity or even extinction of some species in the reefs and the bush. Destroying spirit places, according to a belief shared by many young people too, makes the local people, especially the ones spiritually connected with these places, feel sick.

The term *gumbali* was traditionally used by the Karajarri to designate peo-

---

8. The Western desert elders performed a smoking ritual at the South Australian Museum from which sacred objects were removed to a new storage place so that the room could be used with no danger to the public from spirits (Philip Clarke, pers. com.).

ple who have the same name, that is people who can exchange goods. In Broome Aboriginal English, *gumbali* means "soul brother," in the sense of pal, friend, people of the same generation that you grew up with. The relation between name, place, and spiritual brotherhood refers to an Aboriginal phenomenology which, in my experience, could be generalized to most of the desert and northwest groups: each person is the actualization of virtual names (and often related songs) connected with places. Among the younger generations, where identification with community towns of residence tends to replace links with remote sacred places, specific sacred spots in town are still recognized, and some people still dream spiritual connections between these places and their children to be born (Glowczewski, 1998b, ed. n.d.).

The existential threat to individual people from the destruction or harming of spirit-name places also applies to the wrongful manipulation of sacred objects which embody spiritual singularities: when stolen or put in the wrong place, they can threaten the community with sickness, conflict or other disorders. If the wrong people see or touch them, not can only they themselves go mad, or even die, but their behavior also jeopardizes the safety of members of the community, who can be affected in their body, their spirit and through natural phenomena. This belief in the ancestral spiritual power common to places and sacred objects is held by many people in the community, who would rather not see the storage place be located next to where people gather and work, and even prefer not to talk about it, for fear of unknown consequences. It is constantly stressed that the center has to be controlled by people—elders and ritual custodians—who can protect the others from the dangerous powers involved in dealing with traditional culture.

Who Should be the Main People Involved with the Aboriginal Culture Centre?

The survey consensus gave the first voice to traditional elders (80), then people with language and other cultural skills (71); less then a third of the people favored representatives of Aboriginal organizations (38) or people with administrative and technical skills (36). Some expressed the necessity to have representatives of each language group and community (23) and that Yawuru should be "first," because they are the traditional owners of Broome (10).

The issue of who should be the main deciders is the key to the whole process of cultural reappropriation: how to write a constitution for the future incorporated body that will manage the center. Is the center to favor economic self-determination by becoming a place for promotion and retail, giving employment and income to Aboriginal people? Or is the center to be a culture-sharing place without risk of "loss" and lack of traditional control leading to social disorder and supernatural aggression, which can manifest themselves in many ways, such as a cyclone? In that dilemma, many people trusted their elders as the only ones able to protect the whole environment by protecting a culture through the circulation of rituals and sacred objects over hundreds of kilometers in the ways they had learned from their forefathers.

A year after the survey was completed, the vision of the Bugarrigarra Nyurdany Culture Centre was summarized in a conference on "Planning Cultural and Interpretive Centres in the Kimberley" by the coordinator, granddaughter of the deceased Yawuru elder, custodian of the Broome initiations and secret cult mentioned above (Tarran 1997: 25):

— To facilitate the preservation, continuation and management of Aboriginal Law and Culture under the direction of the Old People with the strategic inclusion of Aboriginal Youth.

— To pursue sustainable economic independence through the development of employment, training and business opportunities within a supportive cultural and tourism industry environment.

— To provide appropriate cultural spaces and infrastructure support.

The notion of "appropriate" is very sensitive in the Aboriginal context. For instance, the fact that the possible repatriation of ancient objects in a local Aboriginal culture center and museum will give access, in terms of storage and maintenance, to other people than the traditional elders is a constant worry. At this level, even the photographic representation of such objects is considered to be inappropriate. Images, like the secret words that designate them, are believed to carry some of the power embodied in these objects. The image has this power precisely because the traditional painting of specific signs on the body, the ground or sacred objects was aimed, like the songs, at "nurturing" the medium. In the end such objects, which physically embody the power of the signs, *are* the culture because they are identified with the people. The whole problem of reviving the culture is to find a way of protecting these objects while allowing them to travel in the proper way, that is to stay a live sharing medium.

The Virtual Circulation of Non-Alienable Objects: Giving-Without-Loosing

I used the example of northwest and central Australia to show that, in the case of a traditional model in which cultural differences were produced

by the circulation of inalienable objects and traveling rites, the question of
the cultural repatriation of these objects and the accompanying knowledge
to a sedentary space such as a culture center raises political, economic, spiritual and ethical questions which challenge Western models of property. The
unsuitability of the Western notion of property has also been noted in the
case of Native American culture:

> The most important difference between cultural property and inalien-
> able possessions has to do with the distinction between property and
> possessions... possessions are always implicated in systems of
> exchange... [the] concept of inalienable possessions provides a more
> inclusive and potentially more effective avenue for arriving at resolu-
> tion of cultural property disputes. (Welsh 1997: 17)

We have seen that it is in the discrepancy between cultural property and
inalienable possessions that the problem of restitution, not only of Australian sacred objects but of Aboriginal intellectual knowledge as well,
resides. If the sacred objects which circulate between groups through rituals are inalienable, then the knowledge that goes with these rituals, in the
form of stories, songs, paintings and dances, is also inalienable, as are the
sacred places which, for Aboriginal people, materialize this knowledge just
as the sacred objects do: they are more than a representation, they are the
living manifestation of this knowledge.

One Aboriginal myth from the northern coast, in Arnhem Land, tells the
story of the Djanggawul, two ancestral sisters who, after the men stole their
bags and certain sacred objects, said: "We know everything. We have really lost nothing, for we remember it all, and we can let them have that small
part. For aren't we still sacred, even if we have lost the bags? Haven't we
still our uteri?" (Berndt, 1952: 58). The reproductive organ mentioned here
is also symbolized by the mats produced by women in the north for use as
pubic tassels. In an earlier article, I showed that the circulation of hair strings
which are used, among other things, to make pubic tassels, position desert
women as agents of social reproduction in a way similar to that analyzed
by Annette Weiner (1976) for the production and circulation of mats by
women in Samoa and the Trobriand Islands:

> ...hair string transmission between men occurs through women
> as the sisters. This transmission is reciprocal between brothers-in-
> law to symbolize compensating or attaching sisters with the brother
> or the husband. A woman shares with her brothers the ownership of
> the patriclan territory and at the same time she is a ritual manager of
> her husband's sister's territorial ceremonies... Hair string circulation
> thus symbolizes alliances and economic exchanges (access to anoth-
> er person's territorial resources), affirms a certain dependence of men

on women, and confirms women's responsibility not only as land owners or managers but also as producers of the value (their string made
from their hair) which incarnates the ritual management relations.
(Glowczewski, 1983a: 238)

Ten years later, Annette Weiner (1992), in her book, *Inalienable Pos-
sessions: The paradox of keeping-while-giving*, referred to my analysis of
Warlpiri hair strings with respect to other work on Australian desert groups
(Bell, 1983; Dussart, 1988; Myers, 1986):

... these recent data on women's controlling interests in the circulation of hair strings, rope, threads, and cloth show how essential such
possessions are to men as well as women and how these possessions
constitute social identities as well as rights to territorial associations.
Clearly, Aboriginal women had (and in some cases, still have) access
to sacred objects that, infused with potency, have significant exchange
value. Whether or not some of these possessions take on absolute value
and become inalienable cannot be discerned from the available data.
(Weiner, 1992: 112)

Since my 1983 article, I have gathered new material on hair strings,
notably a myth telling how the Digging-Stick women (*Kana*) wanted to
acquire headbands and makarra ("womb") rope made by an ancestor from
the hair of men in order to seduce them, and so agreed to give men their
knowledge of initiations and hunting (Glowczewski, 1991, ed. 1991). Like
the women of Arnhem Land, the Warlpiri women said that they had "lost"
nothing by agreeing to this gift-exchange. In the Owl conflict-resolution
ceremony—the same one the Warlpiri gave the northwest groups—men
dance around with hair strings and stop in front of the mothers of potential wives, who take these strings: mothers used them to make pubic tassels, which they wore before passing them on to their daughters when they
were old enough to marry the giver of the hair string (Glowczewski, 1991:
209). It is as though the hair strings constantly bound up descent with
alliance through a circulation of substances that were embodied and transmitted in these exchanges. Made from the hair of men or women, by men
or women, hair strings circulate between the genders, who transform
them in their own way.

The hair string pubic belt of a boy who was to be circumcised could be
sent in his stead to invite distant groups—sometimes from different language groups—to participate in his initiation. In former times an initiand
accompanied by his guardians could spend several months traveling hundreds of kilometers to rally various allies to his initiation. Today all kinds
of vehicles, even aircraft, add many more kilometers to these initiation cir-
cuits. Peterson (2000) reports that, in 1994, a boy from a Western Desert

Photo 25: Mangaya sticks connected with the ritual *makarra* (womb) hair string rope aiming at bringing the dancers into the Dreaming space-time. (Photo B. Glowczewski)

group traveled 2,250 kilometers to the north, as far as the Lajamanu Warlpiri, before returning in a ritual convoy totaling some 600 travelers upon arrival. Novice's travels are accompanied by transfers of ritual objects, slabs and hair strings, as well as marriage promises, the circumciser often being obliged to promise the novice one of his daughters. Similar convoys travel the east/west axis linking the Central and Western deserts to the Kimberley groups, as far as Broome. Interestingly, on this coast, boys and girls of marriageable age used to receive a hair string belt garnished with a large pearl-shell. Once this shell, inscribed with Dreaming signs, was transmitted to the desert groups, it became a sacred object reserved for initiated men, especially rain-makers.

Desert men use hair strings to make string crosses; these highly sacred objects are allowed to be seen by women only in exceptional circumstances. In the northwest, wool has replaced string for the manufacture of these crosses which, here, are presented to women as ritual gifts. In desert groups, the "womb" hair string is extremely sacred for women; it is strung between the two meter-high sacred sticks they "plug into" the ground; this ritual device is believed to actualize the Dreaming space-time for the duration of the ritual. Men and women alike use hair strings and rope to wrap other sacred objects, especially wood or stone slabs. Women also use them therapeutically and at times of mourning or initiation: they rub women or men, girls or boys with them in order to infuse them with a power or to extract something from them. The purpose of touching a person with the strings seems to be the same as with the slabs. Something of the power of the Dreaming and the singular identity of all those who have ever touched these objects has become consubstantial with them in the course of the different handlings which bind together all differences: genders, kin, affines, exchangers from various language groups.

Summing up I would say, in answer to Annette Weiner, that hair strings are alienable when they are given in payment for a ritual service, for example, when the temporary custodians of a slab return it to the original owners; but they become inalienable once they have been used in a sacred ritual function by either sex: to make ritual string crosses, to wrap up sacred objects or to rub a sick person, novice or someone in mourning. Then they become sacred objects. All circulations of men, women, objects and rites, which sometimes circulate together, sometimes one instead of another, seem to operate according to the same logic of giving-without-losing, consistent with giving to make what one gives desirable. A logic of desire imbedded in a relation of power, for it is when one succeeds in obliging the other to accept a gift that one can claim to be the strongest (Glowczewski, 1991: 288). This explains the complex negotiations which lead groups to mutually impose the — temporary — adoption of each other's inalienable riches: sacred objects, rites, young people for initiation and marriage.

The idea of giving-without-losing, found in all Aboriginal ritual circulations, is in its own way like the logic of certain software designers who argue for the free circulation of their product as opposed to the principle of intellectual copyright, which benefits only the big monopolies. In what they humorously call "copyleft," which consists in allowing copies to be made of a program while acknowledging the creator's origin, they see a better means of controlling their creations than in the present application of the copyright laws, which transfer the original author's rights to whoever buys the product for the purpose of commercialization. As Stephenson suggests (1994), there is certainly a parallel to be explored with indigenous peoples' claims to their inalienable possessions. Such a parallel would also evoke the similarity between the non-linear synchronous nature and the hyperlinks of the Web and the Internet with the linked-up thinking and the cognitive networks of a certain kind of mythic thought.

I would like to add here that myth does not seem to me to oppose history in the way Kolig (2000) opposes the cognitive perception of the desert groups — as mythic and synchronic — to that of the Aboriginal peoples of the northwest — as historic, diachronic and post-colonial. We have seen that, over and beyond their cultural, social and geographical differences, Aboriginal groups of the two regions exchange cults which they re-adapt to suit themselves while reproducing local differences which go beyond simple dualism. Although it is true that northwestern Aboriginal groups felt the effects of colonization long before the desert groups did, it remains that the circulation of objects and songs as well as kinship systems between the two regions pre-dates colonization. It is this ritualized circulation of tangible and intangible artifacts back and forth on linear journeys stretching across time which enables mythic thinking to be reproduced in the form of a living network: mythic thinking manufactures transformations and connections which singularize and reposition anchor points, sacred places, in a continually evolving structure of narrative and performance. Compared with this logic, the merely encompassing West is constantly threatening to dis-authenticate those who create these anchor points. Hence the urgent need for museums, and anthropologists, not to go on "alienating these cultures" by alienating their objects, but instead to recognize their inalienability by authenticating their creators rather than their acquirers.

Translated by Nora Scott

Chapter 11

Time, Objects and Identities
The Destiny of Kanak Art *

Alban Bensa

Will the virgin, lively and beautiful today
Rip with its drunken wingbeat this hard
Forgotten lake of ours haunted under frozen dew
By the transparent glacier of unfled flights!

S. Mallarmé (1913)

...to go against the too sleek grain of history

W. Benjamin (1991: 343)

History of a Collection

For contemporary visitors, objects displayed in ethnographic museums radiate an unusual force because they were "alive" in the past. Their authenticity is derived exclusively from this privilege, that cannot be attributed to copies, however perfect. These objects are the concretion of an earlier time in history that is constantly intruding into our present. Thus, they can be summoned as testimony, at times an accusation held against the society that created them, sometimes in its defense, for its glorification. For the most

---

* This paper is a revised and unified version of two publications: "La culture kanak au présent. Dialogue sur l'art océanien," *Le Genre Humain (Actualités du contemporain)*, Paris, Seuil, 2000, pp. 65–79, and *Ethnologie et architecture. Le Centre culturel Tjibaou, Nouméa, Nouvelle-Calédonie. Une réalisation de Renzo Piano*, Paris, Adam Biro, 2000, (chapitre VI, "Les objets de la culture kanak").

289

part, colonized peoples and dominated classes have known this pendulum movement which first considers their works as barbarous and crude before hoisting them, at long last, to the pinnacle of great art. Kanak objects have not escaped these ups and downs.

The Long Night of Kanak Objects

During a very long period—the 19th and the 20th century until 1983—museographic ideology viewed the Kanak as evidencing humanity in infancy. Much like the reservations to which they were gradually being confined, the cases displaying their skeletons, stone tools, pottery, and weapons substantiated the idea that a crude and savage society (didn't they practice cannibalism?) was dying out before our eyes. Thus, the anthropometric measurements of skulls made by 19th century scholars substantiated the nonexistent criterion of primitiveness. For a long time, the constitution of ethnographic collections was considerably hindered by scientists' bone collecting and the destruction of objects by missionaries and colonists, although Governor Guillain did create a local depot for various objects as early as 1863. The idea, at the time, was to determine the mining potential of Grande Terre, but there were Kanak objects mixed in with the mineral samples brought back by colonial officers from their inspection rounds "in the bush." In 1895 the small structure created by Guillain became the "Colonial Museum." Its ethnographical pieces were still mixed in with the minerals and the natural history collection of birds, insects, fish, coral, etc. However "the most ancient pieces of the museum's ethnological collections, coming from New Caledonia, but also from Vanuatu, the Solomon Islands, the Marquesas Islands, and Australia, date back to this period." (Néaoutyine, 1995: 22–23)

Until 1920, this more systematic object-collecting was motivated by the very prevalent conviction that the Melanesian world of New Caledonia, including its human representatives, was going to disappear. Thus, while the Kanak rebelled against land spoliation and then were requisitioned as underpaid labor for the colonists and the administration, their real existence in the contemporary world continued to be comprehended in reference to some totally imaginary past. The bones of their dead, their daily-life objects, and their works of art fed speculation and sarcasm over their belonging to obsolete forms of human history. This view, putting them on a par with animals and minerals, led to a museographic presentation governed by the natural sciences. Colonial anthropology, which linked the Kanak people to an immemorial past and refused to see and hear them in their present state, aimed at deepening the gap between what was judged "primitive"—the period before the arrival of White people—and the period thereafter, during which, being subject to French rule, the population had purportedly "evolved" in the right direction. This evolutionary conception was totally predominant at the time, pervading everything from the colonists' pragmatic racism to that of scholars in theoretical disguise. Everyone or almost everyone, from the furiously evangelizing missionary to the convict settled on Kanak land, and including the most progressive political thinkers, held the same opinion: that the Kanak deserved only paleontological and archeological interest. Under these conditions, the presentation of their objects as a fantastic essay on the extent of their savagery or their link to Neanderthal man was necessarily derisive or condescending. Exposure and mockery merged in the solid conviction that only the European bourgeoisie knew what was good morals, art, and "civilization."

To make the colonized into puppets serving their desires and their self-satisfaction, the colonizers had to begin with "pacification." Military operations, massacres and forced population movements were their response to the Kanak revolts which marked the first twenty-five years of French presence in New Caledonia and came to a head in the great uprising of 1878 (Dauphiné, 1989; Merle, 1995; Bensa and Goromido, 1997). The population was first vanquished, then put into museums or on exhibit. Assegais and clubs, war trophies from the "colonial" war, were inevitably a part of displays. It is still striking to see several hundred Kanak weapons piled on shelves in the storerooms of the Musée de l'Homme in Paris. For colonized peoples, this staging is only the final phase of their subjection, a scalp dance organized by those who subdued them, often without real military difficulty. This braggadocio reached its peak when the "natives," in flesh and bone, were brought to Europe to be seen by all. Thus, the "Canaque village on the Esplanade des Invalides," during the 1889 Paris World Fair showed Melanesians, pulled out of their reservations, in a vaguely reconstructed setting. For Europeans of the time, these "Coloreds" could only be "savages." The commentators, as Sylviane Jacquemin explains, citing texts from the period, base their evaluation on the horror with which the Kanak objects fill them: "if the arms correspond 'to the lowest level on the scale of civilization', the numerous taboos (on doorframes and roofing peaks) shown in the villages are hardly better. (...) They combine all the signs of crudeness and poverty of form: 'hideous' or 'grimacing' faces, 'monstrous nostrils' or 'thick-lipped mouths'; these 'misshapen monsters' intervened in sorcery or in anthropophagic rituals, when they were not assimilated with the 'evil spirit' or simply 'park statues.'" At best, other journalists spoke highly of the Kanak exhibited because they had helped France quell the uprising in 1878... In the same tone, the colonial exposition in 1931 put on a demonstration of primitiveness eagerly awaited by the public, showing the Kanak "posed on a float decorated with taboos and totems, dressed in traditional costumes, making ancestral gesticulations and singing their

war songs" (Jacquemin, 1990: 235–237). In addition to these daily festivities, other Melanesians could be seen eating raw meat in cages at Paris'
Jardin d'Acclimatation (the zoo) (Dauphiné, 1998; Douglas, 1998). The
Kanak people, alternately reduced to a decor along with shells and other
exotica, exhibited as monsters, or forced into ridiculous or degrading
exhibitions, had no chance of being taken seriously in those times of tri-
umphant French colonialism.

   Neither their surrender to a firepower that made short shrift of their
traditional weapons nor their Christianity, nor the voluntary enlistment of
many into the French army to combat in Europe (1914–1918 and 1939–1945)
would soften the devastating White judgements. In the 19th century, Louise
Michel was probably the only person to appreciate the world of the Kanak,
their way of living and ability to dialogue. Picasso and Vlaminck were apparently the first to realize the importance of Melanesian art work (Peltier,
1990). Their studios housed several Kanak statues along with other works,
mainly African, bought on the still diminutive "primitive art" market. These
isolated attitudes were of course incapable of reversing the denigrating trend
that repudiated the "natives" all the more vocally inasmuch as it derived
its strength from the colonial settling and exploitation of New Caledonia.

The Reversal of the Situation

   In this concert of injurious remarks, the voice of missionary Maurice
Leenhardt (1878–1954) rang out as a call to get a grip on events. This Protes-
tant pastor, who arrived in the archipelago in 1902, devoted his life to the
study of the various Kanak languages and cultures, although he never abandoned his evangelizing work nor questioned the principle of colonization.
He collected extensive ethnological and linguistic material (Clifford, 1982)
and strove, through his work and intercession with local and national authorities, to give Kanak culture its rightful value within the overseas French
empire. Leenhardt was sensitive to the Melanesians' aesthetic taste, as evidenced in their oral traditions, art work, ceremonies, and appreciation of
landscape. His anthropological endeavor testifies to the richness — scien-
tific as well as moral — of this civilization. This pastor, who claimed to have
been 'converted' by those to whom he was supposed to teach the gospel,
not only formed a documentary base, unparalleled at the time, but also
strove to reveal the Kanak's sensitivity to others and to nature. In doing so,
he introduced a highly personal, philosophical approach to anthropology,
now viewed as questionable (Bensa, 2000b). But his publications definitely marked the entry of the first inhabitants of New Caledonia in the great
sociological debate initiated by Durkheim and Mauss. Likewise, books such
as *Gens de la Grande Terre* (1936) and *Do Kamo* (1947) made the Kanak

example a source of inspiration for the intellectually fashionable philosophical nativism that prevailed in post-1945 France. Although this progress hardly succeeded in shaking the colonial order in New Caledonia nor in substantially reducing prejudice, it did constitute the first positive attention given to the Kanak. They did not disappear, as had been announced, and the vitality of their past and their present was restored, thanks to ethnographic work.

The Melanesians gained access to French citizenship in 1946, and their rapid, decisive entry into the politics of the archipelago was to confirm the findings of Maurice Leenhardt, and later of Jean Guiart (1992), both of whom emphasized the vitality of the Kanak world after a century of colonization. The collections of objects grew with the organization of the "New Caledonian Museum" which replaced the older institution in 1940. In 1970 the museum was finally transferred to the premises it occupies today, and in 1983 it became a museum of Melanesian art, definitively separated from the natural history collections. This slow swing towards an autonomous and enhanced presentation of Kanak society gradually broke with the caricatures which had prevailed for far too long. The relaunching of linguistic and ethnological research in the field, led by André-Georges Haudricourt (1911–1996) at the end of the 1960's (Ozanne-Rivierre, 1979; Rivierre, 1980; Bensa and Rivierre, 1982; Bensa and Leblic, 2000) accompanied this renaissance, which the Kanak people gradually took into their own hands. They took responsibility for the presentation of their own civilization, and imposed their own images both of their past and of their presence in the contemporary world.

It was Jean-Marie Tjibaou (Bensa and Wittersheim, 1998) who took the first major steps in this direction. With the Melanesia 2000 festival, organized in 1975 on the very location of the cultural center that now bears his name, the future president (in 1984) of the Socialist Kanak Liberation Front (the FLNKS, in French), made Kanak culture the focus of political debate. On the Tina site, all regions of New Caledonia were represented and a play portrayed the history of Kanak country in three scenes: the pre-colonial period, the arrival of the White people and the contemporary period. With its splendor and fervor, its ceremonial speeches, large reconstructed huts, songs, dances, and craft exhibitions, the show surprised more than one observer. It displayed the ruptures and continuities with a past brandished like the bloody coat of arms of a wounded and all the more revengeful identity: for the first time, thanks to this festival, the strengths of yesterday and of today merged into one image. This paved the way for growing political protests, and also for the series of organizations through which the Kanak were to take their cultural advancement into their own hands. Melanesia 2000 resolutely showed those people who were reassured by the predicted breakdown of the Kanak world that they, their traditions and their projects for emancipation were very much alive and had to be taken into consideration (Tjibaou, 1978 and 1996).

To be effective, this refusal to be assimilated, in the Western imagination, with a fossil people required new initiatives. These were forthcoming; they were political as well as cultural: the demand for independence (1977), the creation of a coalition of parties supporting that demand (1982 and 1984), the boycott of territorial elections (1984), and even the active preparation of the Caledonia 2000 Festival, which was finally cancelled (1984), and the inauguration of New Caledonia's first Kanak cultural center (1985). Jean-Marie Tjibaou, then mayor of the small district of Hienghène, had three circular buildings topped with pointed metal sheeting edified at the river mouth, well in sight of the territorial road skirting the sea. These are miniature replicas of the very high hut, made of plant materials, erected on the same grounds by the chiefdoms of the valley, at his request. His own collection of ancient objects is exhibited there, while activity leaders attempt to revive interest in traditional music and song. The opening year of this cultural center exemplifying an original political philosophy also saw the inauguration of the reorganized collections at the Museum of Nouméa. This striking display of objects, notably doorframes and roofing peaks, conceived jointly by anthropologist Patrice Godin and by Jean-Marie Tjibaou prompts meditation on the mysteries of this ancestral culture. These inspired works were created long before the shock of colonization threw Kanak artists into a protracted state of despair. Their sober majesty is witness to the spiritual intensity of their civilization. The responsibility for this artistic heritage was soon given to Emmanuel Kasarherou, and its finest pieces, dispersed in museums and private collections the world over, were at long last exhibited, in 1990, first in Nouméa then in Paris. With the exhibition "Jade and Mother-of-pearl," Roger Boulay, curator of the Paris Museum of African and Oceanic Art, put a very complete collection of the most beautiful works of Kanak art on display for the first time (Boulay, 1990).

Present-day Kanak Culture

What a long way we have come: from a hodge-podge of curiosities — stuffed birds, masks, mineral specimens, statuettes, various bones, corals, and ploughing tools piled up indiscriminately, turning an entire civilization into a mere natural species — to the permanent or temporary exhibitions in museums where the consistency and beauty of Kanak works can at last be appreciated; from World Fairs and colonial exhibitions portraying Kanak as savages and their society as folklore to Melanesia 2000, that great festival of a proud people! This ideological change has gone along with a new relationship to the past. It was convenient for Europeans to reject the

Kanak as archaic in order to expel them from the present. If the Kanak were viewed as the last vestiges of a distant human past, their only chance of entering History could be as fossils. But anthropological criticism of this blindness and above all the Kanak's determined struggle for their survival and dignity slowly integrated the past into the present. Since Kanak society had managed to hold its own by adapting its cultural heritage to the contemporary world, there was no justification for banishing it into an inaccessible past or erasing its specific character. In 1988, when the project for a great cultural center took form, past and present were no longer antagonistic, but reconciled on two counts. A very lively tradition was finally to achieve full recognition and Kanak art was to be set on a par with the art of all other civilizations.

Having retrieved their dignity, ancient objects have become the basis of positive identity, and by the same token the Melanesian public has taken new interest in them. Because they are "Kanak, and proud of it," nearly all of the new, often young visitors to the Territorial Museum of Nouméa are discovering masks, doorframes, and roofing peaks that they have never before seen, since they disappeared from homes and villages long ago. These people feel somewhat uneasy about these expressions of their ancestral culture, but at the same time they look for remnants from their own region, and explanations of the bygone practices connected with them. For a majority of present-day Kanak, these objects, souvenirs of the "old people," represent traces of a past that they have not experienced. The testimonial force of the works, like words of an ancestor coming from beyond the grave, creates the impression of a reunion, a feeling that generally partakes of the aesthetic emotion, to the point that the two may merge.

Never is the need for a past felt as strongly as when the future provokes the present. It is because a new political future has opened up for the Kanak people that the younger generations have been able to recreate their ties with the history embodied by the ancient objects. This impulse to embrace their heritage is accompanied by a changed relation to contemporary art, particularly since New Caledonia now possesses two locations—the Territorial Museum and the Tjibaou Center—in which Kanak and Oceanic creations find their natural setting. There was talk, at one point, of having the center replace the museum. This solution would have deprived the Kanak of a memorial located in the heart of the city and made architect Renzo Piano's building seem to be looking back towards the past. To mark both the new enhancement of the past and the desire to participate actively in the present-day world, the Kanak Cultural Development Agency emphasized the necessity to devote an important part of the Tjibaou Center to contemporary Oceanic art. Thus, the guardians of the newly revived memory promised to undertake the promotion of resolutely "traditional" recent artwork as well. Whereas art work had almost totally disappeared from the

Photo 26: The Jean-Marie Tjibaou Cultural Center, Nouméa. (Photo A. Bensa, 1998)

Kanak world since the beginning of the 20th century, there has definitely been a real cultural renaissance over the last few decades, with a multitude of artists, men and women, sculptors and painters. This explosion of creativity is now coming up against a major difficulty, intensified by the issue discussed above: how can these works be supportive of a collective identity? Modern creations do not have the efficiency of the old art that upholds Kanak identity all the more effectively in that it is the main source of its visual foundations. They must therefore invent forms that may also come to symbolize Kanak identity: a most delicate task, since those forms must also make sense for contemporary art.

Objects in Time

Why does the term "contemporary" not figure among the key words in anthropology? There is the fact that anthropologists, those professional observers, are necessarily the contemporaries of what they observe, report and ponder. A more probable reason, however, has to do with the distance that anthropology seeks to take from present-day situations and events in order to better develop its generalizing interpretations in terms of permanency. The price to be paid for taking a distance from what is contemporary is the detemporalizing of the ethnographic experience. But conversely, studying what happens to persons who share the same situation, understanding how human beings collectively experience their own times, or analyzing the various ways in which the notion of "contemporary art" is used, involves shifting our focus toward the temporal reality of objects and singular events—in the present case, Oceanian art work and the way it is presented to an expert committee—as social facts.

An Invisible Heritage

In 1989, France decided to yield to the demand repeatedly voiced by Jean-Marie Tjibaou, the leader of the movement for independence in New Caledonia, that a Kanak cultural center be built in Nouméa. After competitive bidding, an international jury awarded responsibility for the project to Renzo Piano (known in France as the architect, along with Richard Rodgers, of the George Pompidou Center in Paris). The ADCK, the Agency for the Development of Kanak Culture, a public agency set up in 1989 under the so-called "Matignon Agreement,"[1] was to be the contractor for the project. In 1994, the ADCK formed an "international steering committee" made up of Europeans and Pacific islanders along with representatives of the French administration to draw up plans for this center's activities. During its second meeting in April 1996, this committee discussed creating a contemporary Oceanic art collection. The verbal exchanges that took place at that meeting in Nouméa will guide my comments on the semantic destiny of objects and the many facets of the concept of what is "contemporary."

As I pondered on the meeting, which I had the good fortune to attend, the understanding of the present in general and of the contemporary period as an era, a way of life and a singular way of appraising works of art seemed to present endless reflections as in parallel mirrors, what is called *mise en abîme* in French. As viewpoints were exchanged, the enigmatic magic of the present, with its simultaneous sameness and constant difference intimately disclosed the originality of our contemporariness. I resorted to intuition, then, as I embarked on the adventure of exploring these two domains: an intuition formulated by the poet Mallarmé in the stanza that heads this paper, and which sets a framework for any reflection on the present, along with some of Walter Benjamin's thoughts on the relations between the modern world and its past.

The brilliancy of the present is dazzling. What do we know about what

---

1. Following a troubled period of several years, Prime Minister Michel Rocard's government succeeded in convincing both the pro- and anti-independence parties to commit themselves to a ten-year process of correcting the economic, political and cultural imbalances so as to reduce the inequalities of which the Kanak remained the main victims in this French Overseas Territory (TOM in French).

is happening to different people at the same time, here and now? In its most tangible form (words exchanged, the contemplation of a work of art), the present is a series of events being lived. But this form is highly uncertain, for the outcome is yet to come (but where, and when?). Social scientists often dodge the obscure brilliancy of what is happening before their eyes. They do this by relating the event to something else, transcendent and out of sight — a structure or rule — that governs actual social interplay. Everything seems to be prepared on another stage, "out of time," as N. Thomas would have said (Thomas, 1989; Bensa, 2000a). But by thus detemporalizing the present, with the objects and art work it contains, we shift its meaning onto improbable divinities (such as society, cognitive representations or culture), and deprive it of any singularity. Is it impossible to grasp the present from within by seeing how it is happening?

The present brings individuals and concrete objects into interaction. This being-present-together involves exchanges: talking, seeing and commenting. The mysterious materiality of works of art, and the words that come and go in their wake reveal the thick of a situation.

The dialogues that follow are taken from my notes of the aforementioned meeting.[2]

— Kanak institutional discourse: "... We would like the Jean-Marie Tjibaou Cultural Center to give our culture the full place it deserves in its own country. In compliance with Article 75 of the French Constitution, we are governed under a 'particular law' status that legally recognizes our historical specificity. We intend to give full political strength to this specific identity."[3]

— French ministerial authorities: "Certainly, but over and beyond these principles, your task is to present Kanak and, more broadly, Oceanic works of art. These exhibited objects provide the best proof of your presence in the contemporary world."

Running through the present, a thread of words refers to distinct experiences. The colonial context highlights a structural heterogeneity by jux-

---

2. I shall present excerpts from exchanges during this meeting by indicating the speaker's institutional position or occupational status. Although I took notes during the meeting, participants have not reread them. I therefore take full responsibility for presenting and interpreting these exchanges.

3. According to articles 45 and 75 of the French constitutions of 1946 and 1958 respectively, persons "originating in the Overseas Territories" or "citizens of the Republic whose civil status is not that of common law" are granted a "personal status" whereby they are granted the right to administer themselves according to their own customs in matters of inheritance, matrimony and land (see Constitutions, 1995). All Kanak of New Caledonia have this status, except those who have voluntarily relinquished it.

taposing two separate memories: that of the natives and that of the invaders.[4] When a solid national melting pot exists, institutions are, in one way or another, grounded in a consensus. But in New Caledonia, where parties have not yet reached an agreement about the island's political future,[5] the two parties have quite dissimilar expectations.[6]

The museographic project associated with the Jean-Marie Tjibaou Cultural Center enjoins "the natives" to exhibit their specificity—their culture—something the Kanak hardly ever think of doing. To do so implies that the Kanak people solve several problems. They must overcome the barriers between their 28 different linguistic zones. They must disentangle themselves from the overall structure of a French Overseas Territory and distinguish themselves from the other communities forming that entity (people from Wallis and Futuna, Tahitians, Indonesians, Europeans, etc.), and they must manage to see themselves in the context of an Oceanic civilization. These wider horizons oblige them to come up with another image of themselves.[7] The task is arduous since they must transform the medium governing their immediate universe, with a switch from confidential relations to official ones—from private to public—and from "just-between-us" to international forms of communication. This is the very situation analyzed by J. Clifford, where "marginal populations come into a historical or ethnographic space that has been defined by the Western imagination" (Clifford, 1988:5; Bensa, 2000d). The Cultural Center forces the Kanak to transgress their own temporal framework insofar as it is strongly conditioned

4. "The relation (of colonial powers) to universality has never involved a true experience of plurality. The colonized, on the other hand, have—usually painfully—had a triple experience associated with discovering others, namely: the acceleration of history, the narrowing of space and the individualization of destinies" (Augé, 1994: 145).

5. See Bensa, 1995. In April 1996, during the discussion I have analyzed here, the leaders present were unable to reach an agreement. It was only two years later, with the signing of the Nouméa agreement on May 5, 1998, that a solution was found. The Tjibaou Center had just been inaugurated. The agreement stipulates that New Caledonia will gradually take over responsibility for the broad domains of activity that will be turned over to it by the French government. Through this progressive change of status, it will cease to be an Overseas Territory, and will have the option, fifteen to twenty years from now, and following a referendum, of achieving full sovereignty.

6. France took possession of New Caledonia in 1853. Starting in 1970, the native peoples of this Overseas Territory began asserting their rights to self-determination and independence. New Caledonia was governed under the Matignon Agreement from 1988 to 1998. See note 1.

7. By its use of the term Kanak, instead of canaque (as it is written in French), the independence movement sought to put its own mark on the spelling of the word used indiscriminately and pejoratively by colonists to designate the first people to inhabit the archipelago. We have attempted to comply with this attempt to reconstruct the collective self-image through spelling.

by very local affairs involving their family, political and economic relations with their kin, their chiefdoms, their gardens or development projects. Through this building, the Kanak would be obliged to tune in on global time, dictated by the major stock markets, the famous art galleries, and the Olympic games, those places that epitomize "contemporariness" for those members of the Western elite who have the least roots in their home-land—I am thinking of economists, business people, computer scientists, etc. However, the present as lived by the Kanak people is not in phase with the rhythm of globalization that museum curators have in mind when they talk about "being contemporary." And what makes this temporal difference particularly acute is the fact that the Melanesians of New Caledonia think of their "culture" as a cornerstone for their future nation: Kanaky.

For each party in this debate, the notion of culture conveys different meanings, or rather, different perspectives. The Kanak are involved in a struggle for decolonization, and take this notion as the starting point for all of their demands. Since independence is supposed to provide political room for total cultural fulfillment, expectations for a new era completely predetermine how the term "culture" is used. The militant, linear temporal framework which underlies political arguments and objectives is not shared by specialists in art, who construe cultures in reference to the instantaneity of juxtaposed objects exhibited to the empty gaze of visitors. Echoing this attitude, the colonial administration's notion of culture grants the Kanak people the status of a regional culture within the French Republic, at the very most. Accordingly, the cultural center should be a monument that materializes and glorifies Kanak culture while simply placing it alongside other cultures.

— The French ministerial authority: "By opting for the creation of a collection of contemporary Oceanic art, we will make your image a part of a worldwide project of artistic promotion."

— Kanak institutional discourse: "We do not feel comfortable with the idea of being in the spotlight. Our society has less to do with showing than with sharing. What is essential in our culture still has to do with what is immaterial and hard to grasp. This showcase approach must therefore be balanced by projects more oriented toward our heritage and toward a documentary approach, in the library for example, to compensate for the risks of museological reification."

The fear of being objectified in a collection of exhibited museum pieces is counterbalanced by placing value on what cannot be shown and, as such, belongs to the "true" heritage. The essence of the Kanak world must remain secret and nearly inaccessible. The reference to culture as a hidden, immaterial and indescribable god may sometimes serve as a sort of incantation for people who feel intimidated by the elitism of international art specialists. A series of contrasting terms—authenticity/artificiality, invisible/show-able and popular/fashionable—runs through the classificatory system used by those Kanak who work with the institutions responsible for promoting their culture. Unlike the natural passing of time in social activities, the temporality of museums can be said to be a sort of "non-time", like the "non-places" (Augé, 1992), those meaningless spaces that form whenever individuals and peoples "rub shoulders" without meeting each other. The visitor's outside view of objectified pieces of Kanak culture is the way tourists use time to consume cultural commodities. The Jean-Marie Tjibaou Cultural Center presents a strong image of the Kanak world but nonetheless fits into a chain of exhibitions on any tourist itinerary. At the very point at which the Kanak world is asserting its political singularity it is, paradoxically, being trivialized through its integration in the international network of art shows. In showrooms, historical temporality vanishes. Room is made for the illusion of simultaneity, an illusion arising out of references to planetary contemporaneity, through which the expanding Western world believes it can achieve universal presence unto itself.

"Contemporary Art is Universal"

It is no surprise, therefore, that "culturally exhibited" populations say they do not recognize themselves in the images intended to present them. The difference between a way of life and the way of showing it often causes an outcry. Cultural centers, museums and even ethnological work expose the skeleton of things, but this exposure is criticized as a fake or a lie. True, the work of transforming a social world into a "culture" breaks the ordinary course of life. Like any "work of art," a building, museum show or book creates a distance between the architect, curator or anthropologist and those people about whom the latter wish to speak. A local world feels betrayed when its present is exhibited on the stage of the global present of the contemporary world. Changing the temporal frame of reference creates the impression of switching from truth to falsehood, from authentic to fake, from a model to a copy. Being put into words and shown creates a split image and elicits the comparison of oneself with this image. The mirror effect produced by the modern mass media tends to spawn an ever-increasing number of claims to an identity. These claims construct microcosms whose diversity contrasts strikingly with the out-of-place-and-time omnipresence of our modernity, so characteristic of what "being contemporary" means to the most mobile and international of its followers (Chesneaux, 1989). Events, on the other hand, unfold the historical logic of their sequences in a bounded time and space. But contemporaneity, inasmuch as it is the public expression of the practices and discourse of the political, intellectual and artistic elite of the most affluent nations, seeks to escape from the bounds of time and space, and to settle into an ongoing instantaneity. In this sense, "contemporary art" is necessarily a deterritorialized art, judged according to aesthetic criteria set by specialists accustomed to comparing all works of art from all periods of time. However, "folks" do not experience their own art in this universalizing way.

— A Maori professor of art history: "We are irritated by feeling defined from the outside. Our artists' works must be representative of Maori identity. We should not revert to the typically colonial practice of forming a European collection of Oceanic art out of pieces created by those people whom you select as 'sophisticated artists'. The Maori language has no word for designating art. Works [of art] and the places where they are exhibited are sacred. The fundamental question is what does one want to say to visitors through the objects exhibited."

— A European art gallery owner: "The last exhibition, in Singapore, of contemporary art from the Asia-Pacific zone has guided our choices. We tend to turn more toward the future than toward people's cultural background. Contemporary art is universal."

— Kanak institutional discourse: "A link must be kept up between the contemporary and the traditional. Kanak works [of art] created today must be in harmonious complementarity with the older Kanak objects now on display at the Nouméa Museum.[8] The solution would be to show the universality at the heart of what is most specific."

Underlying this discussion is a conflict over legitimacy. Who is qualified to present an authentic image of someone else? Who can authenticate an object or a culture? As Clifford (1988: 12) points out, "If authenticity is relational, there can be no essence except as a political, cultural invention, a local tactic."

In today's world of speech-as-event, remarks which, if separated, would have no reason for being or would be taken for granted rebound on each other. Viewpoints crystallize into arguments. Traditional *vs.* contemporary, art *vs.* society, international elite *vs.* Oceanic peoples, such cross-references make the present dazzle. We cannot unravel this present without paying attention to the specific language games whereby speakers adopt stances with regard to each other. Through confrontations or misunderstandings during these games, they work out the meaning that can be assigned to

---

8. There is now a museum of traditional Kanak and Oceanic art located in downtown Nouméa. The Tjibaou Center, on the other hand, is on the outskirts of the city.

things at that point in time. Each party's plans affect those of all other parties, and ideas develop out of specific intentions and memories. Speakers seek to bend the images and events now taking shape to suit their own temporal requirements. But they are forced to express their own intentions euphemistically in order to bridge the gap between the different temporalities running through debates. They thus resort to seemingly unequivocal words that are actually nothing but the conventional packaging used for their differing intentions. The experience of the present skirts around the deadlocks or violence that would result were each party to straightforwardly expose the "truth." It does this by using words that "do not spell things out" and by resorting to notions (such as tradition, contemporary, modernity and, above all, in the present instance, Kanak culture) that can be reinterpreted because they lack precision. In talks between the directors of the future Cultural Center and other parties (high-ranking French civil servants, art historians, museum curators and anthropologists), the notion of culture is like a baton passed from hand to hand, to which each party, in turn, gives a particular meaning. It may thus serve as the grounds for a claim to an identity or for thought about aesthetics, all the more easily since the objects substantiating these claims are speechless, by definition. But the notion itself is sufficiently vague—who knows what the words "culture" or even "Kanak" really mean?—to be passed on without clashes between parties motivated, deep within, by different historical experiences and therefore pursuing distinct goals. Is "Kanak culture" the means for French culture to shine in the Pacific or a popular slogan among the Kanak for winning independence? As a constant but ambiguous referent, this notion, like a password or a compact token, circulates between players all the more easily because its contradictory origins are kept out of sight. *"This hard forgotten lake"* is not a series of meaningless or vague words. Rather, it is a form everyone can fill, each in his or her own way, with no risk that anyone will destroy it. Wordplay sometimes masks the past, and sometimes summons it to be present. The synchronous present can only settle in by denying the past: a time is lost so that a forthcoming time may take its place.

The present necessarily partakes of phatic speech, which keeps communication lines open by allowing for several possible meanings while emitting a message without specific contents. But this masked game leaves many openings for an unmasking move. The fragile lines of communication between speakers, that accepted weightiness of the situation, may crack at any time under the pressure of the *beautiful today*. Will its *drunken wingbeat* rip us out of this situation? Not much is needed for the past to erupt into the present: any player needs but turn a card over and scream, "Cheater!" Many a time when the expert's detemporalized viewpoint on objects has too strong a sway, the Kanak have intervened, to develop the cherished ideas of their deceased leader:

— Jean-Marie TJIBAOU: "You must recall, to understand our troubled state and our aspirations, that we are not yet decolonized (...). We want to proclaim our cultural existence. We want to say to the world that we are not survivors out of prehistory. Nor are we archeological relics. We are human beings of flesh and blood." (Tjibaou, 1996: 48)

Through the project of creating a cultural center, the French Republic is attempting to clear itself of its colonial past. Its own references to "contemporary" art may be read as deriving from the political allusions strewn here and there by the other side. Each party may think it urgent to put off this extremely ticklish debate by engaging in discussions that focus on apparently aesthetic or technical matters. But the paving stones of history soon show up under this beach of good intentions. In this situation, as in many others, parties swing back and forth between sacrificing history in order to maintain minimal agreement and exposing history in full daylight in order to give meaning to the present but at the risk of opening the way to memory and, therefore, to passions.

In the particular situation discussed here, the paradox resides in the fact that these events are being played out around a decision—to build a cultural center—made following an intense period of political disturbance and violence. The occasional guarded, verbal fencing between Kanak cultural professionals and the other parties over a collection of Oceanic works of art always tends to refer to the events of ten years ago that made today's discussions possible. The Jean-Marie Tjibaou Cultural Center erects a memory. It would never have existed without the events by which the Kanak burst onto the national and international political scene between 1984 and 1989. The building designed by Renzo Piano and his colleagues is, indeed, one of those grandiose projects of which French presidents are so fond. But for the Kanak, it is the remembrance of a struggle and of Jean-Marie Tjibaou, the leader who embodied that struggle. The Center asserts the presence of the Kanak in our modern world. Because it bears witness that a people is being admitted into global temporality, the building represents "a breach in time", in H. Arendt's words, of the sort that opens all periods during which men and women collectively invent a new future. Of those revolutionary, founding periods, they retain the memory of extraordinary public elation (Arendt, 1972: 13). Between 1984 and 1988, the Kanak accelerated New Caledonia's history by physically opposing the French colonial system. Their determination to gain emancipation led them to break down the barriers of languages, chiefdoms, clans, religions and political parties in order to set up new public forums: a liberation front, a radio, a proposal for a constitution, a cultural center, etc. Out of this movement for acquiring potentially national institutions grew a strong, unified image of Kanak culture. The concrete realization of this image through an architectural project bears the marks of this past. This project, along with the creation of the contemporary art collection that grew out of it, constitutes both an outcome and a threshold. The Jean-Marie Tjibaou Cultural Center lies at the point where several temporalities flow into each other: the temporality of the construction by the Kanak people of a self-image to be viewed by others, that of the non-Kanak communities of New Caledonia, and last, the time frame of the discussions under way about the institutional future of the Overseas Territory.

— Kanak institutional discourse: "The Center must be an opening instead of a ghetto. But how can we control this overture? Given New Caledonia's sorrowful past, the Cultural Center must be a place for encounters and exchanges between cultures, rather than simply a place for exhibitions."

While the promotion of the Kanak heritage and culture is on its agenda, the Center's architecture and museological plans also offer the possibility for constructing new relations between Kanak and non-Kanak people. The Center implicitly invites all New Caledonians to experience the present differently. In this respect, the building is typically urban in character: from the start, it does not reduce its space to a single meaning, but as a part of the city, it offers many meanings. It refers, ultimately, to a major element in New Caledonian history: to the shock between two civilizations, to what the colonized had to offer to the colonizers, and vice versa, and to how, after two centuries, the Kanak again became landowners in Nouméa.[9] The Cultural Center intensifies what architect Christian de Portzamparc describes as an essential dimension of a city, namely: "the ongoing conversation across the centuries (...). In this game with eras, we link the past to the future, and dialogue with our fathers and sons" (Portzamparc, 1995: 69). Besides this sought-for convergence between the temporalities of different communities in order to identify, if possible, "a common heritage," as the participants at the meeting said, there is the temporality of the contemporary world, with its specific relation to time, made of speed, ubiquity, the juxtaposition of images and meanings, and so forth. Various temporal tensions already crisscross the building, tensions embodied in materials and a shape that both reveal and hide them. But perhaps the force of any object comes from the fact that it is always exhibited in the present, while

---

9. The land on which the Cultural Center is built was turned over to the ADCK by the city of Nouméa. This was the first time that Kanak land in the Nouméa area was handed back to its former owners. On land claims in New Caledonia, see: Naepels, 1998.

at the same time it bears witness, in some obscure way, to the multitudi-
nous past that made it possible?

Histories of Identities

The present, like a blotter, is saturated with elements of the past that are
always ready to re-emerge. *Under the frozen dew* of conventional, toned-
down speech, the memories of individuals and, through them, of communities are beating their wings. As William Faulkner says, the past is never
dead, nor even past.[10] A situation cannot be frozen into some underlying,
timeless principles. The metamorphoses of past histories crop out into the
present and join together, just as floaters on the water's surface signal the
presence of nets deep down in the ocean. If we are to understand how people maintain interactions and develop relations to objects within a shared
time frame, we must have the possibility of relating their present and their
past, and of showing how the memory of what probably happened is brought
up to daylight and subjected to the requirements of the present. This may
provide an explanation of the "mysterious meeting between deceased generations and our own". Should not the anthropology of the contemporary
world respond to Walter Benjamin's invitation (Benjamin, 1991: 340)? To
do so, the past must be reactivated out of the present. To extend Mallarmé's paradox, the vivacity of *today* must be used to explore *the transparent glacier of unfled flights*. There can be no real comprehension of the
presence of objects and beings, seized in their frail passage in this morning's
sunlight, unless the ghosts that haunt them can rejoin the essence of that
moment.

The insistence on the need for the Center to refer to New Caledonia's
history is concrete proof of the smarting scars left on the present by the past:

— A European anthropologist: "It is essential that the history of
New Caledonia be present in one way or another in the future cultural center."

— A Pacific islander, member of the Museum staff: "But this history should be stated from several points of view, to avoid having West-
erners monopolize its telling."

As we know, history is written from the perspective of the present. Contrary to what the idea of tradition implies, the past does not subsist intact
in the present. Instead, it is converted into the present. The return of the past
as identical to itself is unverifiable, since going back into the past is not like

---

10. Quoted by Hannah Arendt, 1972: 20.

Photo 27: Objects displayed in the Jean-Marie Tjibaou Center, Nouméa. (Photo R. Boulay, 1990)

going into the room next door (Wittgenstein, 1975: 95–101). "To go against the too sleek grain of history" (Benjamin, 1991: 343) is to travel upstream from the present to the past. This road takes us a long way from that terribly artificial "ethnographic present tense" which, by treating social facts like things, abolishes both time and movement in a social eternity whenever it formulates statements such as: "Society x is patrilineal." To grasp the at-present involves putting time at the center of ethnographic descriptions. This means neither lining up practices, be they linguistic, artistic or other, side by side chronologically, nor staking them out with "places of memory" (*i.e.*, monuments, events, individuals, collections of objects) that serve as historical landmarks. It means understanding attitudes with respect to efforts to reactivate the past. By discovering references to the past within the present process of socially constructing the meaning of events and objects, anthropologists are led to refuse the dictatorship of the rule of sequentiality. "*A* precedes *B*" does not necessarily mean that *A* explains *B*. In fact, it is better to start out from *B* to go back toward *A* by trying to show how *B* is the fulfillment of *A*. Indeed, as anthropologist Edmund Leach clearly pointed out, we are not obliged to conceive of time as a constant flow: time may slow down or sometimes stop or even flow backwards (Leach, 1968: 225). In a forward-looking direction, it is just as important to identify those elements of the present that point toward the future. True, as Paul Valéry observed, we are backing into the future. But this future leaves marks on our contemporaneity—marks in the form, today, of relentless trends toward massive urbanization, environmental destruction, the globalization of technical progress, the deadening of living heritages, etc., so that those last communities to enter on this path prepare themselves—preventively, so to speak—to bear the consequences of this trend. Our present is stretched taut between the past, still clinging to us, and the future that already absorbs us. "Contemporaneity", with its works of art, its projects and its architecture, scrutinizes, announces and anticipates this destiny.

The Jean-Marie Tjibaou Cultural Center, with its collections, would recount the past events that marked its construction and made it possible, and atemporal anthropology would be content with interpreting the Center as an element in a symbolic structure that fits into the immediate eternity of the community. Critical anthropology,[11] on the other hand, takes the Center as it now exists as its starting point and proceeds to investigate the practices and memories of its contemporaries to determine how people take possession of and inhabit time nowadays. Recognizing that time has its own force, understanding it as an essential dimension of action, language and objects by reinjecting it, as Benjamin and Heidegger do, into our investigative and analytic horizons does not mean describing cultural representations of time and of objects—be they those of the Chinese, the Eskimos or the Maori. It consists in analyzing the internal temporality of social processes (Bensa, 1997: 5–18). The best way to go beyond the contrived reasoning that opposes culture and history is to pay attention to how people use the past to construct the present. The emotional and intellectual faculties activate a pattern of relations, of varying depth, with what happened, is happening or is expected to happen. This multidimensional experience cannot be reduced to a simple linearity. It plunges into the depths of the humus of time, and thus makes much room for the present inasmuch as it holds several types of temporalities together.

We cannot consider that the past continues as such in the present or in objects, thus fostering the utopian idea of a tradition preserved unchanged as time goes by. The social forms that ethnography can observe and museums can display are the outcome of efforts to take possession of the past. This work is subject to the contingencies of the present, and therefore eternally unfinished: it underlies the relations uniting people within a group existing in a specific time and place. These persons think of themselves as a group because they share, if only momentarily, the same practices with respect to their past. The transmission of objects, the social processes of memory and inherited customs, as well as action determined by the pre-

---

11. See Bensa, 1996: 37–70, and on the cultural center of Nouméa: Bensa, 2000c.

sent juncture all contribute to forming an original precipitate, which is the present. The task of anthropology is to study the formula of that precipitate without forgetting that like aging wine, it never stops changing, not only over time but also as a function of the variable ways whereby the observer enters into the situation under study.

The same ancient Kanak objects have been displayed in a wide variety of ways, and received comment ranging from the extremely disparaging to the most appreciative, and when Kanak art—and Pacific island art in general—aims at being contemporary, it is exposed to assessment based on other, new criteria. The unending effort to appraise works of art is based on exchanges of words constantly caught up in specific interactions. Meanings follow one another, are superimposed and intertwine, but they take place outside of the object itself. Through this process, identities may be created and undone. No interpretation ever exhausts the silent materiality of an object, its "thingness"; that is to say, fundamentally, its freedom.

Translated from French by Janet Pawelko and Noal Mellot
Revised version, Helen Arnold

Bibliography

ACKERMAN, Kim — 1979, "Material Culture and Trade in the Kimberleys Today," in R.M. & C.H. Berndt (eds.), *Aborigines of the West. Their Past and their Present*. Nedlands, University of WA Press: 243–251.

AKIN, David and Joel ROBBINS — 1999, *Money and modernity. State and local currencies in Melanesia*. Pittsburgh, University of Pittsburgh Press.

ANDERSON, Christopher — 1990, "Repatriation of Cultural Property: a Social Process," *Museum* 156, 42 (1): 54–55.

ANDERSON, Christopher — (ed.) 1995, *Politics of the Secret, Oceania Monograph* 45.

ARENDT, Hannah — 1972, *La crise de la culture. Huit exercices de pensée politique*. Paris, Gallimard Folio.

AUGÉ, Marc — 1988, *Le dieu objet*. Paris, Flammarion.
— 1992, *Non-lieux. Introduction à une anthropologie de la surmodernité*. Paris, Seuil. Translated as *Non-Places: Introduction to an Anthropology of Supermodernity*. London, New York, Verso, 1995.
— 1994, *Pour une anthropologie des mondes contemporains*. Paris, Aubier Critiques. Translated as *An Anthropology for Contemporaneous Worlds*. Stanford, Stanford University Press, 1999.

BAAL, Jan van — 1966, *Dema: Description and Analysis of Marind-Anim Culture*. The Hague, Martinus Nijhoff.

BABADZAN, Alain — 1993, *Les dépouilles des dieux. Essai sur la religion tahitienne à l'époque de la découverte*. Paris, Ed. de la Maison des sciences de l'homme.

BARRAU, Jacques — 1965, "L'humide et le sec: An Essay on Ethnobiological Adaptation to Contrastive Environments in the Indo-Pacific Area," *Journal of the Polynesian Society* 74: 329–346.

BARTH, Fredrik — 1975, *Ritual and Knowledge among the Baktaman*. Oslo, Universitetsforlaget, New Haven, Yale University Press.

BATAILLE-BENGUIGUI, Marie-Claire — 1994, *Le Côté de la mer. Quotidien et imaginaire aux îles Tonga, Polynésie occidentale*. Bordeaux-

Talence, Centre de Recherche des Espaces Tropicaux de l'Université de Bordeaux III (CRET), collection "Iles et archipels" n° 19.

BATAILLON, Pierre — 1841, "Notice sur l'île et la mission de Wallis, adressée au R.P. Colin, supérieur-général de la Société de Marie," *Annales de la Propagation de la Foi* 13: 5–34.

BATESON, Gregory — 1958 [1936], *Naven.* Stanford, Stanford University Press.

BELL, Diane — 1983, *Daughters of the Dreaming.* Melbourne, McPhee Gribble/George Allen and Unwin.

BENJAMIN, Walter — 1991, *Ecrits français.* Paris, Gallimard.

BENSA, Alban — 1995, *Chroniques kanak. L'ethnologie en marche.* Paris, Ethnies-Documents n° 18–19.

— 1996, "De la micro-histoire vers une anthropologie critique," in Jacques Revel (ed.), *Jeux d'échelles. De la micro-analyse à l'expérience.* Paris, EHESS-Gallimard-Le Seuil: 37–70.

— 1997, "Images et usages du temps," *Terrain* 29: 5–18.

— 2000a, "De l'interlocution. Dialogue anthropologique," in B. Masquelier and J.-L. Siran (eds.), *Anthropologie de la parole. Rhétoriques du quotidien.* Paris, L'Harmattan: 59–79.

— 2000b, "Les réalités mythiques de Maurice Leenhardt," in A. Bensa et J. Jamin, "Formes mythiques de la vie chez les Mélanésiens. Maurice Leenhardt. Notes de conférences prononcées au Collège de France prises en 1943 par Michel Leiris," *Gradhiva* 27: 1–14.

— 2000c, *Ethnologie et architecture. Le Centre culturel Tjibaou. Une réalisation de Renzo Piano.* Paris, Adam Biro.

— 2000d, "The End of Other Worlds or the Cultural Cenotaph," in *Partage d'exotismes,* 5e Biennale d'Art Contemporain de Lyon: 79–88.

BENSA, Alban and Antoine GOROMIDO — 1997, "The Political Order and Corporal Coercion in Kanak Societies of the Past (New Caledonia)," *Oceania* 68 (2): 84–106.

BENSA, Alban and Isabelle LEBLIC (eds.) — 2000, *En pays kanak. Ethnologie, linguistique, archéologie, histoire en Nouvelle-Calédonie.* Paris, Maison des sciences de l'homme.

BENSA, Alban and Jean-Claude RIVIERRE — 1982, *Les Chemins de l'alliance. L'organisation sociale et ses représentations en Nouvelle-Calédonie (région de Touho, aire linguistique cèmuhî).* Paris, SELAF ("Langues et cultures du Pacifique" 1).

BENSA, Alban and WITTERSHEIM, Éric — 1998, "Nationalism and interdependence: the political thought of Jean-Marie Tjibaou," *The Contemporary Pacific* 10 (2): 369–390.

BERDE, Stuart — 1973, "Contemporary Notes on Rossel Island Valuables," *Journal of the Polynesian Society* 82 (2): 188–205.

BERNDT, Ronald — 1983 [1952], *Djanggawul, an Aboriginal Religious Cult in North-Eastern Arnhem Land*. New York, Philosophical Library.

BIERSACK, Aletta — 1991, "Kava'onau and the Tongans Chiefs," *Journal of the Polynesian Society* 100 (3): 231–268.

BIERSACK, Aletta (ed.). — 1991, *Clio in Oceania. Toward a Historical Anthropology*. Washington-London, Smithsonian Institution.

BILLINGS, Dorothy K. and Nicolas PETERSON — 1967, "Malangan and Mamai in New Ireland," *Oceania* 38 (1): 24–32.

BLOCH, Maurice — 1974, "Symbols, song, dance and features of articulation. Is religion an extreme form of traditional authority?," *Revue européenne de sociologie* 15: 55–81.

BODROGI, Tibor — 1967, "Malangans in North New Ireland: L. Biro's Unpublished Notes," *Acta Ethnographica Academiae Hungaricae* 16: 61–77.

BOELAARS, J.H.M. — 1981, *Head-Hunters About Themselves. An ethnographic report from Irian Jaya, Indonesia*. The Hague, Martinus Nijhoff.

BONNEMÈRE, Pascale — 1994, "Le Pandanus rouge dans tous ses états. L'univers social et symbolique d'un arbre fruitier chez les Ankave-Anga (Papouasie Nouvelle-Guinée)," *Annales Fyssen* 9: 21–32.

— 1996, *Le pandanus rouge. Corps, différence des sexes et parenté chez les Ankave-Anga*. Paris, CNRS-Editions, Editions de la Maison des sciences de l'homme.

BONNEMÈRE, P. Forthcoming. "When women enter the picture: Looking at Anga initiations from the mother's angle", in P. Bonnemère (ed.), *The Unseen Characters. Women in male rituals of Papua New Guinea*, ASAO 1999 Symposium.

BOTT, Elizabeth — 1982, *Tongan Society at the Time of Captain Cook's Visits*. Wellington, The Polynesian Society, Memoir 44.

— 1987, "The Kava Ceremonial as a Dream Structure," in Mary Douglas (ed.), *Constructive Drinking: Perspectives on Drinks from Anthropology*. Cambridge, Cambridge University Press / Paris, Editions de la Maison des sciences de l'homme.

BOTT, Elizabeth and Edmund LEACH — 1972, "The Significance of Kava in Tongan Myth and Ritual," in J.S. la Fontaine (ed.), *The Interpretation of Ritual*. London, Tavistock: 205–284.

BOTTÉRO, Alain — 1992, "La consomption par déperdition séminale en Inde et ailleurs," *Annales de la Fondation Fyssen* 7: 17–32.

BOULAY, Roger (ed.) — 1990, *De Jade et de nacre, Patrimoine artistique kanak*. Paris, Réunion des Musées Nationaux.

BOURDIEU, Pierre — 1998, *La domination masculine*. Paris, Editions du Seuil.

BOYER, Pascal—1986, "The 'Empty Concepts' of Traditional Thinking. A Semantic and Pragmatic Description," *Man* (n.s.) 21:50–64.

BRETON, Stéphane—1999a, "Le spectacle des choses: considérations mélanésiennes sur la personne," *L'Homme* (special issue, "Anthropologie psychanalytique") 149: 83–112.

—1999b, "To Kill the Bride: Matrimonial Compensations among the Wodani, Western Highlands of Irian Jaya," paper read at the Department of Anthropology Colloquium, Pittsburgh University, 26 February 1999.

—1999c, "De l'illusion totémique à la fiction sociale," *L'Homme* 151: 123–149.

—1999d, "Death and the Ideology of Compensation among the Wodani, Western Highlands of Irian Jaya," *Social Anthropology* 7(3): 297–326.

—1999e, "Social Body and Icon of the Person: A Symbolic Analysis of Shell Money among the Wodani, Western Highlands of Irian Jaya," *American Ethnologist* 26 (4): 558–582.

—Forthcoming, "Tuer, manger, payer: l'alliance monétaire des Wodani de Papouasie occidentale," *L'Homme* (special issue, "Les liens de la monnaie").

BROMBERGER, Christian (avec la collaboration de A. Hayot and J. M. Mariottini)—1995, *Le match de football. Ethnologie d'une passion partisane à Marseille, Naples et Turin*. Paris, Editions de la maison des sciences de l'homme.

BRUNTON, Ron—1989, *The Abandonned Narcotic. Kava and Cultural Instability in Melanesia*. Cambridge, Cambridge University Press.

BRUSSET, Bernard—1988, *Psychanalyse du lien. La relation d'objet*. Paris, Le Centurion.

CARRIER, James G. (ed.)—1992, *History and Tradition in Melanesian Anthropology*. Berkeley, Los Angeles-Oxford, University of California Press.

CHAVE, Sophie—1992, *La cérémonie du kava à l'île Wallis*. Mémoire de Diplôme d'Etudes Approfondies, Paris, Ecole des hautes études en sciences sociales.

CHESNEAUX, Jean—1989, *Modernité-Monde, Brave Modern World*. Paris, La Découverte.

CHINNERY, Edward W. P.—1929, *Notes on the Study of the Native Population of the East Coast of New Ireland*. Territory of New Guinea Anthropological Report n° 6, Canberra, H.I. Green.

CHURCHWARD, Clerk M.—1959, *Tongan Dictionary; Tongan-English and English-Tongan*. Oxford, Oxford University Press.

CLARK, Jeffrey—1991, "Pearl-shell symbolism in highlands Papua New Guinea, with particular references to the Wiru people of Southern Highlands Province," *Oceania* 61: 309–339.

CLARK, Philip and Christopher ANDERSON—1997, "Unlocking museums—The proceedings," 4th National Conference of Museums Australia Inc, Darwin, NT.

CLAY, Brenda J.—1977, *Pinikindu: Maternal Nurture, Paternal Substance.* Chicago, University of Chicago Press.

CLIFFORD, James—1982, *Person and Myth. Maurice Leenhardt in the Melanesian World.* Berkeley, University of California Press.

—1988, *The Predicament of Culture. Twentieth-Century Ethnography, Literature, and Art.* Cambridge (Mass.), Harvard University Press.

CODRINGTON, Robert H.—1972 [1891], *The Melanesians. Studies in their Anthropology and Folk Lore.* New York, Dover Publications.

COLLOCOTT, E.E.V.—1927, "Kava ceremonial in Tonga," *Journal of the Polynesian Society* 36: 21–47.

CONSTITUTIONS—1995, *Les Constitutions de la France depuis 1789.* Paris, Garnier-Flammarion.

COOMBE, Rosemary—1991, "Objects of Property and Subjects of Politics: Intellectual Property Laws and Democratic Dialog," *Texas Law Review* 69: 1853–80.

—1997, "The Properties of Culture and Possession of Identity: Postcolonial Struggle and the Legal Imagination," in B. Ziff and P. Rao (eds.), *Borrowed Power: Essays on Cultural Appropriation.* New Brunswick, Rutgers University Press: 74–96.

COPPET, Daniel de—1968, "Pour une étude des échanges cérémoniels en Mélanésie," *L'Homme* 45–57.

—1985, "Land Owns People," in R.H. Barnes, D. de Coppet and R.J. Parkin (eds.), *Contexts and Levels. Anthropological Essays on Hierarchy.* Oxford, JASO Occasional Papers Nr 4: 78–90.

—1995, "Are'are Society: A Melanesian Socio-cosmic Point of View. How are Bigmen the Servants of Society and Cosmos ?," in D. de Coppet and A. Iteanu (eds.), *Cosmos and Society in Oceania.* Oxford-Washington, Berg: 235–274.

COPPET, Daniel de and André ITEANU (eds.)—1995, *Cosmos and Society in Oceania.* Oxford-Washington, Berg.

CRAIG, Ruth—1969, "Marriage among the Telefolmin," in R.M. Glasse and M.J. Meggitt (eds.), *Pigs, Pearlshells, and Women. Marriage in the New Guinea Highlands.* Englewood Cliffs, N.J., Prentice-Hall: 176–197.

CRAIG, Barry, Bernie KERNOT and Christopher ANDERSON (eds.)—1999, *Art and Performance in Oceania.* Bathurst, Crawford House Publishing.

CROCKER, William and Jean CROCKER—1994, *The Canela: Bonding through Kinship, Ritual and Sexuality.* Fort Worth, Harcourt Brace.

CROCOMBE, Ron G. — 1974, "An Approach to the Analysis of Land Tenure Systems," in H. P. Lundsgaarde (ed.), *Land tenure in Oceania*. Honolulu, University Press of Hawaii: 1–17.

CUZENT, G. — 1940, "Du kava ou ava. Communiqué par M. le Pharmacien Pétard," *Bulletin de la Société des Etudes Océaniennes* 68 (7): 276–283.

DAUPHINÉ, Joël — 1989, *Les spoliations foncières en Nouvelle-Calédonie (1853–1913)*. Paris, L'Harmattan.

— 1998, *Canaques de la Nouvelle-Calédonie à Paris en 1931. De la case au zoo*. Paris, L'Harmattan.

DEBORD, Guy — 1971 [1967], *La société du spectacle*. Paris, Champ Libre.

DERLON, Brigitte — 1990–1991, "L'objet malanggan dans les anciens rites funéraires de Nouvelle-Irlande," *Res* 19–20: 178–210.

— 1997a, *De mémoire et d'oubli. Anthropologie des objets* malanggan *de Nouvelle-Irlande*. Paris, CNRS Editions-Editions de la Maison des sciences de l'homme.

— 1997b, "Sacrifice humain et culte du 'cargo' en Nouvelle-Irlande," in Tcherkézoff and Douaire-Marsaudon (eds.), *Le Pacifique-sud aujourd'hui. Identités et transformations des sociétés océaniennes*. Paris, CNRS Editions: 135–166. English translation forthcoming.

— 1997c, "La mort à bras-le-corps. Jeux de substitution et régénération en Nouvelle-Irlande," *Ateliers* 18: 49–73.

— 1998, "Corps, cosmos et société en Nouvelle-Irlande", in M. Godelier and M. Panoff (eds.), *La Production du corps*. Amsterdam, Les Archives contemporaines: 163–186.

— Forthcoming 2002, "L'intestinal et le matriciel. Aux origines mythiques d'une "monnaie" mélanésienne (Nouvelle-Irlande, plateau Lelet)," *L'Homme* (special issue, "Les liens de la monnaie").

DERLON Brigitte and Monique JEUDY-BALLINI — Forthcoming "'Quoi? — L'Éternité.' Objets de l'Archipel Bismarck en perspective."

DOUAIRE-MARSAUDON, Françoise — 1996, "Je te mange, moi non plus. Meurtre et sacrifice cannibales en Polynésie," in M. Godelier and J. Hassoun (eds.) *Meurtre du Père Sacrifice de la Sexualité, Approches anthropologiques et psychanalytiques*. Paris, Arcanes: 79–100.

— 1997, "Nourritures et richesses: les objets cérémoniels du don comme signe d'identité à Tonga et à Wallis," in S. Tcherkézoff and F. Douaire-Marsaudon (eds.), *Le Pacifique-sud aujourd'hui. Identités et transformations des sociétés océaniennes*. Paris, CNRS Editions: 261–287.

— 1998a, "Le meurtre cannibale ou la production d'un homme-dieu. Théories des substances et construction hiérarchique en Polynésie," in M. Godelier and M. Panoff (eds.), *Le corps. Supplicié, possédé, cannibalisé*. Amsterdam, Les Archives contemporaines: 137–167.

— 1998b, *Les premiers fruits. Parenté, identité sexuelle et pouvoirs en Polynésie occidentale (Tonga, Wallis et Futuna)*. Paris, CNRS-Editions, Editions de la Maison des sciences de l'homme.

DOUGLAS, Brownen — 1998, *Across the Great Divide. Journeys in History and Anthropology: selected essays, 1979–1994*. Amsterdam, Harwood Academic Publishers.

DUMONT D'URVILLE, Jules — 1830–1835, *Voyages de découvertes de l'Astrolabe, exécutés pendant les années 1826, 1827, 1828, 1829, sous le commandement de M. J. Dumont d'Urville, Histoire du voyage*, 5 tomes en dix vol. et 2 vol. d'atlas. Paris, Tastu.

DURKHEIM, Emile — 1968 [1912], *Les formes élémentaires de la vie religieuse*. Paris, Presses Universitaires de France. Translated as *The Elementary Forms of Religious Life*. New York, The Free Press, 1965.

DUSSART, Françoise — 1988 *Warlpiri Women's Yawulyu Ceremonies: A Forum for Socialization and Innovation*. PhD thesis, Australian National University.

— 2000, *The Politics of Ritual in an Aboriginal Settlement: Kinship, Gender and the Currency of Knowledge*. London-Washington, Smithsonian Institution Press.

EIDE, D. B. — 1966, Cultural Correlates of Warfare among the Asmat of South-West New Guinea. Ph. D. thesis, Yale University.

ELKIN, A. Peter — 1961 [1938], *The Australian Aborigines. How to understand them*. Sydney, Angus and Robertson.

ELLEN, Roy — 1988, "Fetishism," *Man* (n.s.) 23 (2): 213–235.

EPSTEIN, A. L. — 1979, "Tambu: The Shell-Money of the Tolai," in R. Hook, (ed.), *Fantasy andSymbol: Studies in Anthropological Interpretation. Essays in Honour of Georges Devereux*. London, Academic Press: 149–205.

FAJANS, Jane — 1997, *They Make Themselves. Work and Play among the Baining of Papua New Guinea*. Chicago-London, The University of Chicago Press.

FEIL, Daryl K. — 1978, "Women and Men in the Enga *tee*," *American Ethnologist* 5: 263–279.

— 1984, *Ways of Exchange: the Enga Tee of Papua New Guinea*. Townville the University of Queensland Press.

— 1987, *The Evolution of Highland Papua New Guinea Societies*. Cambridge, Cambridge University Press.

FISCHER, Hans — 1968, *Negwa. Eine Papua Gruppe im Wandel*. München, Klaus Renner Verlag.

FOSTER, Robert J. — 1995, *Social Reproduction and History in Melanesia: Mortuary Ritual, Gift Exchange, and Custom in the Tanga Islands*. New York, Cambridge University Press.

FREUD, Sigmund — 1953a [1900–1928], *The Interpretation of Dreams*. Standard Edition, vol. 4–5, London, The Hogarth Press.
— 1953b [1905], *Three Essays on Sexuality*. Standard Edition, vol. 7, London, The Hogarth Press.
— 1953c [1922] "Medusa's Head", Standard Edition, vol. 5, London, The Holgarth Press.
— 1955a [1912–1913], *Totem and Taboo*. Standard Edition, vol. 13: 1–164, London, The Hogarth Press.
— 1955b [1916–1917], "On Transformations of Instinct as Exemplified in Anal Erotism," Standard Edition, vol. 17: 125–133, London, The Hogarth Press.
— 1955c [1920], "Beyond the Pleasure principle," Standard Edition, vol. 18: 7–64, London, The Hogarth Press.
— 1955d [1921], "Group Psychology and the Analysis of the Ego," Standard Edition, vol. 18: 69–143, London, The Hogarth Press.
— 1957a [1910], "A Special Type of Choice made by Men," Standard Edition, vol. 11: 163–176, London, The Hogarth Press.
— 1957b [1914], On Narcissism: An Introduction," Standard Edition, vol. 14: 73–102, London, The Hogarth Press.
— 1957c [1915], "Instincts and their Vicissitudes," Standard Edition, vol. 14: 109–140, London, The Hogarth Press.
— 1958a [1911], "Psycho-analytic Notes on an Autobiographical Account of a Case of Paranoia (Dementia paranoides)," Standard Edition, vol. 12: 9–82, London, The Hogarth Press.
— 1958b [1911], "On the Two Principles of Mental Functioning," Standard Edition, vol. 12: 213–226, London, The Hogarth Press.
— 1961a [1921], "The Ego and the Id," Standard Edition, vol. 19: 12–66, London, The Hogarth Press.
— 1961b [1923], "The Infantile Genital Organization: an Interpolation into the Theory of Sexuality," Standard Edition, vol. 19: 141–145, London, The Hogarth Press.
— 1961c [1924], "The Dissolution of the Œdipus Complex," Standard Edition, vol. 19: 173–179, London, The Hogarth Press.
— 1961d [1925], "Some Psychical Consequences of the Anatomical Distinction between the Sexes," Standard Edition, vol. 19: 248–258, London, The Hogarth Press.
GEFFRAY, Christian — 2001, *Trésors, Anthropologie analytique de la valeur*. Strasbourg, Ed. Arcanes.
GELL, Alfred — 1975, *Metamorphosis of the Cassowaries. Umeda Society, Language and Ritual*. London, Athlone Press.
GIAY, Benny and GODSCHALK Jan A. — 1993, "Cargoism in Irian Jaya Today," *Oceania* 63: 330–344.
GIFFORD, Edward — 1924, *Tongan Myths and Tales*. Honolulu, Bernice P. Bishop Museum. Bulletin 8.

— 1929, *Tongan Society*. Honolulu, Bernice P. Bishop Museum. Bulletin 61.

GILLISON, Gillian — 1993, *Between Culture and Fantasy: A New Guinea Highlands Mythology*. Chicago, The University of Chicago Press.

GLOWCZEWSKI, Barbara — 1983a, "Death, Women, and 'Value Production': the Circulation of Hair Strings among the Walpiri of the Central Australian desert," *Ethnology* 22 (3): 225–239.

— 1983b, "Manifestations symboliques d'une transition économique — Le *Juluru*, culte intertribal du 'cargo' (Australie occidentale et centrale)", *L'Homme* 23 (2): 7–35.

— 1998a, "'All One but different': Aboriginality: National Identity versus Local Diversification in Australia," in J. Wassmann (ed.), *Pacific Answers to Western Hegemony — Cultural Practices of Identity Construction*. Oxford-New York, Berg: 335–354.

— 1998b, "The Meaning of 'One' in Broome, Western Australia: From Yawuru Tribe to Rubibi Corporation", *Aboriginal History* vol 22: 203–222.

— 1991, *Du rêve à la loi chez les Aborigènes — Mythe rites et organisation sociale en Australie*. Paris, P.U.F.

— 1996, *Les Rêveurs du désert*. Arles, Actes Sud, Babel (1st publ. by Plon 1989). English translation forthcoming: *Desert Dreamers*.

— 1997, "En Australie, aborigène s'écrit avec un grand 'A'. Aboriginalité politique et nouvelles singularités identitaires," in Serge Tcherkézoff and Françoise Douaire-Marsaudon (eds.), *Le Pacifique-sud aujourd'hui. Identités et transformations des sociétés océaniennes*. Paris, CNRS Editions: 169–196. (English translation forthcoming).

— 2000, *Dream Trackers — Yapa art and knowledge of the Australian Desert*. CD-ROM. Paris, Unesco Publishing.

GLOWCZEWSKI, Barbara (ed.) — 1991, *Yapa, peintres de Balgo et Lajamanu*, Paris, Baudoin Lebon (French/English).

— 1996, *Language and culture survey in the Kullari Region, March-April, for the Aboriginal Arts and Culture Centre working party*. Broome, WA (conducted by Wayne Barker, Quentin Bruce, Mary Lou Farrell, Veronica Francis, Barbara Glowczewski, Brian Lee, Mary Manolis, Veronica Francis, Veronica McKeon, Mary Tarran).

— nd, *Liyan — A Living Culture: Jarndu Yawuru Oral History Project*. Broome, WA, Magabala Books.

GODBOUT, Jacques — 1992, *L'esprit du don*. Paris, Ed. La Découverte.

GODELIER, Maurice — 1969, "La monnaie de sel des Baruya de Nouvelle Guinée", *L'Homme*, 9 (2): 5–37. Translated as "Salt Currency' and the Circulation of Commodities Among the Baruya of New Guinea". *Studies in Economic Anthropology*, ASA Monograph 8, 1971: 52–73.

— 1978, "Les Rapports hommes-femmes: le problème de la domination masculine". *La condition féminine*. Paris, Editions Sociales. Translated as "The Origins of Male Domination," *New Left Review* 127, 1981: 3–18.

— 1982, *La Production des grands hommes. Pouvoir et domination masculine chez les Baruya de Nouvelle-Guinée*. Paris, Fayard. Translated as *The making of Greatmen. Male domination and power among the New Guinea Baruya*. Cambridge, Cambridge University Press, 1986.

— 1984, *L'Idéel et le Matériel*. Paris, Fayard. Translated as *The Mental and the Material. Thought, Economy, and Society*. London, Verso, 1986.

— 1990a, "Sociétés à Big men, sociétés à Grands Hommes: Figures du pouvoir en Nouvelle-Guinée," *Journal de la Société des Océanistes* 91, 2: 75–94.

— 1990b, "Avant-propos," in P. Lemonnier, *Guerres et festins. Paix, échanges et compétition dans les Highlands de Nouvelle-Guinée*. Paris, Editions de la Maison des sciences de l'homme: 9–19.

— 1991, "An unfinished attempt at reconstructing the social process which may have prompted the transformation of great-men societies into big-men societies", in M. Godelier and M. Strathern (eds), *Big Men and Great Men. The Personifications of Power in Melanesia*. Cambridge, Cambridge University Press: 275–304.

— 1992, "Corps, parenté, pouvoir(s) chez les Baruya de Nouvelle-Guinée," *Journal de la Société des Océanistes* 94: 3–24.

— 1993, "L'Occident—miroir brisé," *Les Annales E.S.C.*, 5: 1183–1207. Translated as "'Mirror, mirror on the Wall...' The Once and Future Role of Anthropology: A Tentative Assessment", in R. Borofsky (ed.), *Assessing Cultural Anthropology*. New York, McGraw-Hill, 1993: 97–112.

— 1994, "Monnaies et richesses dans divers types de sociétés et leur rencontre à la périphérie du capitalisme", *Actuel Marx*, (n° spécial "L'inconscient du social"): 77–97.

— 1996, *L'énigme du don*, Paris, Fayard. Translated as *The Enigma of the Gift*. Cambridge, Polity Press; Chicago, The University of Chicago Press, 1999.

GODELIER, Maurice and Marilyn STRATHERN. (eds.)— 1991, *Big Men and Great Men. Personifications of Power in Melanesia*. Cambridge, Cambridge University Press.

GOODY, Esther N.— 1982, *Parenthood and Social Reproduction. Fostering and Occupational Roles in West Africa*. Cambridge, Cambridge University Press.

GREEN, André— 1977, "Atome de parenté et relations œdipiennes," in C. Lévi-Strauss (éd.), *L'identité*. Paris, Grasset: 81–107.

— 1995, *Propédeutique. La métapsychologie revisitée*. Seyssel, Champ Vallon.

GREGORY, Chris A.—1980, "Gifts to Men and Gifts to God: Gift Exchange and Capital Accumulation in Contemporary Papua New-Guinea", *Man* 15 (4): 626–652.

—1982, *Gifts and Commodities*. New York, Academic Press.

GROVES, W. Colin—1934–1935, "Tabar To-day: A Study of a Melanesian Community in Contact with Alien Non-Primitive Cultural Influences," *Oceania* 5 (2): 224–240; (3): 346–360.

GUIART, Jean—1992 [1963], *Structure de la chefferie en Mélanésie du Sud* (seconde édition remaniée et augmentée), vol. I. Paris, Musée de l'Homme, Institut d'ethnologie.

GUIDIERI, Remo—1984, *L'Abondance des pauvres*. Paris, Seuil.

GUNN, Michael—1987, "The Transfer of Malagan Ownership on Tabar," in L. Lincoln (ed.), *Assemblage of Spirits: Idea and Image in New Ireland*. New York, G. Braziller and The Minneapolis Institute of Arts: 74–83.

HARRISON, Simon—1989, "The Symbolic Construction of Aggression and War in a Sepik River Society," *Man* 24: 583–599.

—1993, *The mask of war. Violence, ritual and the self in Melanesia*. Manchester-New York, Manchester University Press.

HAUSER-SCHÄUBLIN, Brigitta—1989, *Kulthäuser in Nordneuguinea*. Berlin, Akademie Verlag.

HELU, Futa—1992, "Identity and Change in Tongan Society Since European Contact," *Journal de la Société des Océanistes* 97: 187–194.

HERDT, Gilbert—1981, 1994, *Guardians of the flutes. Idioms of masculinity*. New York, McGraw-Hill.

—1987, *The Sambia. Ritual and gender in New Guinea*. New York, Holt, Rinehart and Winston.

HERDT, Gilbert (ed.)—1984, *Ritualized Homosexuality in Melanesia*. Berkeley, University of California Press.

—1993, "Introduction to the paperback edition," in G. Herdt, *Guardians of the Flutes. Vol. 1: Idioms of Masculinity*. New York, McGraw Hill: xi–xvi.

HERENIKO, Vilsoni—1995, *Woven gods: female clowns and power in Rotuma*. Honolulu, University of Hawaii Press ("Pacific Islands Monograph Series," 12).

HÉRITIER, Françoise—1989, "Parenté, filiation, transmission," in *Le Père, métaphores paternelles et fonctions du père: l'Interdit, la Filiation, la Transmission*. Paris, Denoël, L'Espace Analytique

HEUSCH, Luc de.—1970, "Pour une pensée structuraliste de la pensée magico-religieuse bantoue," in J. Pouillon and P. Maranda (éds.) *Echanges et communications*. Paris-The Hague, Mouton.

HOCART, Arthur M.—1915, "The Chieftainship and the Sister's Son in the Pacific," *American Anthropologist* 17 (4): 631–646.

HOWARD, Alan—1986, "Cannibal Chiefs and the Charter for Rebellion in Rotuman Myth," *Pacific Studies*, 10 (1): 1–27.

HUMPHREY, Caroline—1993, "Material Objectifications of the Self in Mongolian Rituals of Death," in Pascal Boyer (ed.), *Cognitive Aspects of Ritual Symbolism*. Cambridge, Cambridge University Press.

ITEANU, André—1983, *La ronde des échanges. De la circulation aux valeurs chez les Orokaiva*. Cambridge-Paris, Cambridge University Press et Editions de la Maison des sciences de l'homme.

JACKSON, Sue—1996, *When History Meets the New Native Title Era at the Negociating Table. A Case study in reconciling land use in Broome, Western Australia*. Darwin, North Australia Research Unit, the ANU.

JACQUEMIN, Sylviane—1990, "Une journée en Nouvelle-Calédonie à Paris. Les expositions universelles et coloniales," in R. Boulay (éd.), *De Jade et de nacre, Patrimoine artistique kanak*. Paris, Réunion des Musées Nationaux: 235–237.

JAMES, Kerry—1990, *'Rank Overrules Everything': Religious Hierarchy, Social Stratification and Gender in the Ancient Tongan Polity*. Christchurch (New-Zealand), Macmillan Brown Center for Pacific Studies, The University of Canterbury.

JANKE, Terri—1998, *Our culture: Our Future. Report on Australian Indigenous Cultural and Intellectual Property Rights*, Canberra Michael Frankel and C°, ATSIC.

JESSEP, Owen—1977, *Land Tenure in a New Ireland Village*. Ph. D. Dissertation, Australian National University.

—1980, "Land Demarcation in New Ireland," *Melanesian Law Journal* 8 (1–2): 112–133.

JEUDY-BALLINI, Monique—1992, "De la filiation en plus: l'adoption chez les Sulka de Nouvelle-Bretagne," *Droit et Cultures* 23: 109–135.

—1995, "Les Formes de la coopération chez les Sulka de Nouvelle-Bretagne," *Anthropologie et Sociétés* 19 (1–2): 207–228.

—1997, "Culte du Cargo ou culte du péché? Un rite mélanésien pour rendre Dieu meilleur," in S. Tcherkézoff and F. Douaire-Marsaudon (eds.), *Le Pacifique-Sud aujourd'hui*: 111–134. Translation forthcoming.

—1998a, "Naître par le sang, renaître par la nourriture: aspects de l'adoption en Océanie," in Agnès Fine (éd.), *Adoptions. Ethnologie des parentés choisies*. Paris, Mission du Patrimoine ethnologique, Éditions de la Maison des sciences de l'homme: 19–44.

—1998b, "Appropriating the Other: a Case Study from New Britain," in Verena Keck and Jürg Wassmann (eds.), *Common Worlds and Single Lives. Constituting Knowledge in Pacific Societies*. Oxford, Berg: 207–227.

— 1999a, "Homonymie et sobriquets: le lien de nom dans une société de Nouvelle-Bretagne," in J. Massard-Vincent and S. Pauwels (éds.), *D'un nom à l'autre en Asie du Sud-Est. Approches ethnologiques.* Paris, Éditions Karthala: 83–104.

— 1999b, "'Compensating desire': the price of emotion in New Britain (Papua New Guinea)," *Pacific Arts* 19–20: 12–26.

— Forthcoming, "The Fate of the masks. A few questions about the commercial valuation of the Sulka's ritual artifacts, New Britain," in T. van Meijl and J. Miedema (eds.), *What Happens When a Community Becomes Diffuse? Cultural Identity and Politics in the Pacific.*

JORGENSEN, Dan — 1993, "Money and marriage in Telefolmin: From sister exchange to daughter as trade store" in R. Marksbury (ed.), *The Business of Marriage. Transformations in Oceanic Matrimony.* Pittsburg, London, University of Pittsburg Press: 57–82.

JOSEPHIDES, Lisette — 1985, *The Production of Inequality. Gender Exchange among the Kewa.* London New York, Tavistock.

JUILLERAT, Bernard — 1975, "Transe et langage en Nouvelle-Guinée. La possession médiumnique chez les Amanab," *Journal de la Société des Océanistes* 47: 187–212.

— 1978, "Vie et mort dans le symbolisme iafar des couleurs," in S. Tornay (éd.), *Voir et nommer les couleurs.* Nanterre, Université Paris X, Labethno: 497–524.

— 1986, *Les enfants du sang. Société, reproduction et imaginaire en Nouvelle-Guinée.* Paris, Maison des sciences de l'homme. Translated as: *Children of the Blood. Society, Reproduction and Cosmology in New Guinea.* Oxford-New York, Berg Publishers, 1996.

— 1991, *Œdipe chasseur. Une mythologie du sujet en Nouvelle-Guinée.* Paris, Presses universitaires de France (Coll. "Le Fil Rouge").

— 1992, "'The Mother's Brother is the Breast'. Incest and its Prohibition in the Yangis Ritual of the Yafar," in B. Juillerat (ed.), *Shooting the Sun. Ritual and Meaning in West Sepik.* Washington, The Smithsonian Institution Press.

— 1993, *La Révocation des Tambaran. Les Banaro et Richard Thurnwald revisités.* Paris, CNRS Editions.

— 1995, *L'avènement du père. Rite, représentation, fantasme dans un culte mélanésien.* Paris, Ed. du CNRS / Ed. de la Maison des sciences de l'homme.

— 2001, "L'atome de parenté est-il soluble dans la psychanalyse ?," *Topique* 75: 81–103.

— (ed.) 1992, *Shooting the Sun. Ritual and Meaning in West Sepik.* Washington, The Smithsonian Institution Press.

KABERRY, Phyllis — 1939, *Aboriginal Woman, Sacred or Profane.* London, Routledge and Kegan Paul.

KANTOROWICZ, Ernst — 1957, *The King's Two Bodies: A Study in Mediaeval Political Theology*. Princeton, Princeton University Press.

KEESING, Roger — 1984, "Rethinking Mana," *Journal of Anthropological Research* 40(1): 137–156.

1985, "Conventional Methaphors and Anthropological Metaphysics: the Problematic of Cultural Translation," *Journal of Anthropological Research* 41: 201–217.

KELLY, Raymond C. — 1977, *Etoro Social Structure. A Study in Social Contradiction*. Ann Arbor, University of Michigan Press.

KILANI, Mondher — 1990, "Que de *Hau* ! Le débat autour de l'*Essai sur le don* et la construction de l'objet en anthropologie," in J.-M. Adam, M.-J. Borel, C. Calame and M. Kilani (eds.), *Le discours anthropologique. Description, narration, savoir.* Lausanne, Ed. Payot: 123–151.

KIRCH, Patrick V. — 1984, *The Evolution of the Polynesian Chiefdoms*. Cambridge, Cambridge University Press.

— 1994, "The pre-Christian Ritual Cycle of Futuna, Western Polynesia," *Journal of the Polynesian Society* 103 (3): 255–298.

KIRCH, Patrick V. and Marshall SAHLINS — 1992, *Anahulu. The Anthropology of History in The Kingdom of Hawaii*, vol. I, Historical Ethnography. Chicago-London, The University of Chicago Press.

KLEIN, Mélanie — 1957, *Envy and gratitude. A study of unconscious sources*. London, Tavistock.

KNAUFT, Bruce M. — 1985, *Good Company and Violence: Sorcery and Social Action in a Lowland New Guinea Society*. Berkeley, University of California Press.

— 1987, "Homosexuality in Melanesia," *The Journal of Psychoanalytic Anthropology* 10 (2): 155–191.

— 1993, *South coast New Guinea cultures. History, comparison, dialectic*. Cambridge, Cambridge University Press.

KOLIG, Erich — 1979, "Djuluru: Ein synkretistichen Kult Nordwest-Australiens," *Baessler-Archiv*, Neue Folge 27: 419–48.

— 1981, *The Silent Revolution. The Effects of Modernization on Australian Aboriginal religion*. Philadelphia, Institute for the Study of Human Issues.

— 2000, "Social causality, human agency and mythology: Some thoughts on history-consciousness and mythical sense among Australian Aborigines," *Anthropological Forum* 10(1): 9–30.

KRÄMER, Augustin — 1902, *Die Samoa-Inseln* (2 vol.). Stuttgart, E. Nägele [English translation: 1995, *The Samoa Islands* (2vol.). Honolulu, University of Hawaii Press].

KROEF, Justus van der — 1952, "Some Head-Hunting Traditions of Southern New Guinea," *American Anthropologist* 54: 221–235.

KÜCHLER, Susanne — 1983, "The Malangan of Nombowai," *Oral History* 11 (2): 65–98.

— 1987, "Malangan: Art and Memory in a Melanesian Society," *Man* (n.s.) 22: 238–255.

— 1988, "Malangan: Objects, Sacrifice and the Production of Memory", *American Ethnologist* 15 (4): 625–637.

— 1992 "Making Skins: *Malangan* and the Idiom of Kinship in Northern New Ireland," in J. Coote and A. Shelton (eds.), *Anthropology, Art and Aesthetics*. Oxford, Clarendon Press: 94–111.

LABILLARDIÈRE, Jacques H. J. de — 1799, *Relation du voyage à la recherche de La Pérouse, fait sur ordre de l'Assemblée Constituante, pendant les années 1791, 1792 et pendant la 1ère et 2ème année de la République française*, 2 vol., Paris.

LACAN, Jacques — 1966 [1949], "Le stade du miroir comme formateur de la fonction du Je, telle qu'elle nous est révélée par l'expérience psychanalytique," in *Écrits*: 93–100. Paris, Seuil. English translation by Alan Sheridanin: *Ecrits: a Selection*. London, Tavistock, 1977.

— 1973 [1964], *Le Séminaire, livre XI. Les quatre concepts fondamentaux de la psychanalyse*. Paris, Seuil.

— 1978 [1954–1955], *Le Séminaire, livre II. Le moi dans la théorie de Freud et la technique de la psychanalyse*. Paris, Seuil.

— 1994 [1956–57], *Le Séminaire, livre IV. La relation d'objet*. Paris, Seuil.

LANDTMAN, Gunnar — 1970 [1927], *The Kiwai Papuans of British New Guinea: a nature-born instance of Rousseau's ideal community*. London, Macmillan and C°; New York, Johnson Reprint Corporation, 1970.

LAPLANCHE, Jean and J.-B. PONTALIS — 1967, *Vocabulaire de la psychanalyse*. Paris, Presses universitaires de France.

LARGY HEALY, Jessica de — 2000, "Football aborigène et réconciliation nationale", *Les Nouvelles de Survival* 40–41: 11.

LATTAS, Andrew — 1989, "Trickery and sacrifice: Tambarans and the appropriation of female reproductive powers in male initiation ceremonies in West New Britan", *Man* (n.s) 24: 451–469.

— 1992, "The Punishment of masks. Cargo cults and ideologies of representation in West New Britan", *Canberra Anthropology* 15 (2): 69–88.

LEACH Edmund — 1968, *Rethinking Anthropology*. London, The Athlone Press.

LEBOT Vincent — 1991, "Kava: the Polynesian Dispersal of an Oceanian Plant", in P. A. Cox and S. A. Banack (eds), *Islands, Plants and Polynesians*. Portland, Discorides Press.

LEDERMAN, Rena — 1986, *What Gifts Engender. Social Relations and Politics in Mendi, Highlands Papua New Guinea*. New York-Cambridge, Cambridge University Press.

LEGENDRE, Pierre—1994, *Leçons III. Dieu au miroir: étude sur l'institution des images*. Paris, Fayard.

—1998, *Leçons I. La 901e conclusion: étude sur le théâtre de la raison*. Paris, Fayard.

LEMONNIER, Pierre—1990, *Guerres et festins. Paix, échanges et compétition dans les Highlands de Nouvelle-Guinée*. Paris, Editions de la Maison des sciences de l'homme.

—1991, "From 'Great men' to 'Big men': Peace, substitution and competition in the Highlands of New Guinea," in M. Strathern & M. Godelier (eds.), *Big Men and Great Men. Personifications of Power in Melanesia*. Cambridge, Cambridge University Press: 7–27.

—1993, "Pigs as Ordinary Wealth. Technical Logics, Exchange, and Leadership in New Guinea", in P. Lemonnier (ed.), *Technological Choices. Transformation in Material Cultures from the Neolithic*. London, Routledge.

—1997, "*Mipela wan bilas*. Identité et variabilité socio-culturelle chez les Anga de Nouvelle-Guinée," in S. Tcherkézoff and F. Marsaudon (eds.), *Le Pacifique-sud aujourd'hui. Identités et transformations des sociétés océaniennes*, Paris, CNRS Editions: 197–227. English translation: Forthcoming, "Mipela was bilas". Identity and sociocultural variability among the Anga of Papua New Guinea," in S. Tcherkézoff and F. Marsaudon (eds.).

—n.d., "The Variability of Women's "Involvement" in Anga Male Initiations," paper presented at the workshop on "*Women in Male Rituals of Papua New Guinea*" convened by P. Bonnemère at the 1999 (Hawaii) meeting of the Association for Social Anthropology in Oceania.

LEROY, John D.—1979, "The ceremonial pig kill of the south Kewa," *Oceania* 49 (3): 179–209.

LESTER, R. H.—1941-2, "Kava drinking in Vitilevu, Fiji", *Oceania* 12: 97–121, 226–254.

LÉVI-STRAUSS, Claude—1950, "Introduction à l'œuvre de Marcel Mauss," in M. Mauss, *Sociologie et anthropologie*. Paris, Presses universitaires de France: IX–LII.

—1958, *Anthropologie structurale*. Paris, Plon. Translated as *Structural Anthropology*. New York, Basic Books, 1963.

—1962a, *La pensée sauvage*. Paris, Plon. Translated as *The Savage Mind*. Chicago, The University of Chicago Press, 1969; *The Savage Mind*. London, Weidenfeld and Nicolson, 1969.

—1962b, *Le totémisme aujourd'hui*. Paris, Presses universitaires de France. Translated as *Totemism*. Boston, Beacon Press, 1963.

—1971, *L'Homme Nu*. Paris, Plon. Translated as *The Naked Man*. London, Jonathan Cape, 1981.

LEWIS, P. H.— 1969, *The Social Context of Art in Northern New Ireland*. Chicago, Field Museum of Natural History, "Fieldiana, Anthropological Series" 58.

LIEP, John— 1999, "Pecuniary Schismogenesis in the Massim," in David Akin and Joel Robbins (eds.), *Money and Modernity. State and Local Currencies in Melanesia*. ASAO Monograph 17, University of Pittsburgh Press: 131–150.

LIKUVALU, Apeleto— 1977, "Cérémonial d'investiture de Tuiagaifo, roi d'Alo (Futuna) le 20 avril 1974," *Journal de la Société des Océanistes*, 56–7: 219.

LINDENBAUM, Shirley— 1984, "Variations on a Sociosexual Theme in Melanesia," in G. Herdt (ed.), *Ritualized Homosexuality in Melanesia*. Berkeley, California University Press: 79–89.

LINGE, O.— 1932, *The Erstwhile Savage: An Account of the Life of Ligeremaluaga*. Melbourne, Cheshire.

LIPSET, David— 1997, *Mangrove Man. Dialogics of Culture in the Sepik Estuary*. Cambridge, Cambridge University Press.

LiPUMA, Edward— 1988, *The gift of kinship. Structure and practice in Maring social organization*. Cambridge, Cambridge University Press.

— 1999, "The Meaning of Money in the Age of Modernity", in D. Akin and J. Robbins (eds.), *Money and Modernity. State and Local Currencies in Melanesia*. Pittsburgh, University of Pittsburgh Press: 192–213.

LLOYD, J.A.— 1992, *A Baruya Tok Pisin / English Dictionary*. Canberra, Pacific Linguistics (Series C-n° 82).

LOMAS, Peter W.— 1979, "Malanggans and Manipulators: Land and Politics in Northern New Ireland," *Oceania* 50 (1): 53–66.

LORY, Jean-Luc— 1981–1982, "Quelques aspects du chamanisme baruya (Eastern Highlands Province)," *Cahiers O.R.S.T.O.M. (série sciences humaines)* 18(4): 543–559.

MCDOWELL, Nancy— 1978, "Flexibility of Sister Exchange in Bun," *Oceania* 68 (4): 297–231.

MCGREGOR, William— 1988, *Handbook of Kimberley languages, V.1: General information* (A project of the Kimberley Language Resource Centre). Canberra, The Australian National University ("Pacific Linguistics, series C, 105").

MALINOWSKI, Bronislaw K.— 1922, *Argonauts of the Western Pacific. An Account of Native Enterprise and Adventure in the Archipelagoes of Melanesian New Guinea*. London, Routledge and Kegan Paul.

MALLARMÉ, Stéphane— 1913, *Poésies*. Paris, Gallimard-NRF.

MARCK, Jeff— 1999, "Polynesian Language and Culture History," Ph.D. Thesis. Canberra, Australian National University (Research School of Pacific and Asian Studies, Department of Linguistics).

MARTIN, John—1981 [1817], *An Account of the Natives of the Tonga Islands [...]; Compiled and Arranged from the Extensive Communications of Mr. William Mariner, Several Years Resident in Those Islands.* Edition facsimile. Neiafu, Vava'u Press.

MAUSS, Marcel—1925, "Essai sur le don. Forme et raison de l'échange dans les sociétés archaïques," *L'Année sociologique*, new series, vol.1 ; also in *Sociologie et anthropologie.* Paris, Presses Universitaires de France, (Introduction de C. Lévi-Strauss), 1950: 143–279. English translations: see below.
—1968–1974, *Oeuvres,* 3 vol. Paris, Editions de Minuit.
—1954 [1925], *The Gift: Forms and Functions of Exchange in Archaic Societies.* London, Cohen & West. (Introduction by Evans-Pritchard).
—1990 [1925], *The Gift. The Form and Reason for Exchange in Archaic Societies,* foreword by Mary Douglas, New York-London, W.W. Norton.

MEAD, Margaret—1935, *Sex and Temperament in Three Primitive Societies.* London, George Routledge.

MELEISEA, Malama—1987, *The making of modern Samoa: traditional authority and colonial administration in the modern history of Western Samoa.* Suva, University of the South Pacific (Institute of Pacific Studies).

MENDEL, Gérard—1972, *Anthropologie différentielle.* Paris, Payot.

MERLE, Isabelle—1995, *Expériences coloniales, Nouvelle-Calédonie 1853–1920.* Paris, Belin.

MICHA, Franz Josef—1970, "Trade and Change in Australian Aboriginal Cultures: Australian Aboriginal Trade as an Expression of Close Culture Contact and as a Mediator of Culture Change," in Piling and Waterman (eds.), *Diprotodon to detribalization.* Michigan State University Press.

MIMICA Jadran—1981, "Omalyce. An ethnography of the Ikwaye view of cosmos," Doctoral dissertation, Australian National University, Canberra.
—1991a, "The Incest Passions: An Outline of the Logic of the Iqwaye Social Organization, Part 1," *Oceania,* 62 (1): 34–58.
—1991b, "The Incest Passions: An Ouline of the Logic of the Iqwaye Social Organization (Part 2)," *Oceania* 62 (2): 81–113.

MISSIONS MARISTES—1890, *Dictionnaire Toga-Français-Anglais.* Paris, Chadenat.

MODJESKA, C. Nicholas—1982, "Production and inequality: perspectives from Central New Guinea," in A. Strathern (ed.), *Inequality in the New Guinea Highlands Societies.* Cambridge, Cambridge University Press: 50–108.

MOISSEEFF, Marika—1989, "Représentations non figuratives et singularité individuelle: les *churinga* du désert central australien," in L. Perrois (éd.), *Anthropologie de l'art: Faits et significations (Arts de l'Afrique, de l'Amérique et du Pacifique).* Paris, ORTSOM.

— 1995, *Un long chemin semé d'objets cultuels: le cycle initiatique aranda*. Paris, Ecole des hautes étude en sciences sociales (Coll. Les Cahiers de l'Homme).

MONNERIE, Denis— 1996, *Nitu: les vivants, les morts et le cosmos selon la société Mono-Alu (îles Salomon)*. Leiden, Research School Center for Non Western Studies.

MORTON, J.— 1985, *Sustaining Desire. A Structuralist Interpretation of Myth and Male Cult in Central Australia*. Ph. D. thesis, The Australian National University.

— 1987, "The Effectiveness of Totemism, 'Increase Ritual' and Resource Control in Central Australia," *Man* (n.s.) 22: 453–74.

MOSKO, Mark— 1985, *Quadripartite structures. Categories, relations, and homologies in Bush Mekeo culture*. London, Cambridge Univesity Press.

MOYLE, Alice M.— 1981, *Songs from the Kimberleys*— Companion booklet for a 12-inch LP Disc and tapes recorded in 1968, Cat.n°AIAS/13. Canberra, Australian Insititute of Aboriginal Studies.

MOYLE, Richard (ed.)— 1984, *The Samoan journals of John Williams, 1830 and 1832*. Canberra, Australian National University Press.

MUNN, Nancy— 1964, "Totemic Designs and Group Continuity in Walbiri Cosmology," in M. Reay (ed.), *Aborigines Now. New Perspectives in the Study of Aboriginal Communities*. Sydney, Angus and Robertson.

— 1970, "The Transformation of Subjects into Objects in Walbiri and Pitjantjara Myth," in R. Berndt (ed.), *Australian Aboriginal Anthropology*. Nedlands, University of Western Australia Press.

— 1973, *Walbiri Iconography*. Ithaca, Cornell University Press.

MYERS, Fred— 1979, "Emotions and the Self. A theory of Personhood and Political Order among Pintupi Aborigines," *Ethos* 7: 343–70.

— 1986, *Pintupi Country, Pintupi Self. Sentiment, Place and Politics among Western Desert Aborigines*. Washington, Smithsonian Institution Press/Canberra, Australian Institute of Aboriginal Studies.

— 1994, "Culture-Making: Performing Aboriginality at the Asia Society Gallery", *American Ethnologist* 21 (4): 679–699.

—nd, "What is the Business of the 'Balgo business'? A Contemporary Aboriginal Religious Movement". Manuscript.

NAEPELS, Michel— 1998, *Histoires de terres kanakes. Conflits fonciers et rapports sociaux dans la région de Houaïlou (Nouvelle-Calédonie)*. Paris, Belin.

NASH, Jill— 1974, *Matriliny and modernisation: The Nagovisi of South Bougainville*, Port-Moresby-Canberra, New Guinea Research Bulletin 55, The Australian National University.

NÉAOUTYINE, S.— 1996, *Le centre culturel Jean-Marie Tjibaou et la construction de l'identité kanak: contribution à une réflexion sur la notion de patrimoine.* Paris, Ecole des hautes études en sciences sociales, ms. 73p.

NEWELL, W. H.— 1974, "The Kava ceremony in Tonga," *Journal of the Polynesian Society* 56: 364–417.

O'BRIEN, Denise— 1969, "Marriage among the Konda Valley Dani," in R.M. Glasse and M.J. Meggitt (eds.), *Pigs, Pearlshells, and Women. Marriage in the New Guinea Highlands.* Englewood Cliffs, N.J., Prentice-Hall: 198–234.

OLIVER, Douglas L.— 1967, *A Solomon Island Society. Kinship and Leardership among the Siuai of Bougainville.* Boston, Beacon Press.

OZANNE-RIVIERRE, Françoise— 1979, *Textes nemi (Nouvelle-Calédonie),* vol. 1 (Kavatch et Tendo) et vol. 2 (Bas-Coulna et Haut-Coulna), with a Nemi/French lexicon. Paris, Selaf.

PANNELL, Sandra— 1994, "Mabo and Museums: The Indigenous (Re)Appropriation of Indigenous Things," *Oceania* 65: 18–39.

PANOFF, Michel— 1976, "Patrifiliation as Ideology and Practice in a Matrilineal Society," *Ethnology* 15 (2): 175–188.

— 1980, "Objets précieux et moyens de paiement chez les Maenge de Nouvelle-Bretagne," *L'Homme* 20 (2): 6–37.

PEEKEL, Gerhard— 1927, "Die Ahnenbilder von Nord-Neu-Mecklenburg: eine Kritische und Positive Studie," *Anthropos* 21: 806–824; 22: 16–44.

PELTIER, Philippe— 1990, "Pablo Picasso et les "fétiches" de Nouvelle-Calédonie", in R. Boulay (éd.), *De Jade et de nacre, Patrimoine artistique kanak.* Paris, Réunion des Musées Nationaux: 239–243.

PETERSON, Nicolas— 1970, "Buluwandi: a Central Australian Ceremony for the Resolution of Conflict," in R. M. Berndt (ed.), *Australian Aboriginal Anthropology.* Nedlands, University of Western Australia.

— 2000, "An Expanding Aboriginal Domain: Mobility and the Initiation Journey," *Oceania* 70 (3): 205–218.

PETITAT, André— 1995, "Le don: Espace imaginaire normatif et secret des acteurs," *Anthropologie et Sociétés.* 19 (1–2): 17–44.

POIRIER, Sylvie— 1990, *Les jardins du nomade. Territoire, rêve et transformation chez les groupes aborigènes du désert occidental australien.* Ph. D. thesis, Université de Laval.

— 1992a, "Cosmologie, personne et expression artistique dans le désert occidental australien," *Anthropologie et Sociétés* 16 (1): 41–58.

— 1992b, "Nomadic Rituals: Networks of Ritual Exchange among Women of the Australian Western Desert," *Man* 27 (4): 757–776.

— 1996, *Les Jardins du nomade. Cosmologie, territoire et personne dans le désert occidental australien.* Münster, Lit Verlag.

PORTZAMPARC, Christian de — 1995, "La ville: Réflexions sur dix thèmes," *L'architecture d'aujourd'hui* 302: 68–79.

POUILLON, Jean — "Fétiches sans fétichisme," *Nouvelle Revue de Psychanalyse* 2: 135–147. Reedited in *Fétiches sans fétichisme*. Paris, François Maspero, 1975: 104–119.

POWDERMAKER, Hortense — 1933, *Life in Lesu. The Study of a Melanesian Society in New Ireland*. New York, Norton.

RAPPAPORT, Roy A. — 1969, "Marriage among the Maring," in R.M. Glasse and M.J. Meggitt (eds.), *Pigs, Pearlshells, and Women. Marriage in the New Guinea Highlands*. Englewood Cliffs, N.J., Prentice-Hall: 117–137.

RIVERS, William H. R. — 1968 [1914], *The History of Melanesian Society*. 2 vol., Oosterhout N.B. (The Nederlands), Anthropological Publications.

RIVIERRE, Jean-Claude — 1980, *La langue de Touho. Phonologie et grammaire du cèmuhî (Nouvelle-Calédonie)*. Paris, SELAF.

— 1983, *Dictionnaire paicî-français (Nouvelle-Calédonie)*. Paris, SELAF.

RMIT, Royal Melbourne Institute of Technology — 1995, *Keeping country — a Draft Report Submitted to the Rubibi Working Group*. Melbourne.

RODMAN, Margaret C. — 1981, "A Boundary and a Bridge: Women's Pig Killing as a Border-Crossing Between Spheres of Exchange in East Aoba," in M. Allen (ed.), *Vanuatu: Politics, Economics and Ritual in Island Melanesia*. Sydney, Academic Press: 85–104.

ROGERS, Garth — 1975, *Kai and Kava in Niuatoputapu. Social Relations, Ideologies and Contexts in a Rural Tongan Community*. Ph. D. thesis, University of Auckland.

ROHEIM, Geza — 1970 [1945], *The Eternal Ones of the Dream*. New York, International Universities Press.

— 1972 [1932–1952], *The Panic of the Gods and Other Essays*. New York, Harper and Row.

— 1974 [1934], *The Riddle of the Sphinx, or Human Origins*. New York, Harper and Row.

ROSOLATO, Guy — 1969, *Essais sur le symbolique*. Paris, Gallimard.

ROSSILLE, Richard — 1986, *Le kava à Wallis et à Futuna. Survivance d'un breuvage océanien traditionnel*. Bordeaux-Talence, Centre de Recherches sur les Espaces Tropicaux de l'Université de Bordeaux III (CRET), collection "Iles et archipels" n° 6.

RYAN, d'Arcy — 1969, "Marriage in Mendi," in R.M. Glasse and M.J. Meggitt (eds.), *Pigs, Pearlshells, and Women. Marriage in the New Guinea Highlands*. Englewood Cliffs, N.J., Prentice-Hall: 159–175.

SAHLINS, Marshall — 1963, "Poor man, rich man, big man, chief: Political types in Melanesia and Polynesia," *Comparative Studies in Society and History* 5: 285–303.

— 1974, *Stone Age Economics*. London, Tavistock.

— 1981, "The Stranger-King, or Dumezil among the Fijians," in *Islands of History*. Chicago, The University of Chicago Press.

SALES, Anne de— 1991, *Je suis né de vos jeux de tambours. La religion chamanique des Magar du nord*. Nanterre, Société d'ethnologie.

SALISBURY, Richard— 1962, *From stone to steel*. Melbourne, Melbourne University Press.

SAUSSOL, Alain— 1979, *L'Héritage. Essai sur le problème foncier mélanésien en Nouvelle-Calédonie*. Paris, Société des Océanistes n° 40.

SCHNEIDER, David M.— 1961, "Introduction: The Distinctive Features of Matrilineal Descent Groups," in D. M. Schneider and K. Gough, (eds.), *Matrilineal Kinship*. Berkeley-Los Angeles, University of California Press: 1–29.

SERPENTI, L.M.— 1977, *Cultivators in the Swamps. Social structure and horticulture in a New Guinea society (Frederik-Hendrik Island West New Guinea)*. Assen-Amsterdam, van Gorcum.

SILVERMAN, Eric Kline— 2001, *Masculinity, Motherhood, and Mockery: Psychoanalyzing Culture and the Iatmul Naven Rite in New Guinea*. Ann Arbor, The University of Michigan Press.

SIMMEL, Georges— 1978, *The Philosophy of Money*. Boston, Routledge and Kegan Paul.

SMITH, S. Percy— 1892, "Futuna; or, Horne Island and its People. Western Pacific," *Journal of the Polynesian Society* 1: 33–52.

SOWADA, A.A.— 1961, *Socio-Economic Survey of the Asmat Peoples of Southwestern New Guinea*. MA dissertation, Washington, The Catholic University of America.

SPENCER, Baldwin et Frank GILLEN— 1899, *The Native Tribes of Central Australia*. London, MacMillan.

— 1904, *The Northern Tribes of Central Australia*. London, MacMillan.

— 1927, *The Arunta*. London, MacMillan.

STAIR, John B. Stair— 1896, "Jottings on the mythology and spirit-lore of old Samoa," *Journal of the Polynesian Society* 5: 33–57.

— 1897, *Old Samoa, or flotsam and jetsam from the Pacific ocean*. London, The Religious Tract Society.

STANTON, John— 1999, "At the Grass-roots: collecting and communities in Aboriginal Australia," in S. Toussaint and J. Taylor (eds.), *Applied Anthropology in Australasia*. Nedlands, University of Western Australia Press: 282–294.

STEPHENSON, David— 1994, "A Legal Paradigm for Protecting Traditional Knowledge," in T. Greaves (ed.), *Intellectual Property Rights for Indigenous People*. Oklahoma City, Society for Applied Anthropology: 179–189.

STRATHERN, Andrew J.—1969, "Finance and production: two strategies in New Guinea exchange systems," *Oceania* 40: 42–67.
—1971, *The rope of moka. Big-men and ceremonial exchange in Mount Hagen, New Guinea.* Cambridge, Cambridge University Press.
—1978, "Finance and Production revisited: In Pursuit of a Comparison," *Research in Economic Anthropology* 1: 73–104.
—1980, "Bridewealth among the Melpa and the Wiru," in J. Comaroff (ed.), *The meaning of marriage payments.* New York, Academic Press: 49–66.
—1982. "Witchcraft, greed, cannibalism, and death. Some related themes from the New Guinea Highlands," in M. Bloch and J. Parry (eds.), *Death and the regeneration of Life.* New York, Pergamon: 111–133.
STRATHERN, Marilyn—1984, "Marriage Exchanges: A Melanesian Context," *Annual Review of Anthropology* 13: 41–73.
—1988, *The Gender of the Gift. Problems with Women and Problems with Society in Melanesia.* Berkeley, University of California Press.
—1992, "Qualified value: the Perspective of Gift Exchange," in C. Humphrey and S. Hugh-Jones (eds.), *Barter, Exchange and Value. An Anthropological Approach.* Cambridge, Cambridge University Press: 169–191.
—1999, *Property, Substance and Effect: Anthropological Essays on Persons and Things.* London-New Brunswick (N. J.), The Athlone Press.
STRATHERN, Andrew and Marilyn—1969, "Marriage in Melpa," in R. Glasse and M.J. Meggitt (eds.), *Pigs, pearshells, and women. Marriage in the New Guinea Highlands.* Englewood Cliffs, N.J., Prentice-Hall: 138–158.
STRATHERN, Marilyn and GODELIER, Maurice (eds.)—1991, *Big men and great men. Personifications of power in Melanesia.* Cambridge, Cambridge University Press.
STREHLOW, Carl—1907–21, *Die Aranda—und Loritja-Stamme in Zentral-Australien.* 7 Vol., Francfort, J. Baer.
STREHLOW, Theodor G. H.—1964a, "Personal Monototemism in a Polytotemic Community," in E. Haberland, M. Schuster and H. Straube (eds.). *Festschrift für A.E. Jensen.* München, Klaus Renner Verlag.
—1964b, "The Art of Circle, Line and Square," in R. Berndt (ed.), *Australian Aboriginal Art.* Sydney: Ure Smith.
—1968 [1947], *Aranda Traditions.* Melbourne, Melbourne University Press.
—1971, *Songs of Central Australia.* Sydney, Angus and Robertson.
SURGY, Albert de (ed.)—1985, "Fétiches. Objets enchantés. Mots réalisés". *Systèmes de pensée en Afrique Noire* 8. Paris, EPHE (section des sciences religieuses).

SWAIN, Tony—1993, *A Place for Strangers. Towards a History of Australian Aboriginal Being*. Cambridge, Cambridge University Press.

TAHON, Marie-Blanche—1995, "Le don de la mère," *Anthropologie et Sociétés* 19 (1–2): 139–155.

TARRAN, Mary—1997, "Overview of the Bugarrigarra Nyurdany Aboriginal Culture Center", in Kimberley Culture and Natural History Centre Steering Committe Inc. (ed.), *Planning Cultural and Interpretative Centres in the Kimberley*. Regional Conference, Broome: 23–27.

TCHERKÉZOFF, Serge—1985, "The expulsion of illness or the domestication of the dead: a case study of the Nyamwezi of Tanzania," *History and Anthropology* 2: 59–92.

—1986, "Les amendes au roi en pays nyamwezi. La continuation du sacrifice par d'autres moyens," *Droits et cultures* 11: 89–110.

—1987, *Dual Classification Reconsidered*. Cambridge, Cambridge University Press.

—1993, "Une hypothèse sur la valeur du 'prix de la fiancée' nyamwezi," in F. Héritier et E. Copet-Rougier (eds.), *Les complexités de l'alliance. Economie, politique et fondements symboliques de l'alliance. Volume 3: Afrique*. Paris, Ed. des archives contemporaines ("Ordres sociaux"): 51–80.

—1994a, "Hierarchical Reversal, ten years on (Africa, India, Polynesia)," *Journal of Anthropological Society of Oxford* 25 (2): 133–167 and 25 (3): 229–253.

—1994b, "L'inclusion du contraire (L. Dumont), la hiérarchie enchevêtrée (J.P. Dupuy) et le rapport sacré/pouvoir. Relectures et révision des modèles à propos de l'Inde. Ière Partie: un modèle asymétrique," "IIème Partie: statut et pouvoir en Inde: la logique concrète de l'inclusion du contraire," *Culture* 14 (2): 113–134 et 15 (1): 33–48.

—1995, "L'autocar à Samoa ou la hiérarchie au quotidien," *Gradhiva* 18: 47–56.

—1997a, "Culture, nation, société: changements secondaires et bouleversements possibles au Samoa Occidental. Vers un modèle pour l'étude des dynamiques culturelles," in S. Tcherkézoff and F. Douaire-Marsaudon (eds.), *Le Pacifique-Sud aujourd'hui*: 309–373.

—1997b, "Le *mana*, le fait "total" et l'"esprit" dans la chose donnée. Marcel Mauss, les "cadeaux à Samoa" et la méthode comparative en Polynésie," *Anthropologie et Sociétés* (numéro spécial "Comparaisons régionales") 21 (2–3): 193–223.

—1998, "Identités en mutation aux Samoa" [le développement acceptable et la tenure foncière], in D. Tryon and P. de Deckker (eds.), *Identités en mutation dans le Pacifique à l'aube du 3e millénaire*. Talence, Université Bordeaux-3, Centre de recherches sur les espaces tropicaux CRET ("Iles et archipels," 26): 111–157.

—Forthcoming, "'Soeur ou épouse, il faut choisir!' — L'énigme de l'exogamie villageoise à Samoa: mariage, résidence et asymétrie des sexes dans une société polynésienne," in F. Héritier and E. Copet-Rougier (eds.), *Frère/soeur: la relation essentielle de la parenté*. Paris, Ed. des Archives Contemporaines (coll. "Ordres Sociaux").

—n.d. 1, Forthcoming, *La Polynésie et l'Occident: du malentendu au dialogue anthropologique (économie, politique, sexualité)*.

—n.d. 2, Forthcoming, "The Samoan *ie toga* as a "cover" of an initial gift" (Acts to appear of the Symposium on "Objets and Persons in Western Polynesia including Fiji," in St. Hooper and M. Sahlins (eds.), Sainsbury Center, University of North Anglia, Norwich, november 1998).

—n.d. 3, Forthcoming, "Fine mats, Maussian gift and "covering" in Polynesia. From Ancestral Polynesia to the Tongan-Samoan connection," *Journal of the Polynesian Society*.

TCHERKÉZOFF, Serge and Françoise DOUAIRE-MARSAUDON (eds.)
— 1997, *Le Pacifique-sud aujourd'hui: identités et transformations culturelles*. Paris, Ed. du CNRS ("Ethnologie"). Translation forthcoming.

TESTART, Alain — 1992, *De la nécessité d'être initié. Rites d'Australie*. Nanterre, Société d'Ethnologie.

— 1993, *Des dons et des dieux. Anthropologie religieuse et sociologie comparative*. Paris, Armand Colin.

THOMAS, Nicholas — 1989, *Out of Time. History and Evolution in Anthropological Discourse*. Cambridge, Cambridge University Press.

— 1991, *Entangled Objects. Exchange, Material Culture, and Colonialism in the Pacific*. Cambridge (Mass.)-London, Harvard University Press.

THOMAS, Yan — 1991, "L'institution de l'origine. *Sacra principiorum populi romani*," in M. Détienne (éd.), *Tracés de fondation*. Paris-Louvain, Peeters: 143–170.

THURNWALD, Richard — 1910, "Das Rechtleben der Eingeborenen der deutschen Südseeinseln, seine geistigen und wirtschaftigen Grundlagen," *Blätter für vergleichende Rechtswissenschaft und Volkswirtschaftslehre* VI (5–6).

— 1912, *Forschungen auf den Salomo-Inseln und dem Bismarck-Archipel*. Vol. III ("Volk, Staat und Wirtschaft"). Berlin, Dietrich Reimer.

— 1936, "Gegenseitigkeit im Aufbau und Funktionieren der Gesellungen und deren Institutionen," in *Reine und angewandte Soziologie*. Leipzig, Hans Buske Verlag ; and in *Grundfragen menschlicher Gesellung. Ausgewählte Schriften*, 1957.

TITCOMB, Margaret — 1948, "Kava in Hawaii," *Journal of the Polynesian Society* 57: 105–171.

TJIBAOU, Jean-Marie — 1978, *Kanaké: The Melanesian Way*. Translated by C. Plant from the French edition [1976], Tahiti, Editions du Pacifique.

— 1996, *Présence kanak*. A. Bensa and E. Wittersheim (eds.), Paris, Odile Jacob.

TONKINSON, Richard— 1981, "Sorcery and Social Change in Southeast Ambrym, Vanuatu," *Social Analysis* 8: 77–88.

TRENKENSCHUH, F.A.— 1982, *An Asmat Sketch Book N° 1 & 2*. Hastings (USA), Crosier Missions.

TROMPF, Garry W.— 1990, "Keeping the *lo* under a Melanesian Messiah: an analysis of the Pomio *Kivung*, East New Britain," in J. Barker, (ed.), *Christianity in Oceania. Ethnographic Perspectives*. ASAO Monograph n°12. University Press of America: 59–80.

TSOSIE, Rebecca— 1997, "Indigenous Peoples Claims to Cultural Property: A legal Perspective," *Museum Anthropology* 21 (3): 5–11.

TUZIN, Donald— 1976, *The Ilahita Arapesh. Dimensions of Unity*. Berkeley, University of California Press.

— 1980, *The Voice of the Tambaran. Truth and Illusion in Ilahita Arapesh Religion*. Berkeley-Los Angeles-London, University of California Press.

VALERI, Valerio— 1985, *Kingship and sacrifice: ritual and society in ancient Hawaii*. Chicago, The University of Chicago Press.

— 1989, "Death in Heaven: Myths and Rites of Kinship in Tongan Kingship," *History and Anthropology* 4: 209–247.

VALÉRY, Paul— 1958, *Poésies*. Paris, Gallimard.

VIENNE, Bernard— 1984, *Gens de Motlav. Idéologie et pratique sociale en Mélanésie*. Paris, Publications de la Société des Océanistes n° 42.

WAAL, Frans de— 1989, *Peacemaking among primates*. Cambridge (Mass.), Harvard University Press.

WAGNER, Roy— 1981, *The Invention of Culture* (revised and expanded edition). Chicago-London, The University of Chicago Press.

— 1986, *Asiwinarong: Ethos, Image, and Social Power among the Usen Barok of New Ireland*. Princeton, Princeton University Press.

— 1987, "Figure-Ground Reversal Among the Barok," in L. Lincoln, (ed.), *Assemblage of Spirits: Idea and Image in New Ireland*. New York, G. Braziller & The Minneapolis Institute of Arts: 56–62.

— 1991, "The Fractal Person," in M. Godelier and M. Strathern (eds.), *Big Men and Great Men: Personifications of Power in Melanesia*. Cambridge, Cambridge University Press: 159–173.

WEDLOCK, Thomas— 1992, "Practice, politics and ideology of the 'travelling business' in Aboriginal religion," *Oceania* 63: 114–136.

WEINER, Annette— 1976, *Women of Value, Men of Renown: New Perspectives in Trobriand Exchange*. Austin, University Press.

— 1985, "Inalienable Wealth," *American Ethnologist* 12 (2): 210–227.

— 1992, *Inalienable Possessions: The Paradox of Keeping-while-Giving*. Berkeley, University of California Press.

WEINER, James F. — 1982, "Substance, siblingship and exchange: aspects of social structure in New Guinea," *Social analysis* 11: 3–34.
— 1995, *The Lost Drum: The Myth of Sexuality in Papua New Guinea and Beyond*. Madison, The University of Wisconsin Press.
WELSH, Peter H. — 1997, "The Power of Possessions: The Case Against Property," *Museum Anthropology* 21 (3): 12–18.
WHITEHOUSE, Harvey — 1992, "Leaders and logics, persons and polities," *History and Anthropology* 6 (1): 103–124.
— 1995, *Inside the Cult. Religious Innovation and Transmission in Papua New Guinea*. Oxford, Clarendon Press.
WILKINSON, G.N. — 1978, "Carving a Social Message: The Malanggans of Tabar," in M. Greenhalgh and V. Megaw (eds.), *Art in Society: Studies in Style, Culture and Aesthetics*. London, Duckworth.
WILL, Edouard — 1954, "De l'aspect éthique des origines grecques de la monnaie," *Revue historique* 112: 209–231.
WILLIAMS, Francis E. — 1936, *Papuans of the Trans-Fly*. Oxford, Clarendon Press.
WILLIAMSON, Robert W. — 1975, *Essays in Polynesian Ethnology*. New York, Cooper Square Publishers.
WINNICOTT, Donald W. — 1971, *Playing and Reality*. London, Tavistock.
WITTGENSTEIN, Ludwig — 1975, *Remarques philosophiques*. Paris, Gallimard.
WORMS, Ernest A. and Helmut PETRI (eds.) — 1986, *Australian Aboriginal religions*. Nelen Yubu missilogical, series 3 (transl. from German, "Australische Eingeborenen-Religionen," in H. Nevermann, H. Petri and E.A. Worms (eds.), *Die Religionen der Suedsee und Australiens*. Stuttgart.
YOUNG, Michael W. — 1971, *Fighting with Food*. Cambridge, Cambridge University Press.
ZEGWAARD, Gerard A. and J.H.M. BOELAARS — 1955, "De sociale Structuur van de Asmat-Stam" [Asmat social organization], *Adatrechtbundels* 45 (serie S. Nieuw-Guinea, n° 53): 244–301.

The Authors

(By chapter order)

Serge TCHERKÉZOFF is Directeur d'étude (professor) at the Ecole des Hautes Etudes en Sciences Sociales (EHESS) and the head of the Centre de Recherches et de Documentation sur l'Océanie (CREDO, Marseille). He has worked on East African ethnography (1975-1987) and has published on the ritual system, on dual classification (his PhD), on the anthropological tradition in this area and on the epistemology of the comparative approach in anthropology. Since 1982, he has turned to the culture of Samoa and Western Samoan society, examining the system of traditional ranks, the construction of social gender relations and contemporary changes in these areas. He has published a book on gender and sexuality in Samoa and is working on gift-exchange, the kinship system and on the anthropological myths that have grown up around these questions.

Françoise DOUAIRE-MARSAUDON is Chargée de recherche at the Centre National de la Recherche Scientifique (CNRS) and a member of the Centre de Recherches et de Documentation sur l'Océanie (CREDO, Marseille). She has conducted an 18-month ethnographic study in the three Polynesian societies of Tonga, Wallis and Futuna. The main thrust of her research is the relationship between representations of (sexual, personal, etc.) identity and politics. After a doctoral dissertation devoted to the relationship between kinship, body representations—among which gender differences—and political hierarchy in Western Polynesia, she published *Les premiers fruits. Parenté, identité sexuelle et pouvoirs en Polynésie occidentale (Tonga, Wallis et Futuna)*, in which she further develops these issues, stressing an approach that takes account of historical change. In parallel, she has continued her comparative analyses of "Hawaiian" kinship systems in view of a general study of the "sister's children, sacred children" complex in Polynesia.

Maurice GODELIER is Directeur d'étude (professor) at the Ecole des Hautes Etudes en Sciences Sociales (EHESS) and a member of the Centre de Recherches et de Documentation sur l'Océanie (CREDO, Marseille). He has done extensive fieldwork among the Baruya of Papua New Guinea between 1967 and 1988. He has published *The Making of Great Men. Male Domination and Power among the New Guinea Baruya* and, in collaboration with Marilyn Strathern, has edited the acts of an international conference on this subject, entitled *Big Men and Great Men. Personifications of Power in Melanesia.* Recently he has reconsidered the question of gift-giving with his book *The Enigma of the Gift.* Another major theme of his research is the relationship between the body, kinship and power (*La Production du corps* and *Le Corps humain: possédé, sacrifié, cannibalisé*, co-edited with Michel Panoff). Recently he has published a work on kinship, edited in collaboration with Thomas Trautmann and Tjon Sie Fat Franklin, *Transformations of Kinship* (Washington & London, The Smithsonian Institute Press, 1998).

Pierre LEMONNIER is Directeur de recherche at the Centre National de la Recherche Scientifique (CNRS), and a member of the Centre de Recherche et de Documentation sur l'Océanie (CREDO, Marseille). He has studied the economic anthropology and cultural technology of the salt-producers of France's Atlantic coast (*Les Salines de l'Ouest, Paludiers de Guérande*, his PhD). Between 1978 and 1985, as a specialist in the ethnology of techniques (*Elements for an Anthropology of Technology*; *Technological Choices; De la préhistoire aux missiles balistiques*, with Bruno Latour), he investigated the technical system of the Anga people of Papua New Guinea. Together with Pascale Bonnemère, he has undertaken a monographic study of one particular Anga group, the Ankave. He is presently preparing a work on cannibalism and sorcery among the Anga, and with P. Bonnemère, a study of Anga initiations. He has also published several overviews of the socio-cultural systems of different areas of New Guinea—the Highlands in *Guerres et Festins*—but other societies on the south coast as well.

Stéphane BRETON is Maître de conférences (associate professor) at the Ecole des Hautes Etudes en Sciences Sociales (EHESS), and a member of the Centre de Recherche et de Documentation sur l'Océanie (CREDO, Paris). He has done 28 months of fieldwork among the Wodani of the Highlands of West Papua (ex-Irian Jaya). His publications include: *La mascarade des sexes: fétichisme, inversion et travestissement rituels* (Paris, Calmann-Lévy, 1989, a revised version of his PhD dissertation) and several articles (see bibliography). He is particularly interested in the theory of exchange in Melanesia and beyond. He is currently working on the grammar and lexicon of the as yet undescribed Wodani language, West Papua Highlands. He is a documentary filmmaker and has just finished a one-hour film on the Wodani, *Eux et moi*, produced and broadcast by the German-French TV channel "Arte".

Bernard JUILLERAT is Directeur de recherche at the Centre National de la Recherche Scientifique (CNRS) and a member of the Laboratoire d'Anthropologie Sociale (Collège de France, Paris). In the 1960s he did fieldwork for his PhD in a non-Islamized society in North Cameroon. In 1970, he began his study of a group of Papua New Guinea forest-dwellers, the Yafar (West Sepik). His fieldwork has resulted in a monograph (*Children of the Blood*), a psychoanalytical interpretation of Yafar mythology (*Œdipe chasseur*), and an ethno-psychoanalytical study of the Yafar male cult (*Shooting the Sun* and *L'Avènement du Père*). In 1989, he conducted a field study on the Banaro of East Sepik, based on the early 20th-century publications of the Austro-German anthropologist, Richard Thurnwald (*La Révocation des Tambaran*). A selection of his articles on psychoanalytical anthropology has just been published (*Penser l'imaginaire*, Payot-Lausanne, 2001).

Monique JEUDY-BALLINI is Chargée de recherche at the Centre National de la Recherche Scientifique (CNRS) and a member of the Laboratoire d'Anthropologie Sociale (Collège de France, Paris). Since 1980 she has been working on the ethnography of the Sulka people of New Britain (Papua New Guinea). After devoting her doctoral dissertation to Sulka representations of sexual identity, she pursued her analysis of gender relations in articles dealing with the status of chiefs' daughters, work-related mythology, the violation of contemporary prohibitions, and the practice of adoption. Her most recent research deals with the local messianic movement, ceremonial exchanges, the dialectical ties between the local competing Churches (notably Catholics and Seventh-Day Adventists) and Sulka ritual art. She is presently publishing a monograph on Sulka ceremonial exchanges.

Brigitte DERLON is Maître de conférences (associate professor) at the Ecole des Hautes Etudes en Sciences Sociales (EHESS, Paris) and a member of the Laboratoire d'Ethnologie et de Sociologie Comparative (University of Paris X Nanterre). She spent 18 months (1983-84 and 1993) carrying out an ethnographic study in the mountainous central part of the island of New Ireland (Papua New Guinea). She has studied funeral rituals, and in particular the *malanggan* objects and rites as well as traditional beliefs, gender relations, land-holding, exchanges between dual units, the political system and the importance of the body in socio-cosmic relations. Her doctoral dissertation, a revised version of which has been published under the title *De mémoire et d'oubli. Anthropologie des objets* malanggan *de Nouvelle-Irlande*, is an exhaustive study of the *malanggan* that formerly were made in the northern part of the island.

Marika MOISSEEFF is Chargée de recherche at the Centre National de la Recherche Scientifique (CNRS), a member of the Centre of Research and Documentation in Oceania (CREDO, Paris), as well as a consultant psychiatrist. She has been a Visiting Research Fellow at the Australian Institute of Aboriginal and Torres Strait Islander Studies (AIATSIS) between 1991 and 1995 and is the author of *Un long chemin semé d'objets cultuels: le cycle initiatique aranda* (MA in Anthropology, Paris, EHESS, coll. Cahiers de l'Homme, 1995) and of *An Aboriginal Village in South Australia : A snapshot of Davenport* (Canberra, Aboriginal Studies Press, 1999). Her current work concerns the representation of sexuality and procreation in contemporary Western societies and the processes underlying the construction of identity in present-day Australian Aboriginal communities.

Barbara GLOWCZEWSKI is Chargée de recherche at the Centre National de la Recherche Scientifique (CNRS) and a member of the Laboratoire d'Anthropologie Sociale (Collège de France, Paris). She has worked in Australia since 1979. She has published a book on her research in the central desert and on Aboriginal land issues (*Les Rêveurs du désert*; German translation: *Träumer der Wüste*, Promedia, 1989), a doctoral dissertation comparing the articulation of the rites, myths and social organization among the Warlpiri and other Aboriginal groups (*Du rêve à la loi chez les Aborigènes*), and numerous articles in journals and collective works, in particular on gender relations and on the dynamics of the constant re-elaboration of mythic and ritual patrimony. She also designs multimedia resources (*Dreamtrackers — Yapa art and knowledge of the Australian desert*, Unesco, produced for the Lajamanu Aboriginal school for museums and universities). Currently she co-ordinates an international program on "New technologies, anthropology and multimedia" with Dr John Stanton, Director of the Berndt Museum of Anthropology in Perth, Australia.

Alban BENSA is Directeur d'étude (professor) at the Ecole des Hautes Etudes en Sciences Sociales (EHESS, Paris). After his PhD on a cult of saints in a region of France (Le Perche), he has been conducting anthropological and historical investigations since 1973 on the political practices specific to the Kanak chiefdoms in a particular area of New Caledonia. Since 1984, he has been studying the most recent changes in this French overseas archipelago, so as to throw new light on the forms and issues of Kanak independentist claims. Between 1990 and 1997, Bensa worked with the architect Renzo Piano's team and the Agence pour le Développement de la Culture Kanak for the construction at Nouméa of the Jean-Marie Tjibaou Cultural Center. At the same time, he has been developing a theoretical reflection on the relationship between anthropology and history and on such key anthropological concepts such as "myth", "structure", "culture", and "symbol", etc.

Summaries

1 — Serge Tcherkézoff

In Samoa (Polynesia), fine mats made of strips of plaited vegetal material are the most prestigious gifts one may give. These mats symbolize the genealogy of a family, and their value increases with their circulation through exchanges. For possessors of the mats, the obligation to put them in circulation at each important event either marking the life of the family or involving the village community as a whole conditions any reassertion of their social identity. The "beauty" of a mat depends on its age, its size and its fine plaiting, and is the basis of its sacred character, and consequently of its symbolic efficacy. According to the myths and rites, it has the power to restore life and to preserve the "souls" of deceased individuals from eternal wandering.

2 — Françoise Douaire-Marsaudon

The *kava* ritual was traditionally one of the major Polynesian rites, in that some crucial issues hinged on it. There were issues of a directly political nature and others pertaining to the construction of the person's identity. The present article places emphasis on how one of these identity-linked aspects was dealt with. Its purpose is to show that the *kava* ritual not only partook in the ongoing development of a religious hierarchy, but that it was also the locus of transmission, between those men who assumed leadership, of an idealized image of manliness. If this is truly the case, then the *kava* ritual may be seen to fulfill the same main function as the great initiation ceremonies for men found in so many other Pacific island societies, which is to say the reproduction of at least one part of the male identity. Moreover, there seems to be a specific, essentially paradoxical issue at stake in the reproduction of men's identity: that is, the fact that men originate within women.

343

To make her point, the author will discuss the example of *kava* rituals in several Polynesian societies, and more specifically in the kingdom of Tonga.

3 — Maurice Godelier

Among the Baruya of New Guinea, the category of sacred objects appears to stem from gifts given by the gods to the ancestors of men: these are objects that must be kept and can therefore not be given. The analysis shows that, in order for potlatch societies to emerge and develop, two sociological conditions must be present. First, marriage must rest on the exchange of wealth for women and, second, some of the positions of power in the society must be acquired through competition which combines the amassing and the giving of wealth. The precious objects and "monies" circulating in both bridewealth and potlatch therefore appear as substitutes for humans or the gods. The analysis thus sheds light on Mauss' until now vague distinction between the giving of total services (without competition) and agonistic gift-giving (potlatch).

4 — Pierre Lemonnier

On the basis of his fieldwork among the Ankave, a group belonging to the "Anga" cultural complex (Eastern Highlands, Gulf and Morobe, Papua New Guinea), like the Baruya studied by Maurice Godelier, the author challenges Godelier's hypothesis concerning a possible relation between "Great-Men" societies (those without ceremonial exchange systems that create Big Men, but with male initiation) and a marriage system based on "sister" exchange. Lemonnier shows that there is no systematic relation between the two types of phenomena using material collected among the Ankave, and other Anga groups, as well as a few societies on the south coast of New Guinea. In particular, he points up a new fact in the anthropology of alliance: that money or valuables are in fact used, not only in bridewealth systems, but also on the fringes of direct sister exchange (in cases in which the exchange is often completed only after a long lapse of time), when a matrimonial debt could not be paid off by another woman.

5 — Stéphane Breton

Starting from two typical Melanesian object-relationships — head hunting and shell money transactions — it is shown how the object, while being used in symbolic exchanges through a metaphor (the head of a victim, sign of the name the person will bestow on his offspring), or a metonym (shell money, sign of the transactions constitutive of the person) is to play a role in the definition of the self, characterized by a missing part. The complex interplay mediated by objects of transactions between the self and the social *persona* leads to the conclusion that the self itself is socially instituted, and that it cannot be properly understood without recourse to a definition of society as a third party in the transactional space—of society as a spectacle of missing objects.

6 — Bernard Juillerat

This contribution draws out the logic of gift-giving and exchange from the relationships the Yafar of Papua New Guinea maintain with their totemic gods, the primordial parental couple (symbolic ingestion of the divine semen and milk, or search for the "cargo" within the chthonian womb). The mother is supposed to give her milk to her "children" for nothing, whereas the access to her fecundity (cargo and game) supposes the introduction of the father's law. The relation with the spirits of the dead during daily cynegetic activity, dream interpretation and possession shed some light on a similar underlying œdipal structure. This also enables us to understand why gifts are absent on the occasions of birth and death. The essentially juridical nature of Mauss' theory of the gift as seen here thus seems incomplete with regard to the primacy of the desire to receive over the "obligation to give."

7 — Monique Jeudy-Ballini

Among the Sulka of New Britain (Papua New Guinea) any ceremonial exchange challenges the protagonists' capacity to bring together the required quantity of goods they will give and to make sure, once they are assembled, that they do reach their recipients. For the main threat hanging over a ceremonial exchange seems not so much the shortage of resources as the presence of an impediment that would immobilize the gift circuit. As Monique Jeudy-Ballini shows, ensuring that these prestations are able to change hands calls for the same kind of know-how exchange partners need to manage the assistance they receive. In her analyze of the Sulka ceremonial exchanges, the author discusses the different forms of cooperation, their underlying representations as well as their implications on the formation of social links.

8 — Brigitte Derlon

The rules governing the patterns of the *malanggan* objects formerly used in funerary rites on the island of New Ireland, with the social entities exerting rights of control and individuals retaining copy rights, were modeled along the same lines as the legal system of land tenure. The advantage of the land-tenure system resided in its consolidation of matrilineal filiation along with concomitant allowance of the expression of strong patrilateral bonds, justified by theories of procreation in which the father is viewed as wholly responsible for creating the substance of the fœtus. This ensured the perpetuation of dialectic relations of identity and exchange between two interdependent, perpetually asymmetric exogamous units.

9 — Marika Moisseeff

The author examines the link between the formal qualities of certain ritual objects and the way these objects are used, to account for the role they play on the level of the ritual's efficacy. She does this by reconsidering the *tjurunga*, a sacred object of the Aranda. She first briefly summarizes Aranda cosmology, with its holistic representation of the world, in which *tjurunga* occupy a central role. She then goes on to discuss these objects, laying particular emphasis on those that may be qualified as prototypical (personal *tjurunga*). The representational properties of these artifacts are examined. They are alternately and simultaneously representations of the Aranda's key concept/the Dreaming/of prodigious beings and of an individual person's singularity. In the last analysis, however, the only thing a *tjurunga* refers to is itself. It is, indeed, the self-referential nature of this ritual object — the underpinning of which is its material nature — that makes it so effective in the rites in which it is deployed. This is illustrated by the description of one of these rites. Finally, some hypotheses of a more general nature pertaining to ritual objects are presented.

10 — Barbara Glowczewski

Against a backdrop of political solidarity, the Aboriginal peoples of northern and central Australia have continued to exchange objects and cults which they readapt to their own needs while reproducing local differences in their languages and social organizations. Tangible and intangible artifacts circulate ritually along a network in which, through reactualized mythic connections, sacred sites are transformed and repositioned within a dynamic structure of narrative and performance. Confronted with this logic which recognizes the inalienable claim of the original owners of these objects, songs, paintings or ritual dances, the West is always threatening to disauthenticate them. The author stresses the urgent need for museums and anthropologists to stop alienating these cultures by alienating their objects and instead to recognize that such knowledge and objects are inalienable by authenticating their creators rather than their purchasers. With regard to the international context of contemporary title claims to cultural property, the author shows the inalienability surrounding the ritual circulation of sacred objects and the cults to which they belong, in central and northwestern Australia. Examination of the elaboration of a cultural center by representatives of a dozen Aboriginal language groups and organizations based in the coastal town of Broome will illustrate a process of deliberate reappropriation of indigenous objects and knowledge. Whether internal or external, single-gendered or mixed, transmission of the Aboriginal heritage today seems to bring together into one problematic of "giving-without-loosing" indigenous peoples and software developers who argue for the authentication of their products through their free circulation.

11 — Alban Bensa

There is a long tradition of using ancient Kanak artwork (including sculpture, engravings, stone carving, etc.) to classify the native people of New Caledonia on the lower echelons of the imaginary hierarchy of civilizations. Following a long political and academic struggle, this evolutionist perspective has finally given way to admiring attention. The Kanak people came all the more clearly into their own with the creation in Nouméa of the Tjibaou Cultural Center built by the architect Renzo Piano and which opened concomitantly with the constitution of a collection of contemporary Oceanic art. This initiative aroused much debate among Kanak leaders, museum curators and anthropologists. Analysis of these discussions shows how difficult it is to reduce contemporary Pacific art work to the function of unambiguous props for cultural identity. The discussion evolves into a reflection on temporality in dialogue. Works of art, be they ancient or contemporary, are seen to be at the heart of a constant restructuring of the relations between present, past and future.

Index of Personal Names

Index of Proper Names

Subject Index